Create, Produce, Consume

Create, Produce, Consume

New Models for Understanding
Music Business

David Bruenger

UNIVERSITY OF CALIFORNIA PRESS

University of California Press, one of the most
distinguished university presses in the United States,
enriches lives around the world by advancing scholarship
in the humanities, social sciences, and natural sciences. Its
activities are supported by the UC Press Foundation and
by philanthropic contributions from individuals and
institutions. For more information, visit www.ucpress.edu.

University of California Press
Oakland, California

Library of Congress Cataloging-in-Publication Data
Names: Bruenger, David, 1953- author.
Title: Create, produce, consume : new models for
    understanding music business / David Bruenger.
Description: Oakland, California : University of
    California Press, [2019] | Includes bibliographical
    references and index. |
Identifiers: LCCN 2019003679 (print) | LCCN 2019007769
    (ebook) | ISBN 9780520972735 (ebook) | ISBN
    9780520303508 (cloth : alk. paper) | ISBN 9780520303515
    (pbk. : alk. paper)
Subjects: LCSH: Music trade. | Popular music—Social
    aspects.
Classification: LCC ML3790 (ebook) | LCC ML3790 B7766
    2019 (print) | DDC 338.4/778—dc23
LC record available at https://lccn.loc.gov/2019003679

Manufactured in the United States of America

28 27 26 25 24 23 22 21 20 19
10 9 8 7 6 5 4 3 2 1

Donna, in stillness, in motion, harmonizing
all that matters.

CONTENTS

Introduction

Music is an art form in the medium of sound. Musical experience involves—at minimum—a maker and a listener and an exchange between them consisting of music, meaning, appreciation, and, sometimes, money. To thrive, a music business must in some way facilitate that exchange in order to monetize the experience.

But it's not just about money. A music experience can also be transformative, life affirming, and culturally powerful. The right popular song at the right time can change the world. Music is the core product and service of a multibillion-dollar industry. Music can make you fall in love, or break your heart.

That's what this book is all about. All of it.

Create, Produce, Consume: New Models for Understanding Music Business is an exploration of the music experience cycle. It looks at artist/audience and producer/consumer relationships—not necessarily the same thing—from creation to production to reception and from creation to consumption. Each chapter offers a different perspective on the processes and structures that provide access and guide listeners to discover, experience, and interact with music and musical artists. The goal is to help the reader to understand and be able to explain why an established music enterprise works, to predict how well an emerging venture may perform, and to plan an entirely new one from the ground up.

The content of this book is not arranged chronologically, but by topic. It begins in the first chapter with an overview of the music experience cycle from creation to reception and, ultimately, consumption. The next two chapters look in detail at the core elements of that cycle, production and reception, from multiple perspectives. From there the chapters spiral outward to consider how reception becomes consumption, is taken to scale, and is monetized, localized, diffused, and disrupted across networks, corporations, and a society increasingly addicted to spectacle and media. At each stage, from chapter to chapter, the experience cycle is viewed from a new perspective and the overall complexity of the music business progressively revealed in greater scope and detail.

Along the way, readers are introduced to a variety of analytical tools and encouraged to develop an adaptive expertise that is well suited to the complex and rapidly evolving economy and culture of music. The reader is also challenged to dive deeper and create conceptual prototypes of as yet unbuilt musical ventures or to enhance ones they have already launched.

The path ends where it started, with the vital importance of creating a song that someone will fall in love with or use to change the world, even if only for three minutes. The difference is that the reader is better prepared to understand how and why that has happened. And, most critically, is empowered to act and make it happen for themselves.

A brief overview of the chapters follows.

I. INCEPTION

Introduces the processes that connect creators to listeners and provide access to musical experiences and products. Defines critical concepts including complexity theory, cycles of stability and disruption, and adaptive expertise. Introduces the principal analytical tools used in the book, including case studies, process models, and conceptual prototypes.

2. PRODUCTION

Begins with a fundamental definition of "production" as the means to create access to musical experiences, whether live or technologically mediated. Explores the impact of production technologies on music creation and distribution. Considers how casual listeners become consumers and how that "journey" is managed.

3. RECEPTION

Examines the ways listeners discover, engage, and interact with music and music creators. Introduces fundamental concepts about the neurobiology of music listening and how production techniques grab and hold a listener's attention and shape musical preferences. Explores how consumers also shape production decisions via Internet-based fandoms.

4. COMMODIFICATION

Focuses on what happens when production and reception are scaled upward for massive distribution and consumption. Explores the pros and cons of turning music and musicians into products and how, on a sufficiently large scale, the music industry is both an economic and a cultural driver for society as a whole.

5. MONETIZATION

Explores how the relationship between ownership and access creates value through the three main sectors of music enterprise: publishing and licensing; concerts, tours, and festivals; and recording and distributive media. Copyright—the primary mechanism for managing ownership of musical productivity—is examined in relationship to each of these sectors. The ongoing effects of technological innovation on copyright law and music business practice are traced throughout.

6. LOCATION

Examines the relationships between local communities, venues, record labels, and musical genre development. Considers whether or not a music scene can be started "from scratch," or must arise organically from the context in which it appears.

7. DIFFUSION

Considers how music is distributed to optimize cultural and economic impact. Begins with the perspective of the previous chapter—the local music scene—and examines the methods by which local music becomes global.

8. DISRUPTION

Uses the concept of *creative destruction* to examine cycles of stability and disruption as applied to music. Explores the concept of "adaptive expertise" as the capacity to respond to disruption by reusing or adapting existing solutions, or creating entirely new ones. Posits that adaptivity is the key to surviving and thriving in the volatile music and entertainment sectors of economy.

9. CONNECTION

Reviews the various structures and processes that connect music, musicians, and music enterprises, including artist-to-audience, artist-to-artist, business-to-artist, and business-to-business relationships. Also examines how music can be the basis for the formation of communities and subcultural groups, from the shared experience of a concert audience, to fan clubs, to the Internet fandoms that impact productivity metrics for the industry.

10. INCORPORATION

Considers business structures that facilitate and monetize production and reception. Introduces theoretical perspectives that address start-ups, adaption/disruption, and the management of creativity and risk. Gives examples that embody the application of these principles to twenty-first-century musical culture and markets.

11. AGGREGATION

Explores the issue of aggregation: of audiences, of artists, and of the music they create. Introduces some of the methods by which producers aggregate information about consumers. Considers how data—about listeners, listening habits, recorded product, and curated playlists— have created a new web of aggregative possibilities, in which artists, producers, and listeners are all—potentially—"product." Introduces the burgeoning field of data analytics as a tool for prediction and control of outcomes in a volatile creative industry.

12. SIMULATION

This final chapter ponders spectacle: the creation and consumption of simulated realities. Considers several kinds of spectacles and their uses (and side effects) in society and commerce. Examines the effects of spectacle in music: technologies that blur distinctions between live and recorded performance, between advertising and content, and the deconstruction of the traditional forms, roles, and institutions of music.

Although, as indicated above, there are deep dives into specific music enterprise structures and theoretical frameworks along the way, the overarching orientation of the book is toward the most critical destination: the place where artists and audiences come together and share music making and cocreate artistic, social, and economic value.

Let's get started.

I

Inception

Creation, Production, Reception

Music most often begins as an idea or a feeling in the mind or heart of one person. Understanding how or why is a mystery beyond the scope of this text. Here, we will take musical creation as a given and focus on what comes after: shared musical experience, what makes it happen, and the forms of value it can generate.

Musical experience depends upon someone making and someone else listening to music. Performance can be technologically mediated so that performer and listener don't need to be in the same space at the same time. Or the performer and listener can be in the same room (or even be the same person). But for music to have wider impact, the minimum "equation" is one performer plus one listener equals a musical experience.

How music moves from an idea—*creation*—to the ears of listeners—*reception*—is where the *production* structures of music enterprise come into play. All forms of music production provide access to musical experience, regardless of venue or technological medium. Access to music and musicians is what brings music commerce, community, and culture to life. Consequently, managing access and the complex relationship between artist and audience is the essential mission of every music enterprise, regardless of where or when or in what genre it happens.

This chapter begins with an overview of the processes through which producers bring music, musical artists, and audiences together. This is followed by an introduction to fundamental concepts, analytical tools, and a methodology for new venture creation, all of which will be referenced throughout the remaining chapters.

PRODUCTION PROCESS: ACCESS, DISCOVERY, ENGAGEMENT

Because the inception of music is so often personal, the first challenge for anyone wanting to use it to create value is to make it possible for someone besides the creator to hear it. At the most fundamental level, this is a question of *access*.

For centuries, access to music meant that the listener had to be in the same space as the performer while the performance was happening. Late in the nineteenth and early twentieth centuries, technologies such as audio recording/playback and radio broadcasting made access possible even when artists and audiences were far apart or the acts of performing and listening were separated in time. A record played on the radio made it possible for a listener in Arizona to hear a performance recorded in Massachusetts, two years earlier.

New technologies that increased access to music—particularly those that made it more convenient or cheaper—changed listening and commercial consumption patterns. Musical styles previously limited to the players and listeners of a specific geographical region could be heard all over the country and, ultimately, the world. The scale of consumption changed as well: "handcrafted," one-of-a-kind local performances could become mass-produced products for audiences of millions. As the musical experiences and social/economic opportunities of creators expanded, creative practices changed too.

In addition, by the mid-twentieth century, broadcast and recording technologies moved musical experiences, previously available only in public spaces, into private ones. Music in a vast array of styles, from all over the world, could be heard in the comfort and convenience of one's own home via radio and records. The digital technologies of the late twentieth and early twenty-first centuries intensified these effects. Today, it is no exaggeration to say that access to any music, anywhere, at any time is a reality across the industrialized world.

Incredibly, this near universal, on-demand access to music is available at minimal or no cost to listeners. Musical experience—from the listener's perspective—has never been richer or more convenient. But at the same time, the emergence of this reception utopia has caused a major crisis for producers.

For music producers there has always been tension between facilitating access and controlling it. If music is too difficult to find, people won't hear it, let alone purchase it. If access is too easy, people don't need to pay and may even be able to function as "pirates," creating and distributing illegal copies.

The point of access to music is always also the point of monetization, whether in the form of a ticket that lets you into a concert or the purchase of a recording. Even broadcast media like radio monetize access—by providing advertisers access to listeners who must listen to or watch ads in order to hear (have access to) music.

When a new technology, a changing social behavior, or a combination of the two changes access it also affects both control and monetization, to which producers must respond. This phenomenon is both cyclic and inevitable (see chapter 8 for a discussion of this cycle) and has happened many times.[1] But, fueled by the "compressive effects" of digital technologies, the conflict between access and control became unusually intense early in the twenty-first century.[2] In later chapters we will look at some of the winners and losers in these rapidly evolving frameworks for production and consumption.

In addition to unparalleled ease of access and an increasing difficulty monetizing it, the contemporary music business faces another issue.

Since the early 2000s, it has been possible for anyone to reach a global audience with musical (really any digital) product via the Internet. The production, distribution, and promotion of such products, ranging from professionally done recordings of original songs to home-made lip synch videos, became possible at minimal cost via web-based media hosting platforms like YouTube, SoundCloud, and Bandcamp (as well as Zoella and KSI for Gen Z-ers), and networking utilities like Facebook, Twitter, Instagram, Snapchat, and Musical.ly (for Boomers, Gen X, Millennials, and Gen Z, in roughly in that order of usage).[3]

The mechanisms of production, distribution, and promotion previously controlled by (and beneficial to) record labels and radio stations were democratized by the Internet. Much more music by many more creators and producers was available than ever before. The downside was that in removing the gatekeeping function of labels and networks, the curatorial function was removed as well. Everything becomes equally available online: good, bad, and ridiculous. The bandwidth is enormous but the signal-to-noise ratio is very poor. Because so much music is discoverable via the Web, for producers the question becomes one of how to ensure that listeners discover their music amid the millions of choices.

For most of the twentieth century, music *discovery* (how listeners find music) depended upon a coordination of radio play, retail record sales, and live shows, supplemented with print and broadcast media advertising and promotional appearances. Traditional discovery was part of a process that was relatively stable and well understood. As explained by Samuel Potts (Head of Radio, Columbia UK): "Previously, in the era of the traditional customer journey, we generated discovery for 8 to 12 weeks (allowing customers to discover new music by promoting through intermediaries such as TV, radio and press), and then the purchase or 'consumption' of music would come afterwards."[4]

Today, discovery increasingly depends on Internet-based platforms that incorporate a social networking component. In one sense this is not new, in that "telling your friends" has always been a valuable tool to promote music. But, like other aspects of the multidirectional networking on the Internet, the speed, scale, and interactivity in the present environment are unprecedented. In addition, Internet-based "fame" is extremely transitory and may last hours, perhaps a day or so at best.

As a result, the question confronting producers today is not only one of driving traffic to a YouTube channel, for example, but also one of fostering listener *engagement* with the content there. It is not now—nor has it ever been—sufficient to lead listeners to find an artist. A listener must personally connect to the artist's music and to the artist as a human being. This connection is the basis for longer-term relationships. Neither economic success nor cultural influence is achieved by way of "one and done" musical encounters. Successful management of the production process requires an integration of artist/music discovery and engagement, followed by consumption—ideally via multiple purchases of products and experiences—over time. As explored in later chapters, this process has been accelerated, compressed, demonetized/remonetized, and fundamentally altered in the digital era.

Developing a working understanding of the creation-production-reception cycle—and its potential to generate commercial consumption—depends upon knowledge of a wide range of historical and contemporary examples, as well as a degree of skill using concepts, theoretical frameworks, and analytical tools to analyze, compare, adapt, and apply them to emerging or entirely new musical ventures.

FUNDAMENTAL CONCEPTS

In this chapter we introduce three concepts and a brief overview of the theories from which they emerge: complex systems, stability/disruption cycles, and adaptive expertise. All are highly relevant to music enterprise across virtually all genres, eras, and locales. As such they are presented as foundational perspectives to which we will return a number of times throughout the text.

Complexity

The term "complex system" has a number of specific meanings that, depending upon context, can range from the casual—that how something works is "complicated"—to formal discipline-based meanings. These include, in mathematics, chaos theory; in biology, the physical processes of organisms; and in computer networking, the Internet. All of these "things" (except the casual, conversational usage) share some critical characteristics: that there are many seemingly independent elements, that these appear to function without central control and yet somehow "act together" to make the whole thing work.

We will take a deeper look at complex adaptive systems in chapter 8. But for now, a basic interpretation of complexity applicable to music enterprise might look something like this: a complex system is one that has many "moving parts" (people, products, processes) that are relatively simple to understand individually, but that act together to be productive and efficient without the benefit of a controlling authority.

Let's take that working definition for a spin.

There is, for example, no individual or organization that can with certainty produce a "number 1 hit single."[5] That distinction is the result of a large number of actions and interactions by and among songwriters, performers, producers, marketers, advertisers, communications experts, retailers, broadcast and web-based media platforms (and more) all acting independently (or at least semi-independently) but whose aggregate actions produce a "hit," a "song of the summer," a Grammy or CMA award nomination, or even the recognition of an artist as the "voice of a generation."

And that's just the production side of the process.

Even the combined expertise of all these actors and the considerable resources at their disposal will not, absent the enthusiastic participation of listeners/consumers, make a song rise to the top spot on the charts. The complex system for hit songs includes the listening public as well as the creators and producers and, since the early years of the twentieth century, music businesses have sought to understand what makes people love a song enough to make it a hit. Despite increasingly sophisticated research, sometimes the "hit-making machine" works exactly as planned, while at other times it does not.

The issue then is, perhaps, not how we see the "machinery" in all its complexity. The greater challenge is to know what specific action— what "button" to push—to make the system reliably and repeatably produce an intended result. In other words, the task for the artist/entrepreneur is doing it "on purpose" rather than waiting for "magic to happen." Consequently, the most critical consideration about the complex system of music production and reception is one of control.

A number of processes were developed by the music industry over the years intended to improve the chances of producing a hit and making a musical artist a star. For example, increasing public awareness of the artist and product via advertising and promotional activities is one such process. Tours to put the artist physically in front of audiences to create a personal connection and shared experience is another. For most of the twentieth century, the synergistic relationship between radio, record sales, and live shows was the foundational method believed to "engineer" successful outcomes most reliably.

Obviously, as a matter of historical fact, these control mechanisms did not always work. A big promotional budget and even an established brand do not necessarily produce a number one hit, a profitable record, or a successful tour. For example, the legendary "sophomore slump," in which artists with a popular debut album disappoint economically or artistically on their second release, is both common and yet not certain.[6] For emerging artists and first albums the results are even less predictable. What catches on and what disappears without a trace can depend upon variables that are not apparent during the creative or production phases or that simply don't work the way they are "supposed to" work.

The embarrassingly negative public response to the U2 and iTunes partnership in which the band provided their album *Songs of Innocence*, released in 2014, free to Apple customers is an example of such unpredicted and unintended results.[7] Fan demands to remove the "unwanted" product from the music libraries of their mobile devices were strident and incredibly well publicized in both social and professional media. The fiasco prompted embarrassed apologies from both Apple and Bono, on behalf of the band. Clearly this was not what the artists or the company intended.

Why one result and not another?

The issue is, complex systems are just that: complicated. There are too many moving parts (people, processes, and motivations) interacting in too many ways, often too quickly, for control to be easy. The Arctic Monkeys' groundbreaking online release of their debut album was initially considered a disastrous mistake by their label (a "leak" of massive proportions) until it turned out to be an industry-changing innovation. "What just happened here?" is not an unusual reaction in the business of breaking new music to the public.

Central to the difficulty of predicting outcomes, or even understanding results after the fact, is that it is possible to look too closely at an individual event and miss the larger picture. The converse is also true: an overarching brand strategy that is timely and appropriate doesn't matter if we (the audience) "don't hear a single." But it is the premise here that it is possible to do both: see the larger pattern as well as the individual elements and, more critically, their constantly morphing interactions.

That said, what this book cannot do—because, arguably, it cannot be done—is explain, once and for all, "how it works." There is no "trick" to it. Complex systems are self-organizing (people like what they like and do what they want), nonlinear (advertising does not necessarily equal sales and neither do social media "likes"), emergent (new technologies, trends, and behaviors appear), and dynamic in their movement from chaotic to ordered conditions and back again. Consequently, what worked beautifully for Band A last week may or may not work at all for Artist B today.

Because complex systems are dynamic and their behaviors are hard to predict, investments tend to be high risk. Much of the history of the music business—the growth of major record labels, as well as the promotional relationships between them, radio networks, and concert promoters—is a quest to control that complexity, or—depending on your point of view—to game the system. If, for example, one could suppress the competition *and* control the choices available to retailers and consumers, a streamlined process could—theoretically—emerge: a "star maker machine" that outputs "stars" and "hits" at a reasonably predictable rate.[8]

Such practices can and do work. Until they don't. This variability is also a process, the result of a recurring cycle between stability and disruption in business, economics, and culture. The next step toward understanding complexity in the music business is found in the relationship between stable and disruptive states.

Stability and Disruption

If we take "culture" to mean the cumulative effects of relationships among people (what we believe and do), institutions (collaborative structures such as governments, private organizations, as well as legal and economic systems), and artifacts (what we make), we can see that these elements are sometimes stable and long-lasting, while at other times highly changeable.

Change occurs in these elements of culture both individually and collectively. For example, the members of different generations may value different things and view what constitutes "normal" behavior differently. Such social shifts drive changes both in the government and in the economy. Music business models rise and fall as a result of shifts in musical styles and patterns of listener preference and consumption. Some musical trends or fads emerge and disappear quickly, while generational tastes and values change relatively slowly. In contrast emerging technologies can have far-reaching effects that manifest rapidly and disrupt established systems of both production and reception.

At other times, conditions seem stable. During such periods people understand how things work and the phrase "business as usual" applies.

In reality, however, the elements of society, economy, and culture are always in flux. It is only the rate of change—as well as the completeness and accuracy of one's situational understanding—that varies. Thus, we move from periods of relative stability, when institutions, social behaviors, and the aspects of life that are valued and important seem solid, to periods when the old rules no longer apply in a "wild west" environment. Such periods, though upsetting in the short term, are followed by the emergence of some new "status quo," which inevitably carries the seeds of its own eventual destabilization (more in chapter 8).

In terms of music, we can observe this cycle in the shift from periods when "mainstream pop" has a particular sound and many imitators to the seemingly sudden appearance of some "rebellious" musical movement that shakes everything up. In the 1920s, it was Jazz. In the 1950s, Rock and Roll was the "menace" to society and the music business. The 1970s saw Punk disrupt the status quo and the 1980s brought the rise of Hip Hop. In the late 1990s Grunge disrupted Glam Metal in the United States, and the 2000s saw the rise of Emo, Crunk, EDM (and its various subgenres), and an increasingly complex eclecticism, which is still unfolding. These artistic innovations caused audience behaviors to change and forced artists and production businesses to adapt.

Adaptive Expertise

If the purpose of music business study is to develop expertise for a rapidly evolving music marketplace, then we must pay attention to what it means to be "expert." If your goal is to become an efficient professional in the music business as it works today, you obviously must acquire knowledge and develop skills relevant to that setting. This is what is known as *routine expertise*. But, if in addition to efficiency in standard settings you want to add the capacity to effectively adapt to changing conditions, then it becomes necessary to consider what is called *adaptive expertise*.[9]

Comparison of the two kinds of expertise reveals the following distinctions. "Routine expertise" is based on the mastery of known procedures and has a goal of developing increased speed and efficiency in their application.[10] In contrast, "adaptive experts" acquire the same practical knowledge, but they do so in order to develop a conceptual understanding of how and why a given process works. Routine experts operate at peak efficiency in the world of known problems. Adaptive experts excel in their ability to analyze problems and repurpose existing solutions or create new ones as needed.

From a problem-solving perspective, the routine expert tends to view all problems categorically, in line with what is known to be standard operating procedure. In contrast, "rather than *assuming* that their current knowledge and their problem definition are correct, adaptive experts draw on their knowledge in light of situational factors or unique aspects of a case to formulate a *possible* explanation or a *theory* of the situation which they test in the given context of the problem at hand."[11] As a result, the adaptive expert is more able to distinguish between what is a "normal" situation and when conditions deviate from the norm, as, for example, the appearance of Napster in 1999 and everything that happened afterward reveal.

TOOLS: CASE STUDIES, PROCESS MODELS, AND PROTOTYPES

The story of Napster, the record labels, and iTunes provides a lesson about adaptive innovation.[12] But interpreting the story in that way requires not only having access to the facts and the sequence of events, as well as an understanding of the context in which they occurred. In addition, in order to apply the lessons of that story, it is critical to be able to take a sequence of events and infer causality: what led to what, which events were pivotal, and which merely circumstantial.

A detailed narrative—more details than in the example above—that provides factual information about a person, event, or institution over time and situates it in the relevant context is a case study. Case studies are used in a number of disciplines and they represent a particularly good tool for the development of adaptive expertise.

Here's why.

Adaptive expertise involves three elements: *factual knowledge, conceptual knowledge,* and *transference. Factual knowledge,* for music enterprise, can be subdivided into two categories: (a) standard practices and current conditions in the music industry and (b) historical structures and events as a basis for recognizing and understanding recurring patterns. Detailed case studies of specific businesses, careers, and events are particularly useful for developing and reflecting upon factual knowledge.

Conceptual knowledge is an understanding of the foundational principles underlying music business practice. Developing a conceptual knowledge framework depends upon the study and comparison of historical and contemporary cases with a particular goal: to identify principles that can be applied to more than one context, era, or music business sector. Conceptual knowledge also depends upon a process of reflection and abstraction, of looking beyond the specific details to underlying structures. *Process models* are the analytical tools that help us move beyond *what* a case is, to *how* and *why* it works.

Process Models

There are several types of process models to consider. First, context-specific process models can deepen your understanding of how specific businesses currently work or have worked in the past. These go hand in hand with case studies.

Second, the *business process model abstraction* has a particular value in the development of adaptive expertise. Abstracted process models are the result of "an operation on a business process model preserving essential process properties and leaving out insignificant details in order to retain information relevant for a particular purpose."[13]

For example, a case study of the early career of the Beatles, up to their first record contract with Parlophone, would be the story of the people, their actions, within the then-current music scene. A process model would define where it began, how it developed, what decisions were made to what effect, as well as what pivotal opportunities and resources became available and how they were leveraged. The abstracted process model would look at those events in a general sense, independently of the specific elements of the case. Consider the following: a case study–based process model and an abstracted process model, both based on the early career of the Beatles (see figure 1 and table 1).

These examples show how one can select elements of a narrative— in this case about a band formed in Liverpool, England, in 1957—to create a streamlined version of events as they occurred over time. The selection process involves deciding the information that seems most significant and putting individual narrative pieces into groups indicating phases of development from beginning to conclusion. In this case, these phases are labeled *initial connections, upping the game, critical opportunity, leveraged opportunity,* and *benchmark.* The abstracted model uses the same labels, but removes the things specific to the Beatles, replacing them with descriptions that could be applied to other startup bands in other times and places.

In terms of adaptive expertise, the value of an abstracted model will most often be to facilitate the application of the insight provided in one case to another situation. It is a particularly useful tool when the model can be transferred from an instance where the outcomes are known to one where they are not, that is, from a historical model to an unfolding event in the present.

To test the validity of this model in comparisons across time and type of musical venture, let's consider what an Early Band Development process model drawn from the late 1950s and early 1960s in Liverpool, England, suggests about the origins and development of a Hip Hop record label in the New York in the 1980s. The Def Jam Recordings case study/process model—based on one of several versions of how the principals met—is found in table 2.[14]

There are both commonalities and disparities between the case and process model for the Beatles and Def Jam Recordings. The two are compared in table 3.

TABLE 1

The Beatles: Early Years

Case Study/Process Model, 1957–1962

Initial Connections	Upping the Game	Critical Opportunities	Leveraged Opportunities	Benchmark
• McCartney and Lennon meet at a gig in Liverpool, 1957; • Lennon was already in a band (with classmates at Quarry HS); McCartney is an aspiring amateur; • McCartney joins Lennon's band on guitar; • They play low-stakes, low-reward, low-status performances.	• Harrison joins band as lead guitar, 1958; he is a classmate of McCartney at Liverpool Institute (HS); • Lennon's other school friends leave band, 1959; • They rebrand as "Johnny and the Moondogs" playing American Rock and Roll; • Stu Sutcliffe joins on bass, 1960; • They become "The Silver Beetles" in tribute to Buddy Holly.	• "Unofficial manager" Alan Williams gets them a tour of Scotland, early 1960; • They get their first permanent and strongest drummer, Pete Best, August 1960; • They get first Hamburg residency, August–November, 1960.	• Reputation boost from Hamburg leads to better gigs at Cavern Club in Liverpool; • They start backing and recording with Tony Sheridan, Hamburg; • They release "My Bonnie" single, 1961, becomes #32 on *Musikmarkt* chart; • Demand for single and live shows in Liverpool leads to Brian Epstein becoming manager, 1962.	• Epstein gets them signed to Parlophone Records, with producer George Martin, May 1962.

Initial Connections	Upping the Game	Critical Opportunity	Leveraged Opportunity	Benchmark
Common location	Personnel changes to increase skill level and reduce weakness	Events/ decisions to improve resources or personnel	Better venues, larger following	Professional management or production contract
Common experience as connector			Attention from management, A&R, other professionals	
Disparate levels of expertise or resources	Brand/style redirection and refinement	Significant engagement or project		Platform for large-scale production/ distribution
Entry-level product and compensation				

Figure 1. Early Band Development, Mid-Twentieth-Century Process Model/Abstraction.

Note that at several points both the label (see tables 2 and 3, below) and the band had to refine both brand and stylistic direction as well as make personnel adjustments in order to advance from one process stage to the next. Both the Beatles and Def Jam were focused early in their development on bringing the right people together and refining their respective brands. The Beatles mission was to assemble an internal creative team and connect it with the right engineer, producer, and label personnel. Def Jam began with the production/label team and brand and sought out the writers and performers to embody it.

The differences include that the Beatles model covers six years from initial meeting to the first edges of professional success—signing with Parlophone—while the Def Jam model is more compressed: one year shorter and going from first efforts to large-scale national success. The Def Jam model also involves much earlier capitalization in the form of a loan from Rubin's parents and then the shared investment by Rubin and Simmons. The Beatles' first capitalization point other than fees for playing gigs—though it is not indicated on the model—would have come with their Parlophone contract with the label paying to produce their first record.

To take the final step, the abstracted model from the Def Jam process is shown in figure 2.

TABLE 2

Def Jam Recordings, Early Years, 1982–1986

Case Study/Process Model

Initial Connections	Upping the Game	Critical Opportunity	Leveraged Opportunity	Benchmark
• Rick Rubin is a struggling artcore/punk musician, aspiring record producer, philosophy major at NYU; • Rubin borrows money from his parents and launches Def Jam Recordings out of his NYU dorm room; • He produces his band's single, "Mobo," Def Jam Recordings #1, 1982; • Rubin meets Jazzy Jay, prominent DJ, who provides insight into Hip Hop music and record production.	• Rubin and Jazzy Jay produce first Def Jam Hip Hop record: "It's Yours" by T La Rock and Jazzy Jay; • Distributed by Streetwise Records/Partytime and out of Rubin's NYU dorm room; • It sold 1000s of copies; • It had huge impact on Hip Hop underground scene and artists;	• Jazzy Jay introduces Rubin to Russell Simmons, established Hip Hop show producer, as the person who produced "It's Yours"; • Rubin was impressed by Simmons's experience and Hip Hop credibility; Simmons was impressed by Rubin's ear for and skill with a hit record; • Both invest in a relaunch and rebranding of Def Jam Recordings as partners, 1983.	• Rubin's/Simmons's Def Jam Recordings produces and release LL Cool J's "I Need a Beat," which sells over 100,000 copies, 1984; • Def Jam produces and releases "Rock Hard" by the Beastie Boys, also 1984.	• Simmons uses success of these Def Jam singles to get a distribution deal with Columbia Records, the first of its kind for a Hip Hop label, 1985. • Def Jam produces LL Cool J's album *Radio*, 1985, sells over 500,000 in four months; • Def Jam produces the Beastie Boys album *Licensed to Ill*, 1986, which reaches #1 on *Billboard* Album Chart, first Hip Hop record to do so.

TABLE 3

Comparison of the Development of Def Jam and the Beatles

Def Jam Recordings	The Beatles
Initial Connections	
Common setting—New York City's music and club community	—Liverpool's youth music scene
Social connections—Rubin and DJ Jazzy Jay become friends based on a common interest in music and record making	—Band members were classmates in Liverpool high schools, aspiring musicians
Upping the Game	
Success in producing underground Hip Hop record	Improved personnel, stylistic rebranding
Critical Opportunities	
Rubin and Simmons meet and re-form Def Jam Recordings as a pure Hip Hop label	"Unofficial" manager arranges first tours: Scotland and Hamburg
Leveraged Opportunities	
Singles by rising Hip Hop stars—LL Cool J and Beastie Boys—produced much larger sales in the 100s of thousands	More prestigious gigs in Liverpool and Germany, professional management
Benchmarks	
Major label distribution deal, massively successful albums by LL Cool Jay and Beastie Boys	Parlophone record and production deal

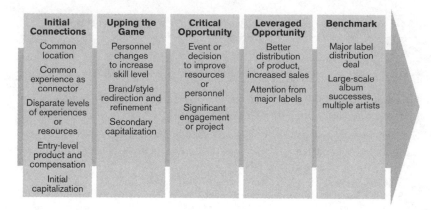

Initial Connections	Upping the Game	Critical Opportunity	Leveraged Opportunity	Benchmark
Common location	Personnel changes to increase skill level	Event or decision to improve resources or personnel	Better distribution of product, increased sales	Major label distribution deal
Common experience as connector	Brand/style redirection and refinement	Significant engagement or project	Attention from major labels	Large-scale album successes, multiple artists
Disparate levels of experiences or resources	Secondary capitalization			
Entry-level product and compensation				
Initial capitalization				

Figure 2. Early Record Label Development Process Model/Abstraction.

In addition to the obvious parallels with the band abstracted model, this one reveals the importance of earlier capitalization points, the creation of a significant product at the critical opportunity stage—modestly successful records—that can be leveraged further and faster than live gigs in the band model. For example, singles by LL Cool J and the Beastie Boys led to a major label distribution deal and then a benchmark of 500k plus record sales by multiple artists. The Beatles, by contrast, found their first critical opportunities in modest foreign tours, which they leveraged to record a cover song single and get better local gigs and management, which in turn—and over more time—led to signing with a label. Large-scale success comes much later in their story and process.

Reflection upon this difference suggests a number of possible causes. First, as noted above, a record label can aggregate the talents and creativity of multiple artists, while a band is limited to their own internal ones. Second, as a label, a first "proof of concept" product can be a record. A band must either build longer to attract the attention of a record label or self-produce and in effect take on the role of label/producer. This is, in fact, a much more common phenomenon in the 2000s than in either the 1960s or the 1980s and we can expect contemporary process models to reflect this DIY production trend, without necessarily discarding other key points of the models above.

It is one thing to critically analyze a music enterprise when it already exists. We all know what a great idea looks like once it is articulated and implemented. It is another thing entirely to recognize an idea, notion, or creative spark before that work is done. Sometimes, this recognition comes as a thought about why somebody isn't already doing something: for example, a question like "Why isn't Spotify finding and producing new artists?" From an entrepreneurial perspective, this is not a complaint about streaming services; it is a potential avenue of innovation. (But see, for example, chapter 11.)

If we take it as a call to action, that Spotify, or some other streaming platform, could take on the A & R discovery, production, and promotion roles for new artists previously held by record labels, how would we go about building such a company or service?

Prototypes

One way to work with an idea like "streaming platform as record label," or any new entrepreneurial project, is to create a prototype for it. The term originally comes from the world of design, where it was used to describe the initial physical model of a new product. Such prototypes were used to test a concept, demonstrate functionality, measure user reactions, and serve as an intermediate step between creation and production.

Beyond basic prototypes, the design approach to problem solving has been adapted to a number of different fields. The foundational application of this creative methodology is the *Design Thinking* (DT) approach, which began with explorations of the creative methods of graphic designers in the 1950s and 1960s.

As DT evolved, it began to be applied to problem solving beyond the field of design and evolved into a way of thinking about problems generally, particularly complex ones. In the 1980s, much work was done at the Hasso Plattner Institute of Design at Stanford University—better known as the *d.school*.[15] In the 1990s, Design Thinking was explicitly applied to business by Stanford researcher David Kelly, who also founded a design consulting and education firm, *IDEO*.[16]

The *Design Thinking Process (DTP) Guide* states: "To create meaningful innovations, you need to know your users and care about their lives." This statement comes from the first mode of the DTP: *empathize*. Beginning with empathy focuses your thinking on the people your project is intended to serve. This phase explores not only who the intended users are, but how well you understand, relative to the prototype you are creating, "their physical and emotional needs, how they think about world, and what is meaningful to them."[17] Thus, to apply the DTP to our streaming/record label question, we begin not with the business model, but with the question "who would this idea serve?" This is a critical issue for design thinking: to begin with a deep understanding of the intended user's wants and needs.

So, for the streaming service/label prototype, who are the intended users? How well do you know them? How would this business fulfill their wants and needs? One consideration seems immediately apparent: If your intended users are music listeners, then how would they benefit from your project? There are many other options for discovering and accessing new music today. Does your concept provide something that is different and better? It isn't just a matter of being aware of current and potential offerings in the streaming marketplace; you have to thoroughly understand the people you are hoping will be your customers and—most critically—care about what is important to them.

Conversely, if your intended users are aspiring musical artists, then the value of a venture that provides production and support for them would be more obvious, given the relative scarcity of these in the current marketplace. But how familiar are you with this group? Do you understand and care about their needs in this situation?

This dual perspective—listener as user versus artist as user—is an issue that is best illustrated with an existing case: the startup and implementation of the Tidal streaming music service. Launched in 2014 and purchased by Jay-Z in 2015, Tidal became the first artist-owned streaming service and was intended to address needs of both artists and listeners by providing better royalty percentages for the producers and both high-fidelity audio and exclusive, curated content for the consumers.

From the perspective of the "empathize" phase of DTP, Tidal was an unmitigated success with artists. The company understood that creators wanted more control over the streaming environment and better payment rates. In contrast, for listeners the monthly subscription costs—initially $20 (compared to the three Spotify tiers of free, $4.99, and $9.99)—proved to be a disincentive.[18] Whether we see this issue as a result of insufficient research about listener wants and needs, an insufficient concern for them, or some combination of the two, it's clear that the Tidal model fails conceptually from the empathy perspective of DTP. TIDAL's continuing difficulties in the marketplace indicate that this failure of concept may have had practical consequences as well.[19]

The next phase of the DTP is the *define* mode. "Framing the right problem is the only way to create the right solution." This phase is about defining the problem you wish to solve, or the question you want to answer. This answer will be "based on what you have learned about your user and about the context." This is a process of both clarification and focus. As the *DTP Guide* states, "crafting a more narrowly focused problem statement tends to yield both greater quantity and higher quality solutions when you are generating ideas."

The definition process depends upon the articulation of three things: the *user* you intend to serve, the *need* you intend to fulfill, and the *insights* you gained from the empathy phase and research into current conditions. Based on the user and their needs, you may need to redefine or clarify your question. Returning to a consideration of Tidal vs. Spotify for a moment, one could argue that if the Tidal model failed it was in not understanding the "gap" that the service could fill for listeners nearly as well as it did the artist gap.

From a DTP perspective, this could be seen as insufficient empathy work and research into consumer/listener wants and needs. It also suggests that Jay-Z, as an artist and an entrepreneur, understood fellow artists much better than listeners/consumers. This is a potentially transferrable issue. How similar are you to your prospective users and customers? How should that affect your thinking in the *empathize* and *definition* modes of the DT process?

Following the definition phase, DTP moves to *ideation*. At this point in the process you come up with multiple solutions/answers to your defined/redefined question—as many as you can. As the *DTP Guide* observes, "It's not about coming up with the 'right' idea, it's about generating the broadest range of possibilities."[20]

The *prototype* mode comes next in the DTP process and it is the place where we can both follow DTP principles and begin to draw on other conceptual frameworks as well. One that is particularly valuable for a music venture is the *minimum viable product* (MVP) from *The Lean Startup*.

Eric Ries first proposed the "lean startup" principles for the high-tech industry in 2008. It has become a widely applied tool for startups in all sectors of the economy since the publication of his book *The Lean Startup* (2011). One aspect of this approach is to begin, like DTP, with the wants and needs of the prospective consumer and, from the beginning, keep building versions of a product or service that better meet those wants and needs; that provide solutions for customers' problems.[21]

Lean Startup thinking centers on the idea that the process for innovation moves from building to measuring consumer response, learning from it, and then starting the loop again with better information. This Build-Measure-Learn loop is repeated and the goal is to repeat it as quickly as possible to improve the product. A critical feature of this loop is that if you build a *minimum viable product* rather than an exhaustively "perfect" one, you can learn and improve much faster.

A good example of an MVP in the music business is the demo recording. If you are trying to grow a band or develop an artist discovery, development, and production business—like a record label—your minimum viable product is likely to be a demo recording of some kind. For a band, demos typically come later in the process, so an earlier MVP might be—as for the Beatles above—low-stakes gigs and local clubs and, later, tours and better venues. Regardless, we can consider each iteration/improvement as a trip around the build-measure-learn loop.

In contrast, the Def Jam model gets to a demo recording early—with Rick Rubin's punk band and then with the T La Rock indie single. The feedback from the second release was especially useful to develop better iterations later on. In both cases—band and label—the segment of the model labeled "Leveraged Opportunity" could also be considered as second, third, and later iterations of the build-measure-learn loop.

From a pure DT perspective, the *prototype* mode is where you create something with which your intended users can interact. This is a point in the process where you could share a conceptual model of your project, perhaps a "story board" of how it would work that would allow potential users to see the concept in action. But in music, hearing is believing. This is why creating a minimum viable product—a demo— for users to see and hear would be most effective.

This could be a recorded song made available on SoundCloud or some other site, or a performance (or a "making of") video via YouTube or another host. It will be hard to avoid making/using music in order to sell a venture concerned with music. For a music streaming and artist discovery/development project, what would the MVP look like? How would users be able to interact with it and how would you be able to gather feedback about it? While it may or may not be practical to actually "build" it, it will be immensely valuable for future endeavors that you intend to test and bring to market if you do the conceptual work thoroughly, considering and discussing your concept with potential users now.

But taking the next step, you could test the prototype with listeners by making a single song recording available via some version of the discovery/distribution method you are planning. If you build user interactivity into that platform (using, for example, the familiar tools of social media, such as likes, comments, and follows), you could gather the feedback data necessary to quickly assess the prototype and make needed changes. While this particular example is not innovative, particularly if using already-available web-based tools, or comprehensive, you could still use it to identify gaps or weaknesses from the user perspective and adjust (or brainstorm adjusting) your prototype to minimize or eliminate them.

If the intended user is the aspiring musical artist and your core goals are to support development and production, the production of the single proves the concept. A "making of" video that shows the work and interactions involved takes that experience further. Feedback from prospective artist-customers as well as any positive listener feedback to the recording/video would be an indication that value is being produced from both production and reception sides of the equation.

In the context of DT, the prototype and testing phases are interrelated. As the DTP process guide states: "Build to think and test to learn." Within this text, however, the focus will be on developing a concept through the prototype phase and leaving actual testing to those who are actively engaged in entrepreneurship, with the understanding that additional resources and guidance beyond the scope of this text will be necessary.

This book is a launching pad. You will need to build your own rocket.

CRITICAL CONCEPTS

Access and Control

- If music is too difficult to find, people won't hear it, let alone purchase it. If access is too easy, people don't need to pay and may even be able to create and distribute illegal copies.
- The point of access to music is always the point of monetization.
- Managing access and the complex relationship between artist and audience is the essential mission of every music enterprise, regardless of where or when or in what genre it happens.

FURTHER CONSIDERATION

Discussion

· Consider this statement: "Radio, film with sound, television, digital audio, the Internet, P2P file sharing, and streaming have all driven changes in the reception, production, and creation of music." Is the order of the terms "reception," "production," and "creation" correct? If not, why not? If so, what does it mean? Doesn't creation drive production and reception? Or doesn't production constrain both creation and reception?

Music Case Studies

· Digital Music Marketing Case Studies—Best of 2015, from Music Ally

http://musically.com/2016/02/05/digital-music-marketing-case-studies-music-allys-pick-of-2015/

Conceptual Prototype Questions

· What happens if the touring market finally becomes oversaturated? What's the next revenue-generating business model for music? How would you go about creating it now so that it's ready next year, or next month?

· If you wanted to start a band or launch a record label next year or week, what resources must you have, what/who must you find, and what would the minimal viable product—the proof of concept product—be?

2

Production

Art, Science, Enterprise

Every artist and every song has an idea, and the producer's job is to capture it.   —Jimmy Iovine, 2016[1]

I grew up obsessed with science fiction, and when I was really young, I wanted to be a scientist. What that meant was, I wanted to work in an environment that looked like the bridge of the Enterprise. I wanted to have oscilloscopes and buttons. Somehow, magically, I've become an electronic musician, and I have a recording studio that looks like the bridge of the Enterprise.   —Moby, 2012[2]

Consumption is the sole end and purpose of all production; and the interest of the producer ought to be attended to, only so far as it may be necessary for promoting that of the consumer.   —Adam Smith, 1776[3]

In almost any context, if there is a producer, there is an expectation that there is also a consumer. In music, production processes refine and realize musical expression, convert "pure" or "raw" musical creativity into consumable products and services, and deliver them to the marketplace and, thus, the consumer. Production processes are the bridge between artist and audience and a two-way conduit both for music and for the value it can generate.

The term "production" is used in a variety of contexts in music. In audio recording it refers to the process of capturing live performance (or the creation of tracks via electronic and/or digital means) on a recording medium, as well as the editing and "postproduction" that lead to the creation of a master recording. Since the master recording is the "original" for all copies that are distributed and sold to the public, producing it is a critical pivot from making music to selling music.

In this context, a producer is the person who connects musical creation/performance and the art and science of audio recording to the commercial enterprise of selling recorded musical experience. In that role, the producer must mediate between and among people with different skill sets, values, and expectations.[4]

The role of record producer has a particular significance because record labels were the most important revenue generator for a twentieth-century music industry large and successful enough to shape popular culture on a global scale. As such, production processes in the recording industry are the primary focus of this chapter.

The term "production," however, can also describe the work involved in putting a live performance onstage in front of an audience. So a brief discussion of concert production, particularly in comparison with (and in relationship to) record production, is worthwhile.

In the recording studio, it is not unusual for creative and performative aspects of a project to be still in flux at the beginning of a session. The producer's work is quite often to refine "raw" creativity through collaborative work with songwriters, performers, and audio engineers. In contrast, the concert business operates with an expectation that songs and performances will be "good-to-go" prior to the event. Most popular artists/groups do, of course, rehearse prior to the first concert of a tour, but that is more about the logistics of sound, lighting, and stage setups than song structure or musical interpretation.[5]

As such, concert "producers" operate more in the realm of the logistical and promotional, rather than the creative. For this reason, perhaps, the terms "concert promoter," "presenter," and, even to an extent, "tour manager" are often used instead of "producer" to describe the people who make it possible for artist and audience to come together in a concert venue.

Despite such differences, what happens onstage in front of an audience is in one essential way the equivalent of what happens when a listener presses "play" on a recording or streaming device/interface. This moment of connectivity is the culmination of all production processes regardless of medium or business model. It's the only thing that really matters in terms of making music, making money, and having social and cultural impact. The production process—whether technologically mediated or live—is designed to facilitate that moment of discovery, engagement, and artist–audience connection.

This connection is also the foundation for a long-term relationship between fans and performers and consequently between consumers and producers. As such, it is the basis for all forms of music enterprise, which underscores the importance of looking at music production from two perspectives: (1) how the musical product is produced and made available to the public and (2) how producers understand their customers and attempt to control their engagement with the product.

The production of classical music—whether the term refers to symphonic music, chamber music, or opera—for live performance or recordings is not profoundly different from production in the popular and commercial sector. Though classical music is often assumed to have higher artistic and cultural ambitions than popular forms, all music ventures are based on a combination of motives: making good music, making it available for public access, and having a sustainable economic model. The relative importance of these factors may vary by musical genre and even from project to project, but all three are almost always present.[6] The role of money and subsidy in music production processes is explored in much more depth in chapter 5.

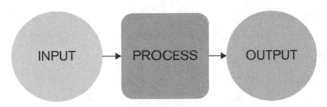

Figure 3. Music Production Model.

A MODEL FOR MUSIC PRODUCTION

To understand music production in a broad, structural sense, it is helpful to consider it as a three-part model: *input, process,* and *output* (see figure 3).

As noted in the first chapter, this book treats musical creativity as preexisting. As such, we can consider such creative productivity as the most fundamental, or "raw," input into any music production system, live or recorded. The process includes all of the artistic, technical, social, and commercial factors that contribute to the transformation of the raw input into the intended product, which is, of course, the output: the thing that you wanted to make and, in the case of a commercial music venture, hope to sell.

To produce records, it is necessary to have both creative musical content and performance as inputs: in essence, a song and a singer. Songwriting is itself a creation-production process that begins with an idea or feeling and culminates in a "song" that, regardless of musical genre, almost always combines words and music. The history and methods of songwriting/arranging are beyond the scope and purposes of this book. But it is important to understand the significance of original music as an input and, combined with recorded performance, the primary output of the system.

In the recording business, placing the right song with the right performer is so critical that there is a job whose purpose is to do exactly that. The Artist and Repertoire (A & R) representative is a crucial part of record making historically and in the present. Just as a recording session cannot really begin until someone makes a musical sound, so must a song be paired with a performer to make that sound.

That's where we begin.

Performance as Input (and Output)

One thing that both record production and concert production share is a focus on performance. The relationship between performance in the studio and on stage was closest in the early days of the recording era. Performers in both settings had to be able to play and sing the music that they wanted their listeners to hear without benefit of amplification or other audio-enhancing technology.

For many years, the purpose of recording was to capture and document live performance. Since early recording quality was far inferior to live sound, it was easy—almost unavoidable, in fact—to sound better in person than on record (or cylinder). During this early recording era, performance was both a critical input and a critical output of every form of music production. Recordings were more of a novelty product, ancillary to the sale of tickets to live performances and the purchase of sheet music, rather than a primary source of musical experience.

Electronic sound transmission and amplification brought benefits to both concert stage and recording studio. The microphone was a truly transformative device that revolutionized the quality of recorded sound and greatly enhanced the quality and projection of live sound, particularly for singers.

These new technologies fostered the creation of new styles of music. Amplification, especially as applied to the guitar both revolutionized popular music and created challenges in recording studios. Early Rock and Roll performers were a problem for engineers attempting to manage the high volume levels of electric guitars (and drum kits) in studio environments built for another era and an acoustic style of music.

By the late 1960s, when recording technology evolved to support multitrack recording (among other breakthroughs), and as studio engineers and producers developed the skill and insight to use them, it became possible to capture the intensity of amplified Rock, R & B, and Country music on recordings. This was a period when excellence in performance, engineering, and production came together to make what have become iconic records. Ultimately, however, evolving technology and marketing processes would fundamentally alter the relationship and relative significance of performance, recording, and production, bringing this balanced excellence to an end (see, for example, the comparative discussion of record making by Marvin Gaye and Maroon 5, below).

The finished musical product on record increasingly became the result of a complex layering of recordings, electronic alterations, and even the capacity to correct performance errors after the fact. As the recording studio became not just a place to capture live sound, but also a tool to create music, records began to transcend the individual performative elements captured on tape. As recorded output became more complex, an unprecedented problem appeared: how to perform live the music from a highly produced record.

This shift had as much to do with economics as it did with technology. Record singles—and later individual album tracks—that became radio hits were the most important output of the music industry. Hit records drove sales, sold tickets, and established the brand of artists. The listening public discovered most new music via records on the radio (or jukeboxes), rather than through live performance. The hit record was what they knew and loved and what they expected to hear when an artist performed in concert.

The shift in importance from live performance to recorded production brought some unintended consequences. The performing expertise that was once an essential precondition for being a professional musician remained a convenience, but was no longer a necessity. What a musician could perform in real time became a "raw" input, easily revised and even fundamentally changed in the studio and, soon after, in concert. See chapter 12 for more on this.

Although charisma and audience appeal have always been an integral part of music enterprise ("artist" is the "A" in A & R), as performance skills became less critical to both input and output, the importance of appearance and personality has increased. There is, after all, an Auto-Tune for vocals. There is no "Auto-Vibe" for performers. Yet.

MAKING RECORDS, MAKING HITS (AND STARS)

Whatever level of performance skill that is input into the record production system, the production process is designed to add value to that input to create a successful commercial record. And, just as there is an element of mystery about the ideas and emotions that lead to the creation of a song, so is there uncertainty about whether or not a given input will result in a hit record. In reality, the majority of records are not successful (just as the majority of musical artists do not become "stars").

For many years, music industry writers talked about the 80/20 rule. That is, that roughly 80% of the income in the recording industry was generated by 20% of the records made. This was an overly generous formula in the twentieth century and it has become even less accurate in the second decade of the twenty-first. In fact, drawing on research by Nielsen Soundscan, in 2011 just under 2% of the albums released produced nearly 80% of the sales. For digital singles, the percentages are even more imbalanced, with less than one percent (.78%) of available songs generating nearly 80% of sales.[7]

While not every production process model is about "hits," economic viability is a factor for everyone, so hits are hardly irrelevant, even if they are not a top priority. One perspective, for example, is offered by Bill Ivey, former director of the Country Music Foundation and former chairman of the National Endowment for the Arts:

> Some 20 years ago, my friend Jim Ed Norman—then head of the Nashville division of Warner Brothers Records—explained to me why he signed a

fine black gospel vocal group, Take 6. "I thought they were really good," he said. "I thought we could sell some product; and I thought it was important that the Southern division of our label have at least one African-American act."[8]

Quality of music is mentioned first, then economic incentive, and then social benefit. And even from the financial perspective, Norman said that his expectation was to "sell some product," not a million units. Making a hit was not the primary motivation.

In contrast, Robbie Williams has stated that, "I want a hit. I don't think anybody spends 12 months writing and recording an album, making something cool, and says, 'Great, I hope this doesn't sell.' I don't understand that mind-set. I want hits: a big bunch of them."[9]

None of this implies that commerce is a "higher" or "lower" motivation than "art" or "public good." But absent some form of subsidy, the market is not only where economic value has been realized, but also where art has been publicly recognized since the 1800s. Economic value, artistic value, and social value are not now, nor have they ever been, mutually exclusive.

As a matter of practicality, making a hit record requires a comparable investment of time and resources to making a flop. So there is an incentive to improve the odds of success for every recording project regardless of the primary motivation for making it. In addition, a "hit" is the result of making good music that people love, and which they purchase. The ideal situation would be to develop a process that ensures that any given input will produce a hit record and do so repeatably and reliably. To date, many have tried to build such a "hit factory," some coming closer than others. We look at two examples, below.

Case Study: Motown, Hitsville USA

The preeminent example of a production system that generated massive financial success and achieved iconic cultural status while producing some of the most recognizable and beloved records of the twentieth century is Motown. The label was founded in the city of Detroit, home to the ultimate benchmark for mass production: the auto industry.

In 1959, Berry Gordy, a young songwriter, producer, and entrepreneur, launched a record label with an $800 loan from his family. Motown Records Corporation (Detroit = Motor City = Motown) was built both on Gordy's musical vision and practical "day gig" experience working on the assembly line at Lincoln-Mercury:

> Every day I watched how a bare metal frame, rolling down the line would come off the other end, a spanking brand new car. What a great idea! Maybe, I could do the same thing with my music. Create a place where a kid off the street could walk in one door, an unknown, go through a process, and come out another door, a star.[10]

Gordy used his knowledge of the rich Detroit Jazz scene to hire top-notch musicians to play on every track cut by every artist at the studio. He hired staff songwriters and producers to ensure that the artists were working with great songs. Further, Gordy's vision for Motown's production model also included what he called "Quality Control" to ensure that only the best output would be produced.

At weekly meetings (9:00 AM on Fridays), songwriters/producers—like Holland-Dozier-Holland, Norman Whitfield, Ashford and Simpson, and Smokey Robinson—would listen to one another's songs and give them a grade. According to songwriter and music critic Helienne Lindvall, "if the song got an A+ it would get released, anything else and it went in the vault. If you arrived at 9:01 AM, you wouldn't get in, says Smokey Robinson, and had to wait until the next meeting to get a chance to get your song cut."[11]

The studio process at Motown was remarkable not only for its consistent productivity, but also for the speed, adaptivity, and technological simplicity of the work. There were only three recording tracks available. According to Lindvall, "The first track was used for drums and bass. All the other instruments went on the second track and the third track was used for vocals."[12] The studio musicians—the house band, nicknamed the Funk Brothers—were paid by the day, so the goal was to record as many backing tracks as possible. Since getting a good first take was critical, performance skill was at a premium in this environment.

Because the lead vocal had its own track, it was possible to do multiple versions. But because the studio was in constant use due to the production schedule, singers were also valued for their ability to get a successful take on the first try. Despite struggling with nervousness in the studio, Marvin Gaye had a reputation for successful first take recordings; his vocal for "How Sweet It Is" (top ten in Billboard Hot 100 and R & B charts in 1965) was, for example, the first take he sang.

When first takes didn't work in the early three-track days, the singer would have to perform the song again. By the later 1960s when multi-track recording had advanced and the Motown studios had sixteen tracks with which to work, vocal production was simplified. But even on a three-track recorder it was possible to "punch in," that is, for a performer to sing along with a previous track in order to make an improvement and have the engineer press a button at the right moment in order to record the new sounds over the old.

Punching in like this, however, produced a slight time delay, so it was only possible at a point where there was a significant break in the vocals. With sixteen tracks, the producer and engineer could keep multiple versions of the vocal and combine the best moments of several without any delay—called "comping the vocals"—in the final version.[13]

Though new technologies simplified the process, some have argued that the early technical and logistical limitations were good for the music. As Lindvall observes:

> The musicians were forced to truly master their craft and the recordings captured the magic that happens when a song is fresh (Motown singers usually learned the track about an hour before recording) and everyone plays together. Today, the digital revolution allows us to do hundreds of takes and comp them all together, to Auto-Tune the bits that aren't in key

and move the bits that are out of time. And so we end up with tracks that are technically "perfect" but lack the soul, groove and magic of Motown recordings that were made in a couple of hours, in a converted garage, 50 years ago, and are still played all over the world.[14]

Not everyone liked the Motown approach, however, even as it produced hit records and transformed young musicians into celebrities. There is almost always tension between the creative and the commercial impulses in the music business (and other creative industries). Artists can end up feeling exploited even as they collaborate with producers and labels to leverage their creativity to increase their cultural status and economic success. Motown was by no means unique in this regard.

There are a number of reasons why this has so often been the case. As high-risk ventures (see 80/20 rule above), labels mitigate risk by aggressively negotiating contracts, sometimes by cheating songwriters and performers of the compensation they are due. In addition to financial concerns, the volatility of popular taste, especially in a youth-oriented market like popular music, increases the pressure to balance novelty with consistency.

Finally, but significantly, musical artists often begin their professional careers when still young and poorly informed about their rights and responsibilities in a complex industry. Many artists have had to educate themselves—later in their careers—about copyright and contract law and get legal and accounting support to protect themselves.

Motown was not the only label to "pay" musicians in Cadillacs and fur coats in lieu of royalties. But the success that makes Motown a benchmark for productivity and cultural significance also makes it a high-profile example—like the auto manufacturing industry on which it was modeled—of conflict between "labor" and "management."

According to music historian Arthur Kempton: "Martha Reeves accounts herself the 'first person at Motown to ask where the money was going.' Her apostasy, though not actually original, 'made me an enemy. Did I find out? Honey, I found my way out the door.'"[15]

Others recognized that Gordy's controlling approach was based at least in part on the high stakes of competing in the music "youth market" in the early 1960s.

Everything from charm school to music lessons became part of his plan for artist development, "a means of polishing performers to a satisfactorily high gloss."

"Berry was crazy back then," Marvin Gaye opined. "I can dig the Gordy family approach—work keeps you straight—but Berry carried it too far."[16]

Did the Motown approach in fact go "too far" in the way it developed and exploited talent? To a great extent, it depends on who is telling the story. (See the "Further Consideration" at the end of the chapter for more.) In addition, the human and creative costs of turning original artistic expression and musical artists into products for mass distribution are discussed further in chapter 4, "Commodification."

Taken solely as a music production system, the proof of the Motown concept is in the output: over 190 number one singles (in the United States and internationally) from over three dozen different artists between 1961 and 2000.[17] Others have created "hit factories," notably Cheiron Studios in Sweden and Simon Cowell with *The X Factor* television show, but no one has approached the scale and consistency over time of Motown.

Since Motown, tools for "polishing" and marketing records have continued to develop. In the postmillennial recording studios of the early 2000s, every aspect of a song was controlled and edited to perfectly appeal to a precise listener demographic—based not on Billboard chart categories, but on the far more specific formats of radio.

Case Study: Maroon 5, "Makes Me Wonder"

An example of what is gained and lost by more modern "hit engineering" processes comes from the band Maroon 5 and their work to transform their song "Makes Me Wonder" into a hit (number one, Billboard Hot 100, 2007). Comparing this case to that of Marvin Gaye's "How Sweet It Is" at Motown is instructive. While the inputs are similar—a song and a singer—and output measures are comparable (number one Billboard Hot 100 for Maroon 5 versus number six for Gaye), the production processes differ significantly.

One of the most fundamental differences is time. Adam Levine and Maroon 5 had a much longer production schedule for their work on "Makes Me Wonder." According to writer Tom Whitwell, who analyzed a documentary of the production process, the band discussed the song's lack of a chorus and how much they didn't like it at such length that lead singer Levine observed, *"I'm sick of trying to engineer songs to be hits."*[18] And then he returned to the tedious discussion/analysis /engineering process.

In addition to time and time management, there is an additional factor. Levine and his band did not have the preproduction songwriting resources of Motown. The song was written by Levine, demoed for an earlier album project, and then discarded. It was being recycled for the album in 2007, according to Levine, because "it kept coming up because the label loved it." But he also noted that "it took a lot of work and I hated this song for a long time."[19]

This significantly differs from Motown's "quality control" process for material. Songs that did not "pass muster" at the weekly meetings were rapidly discarded and another songwriting individual or team moved their song to the front of the line. In contrast, Maroon 5 struggled to take an already-discarded input—a song that the band didn't like—and, to please label management, struggled to make it into hit record material.

When released the record received massive radio play in the United States and internationally even though it was not critically well received. Understanding how this kind of success happened depends upon knowing how radio programming formats work (or worked in 2007–2008, when the Maroon 5 song was being broadcast) and how labels optimized releases for best radio format results. This is a definition of output that differs significantly from the one used by Motown—*great artists + great songs = great records*—being replaced by *marginal song + persistent artists + production tweaks oriented toward radio formats = radio play = hit record.*

As Whitwell explains:

> Every element of the recording process, from the first takes to the final tweaks, has been evolved with one simple aim: control. And that control often lies in the hands of a record company desperate to get their song on the radio. So they'll encourage a controlled recording environment (slow, high-tech and using malleable digital effects).
>
> Every finished track is then coated in a thick layer of audio polish before being market-tested and dispatched to a radio station, where further layers of polish are applied until the original recording is barely visible. That's how you make a mainstream radio hit, and that's what record labels want.[20]

At Motown and other record studios in the 1960s and 1970s, songwriters, producers, and performers came together to make great music and records with the intention and expectation of achieving financial success. For Maroon 5 and other artists/entrepreneurs of the 2000s, "there are armies of producers, engineers, software programmers and statisticians lining up to help . . . craft the perfect innocuous but shiny-sounding research-ready pop hit."[21]

In addition to comparing record production models that—while separated by forty to fifty years and different production processes—share a common interest in using songs and singers to make records, there are other, more fundamentally different models to consider. These include using previously produced content as a "raw" input for a new production process—*secondary input*—as well as models designed for the *curation*—rather than creation—of musical experience.

SECONDARY INPUT MODELS

For many decades of the recording era, songs and performances of them were the raw materials for the recording process. The finished record was the output. The turntabling, sampling, and remix techniques of Hip

Hop musical culture represent a fundamental change to that model. Already produced records became raw material for rappers, DJs, and producers in the new musical idiom. For example, James Brown records have been extensively sampled by Hip Hop/Rap/R & B artists from B-Boy in 1986 to Jay-Z in 2001 to Kendrick Lamar in 2015.[22] In addition, the Hip Hop era not only introduced new musical genres and subgenres and disrupted basic concepts about music making; it challenged established compensation mechanisms for creativity and production.

A track based on samples from produced records requires permission from the publisher and the record label that originally recorded the music being sampled. Because sampling and remix music may use many disparate sources on a single track, the complexity of getting permission and the risk of copyright litigation have risen to unprecedented levels. This has brought challenges to ideas about the fair use of material and the danger of creating constraints on the creativity of "remix culture,"[23] and even when permissions have been sought and given, lawsuits can still result if the finished product surpasses early expectations for success.[24] Chapter 5, "Monetization," explores various forms of music licensing in more detail.

In addition to sampling/remixing, there is another kind of secondary input model to consider. As revenue from record sales has declined, record labels have reduced their investment in discovering and developing new artists. One result of this has been an increase in DIY production by aspiring musicians. As a consequence, labels that might have previously signed a relatively unknown band are now only looking at musical artists who already have demo recordings, performance videos, successful live experience, and the supporting evidence of a social media following of perhaps one hundred thousand follows, likes, and so on.

In this context, the input that a label gets from a self-developed artist is in effect preproduced. The label adds value in the form of enhanced promotion or distribution rather than the creative development and transformation of the traditional A & R model. This is a similar approach to the distribution deals that small independent labels have historically signed with larger labels to distribute their already-produced records.

This comparison of these two different kinds of secondary input business models raises a question. What happens if we use outputs to define music business models? In other words, as a consideration not of what constitutes an input, but rather of what being produced? Is it new art? New access? New experience? A set of criteria based on these questions could be that a model that produces new art is a *production* model (like Motown above or Def Jam in the first chapter). A model that produces new access is a *distribution* model—iTunes, for example. And one that creates a new experience without necessarily producing new art is a presentation or *curation* model.

CURATION MODELS

A production model is designed to find, develop, and make new music, and provide it to the public. In contrast, a curation model collects and organizes preexisting musical catalogs and presents them to the listener in such a way as to optimize a particular listening experience. A production model, like a label, makes records. A curation model, like Spotify or Pandora, makes playlists and recommendations.

In terms of roles, in a production setting the A & R representative puts the right artist with the right song in the studio. In the domain of curation, it is the Music Supervisor of a media, advertising, or licensing agency who finds and places music in the right relationship to another creative product, film, television program, advertising, or brand. In a streaming service, while some playlists and recommendations are generated by algorithms, many of the most popular are chosen by a still relatively small number of expert human "curators."

The rise of curation is actually the result of the astonishing increase in available music brought on by file sharing and downloading early in the twenty-first century. According to the senior vice president of Global Streaming Marketing for Universal Music Group:

"People go to streaming services because they love the idea of being able to listen to all the music that they want, when they want it," says Jay Frank. "But then when they get there, they find that that may not actually be what they want most of the time. The prospect of digging through 40 million tracks is just too much."

In addition, if bringing music to the public is more than getting people to find your song, but also to care about it and the people who made it (see the discussion of the customer experience journey, below), then playlists are about more than discovery. That's where, for companies like Spotify, Apple, and Google, human curation comes in:

> We've come to expect that virtually all of our problems can be solved with code, so much so that we summon it unthinkingly before doing almost anything: from choosing what movie to watch, to finding a doctor, to deciding where to wake up the next morning and who with. But what if music is somehow different? What if there's something immeasurable but essential in the space between what is now called "discovery" and, you know, that old stupidly human ritual of finding and falling in love with a song?[25]

CURATION VS. DISTRIBUTION MODELS

A way to compare music businesses like iTunes and Spotify is to consider whether they are built on production, distribution, or curation models. To date, neither Spotify nor iTunes is primarily engaged in finding, developing, or producing original creative content. So neither is a production model business (so far).

iTunes is an aggregator of produced musical products. It provides access using a retail framework. In fact, it's even called a "store." There is an experiential element in using iTunes, in the sense that any store has a "retail-scape" designed to encourage purchasing. But ultimately, a business whose main purpose is to provide access to products and a path to buy them is fundamentally a distribution model.

Spotify also provides access, via streaming as opposed to downloading.[26] Where iTunes was styled and experienced as a "store," Spotify, on the other hand, is more like a radio station. Though radio broadcasting can also be considered distributive—in that it provides access to music—it is more experiential than transactional. No product or money changes hands between music provider and listener. Broadcast radio incorporated playlists, DJ talk, and other content to create formats to attract a specific listener demographic. Satellite radio channels are even more content-specific, even to the point of being based on the work of individual artists or bands, often coordinated with tours or new music releases.

Spotify creates playlists, extended musical tags, and other recommendation mechanisms for a highly customizable musical experience. It also offers on-demand access that neither broadcast nor satellite radio can. As such, as a provider of a purchase-optional, personalizable listening experience, Spotify (as well as Google Play Music and Apple Music) is a curation model.

Neither distribution nor curation models engage in finding or providing production support for new artists. In addition, because streaming services generate less income than did retail/radio relationships in the twentieth century, record labels no longer make the same investment in new artist development that they did previously. As a result, new artists are supported neither by the legacy production models—labels—nor by the new, curated streaming service models.

The good news is that DIY tools make labels less important than ever and make it far easier to "do it yourself." As Bono states:

> What turns me on about the digital age, what excited me personally, is that you have closed the gap between dreaming and doing. You see, it used to be that if you wanted to make a record of a song, you needed a studio and a producer. Now, you need a laptop.[27]

The bad news is that you *have* to do it—all of it, including capitalization, promotion, and distribution—yourself.

This is not, however, bad news for listeners and consumers. Thanks to new production, distribution, and curation platforms, there is more music available today than at any time in human history. How you manage your musical experience is a topic for the next chapter. How producers manage you follows.

MANAGING THE CONSUMER

As noted above, the process of making records (or presenting concerts)—moving from creativity to product—involves some consideration of who the prospective listeners and potential customers will be. This effort is always made by the label and sometimes by the artist. Consideration of the end user takes a variety of forms. It could be based, in the case of an artist, on prior experience playing live and seeing what people enjoy. From a marketing perspective, demographics may suggest who the potential audience is, where they live, how much money they have, and what they like, based on past purchasing patterns. This aspect of music enterprise is also explored in chapter 11, "Aggregation."

Also, in addition to the issue of "who," there is the question of "how." There are a variety of methods for thinking about how to find listeners and then how to turn them into customers, including various versions of the customer experience (CX) journey, discussed below.

But in the broadest terms, once a production process has produced an output—a record, for example—the next steps involve making it available to people, getting them to listen to it, engage with the artist, and ultimately make a purchase. From a production perspective, reception is about moving from discovery to engagement to consumption.

For most of the twentieth-century, consumer music purchases were understood to be the result of a weeks-long process of "generating discovery." Planning for new releases (and supporting tours) was based on successful past practice. Success or failure was evaluated after the fact using either retail record or concert ticket sales as a metric.

As the idea of a "customer experience journey" (CX) was more fully developed and implemented across most business sectors in the late

1990s and early 2000s, the industry was being disrupted by new technologies and social behaviors. Both Potts and Eric Sheinkop, founder of brand/music licensing company Music Dealers,[28] consider that the "academic" version of the CX—awareness, discovery, interest, interaction, purchase, use, cultivation, and advocacy[29]—lost relevance to music production and consumption during this period.

Potts observes that while "the traditional 'sale' was usually somewhere near the end" of the journey, "in a world led by music-streaming, we are directly monetizing both discovery and consumption at the same time."[30] Sheinkop finds that modern "consumers are virally sharing the stories of their real-life experiences. Content is repurposed and personalised to fit individual tastes. Places of engagement and interaction [whether online or physical] are blossoming where consumers can cultivate their own experience without the intrusion of advertisements."[31] See chapter 9, "Connection," for more of Sheinkop's perspective.

In fact, it can be argued, as does Potts, that purchased products have been replaced by experiences. "We are monetizing the public's engagement with music and the currency of that engagement is a 'play' on a streaming service."[32] This point is underscored by Mark Mulligan, who states that "streaming has melded discovery and consumption into a single whole."[33]

As disruptive as these trends may seem from a traditional music producer's point of view, they do not necessarily uproot the fundamental structure of the record production model. As Potts states, "To be clear, the lifeblood of our business—signing, developing, nurturing and guiding creative artists—will not change. But the way we translate this creativity into monetizable, digitally-mediated experiences requires a culture change."[34]

From this perspective, the core function of transforming musical creativity into marketable content remains valid. But redefining what is produced and why listeners value it requires a new mind-set. For example, per Potts, label thinking about outputs must change from "records" (in whatever medium) to "digitally mediated experiences."

In addition, success metrics for such experiences must be measured in something in addition to dollars and sales. Potts suggests that "shares" via digital media (following *Buzzfeed's* "viral lift" metric)[35] could become a significant measure of not only how many consumers are experiencing a musical stream, but also if they value the experience enough to share it with others.[36]

This kind of success metric—and its relationship to monetary value—will be explored in more detail in chapter 5, "Monetization." The increasingly significant role of data collection, management, and interpretation is discussed in chapter 11, "Aggregation."

CONCLUSIONS

In considering the role of production in the music experience cycle—moving from creation to reception and facilitating access and monetization—we find that although production must precede consumption, consumers are a critical element in the process. Musical products and experiences must be accessible and appealing for the process to work. The most critical challenge is to manage listener experience in such a way as to encourage a progression from discovery to engagement to the purchase of musical products and services.

Looking at production as a model consisting of input—process—and output, we observe consistent factors. Even across widely disparate approaches, separated in time and by genre, and using different process tools and techniques, we find that any entity called a "record label" has an interest in discovering and developing songs and singers, making records, and getting them to the public.

We can also identify other structures with differing input/output goals. These include models that emphasize the use of preproduced music as a "raw" input, access/distribution of existing music, and curation of musical experience.

Finally, we observe that how producers see the "customer experience journey" is integral to the business of music production, how producers understand reception must change as tastes and opportunities for discovery and engagement evolve, and, finally, products—even digital ones—are increasingly replaced by listener experiences, as sales become less important than shares.

CRITICAL CONCEPTS

Production Models Based on Output

- one that produces new art is a *production* model;
- one that produces new access is a *distribution* model;
- one that produces a new experience is a *curation* model.

Production View of Reception

- From a production perspective, reception is about transforming listeners into customers by moving from discovery to engagement to consumption.

Label Productivity Shift

- Record labels are still in the artist development and production business, just not in the record making business. Labels today are producing digital experiences, not products.

FURTHER CONSIDERATION

Discussion

Did Berry Gordy and the Motown production and artist development processes go "too far"?

Read the following reviews/articles:

- Ludovic Hunter-Tilney, "Motown Stories," *Financial Times,* March 18, 2016, www.ft.com/content/cf5e0372-eb70–11e5-bb79–2303682345c8.

- Mike Zwerin, "The Mean Side of Motown," *New York Times,* December 3, 2003, www.nytimes.com/2003/12/03/style/the-mean-side-of-motown.html.

Then consider these questions:

- Was the popular and commercial success of Motown artists and records the result of the controls instituted by the label? Why do you think so? Why not?
- Were the artists appropriately recognized and/or compensated for their contribution to the label's success? Why or why not?
- Is the "exploitation" of creativity and talent always a bad thing? Is there a way for it to be good?
- To what extent should listeners, fans, and customers be aware of and/or concerned about tensions and inequities in the creation /production process? Why?

Other "Hit Factories"
- Cheiron Studios, Sweden
  - www.cheironmusicgroup.com/cheiron-history.html.
  - www.slate.com/articles/arts/music_box/2015/10/denniz_pop_max_martin_and_cheiron_studios_the_man_who_invented_modern_pop.html.
  - https://youtu.be/tuy8xTjDz5w.
- Simon Cowell, X Factor
  - www.mirror.co.uk/tv/tv-news/where-x-factor-winners-now-11319737.
  - www.ft.com/content/933257b6–4f3d–11e4–9c88–00144feab7de.
- "It's an Old Trope, but How Well Does the Factory Model Explain Pop Music?" www.thenation.com/article/its-an-old-trope-but-how-well-does-the-factory-model-explain-pop-music/.

A & R vs. Curation

- State of A&R Overview
  - ◦ Heather Wood Rudolph, "Artist Development in the Digital Age," *Creators and Creatives,* https://creatorsandcreatives.com /artist-development-in-the-digital-age-88d6f22a9888.
  - ◦ Nick Jarjour, "A & R Today: Why Gut Still Matters More Than Data," *Variety,* March 21, 2018, https://variety.com/2018/music /news/a-and-r-today-why-gut-still-matters-more-than-data-guest-column-1202731829/.
  - ◦ Reggie Uggwu, "Inside the Playlist Factory," *BuzzFeed,* July 12, 2016, www.buzzfeed.com/reggieugwu/the-unsung-heroes-of-the-music-streaming-boom?utm_term=.dcMB-m2o8w#.tnoV3NBzn.

Mike Will, Producer

- · John Seabrook, "How Mike Will Made It," *New Yorker,* July 11 & 18, 2016, www.newyorker.com/magazine/2016/07/11/how-mike-will-made-it.

CONCEPTUAL PROTOTYPE QUESTIONS

- · If you were going to launch a production company in the coming months, how could you use the three-part production model to create a framework for the project? Would you begin with input, output, or process? Why? Does considering the prototype questions in chapter 1—and the tools used there, such as "who is your consumer?" and "what is your minimum viable product or proof of concept?"—help you decide?
- · From another perspective, would your business be built on an input/process model more like Marvin Gaye and Motown, Maroon 5 and A & M/Music Consultants, or Mike Will (see above)? Why? How would this decision affect the output of your

business? How would this output be received by listeners/ consumers? How would you know?

- Finally, how would the melding of the steps of the consumer experience journey and the monetization of all parts of it described by Samuel Potts and Eric Sheinkop impact your thinking about production process output and what comes after? How could your production business take advantage of this situation?

3

Reception

Listeners, Fans, Consumers

The musical experience cycle—creation, production, reception—culminates when someone hears music. There are various descriptors for the people having that experience: listeners, the audience, fans, and customers, among others. While each term has a connotation of "hearing music," they have differing contextual meanings based on several factors. These include means of access: radio "listener," concert "goer," record "buyer," streaming service "subscriber," and so on. In some cases, the term also describes an emotional and/or economic relationship, such as "fan" or "customer."

Consequently, this text uses a global term "reception," because it covers all of the possible circumstances in which someone has a musical experience, distinct from being a part of making it. For the cases where the producer is also a consumer, Alvin Toffler's "prosumer" is useful because it is a term that describes virtually all musicians, but only some listeners. It also carries with it a specifically economic connotation: *prosumers* both produce and consume products.[1]

The latter point is significant for a couple of reasons. First, making music does involve hearing it as it is being made. Musicians listen to themselves and to one another in performance and during the process of recording and the editing phases of production. In that sense, "producers" are always also "receivers." But the converse is not necessarily true. Experiencing music, receiving it, does not require being a musical producer. Further, an audience member can be an active participant in a concert setting—clapping, singing along, dancing, and so on—directly contributing to the atmosphere of the experience for performers and listeners alike, but without creating any part of the primary musical content.

One way to look at the music business as it evolved during the twentieth century is through its relationship to amateur musicians in society. In the early years of the 1900s—and throughout the 1800s—there were many amateur musicians in the United States. Many of the amateur music "producers" also took lessons, practiced, as well as performed regularly in civic and business-sponsored music organizations. They also consumed commercial music products by buying sheet music and musical instruments and attending concerts. Though predating the invention of the term, these were Toffler's prosumers, both consuming and creating musical culture.

As the recording industry began to grow and become integrated with radio broadcasting, there was a decline in musical amateurism. This shift is best understood as a result of the ease and convenience of "playback" activities as opposed to the time and effort involved in developing and maintaining performance skills. As professional musical performances became available both live and recorded via the radio, record player, and jukebox, active participation in music making began to be replaced by passive consumption of music products and experiences.

This shift was a source of concern for many social observers and critics, not least because of the potential impact of recorded music on live professional performance and performance-related products and services like sheet music and music lessons. In retrospect, we can see that these concerns were perhaps misplaced, or at least exaggerated. For one thing, many people who patronized musical performances prior to the recording era had no aptitude for or interest in learning how to perform music. For another, passive consumption became the basis for the emergence of mass music and entertainment industries in the twentieth century (see chapter 4, "Commodification").[2]

In addition, even though many forms of public music making became less common in the recording and broadcast era, musical amateurism persisted. For example, as civic and business-sponsored bands and choirs declined, public music education increased. Sponsored in part by music instrument manufacturers and printed music publishers, school music making has—with periodic ups and downs—remained part of the musical landscape in the United States, Europe, and other industrial countries.

Nonacademic amateurs/aspiring professionals were also a significant factor during the Rock music era. So-called garage bands comprised young musicians imitating professional artists and sometimes—though rarely—achieving that status themselves. For many years, electric guitars and other amplified band gear for amateur performers were a significant part of the income generated by the music products industry.[3]

Despite the fact that patterns of casual music making have changed over time, there remains for many a persistent impulse to make music not only as aspiring professionals, but also for social or personal reasons. One result of this impulse is that business ventures develop to serve the aspiring pro and amateur alike. Some of these will be explored in later chapters.

But the popularity of amateur talent "search" shows like *American Idol, The Voice,* and *The X Factor* represents a phenomenon worth considering here. Traditionally, aspiring musicians have understood that there is a time/effort equation involved in developing the necessary skills to become a professional musician. In contrast, many of the competitors in talent competitions of the *American Idol* type seem to think that their performance skills are far better than they are and that the only things that differentiate them from established musical artists are publicity, lights, costumes, and other celebrity accouterments.

This is an entirely different perspective from that of musical amateurs who start with a love of "heard" music and are inspired to acquire the necessary skills to make it themselves through instruction or practical experience. This effort fundamentally changes their perceptions about music. As a result, serious amateur performers typically became avid and discerning audience members and consumers because they share many of the values and some of the experiences as accomplished professionals.

A decline in the quality of amateur music making and a loss of critical listening skills were predicted, early in the twentieth century, as a consequence of the increasing popularity of recorded music. If this is in fact a true description of the state of modern music reception and if, as noted in the previous chapter, producers must follow the needs of consumers, lowered expectations about musical quality from listeners will inevitably reduce the quality of the music being produced.

There is, however, always a risk that music professionals of a certain standing and/or age will see the current landscape—whenever and wherever that is—as inferior to conditions "back in the day." Generational perspectives aside, however, we need to be able to answer some fundamental questions about reception. How, for example, do musical and other sounds really impact our lives? How much do production techniques matter to listeners looking to "fall in love" with a song? What happens when audiences move away from passivity to resistance and even cocreation of musical experience?

In the previous chapter we explored how production processes transform "pure" creativity into consumable products and services. In this chapter, we begin with "pure" listening and how hearing music affects people physically, emotionally, and cognitively. Then we take a look at the technologies and techniques that shape listening experience, why some songs are instantly likable, and why some get stuck in your head. Then we explore how sounds grab our attention and how the "attentional economy" exploits this. Finally, we examine audiences and what happens when a producer's plan to manage consumers meets audiences who talk and push back.

PURE LISTENING: THE NEUROSCIENCE
OF RECEPTION

According to the Harvard Medical School newsletter article "Music and Health," "like any sound, music arrives at the ear in the form of sound waves."[4] After traveling along various anatomical structures, these waves cause inner-ear cells to "release chemical neurotransmitters that activate the auditory nerve, sending miniature electric currents to the auditory cortex in the temporal lobe of the brain." Once there, according to Töres Theorell, neuroscientist and MD, "music starts processes in the brain, which in turn affect the whole body."[5]

Once in the brain, the effects of music are then mediated

> via two different routes labelled "upper" (cognitive and relatively slow) and "lower" (emotional and relatively fast). The fact that the emotional processes are much faster than the cognitive ones is the basis for the "emotional surprises" that cultural experiences can offer. Part of the music experience literally speaks more directly to the brain than does cognitive reasoning.[6]

This explains how music can act on us emotionally and how rapidly it does so. It also suggests why music is so often used to trigger and amplify emotional effect in dramatic or advertising contexts. This is particularly important when the desired result is an emotional reaction independent of a logical, cognitive response. It is no accident, then, when we "fall in love" with a song (or a product) without understanding why. There is neuroscience as well as musical art behind it.

The activities in the brain are even more complex than the distinctions between upper/slower/cognitive and lower/faster/emotional processing. Listening to music activates various distinct parts of the brain, "which collaborate when musical processes are ongoing."[7] This collaboration across areas of the brain is intensified when the listener likes the music being heard.

In addition, research into music, liking, and brain activity has indicated that

Your brain has a reaction when you like or don't like something, including music. We've been able to take some baby steps into seeing that, and "dislike" looks different than "like" and much different than "favorite."[8]

This research also found that "listening to favorite songs altered the connectivity between auditory brain areas and a region responsible for memory and social emotion consolidation."[9]

Researchers also found that music's effects on the brain transferred broadly:

> Given that music preferences are uniquely individualized phenomena and that music can vary in acoustic complexity and the presence or absence of lyrics, the consistency of our results was unexpected. These findings may explain why comparable emotional and mental states can be experienced by people listening to music that differs as widely as Beethoven and Eminem.[10]

The findings of such research strongly suggest that music increases our social connectivity—it builds community—and the more we like the music, the stronger the effect. Again, the experience of falling in love with a song, with the artist who performs it, and/or with the person(s) with whom you experience it is backed by brain science.

In addition, multiple research studies since the 1990s have indicated that a high percentage of adults reported that music triggered physical/emotional responses "including thrills, laughter or tears" or that a major enjoyment of musical experience came "because it elicits emotions and feelings."[11]

Further, "prolonged learning produces more marked responses and physical changes in the brain. Musicians, who usually practice many hours a day for years, show such effects—their responses to music differ from those of nonmusicians."[12]

This raises an intriguing point in terms of how musical training impacts listening. In theory, it supports the idea that the prevalence of serious amateurs in society—those who have practiced for years to develop musical skills—will impact how music is received and perceived.[13] According to this brain research, the response of that public will inevitably differ from one in which there are far fewer trained and practiced musicians.

Ultimately, the capacity of music to impact the human experience is central to the arts of musical composition and performance. Advertising and consumer behavior specialists, as well as popular music "hit makers," have, for decades, attempted to apply a practical understanding of these effects to commercials, retail environments, and hit songs. Brain research provides some explanation for the impact of music listening, but fully understanding how music affects us requires looking beyond the "pure listening" of neuroscience and into the realm of cognition: what music means to the person hearing it.

MUSIC COGNITION: THE SCIENCE AND ART OF EXPECTATION

Interdisciplinary study of music perception (how you hear music) and cognition (what it means when you do) has been around since the 1960s. As neuroscientific research into music has grown—as discussed above—it has had a large impact on the field. There are many different approaches to music cognition ranging from psychoacoustics, to brain imaging, to computer modeling. Of particular interest to us here is the work of musician, researcher, and professor of cognitive and systematic musicology David Huron.

Huron's work represents a convergence of the academic study of music, music cognition science, and consumer research. In his groundbreaking book *Sweet Anticipation* (2006), Huron built an argument based on the power of expectation to produce emotion based on five distinct response mechanisms: reaction responses, tension responses, prediction responses, imagination responses, and appraisal responses. He also explores how combining these responses can produce complex emotions and how skilled songwriters and record producers understand these effects in a practical sense, and he explains the underlying science for all of it.[14]

Perhaps most intriguing is Huron's statement that his "book attempts to show how both biology and culture contribute to the subjective phenomenal experiences that make listening to music such a source of pleasure."[15] Huron's perspective about the interrelationship of "biology" and "culture" suggests that what a music experience "means" is dependent on at least two essential factors: (1) how effectively music is designed and presented to activate neurological mechanisms in a listener who is (2) located in an appropriate cultural context. Consequently, music reception must be understood as both individual and cultural, as well as both neurological and aesthetic.

Huron's primary theoretical tool to explain the impact of music is expectation. He observes that despite being nonliteral and nonrepresentational, music has been exploited by composers and performers for centuries to provoke emotionally complex and vivid responses. His explanation for this capacity begins, as he notes, in the work of mid-twentieth-century musicologist Leonard Meyer:

> Meyer's seminal book, *Emotion and Meaning in Music,* argued that the principal emotional content of music arises through the composer's choreographing of expectation. Meyer noted that composers sometimes thwart our expectations, sometimes delay an expected outcome, and sometimes simply give us what we expect. Meyer suggested that, although music does contain representational elements, the principal source for music's emotive power lies in the realm of expectation.[16]

Huron observes that expectation is neurological, evolutionary, and culturally based. From this perspective, we can't do much about our hardwired and long-inherited responses, but the cultural context in which music occurs is not only specific, but also plastic. Popular music is uniquely positioned to exploit deep-seated emotional and physical responses—happy/sad, tranquil/kinetic—and be not only place-specific but also genre- and timeframe-specific. Thus, for example, any given "song of the summer" is likely to evoke happy feelings, but the song from last year or ten years ago will soon be forgotten and sound outdated and perhaps even embarrassing if we come across it later in life.

On the most fundamental level, musical expectation produces pleasure when it is fulfilled and stress when it is not. But because our response to positive or negative expectation comes in two parts, the fast emotional phase and a slower "appraisal" phase, the impact is more complex than good/bad. In fact, an initial negative response that, after a bit of time to think about it (appraisal), produces no serious consequence can become a positive. Additionally, one such negative reaction that is followed by validation of expectation can be unusually pleasing.

Another way to understand a negative expectation outcome is to think of it as "surprise." Huron explains how the "three flavors of surprise" are each related to a "violation of expectation," and are capable of producing powerful emotions such as laughter, sorrow, and fear as well as more subdued and complex feelings. Huron notes that these musically triggered responses are typically short-lived and, because listening to music rarely produces serious consequences, any negative feelings dissipate quickly, leaving behind pleasant sensations from the experience. This goes a long way to explain, for example, why we can listen to—and enjoy—the same music over and over again.

It does not explain, however, why certain songs—even ones we don't like—get "stuck" in our heads.

HOOKS, EARWORMS, AND STICKINESS

In the discussion of Motown in the previous chapter, we looked at how the studio produced nearly two hundred number one hit records with dozens of artists. Certainly some of this was due to the artistry of the performers and some to the quality of songs being recorded.

But the production process included more than songs, singers, a "house band" of highly skilled instrumentalists, and a full complement of talented sound engineers and producers. Each track was carefully crafted to have certain critical characteristics that made its success more likely. One of the most important of these factors was the basic "beat" of each record. Motown producers understood that the majority of their records were music for dancing and they wanted to make sure that people of all levels of skill and rhythmic sophistication were able to dance to Motown records. This was a marketing decision every bit as much as it was an aesthetic decision.

An example of a record with a meticulously reinforced beat is "Where Did Our Love Go." The song was written by a top team, Holland-Dozier-Holland, and produced by Brian Holland and Lamont Dozier. Despite that, the song did not appeal to Motown's top artists. The Supremes, still hitless in 1964, didn't particularly like "Where Did Our Love Go" either, considering it to be repetitive and childish. But eager for the opportunity to prove what they could do on record, they were persuaded by producer Lamont Dozier to give it a try.

The repetitive nature of the song was—from a hit-producing perspective—a "feature," rather than a "bug." Repetition enhances familiarity and improves positive expectation fulfillment (see above) and memorability. A common characteristic of popular songs—and a major factor of the Motown approach—is the use of musical "hooks." A "hook" is a short, repeated musical figure, instrumental, vocal, or a combination of the two. Hooks often appear in the chorus of a song, but can happen in multiple places.

"Where Did Our Love Go" has many hooks in its design and execution. There are, for example, many, many repetitions of the word "baby," usually in pairs: "baby, baby." One of the ways you can tell that this was not an "A+" Motown song was that this repetition is not the title of the song. That means that after hearing it on the radio, if a consumer went to a record store and asked for "that baby, baby song," someone would have to identify the internal hook and direct them to "Where Did Our Love Go."

The place where the production is more remarkable is in its treatment of the basic beat of the song. It is a four-beat structure—the most common in popular music. To make the most of the beat and the song's repetitive nature, the producers had the drummer emphasize all four beats, added an extra percussionist on wood block, and, in a stroke of low-tech genius, had Mike Valvano, another Motown performer, march in time on a mic-ed plywood sheet.[17] The resulting recorded beat is prominent and unmistakable. Overall the record was upbeat and unforgettable. It reached number one on the Hot 100 within weeks of its release in June 1964 and was a pivot point in the career of the Supremes.

Another example, a record released by artists at the top of their game and influence at Motown, was the song "My Girl." This record by the Temptations is a master class in memorability. It begins with one of the most iconic instrumental hooks of all time, the three-note bass pattern. The next sound we hear is a six-note rising guitar hook. Within the first eight seconds, the record is already unforgettable. The lyrics begin with a story about some amazingly positive feelings caused by, of course, "my girl." The title of the song is introduced with five repetitions of the words "my girl."

"My Girl" quickly rose to the top of the R & B and Hot 100 charts and earned the Temptations a Grammy, the first ever for a Motown act. Clearly, as evidenced by this example and many others, the Motown hit-making process worked and the songwriters and producers understood how to make it happen. Why it happens and specifically why people respond to familiarity and repetition is another issue. (For the possibility of an overly repetitive hook, see "Millennial Whoop" in "Further Discussion" at the end of the chapter.)

Brain and music listening studies provide a hint as to why familiarity and liking are so closely tied and, thus, why repetition is important. A research abstract from a study in 2011 summarizes the neurological science behind it:

> First, we conducted a listening test, in which participants rated the familiarity and liking of song excerpts from the pop/rock repertoire, allowing us to select a personalized set of stimuli per subject. Brain activation data revealed that ... the reward circuitry [was] significantly more active for familiar relative to unfamiliar music [and negative activity was significantly

lower]. Hence, familiarity seems to be a crucial factor in making the listeners emotionally engaged with music, as revealed by fMRI data.[18]

It is not such a stretch to conclude, then, that the repetitive elements of "Where Did Our Love Go" made it quickly familiar and therefore likeable. Dancers were comfortable with its prominent and predictably repetitive beat. In terms of the larger context of the song, many critics found it to be a breath of positive energy and feeling. This was particularly welcome at a time (the summer of 1964) when many Americans were stressed by the combination of the assassination of John F. Kennedy the previous November, the country's increasing involvement in the Vietnam War, and the passage of the Civil Rights Acts, which was perceived as both hopeful and disruptive.

As noted by Huron, a positively rewarded expectation (happy song) following a stressful negative surprise (cultural conflict) is perceived as especially positive. Viewed from that perspective, "Where Did Our Love Go," thanks to art, production technique, and brain science, was the perfect song at exactly the right cultural moment to heal and energize the country.

Other research examines why some songs stick in our memory and are "catchier" than others. A pioneering study at Durham University in the United Kingdom, conducted by Kelly Jakubowski and others, indicated that "songs that get stuck in your head—called earworms or involuntary musical imagery—are usually faster, with a fairly generic and easy-to-remember melody but with some unique intervals such as leaps or repetitions that set it apart from the average pop song."[19]

So, "sticky" songs tend to be energetic and easy to remember and have elements of familiarity without being *too* familiar.

But while there is a correlation between frequency of exposure—when songs used to be played on the radio every hour, for example—and stickiness, a study in 2017 identified musical characteristics that make a record catchy independently of how often people have heard it. This study found that the songs "most likely to get stuck in people's heads were those with more common global melodic contours, meaning they have very typical overall melodic shapes commonly found in pop music".[20]

> An example of one of the most common contour patterns in Western music is that heard in *Twinkle Twinkle Little Star* where the first phrase rises in pitch and the second falls. Numerous other nursery rhymes follow the same pattern making it easy for young children to remember. The opening riff of *Moves Like Jagger* by Maroon 5, one of the top-named earworm tunes in the study, also follows this common contour pattern of rising then falling in pitch.[21]

Returning to "Where Did Our Love Go" and listening to the first verse—from the first "baby, baby" to the initial statement of "where did our love go"—reveals a simple melody with only five different pitches in a nine-note pattern. It's not so different from "Moves Like Jagger" or "Twinkle, Twinkle Little Star." So it turns out that research suggests that both things that the Supremes disliked about the song—repetitiveness and a childish quality—were essential to its catchiness. Years before perception and cognition science caught up with their professional practices, Motown songwriters and producers knew exactly what they were doing.

From the listener's perspective, the methods—whether art or science—used to make a song memorable and likeable are irrelevant. The issues that matter are how music fills our thoughts and our heart, makes us move and transcend the ordinary. As the discussion so far notes, however, it is music's capacity to act upon us so immediately that allows producers to manipulate our experience and use music to enter our lives for a variety of purposes beyond getting us to "reach for the stars."[22]

SONIC BRANDING AND THE ATTENTIONAL ECONOMY

Music shapes consumer experiences in both physical environments and mediated spaces, including brick-and-mortar retail stores, media-based advertising, gaming, and various user-interface applications. Because music (along with other sounds) has the capacity to grab our attention as well as to evoke specific physical and emotional responses, it has a particular value in situations where attention is at a premium. In extremely content-rich environments, where, as stated by Matthew Crawford, "attention is ... a resource—a person has only so much of it," attention becomes an economic driver.[23]

You can argue that monetizing musical experience has fundamentally always functioned as an attentional economy. It is a listener's attention that must be gained in order to create an opening for every other effect that music can have. Further, as digital and Internet-based media have provided greater access to more and more content, competition for attention has unquestionably increased.

In an essay about the "customer experience journey" in music, Eric Sheinkop (founder of music branding agency, *Music Dealers*) observed that

> [Because of] the proliferation of social media, brands of all kinds have been forced to evolve from traditional product-marketing practices to open and creative conversations with consumers ... that don't rely on annoying jingles and buy-one-get-one-free advertisements anymore. It's comprised of content that is authentic, that is story-based. Creators of all content types, whether that's brands, video games, television or film, use story to guide consumers along the customer experience (CX) journey from awareness to advocacy.[24]

Twenty-first-century music consumers—especially young ones—tend to be heavy users of social media, but highly selective about where they spend their increasingly scarce attention "capital." Music, by virtue of its attention-gathering qualities, as well as its capacity to create emotional experiences that are specific to an individual and context, is both a value and an "authenticity" multiplier in this environment.

The concept is reinforced by Joel Beckerman, author of *The Sonic Boom: How Sound Transforms the Way We Think, Feel, and Buy* (2014): In a recent interview, the author stated that "more and more companies recognize jingles alone don't sell products."[25] Because of that, he explained:

"We are not in the jingle era anymore, because jingles are very catchy. They might be memorable, but ultimately they're not very meaningful," Beckerman said. "What is new is how sound and music are used in association with these brands."[26]

Note that Beckerman does not restrict himself to a consideration of music. He observes that sound in general has an unparalleled capacity to evoke powerful and complicated reactions:

> You make decisions based on subconscious sonic information when choosing what to eat, where to sit, what to wear, how to feel, and more. When the right sound or music is deployed at the right moment to communicate this information and emotion and help you recall memories and forge new experiences you get what I call a boom moment.[27]

Beckerman's "boom moment" is a synergy of experience and memory. As already noted, sounds affect the nervous system and brain extremely quickly and also can evoke "a specific memory or a story."[28] This is comparable to the "biology" and "culture" aspects of David Huron's theory about musical experience. Surprise is a key element of Huron's description of musical effects and it is also essential to understanding what Beckerman means by a "boom moment."

Beckerman cites Huron's work directly in his discussion of the "orienting response" that reflexively follows being surprised—or startled—by a sound:

> In the event of a startle, within 10 milliseconds—30 times faster than the blink of an eye—a five-synapse circuit causes you to jump, sharply shrug your shoulders, dip your head, and turn toward the source of the sound; this is known as the orienting response. Your heart rate and blood pressure spike too. In less than 50 milliseconds—still six times faster than the blink of an eye—you've identified the sound and where it's coming from.[29]

This is how quickly and urgently music and other sounds—with an element of surprise—draw our attention. But there's more:

In the actual time it takes you to blink, sonic input gets directed through your audio cortex to other parts of your brain that control memories and emotions.... That's when a sound can become more than a sound.[30]

This also ties in to the art and business of making pop records. The research by Jakubowski et al., noted above, found that a "sticky" song, despite being generically familiar, also has "unique" elements "that set it apart from the average pop song."[31] The familiarity is important for people to like the song on first hearing, but the unique elements introduce the critical element of surprise. When that surprise pulls the listeners attention and triggers emotions and personal memories, then—like Beckerman's "sound"—a song can become more than a song.

This doesn't always work, because a "boom moment" isn't just about the neurological reaction to surprising sounds. It is also about the "story" behind that sound and how listener's memories are triggered by it. As Beckerman puts it:

Marketers and creative-decision-makers shouldn't choose music just because they like it. Effective use of sound means building a strategy to pick and create music that helps people understand the brand's place in their world. With the right foundation, sound and music can help transform a business or a message by communicating a clear emotional story and helping people feel the brand.[32]

In a pop song, the story is the songwriter's and performer's story. The listener may or may not share the exact experience, but the story is usually relatable, at least in broad strokes. But when you try to blend the story of a band with the story of a car, for example, there is a much greater likelihood that the listener will not make that secondary connection. That is, they may like the song, but not the car. In fact, listeners may reject the entire construct—car and song—as manipulative and inauthentic.

Beckerman calls this "sonic trash":

Sonic trash is when it all goes horribly wrong. When someone uses the wrong kind of music or sound and it's out of synch with the story. You

instantly realize that Modest Mouse can't make minivans cool in a commercial, or that Iggy Pop's "Lust for Life" (a song about a drug dealer and a
hooker) doesn't speak truthfully for the Royal Caribbean family cruise
line. No one wants to be lied to these days. Sometimes used carelessly, your
favorite song can be ruined by a brand.[33]

In terms of damage to a musical brand from an association with a nonmusical product, there are quite a few examples. It is worth noting,
however, that in the digital-streaming era, as record sale revenues have
sharply declined, song licensing has become ever more important for
economic survival. In response, for example, to criticisms for licensing
"Gravity Rides Everything" to Nissan for their Quest minivan commercial in 2000, singer/guitarist Isaac Brock said, "People who don't
play music for a living can criticize my morals while they live off their
parents' money or wash dishes for some asshole." The pros and cons of
licensing original music for secondary branding purposes are discussed
in more detail in chapter 5, "Monetization."

Despite occasional misfires, "ten of the 15 most valuable global brands
have invested in sonic branding as part of their marketing strategy."[34]
From Motown's hit records, to Maroon 5's radio format triggering
seven-second samples, to the sound of fajitas sizzling in a pan,[35] it is
indisputable that reception—how people react to music and sound—
drives production.

AUDIENCES: PASSIVE CONSUMPTION, RESISTANCE, AND COCREATION

The relationship between reception and production can be described in
a number of ways. As noted in chapter 1, we can see this as a complex
system that, for example, can only produce a hit record when all of the
factors and people on both production and reception sides come
together. This system, though it is understandable, is also unpredictable.
Naturally, producers expend a great deal of effort to understand reception and influence listener/consumer behavior (discussed in chapter 2).

Reception is not only a matter of individual biology, memory, and cultural reference points. Because musical experience so often happens in social settings, social psychology and group behavior are also relevant. The fact that large-scale music enterprise depends upon large numbers of listeners becoming consumers intensifies producer interest in the study of audiences and audience behavior.

The most common application of the term "audience" is in the live performance setting. Live audiences tend to come together around a shared interest in particular music and/or musical artists. They all arrive at the time and place of the performance and share the experience. One of the most important interactions is between the performers and audience members. This is perhaps most evident in smaller venues, but even during the arena concert era, this interaction remains important. New technologies (large-screen projections and so forth) balance the scale of the event with the opportunity to be "up close" to a performer, even if that is only on a "JumboTron" screen.[36]

In addition, there are the interactions between and among the audience members themselves. These exchanges create context for the listeners and performers alike. Enthusiastic audiences applaud, yell, dance, and sing along—depending on what is customary for the musical style of the event. Regardless of whether the concert is Hip Hop, EDM, classic rock, or a symphony orchestra, it is no exaggeration to suggest that performers and listeners cocreate the concert experience that they share.

Even as the popular music concert business scaled upward dramatically in the second half of the twentieth century and audiences for major artists got much larger, they still remained audiences: that is, a group of people assembled at a time and place to hear a musical performance, see and, perhaps, interact with musical artists, and share the whole experience with one another.

Although the term "audience" is sometimes also applied to mediated settings, it is more a term of convenience than an accurate description of what is happening. For example, even though those in a broadcast radio "audience" have tuned to the same station and are listening to the same song at the same time, they're not in the same space, so they can't share a social experience. Even the broadcast of a "live" musical performance separates the listeners from the performers who are playing and singing in the broadcast studio while the listeners are driving across town, largely separated from one another. Both satellite and Internet-based radio share this same feature: convenience of access and separation from the performer and other listeners. Radio, in all its forms, is much more an individual than a social experience.[37]

The "audience" for a record is even more disconnected. Depending on what is meant by "record," it could mean that a physical product has been purchased, taken home, and played there. With few exceptions, listening to recorded music tends to be a solitary behavior, disconnected from performers and most other audience members both geographically and temporally. Again, recordings (physical, downloadable, or streamable) provide convenience of access, but increased distancing from artists and other audience members.

Increasing convenience of access and elimination of the geographic and temporal restraints were critical to the development of a mass production music industry. At the same time, the greater the distance between performer and listener, the more difficult it becomes to tell what effect your music is having on your audience. Live audiences provide immediate feedback—both positive and negative. It is no coincidence that for decades—really, centuries—aspiring professional musicians served their apprenticeships playing a long series of live performances, moving from small and poorly paid shows gradually up in event size and compensation. Or not.

Understanding an audience on radio or for a record is obviously more difficult. A performer can't see a radio listener change the station, or a streaming listener skip a song. This loss of the feedback from listeners to music producers is a serious issue.

From a practical perspective, producers in the mass production era have tried to understand listener/consumer behavior through various metrics—most particularly sales figures—and to influence that behavior as much as possible. These control mechanisms include shaping the listening experience via hooks and catchy songs, the concert experience, the radio experience, and the overall consumer experience journey. As skillfully executed as all of this may be, the results vary. Audiences don't always do what producers want them to do. This is obvious because not every concert tour sells out and not every record goes platinum. Academic research also reveals that consumers generally, as well as audiences in particular, are never completely passive.

In music, this is not just an issue of when a member of an audience calls out a request at a concert. Audience members talk to one another, not just at the concert, but afterward. This effect has been amplified greatly by contemporary social media. If producers don't pay attention to consumer-driven media content, they can't hear what their listeners are saying, and so may be unaware of the conversation they are having.[38]

The empowerment of media consumers is described by Eric Sheinkop in his discussion of millennial generation social media users. He talks about the stories they tell, the content they create, and that which they ignore. This is particularly significant because it points out that, while audiences have perhaps never been truly passive consumers, Internet-based social media have dramatically increased the ability of listeners to communicate, build community, and push back against the limitations imposed by producers and production processes. Via the Internet, consumers become participants, curators of their own experience, and producers in their own right.

One example of this can be seen in the phenomenon of Internet "fandoms." For some years now, marketers have been aware of the impact of virality; how content can spread quickly and vastly across the Web and grab attention and amplify a brand. As noted by *Rolling Stone* writer Brittany Spanos, "viral memes have helped songs like Rae Sremmurd's 'Black Beatles' or Baauer's 'Harlem Shake' to capture the zeitgeist."[39]

Groups comprising dedicated fans of musical artists are not new. During the 1960s, the fans of the Beatles were so committed that security teams and police were required to manage their hysterical enthusiasm, which became known as Beatlemania. Still, despite the extremely high levels of commitment, there were practical limits—primarily the one-way communications of broadcast media—on the capacity of fans to organize and act collectively.[40]

Because Internet-based networks are not one-to-many, like legacy broadcast media, and are instead many-to-many, anyone can, at least hypothetically, launch a viral campaign, even a so-called consumer. In fact, fans have increasingly become engaged in the business of web-based promotion for artists they support. For example,

> People like *Pop Crave*'s Will Cosme have been charting the movements of fan Twitter and passionate promotional campaigns initiated via social media for years. The 23 year-old's own account is a collection of chart data, chart predictions, aggregated news and gossip that has racked up more than 100,000 followers in two years and captured the attention of both fans and major artists who have shared the tweets posted to the account.[41]

Cosme's research reveals just how effective the use of Twitter by music fans can be to impact and even fundamentally change the value—the actual metrics—for produced music. An excellent example of this is the Twitter-based campaign by "One Directioners," the highly organized fans of the band One Direction. The band and its label, Syco Records, had consistently encouraged fan support via social media.[42] More recently, however, the fans have taken matters into their own hands.

Project No Control, a campaign launched on twitter by a One Direction fan, was in response to a widespread belief that the label did not correctly promote the album *Four*, released in 2015, or release the best singles. The fans decided to release the song "No Control" themselves via an online campaign. Prior to this fan-driven initiative, the song had peaked at #42 on the Billboard and Top Twitter Tracks chart. Within two weeks of the fans' "release date" for the new single it was at #1.[43]

Any attempt to "game" record charts is complicated at best. It has become more possible in the streaming age because the formulas used to calculate chart position have changed to include streams (2012) and YouTube views (2013). The remainder of the calculation is based on digital sales and, traditionally, radio airplay. But as apps like Shazam have become increasingly influential in the music industry—radio programmers use Shazam analytics to help curate playlists—they have become portals through which fans can influence production and distribution business decisions.

Billboard, Spotify, and other companies are of course aware of this trend and implement "fraud detection" strategies to offset any impact. In the case of Billboard, this is not an entirely new response. It was not, for example, unheard of for record labels to buy all of the albums of a given artist from certain record stores in influential markets to boost the sales figures in an attempt to affect chart standing. Billboard monitored retail activity, and if they noticed unusual sales patterns at a given store, they would discard the data from that location.[44]

Today, Spotify has implemented a similar approach:

> "We have multiple fraud-detection measures in place," a Spotify spokesperson tells Rolling Stone. "The Spotify Content Operations team regularly monitors consumption on the service to look for fraud and any possible fraudulent activity is investigated and dealt with immediately."[45]

Fan groups counter by providing instructions on how "not to look fraudulent," including in a past campaign to support the group One Direction when they were contestants on *The X Factor*. Advice from a fan campaign organizer to other fans included do's and don'ts, such as

- Stream on Spotify, Apple Music, Tidal, etc.
- Stream on a playlist (such as the same song fifty times or have a song in between).
- (Don't) repeat the song alone or on mute.

In the terminology of audience theory, this is a "resistant" audience, one that rejects the imposition of control by producers. It is not an unusual phenomenon, nor is it stoppable. The entrepreneurial question for music producers, particularly aspiring ones, is how to optimize the engagement and participation of such audiences.

CRITICAL CONCEPTS

· Unless listeners become consumers, there cannot be a music business, let alone a large-scale industry.

· Though the situation has intensified in the era of digital media, monetizing musical experience has always been fundamentally an attentional economy.

· Because music inherently draws our attention and triggers emotional experiences that are specific to individual listeners and their context, it is both a value and an "authenticity" multiplier in content-rich environments.

· Though technologies change the processes of production and reception, how people receive, interpret, share, and value music drives production.

FURTHER REFLECTION

Neuroscience, Emotion, and Music

· The Neuroscience of Music

www.wired.com/2011/01/the-neuroscience-of-music/

· When Music Makes You Cry

https://www.psychologytoday.com/blog/the-new-brain/201709 /when-music-makes-you-cry

Repetition and "Catchiness"

· Music Will Get Catchier but More Annoying, Pop Song Study Suggests, by Yasmin Tayag

www.inverse.com/article/31541-pop-music-repetition-earworms-
  psychology

· Vox Pop Earworm (video)

https://www.youtube.com/watch?v=HzzmqUoQobc

· Spice Girls "Wannabe" Is Catchiest Hit Single

www.bbc.com/culture/story/20160708-why-spice-girls-wannabe-
  is-the-catchiest-song-of-all-time

The Economics of Hooks

· Hooked: The Psychology of Pop Music in 2016

http://pigeonsandplanes.com/in-depth/2016/01/pop-music-2016

CASE: THE MILLENNIAL WHOOP

For another take on the power of repetition in music, consider the case
of the so-called "millennial whoop." It is a melodic vocal pattern that
became so common in the 2000s that it triggered multiple copyright
infringement suits and a number of critical essays about excessive repetition in pop music. The following articles provide an overview of the
phenomenon.

· https://thepatterning.com/2016/08/20/the-millennial-whoop-a-
  glorious-obsession-with-the-melodic-alternation-between-the-
  fifth-and-the-third/

· www.slate.com/blogs/browbeat/2016/08/29/the_millennial_
  whoop_the_simple_wa_oh_ing_melodic_sequence_showing_
  up_all.html

· www.billlboard.co/articles/news/7865084/arcade-fire-suing-artists-
  millennial-whoop/

After reading the articles and listening to some musical examples of
"the whoop" consider the following:

· Is this evidence that, in terms of repetitive musical elements, it is
  possible to have too much of a good thing?

· Compare the frequent occurrence of the whoop in recordings by modern artists to the ubiquitous hooks in Motown records. Why are hooks an essential part of the classic sound of that label, but a "problem" in the modern era? What's different?

CONCEPTUAL PROTOTYPE QUESTIONS

· If the concept of the active audience, whose conversations shape social contexts and impact music production, is valid, how would this impact your model for a music production business? Is it a matter of output design or implementation? How could you encourage not only engagement but also participation throughout the consumer journey?

· Conversely, what if you were to create a business whose function—essential output—was to create social engagement and conversation about musical products/services. The musical producers are your customers, your inputs are random music fans and casual consumers, and your output is engaged musical communities targeted to your client. Is this production? Curation? Distribution? Or something else? Is this an aggregation model? What would the process component of your model look like?

4

Commodification

Product, Process, Culture

As noted in previous chapters, the fact that there is a "producer" in a system implies that there is also a "consumer." In this chapter, we focus on the relationship between music producers and consumers from an explicitly economic perspective. Along the way, a number of fundamental economic terms and concepts will be introduced and applied to the production and consumption of musical goods, services, and experiences. We will also examine some of the disruptive effects—on commerce and culture—of digital technologies, communication networks, and the social behaviors they facilitate.

At its core, this chapter looks at what happens to music production and reception when they are scaled upward and become mass production, distribution, and consumption systems. Music business models capable of producing and selling millions of tickets, physical recordings, digital downloads, and streams to millions of customers do not only impact economic systems. When artists from Bob Dylan to Biggie Smalls to Taylor Swift are given an accolade such as "the voice of a generation," it is a recognition of not only monetary success, but also social/cultural status and influence.

At the same time, converting musical creativity into consumer goods on a mass scale inevitably affects music, musicians, and listeners—and not always in positive ways. In fact, the "massification" of production, consumption, communications, and ultimately culture was a source of concern for social observers and critics for most of the twentieth century.

For example, early in the twentieth century, newspaper editorials disparaged the music of Tin Pan Alley[1] publishers for pandering to "the indiscriminate and undiscriminating crowd" with "blurbs and ballads and banalities."[2] Others were more pointed in their criticism of the music production system itself. Consider these comments from a *New York Times* article in 1910:

> The music of the multitude has always been a powerful factor in the social development of nations, but only with the past half-century has the supplying of it become an important industry.
>
> Nowadays, the consumption of songs by the masses in America is as constant as their consumption of shoes, and the demand is similarly met by factory output. Songs may be properly classed with the staples, and are manufactured, advertised, and distributed in much the same manner as ordinary commodities.[3]

While, strictly speaking, the term "commodities" may be economically inaccurate when applied to popular music—we will examine economics terminology below—it reflects a sentiment that the music "industry" was less concerned with original works of creativity than following rules and processes designed to make consistently successful products. The fact that popular songs seemed repetitive or even indistinguishable from one another to some listeners, however, says as much about their musical preferences as about Tin Pan Alley's productivity. But "high-brow" and "low-brow" tastes aside, it was clear that the factory-like effectiveness of music publishing in the early 1900s was widely recognized as both successful and disturbing.

Performance and performers were a critical part of the music publishing business model from the beginning. Songs were often "released" to the public via live performances, first in theaters and later in films. Tin Pan Alley publishers would pay famous performing artists to sing their songs, especially in a popular show. This practice was not only a matter of providing opportunities for audiences to hear new music offerings. Connecting the popularity of an established artist to a song—including by putting their picture on a sheet music cover—boosted sales. As would increasingly become the case during the recording era, performances and performers were already inextricably linked to the creation of value in print music publishing.

Much like other effects of commodification, when artists themselves become the brands that are used to promote and sell music (as well as other products and services) there are consequences. Artist reputations, status, and income all increased as a result of this approach. But, as noted in chapter 2 in the discussion of creative/management conflict at Motown, the potential for negative impact on the performer as an artist and as a human being is indisputable. The troubled and shortened careers and lives of musical artists like Elvis Presley, John Lennon, Kurt Cobain, Notorious B.I.G., Amy Winehouse, and countless more underscore the personal cost of mass-scale success.

Nevertheless, as the twentieth century progressed, the music industry grew, reaching an audience of unprecedented size and producing previously unimaginable revenues. After records surpassed sheet music in sales in the 1920s, the recording industry evolved into a multibillion-dollar-a-year business: US recording sales were (adjusted for inflation) $10.9 billion in 1973 and (even with some ups and downs) $7.65 billion in 2016.[4]

Success on this scale dramatically increased the cultural influence of the music industry. Recording artists led charitable campaigns—"Do They Know It's Christmas?" (Band Aid, 1984) or "We Are the World" (USA for Africa, 1985)—and calls for social justice—"Strange Fruit" (Billie Holiday, 1939), "A Change Is Gonna Come" (Sam Cooke, 1965), "Fight the Power" (Public Enemy, 1989), or "American Idiot" (Green Day, 2004)—that were meant to change the world more than (or at least in addition to) shifting "units."[5] Nevertheless, such changes—for good or ill—begin when the goal of making music and sharing it with the public is connected with the desire to make money. All other economic and cultural results flow from there.

ECONOMICS OF MUSIC PRODUCTION
AND RECEPTION

Any process through which musical experience creates value is, of course, transactional. In its simplest form, that transaction is an exchange between one performer and one listener.[6] All such transactions involving music (really, all transactions involving anything) occur in a social context. And, put as simply as possible, the social demand for a good or service or experience—in this case music—determines economic value. Using that value framework to explain the production and reception of music requires an understanding of several kinds of economic offerings: *commodities, goods, services,* and *experiences.*

Four Kinds of Economic Offering

In broad economic terms, *commodities, goods, services,* and a more recent addition to the list, *experiences,* define the range of things that can be brought to the market. Commodities are raw materials that are "fungible." That is, any given unit of a commodity is considered to be interchangeable with another—for example, grains, gold, or data bandwidth. Most often, commodities are used as inputs to produce goods or services. The most important consideration in the purchase of a commodity— usually by a producer of some good—is price.

When the term *"commodity"* is applied to music, it is often used to describe the perceived similarity—and an implied fungibility—of one popular song to another. More accurately, it would be used to define what raw materials go into the music production process. A musical commodity that is actually a "raw" input and is also relatively fungible would be live performance at the local "cover band" level. For example, if you're looking for a band for a wedding reception, price is probably the main consideration. In the recording industry, unsigned singers and songs are relatively raw inputs—selected by A & R representatives for their potential to be transformed into celebrities and "hits." Popular songs are not literal commodities in that they are produced to be distinguishable from one another in order to sell them. Even if some listeners—especially nonfans—cannot or claim not to be able to make distinctions among them, they are still the results of a refining, transformative system.

This brings us to *goods,* which are the output of a production process designed to transform commodities into differentiated products more valuable than they were when "raw." Transactions involving goods result in ownership. Goods are—from an economic perspective— tangible: something that can be sold from and stored on a shelf. In the digital era there are an increasing number of goods that are not literally tangible—you can't touch your downloaded songs, for example—but they are still goods because (a) they result from a production process, that is, they are made, and (b) there is an ownership transfer—you buy an MP3, download it, and store it on a hard drive.

In contrast to goods, *services* are not tangible or storable, and when purchased do not result in ownership. Examples of services include haircuts, guided tours, or live music performed in a club or private event. Experiences exist in time and when they are over, they're gone. For centuries, the primary economic offering for music was the service of performing it.

Musical service connects with the most recently defined type of economic offering: *experience.* An article published in 1998 by Joseph Pine and James Gilmore (authors of the influential text *The Experience Economy*) defines economic experiences as follows:

> An experience occurs when a company intentionally uses services as the stage, and goods as props, to engage individual customers in a way that creates a memorable event.... Buyers of experiences—we'll follow the lead of experience-economy pioneer Walt Disney and call them "guests"—value what the company reveals over a duration of time.[7]

To summarize, commodities are "raw" and interchangeable; goods are produced, individually distinct, and owned; services are intangible and consumed on demand without conferring ownership; and experiences are distinct from both goods and services (though they are interrelated), memorable, and revealed over time.

Pine and Gilmore further explain how experiences fit into the matrix of possible economic productivity:

> While prior economic offerings—commodities, goods, and services—are external to the buyer, experiences are inherently personal, existing only in the mind of an individual who has been engaged on an emotional, physical, intellectual, or even spiritual level. Thus, no two people can have the same experience, because each experience derives from the interaction between the staged event (like a theatrical play) and the individual's state of mind.[8]

These economic definitions suggest why music is difficult to categorize and why music—either as a good or as a service—tends to behave differently from "normal" examples of those types. For example, performers provide and sell the service of performing, but that performance produces an experience for the listener.

In fact, you can make a strong argument that it is not "music" per se that drives music enterprise. It is, rather, the "music experience." Once you look, it is impossible not to see that the end point of all music production processes is the moment when—regardless of medium or venue—the listener *experiences* the music and also—sometimes—the artists performing it.

We will take a closer look at the experiential economy below, but for most of the twentieth century, the importance of musical goods—first in the form of printed music and then records—increased. Further, the primary challenge to the recording industry in the digital era relates to goods—notably file sharing, downloads, and streaming. So to dig deeper into this facet of the music economy, we consider three subcategories of goods.

Types of Goods

The three kinds of economic goods to consider in relationship to music are public, private, and consumer goods. The distinction between public and private goods is particularly critical to understanding how music production and reception work economically. A *public good* "is a product that one individual can consume without reducing its availability to another individual, and from which no one is excluded."[9] In economics these qualities are termed "nonrivalrous" and "nonexclusionary." This means that with a public good—like a park, for example—"all people within a society benefit from its use without reducing the availability of its intended function."[10]

Music in the public domain, for example, is free for anyone to use and is, therefore, a public good. Not only can anyone sing "Twinkle, Twinkle Little Star" without permission or fee, doing so in no way impacts the opportunity for anyone else to sing it, listen to it, or put it on a T-shirt, for that matter.

Private goods are, as you may expect, the opposite of public goods. "A private good is a product that must be purchased to be consumed, and its consumption by one individual prevents another individual from consuming it."[11] In addition, companies that produce private goods do so with an expectation of making a profit by selling them.

During the twentieth century, records became the most valuable private good that the music industry produced. Records had to be purchased in order to play them, and each copy had a unique and non-transferrable value. Copyright laws prohibited the copying of such recordings for sale or distribution. Consequently, it was possible for an LP to sell out. That's one reason why people would wait all night outside a record store for an album release.

There is one more category that is relevant here—*consumer goods:*

Consumer goods are products that are purchased for consumption by the average consumer. Alternatively called final goods, consumer goods are the end result of production and manufacturing and are what a consumer will see on the store shelf.[12]

The recordings that used to be in bins in record stores and the MP3s listed at an online music store site are both clearly consumer goods.

There are also three sub-types of consumer goods: durable, nondurable, and services. Durable goods last a long time and are used over time (for example, a car). Non-durable items have a shorter lifespan, and are used in a shorter time frame (a fast food meal). Services are not physical goods at all, but are ... provided by one person to another at or over a particular time (a guitar lesson).[13]

So, to sum up, the economic offerings produced by commercial music businesses are private goods (you have to pay to get access) that are also consumer goods (a record is an output of a production process and, at least at one time, was available "on a shelf"). Records and CDs are also arguably durable goods, while the access a concert ticket provides is nondurable, gone when the concert is over. The musicians who play music for your listening enjoyment at a concert (or elsewhere) are providing a service.

All of these situations are exclusionary. In other words, if you don't pay you don't get the product to be able to access the musical experience coded into it. They are also, to some extent, rivalrous. There are, for example, a finite number of concert tickets available by venue and date. If a concert sells out, a date must be added. Physical recordings have traditionally been produced in finite (if very large) numbers. In contrast, digital files can be produced on a virtually limitless scale, a factor that helps explain the disruptive shifts in music production at the beginning of the twenty-first century.

Music Is an Experience Economy—and Always Has Been

Pine and Gilmore's groundbreaking book *The Experience Economy* (1999) had an immense impact on many sectors of the production and service economies. And as they noted in an article published in 1998, predicting a rise in the importance of business-staged spectacle, "experiences have always been at the heart of the entertainment business."[14]

Ironically, the year their book was published, 1999, was the beginning of a digital doomsday for the music industry. While music and other parts of the entertainment sector were being used as models for how to "stage" experiences for businesses, the music industry itself was facing the loss of the most important and profitable private good it produced: the record album.

In the earliest years of the twenty-first century, the music industry attempted to adapt to an increasingly digital culture by embracing— reluctantly at first—digital downloads. Note that this adjustment was still a product-oriented model, in which online stores replaced physical retail outlets and MP3s replaced CDs.

Economically, downloading grew very slowly, far slower than physical product sales declined. Music industry revenue was ultimately stabilized by focusing on experience-based offerings: live shows and streams. In addition, licensing opportunities through which products, services, and experiences created by other businesses used music to enhance the value of their own offerings became increasingly important. Video-sharing sites like YouTube, Vimeo, and Dailymotion, also became revenue sources by implementing both licensing and advertising models for music videos (and other digital content). (See also chapter 5, "Monetization.")

The changing delivery mechanisms and social connectivity facilitated by digital media aside, music and music enterprise have always been about experience in a social setting. But because the recording industry was so profitable and influential for so much of the previous century, that fact had become, if not obscured, at least less relevant to the business of production. For example, during the peak of the major record label era, instead of being seen as intrinsically valuable artistically and socially, concerts and radio play were used primarily to promote and sell records.

The beauty of records from an economic perspective is that even though they provide the purchaser with access to a musical experience—not so different from a concert ticket (albeit with on-demand convenience)—they perform in the market like private goods. Records are rivalrous and exclusionary. You have to pay to play.

But, in reality, what was really happening with records was more complex. The economic framework that supported them was dependent on twentieth-century technologies, copyright laws, and consumer behaviors, all things that would change at the end of the century.

Legal scholar Peter DiCola describes the twentieth-century model this way:

> Recorded music behaves uniquely because it is a strange hybrid of the intellectual and the physical. When music is purchased, a consumer obtains two things: exposure to a set of ideas conceived by the artist and the physical product. The "conceptual" half of recorded music is difficult to put a price tag on. When one person hears a musical idea, that idea is still 100% intact for the next person who experiences it. None of the idea goes away when someone consumes it. In economics, this is known as *non-depletability*.[15]

This dual character of what we call "records"—the idea and the object—is also reflected in copyright law. Publishing copyright applies to words and music as ideas. Sound recording copyright covers those ideas as realized in a performance captured on a recording medium. Even this perspective, however, doesn't fully describe the difference between the object and the embodied idea. During the era when physical products remained central to music business models, even though a record may have worn out or a CD become defective (or, later, an MP3 file become corrupted), neither the ideas nor the sounds themselves were depletable. No matter how many times it is heard or how many people hear it, it is impossible to use "Stairway to Heaven" up.

DiCola continues to describe how this situation began to change at the beginning of the digital recording and distribution era:

> The cost of producing a musical idea is the same whether only the artist herself experiences those ideas, or whether 50 million people experience them. There is no way to prevent one more person from hearing music for free. As was my case, someone's dad could let them make a copy, someone else could sell the music to a re-seller of used CDs, or someone could use Napster to facilitate the downloading of the music from a stranger's computer. This is called *non-excludability*.[16]

Thus, musical ideas are both nondepletable and nonexcludable. The problem with this is not only economic in nature; it is also technological. Once a technology has been invented to facilitate copying musical products in which musical ideas are embedded, there has never been an effective method for preventing nonauthorized copies from being made.

As DiCola concludes:

> This is what makes it impossible to put a price on an artist's creative concepts. These concepts aren't perishable commodities once they've been created, and there's no realistic way to control the number of people who hear them so it's difficult to objectively measure their value. Goods for which these two concepts, non-depletability and non-excludability apply, do not obey the typical laws of supply and demand. Supply is unlimited, demand is unconstrained, and the price does not exist—it is, in effect, zero.[17]

This is the clearest possible explanation of why a number of artists and producers began in the 2000s to discuss the question "what if the future of music is free?" We will explore the implications of this question in more depth in chapter 8, "Disruption." Here we focus on the tactics and strategies to preserve economic value in the music industry with a concept Pine and Gilmore use to describe how businesses modify the status quo for competitive advantage.

Progression of Value

As noted above, commodities are inherently unrefined and one unit is largely interchangeable with another. The main thing that distinguishes one barrel of crude oil from another is price. In the "blue-collar" strata of live music, the most significant difference between, for example, one bar band or one wedding reception DJ and another—from the customer's perspective—is often price.

The production process that makes goods out of commodities not only refines the raw material but also makes it more individual and distinctive. One coffee drinker prefers Peet's to Brooklyn Roasting

Company, so they'll make the effort to get it. The Rolling Stones' *Some Girls* (1972) was not the equivalent of Aerosmith's eponymous first album of the same year. Nor was either album a generic "cup" of "rock music." Both were specialized goods.

Or put another way, they were not "perfect substitutes" for each other. The economic concept of "perfect substitute goods" only applies "if they are perfectly interchangeable with one another, and the consumer is equally satisfied with consuming either one."[18]

Although one artist can rarely, if ever, be a perfect substitute for another, success does breed imitation in popular music. Musical styles share certain characteristics. Musical familiarity is (as noted in chapter 3) a predictor of whether or not a listener will like a song. Repetition leads to familiarity, which increases success. And over time, particularly for the music genre considered "pop" in a given era—typically high-energy, upbeat dance music intended for early and preteen listeners—there is a creep toward interchangeability. Not so much to the ears of committed fans, but rather among more casual music listeners looking for a more generic experience: getting ready to go to a club, to work, to unwind. This is a form of commodification and it is common, in Pine and Gilmore's assessment, to all goods in all sectors.

As a result, any good can become "commodified" by growing numbers of increasingly similar competitors. When this happens, companies must reduce cost, improve quality, or attempt to add value. Thus, Best Buy not only sells appliances (consumer goods); they also sell service contracts via the Geek Squad. And, as noted above, when competition in the service sector increases, businesses begin to emphasize the experience of using that service:

> An experience is not an amorphous construct; it is as real an offering as any service, good, or commodity. In today's service economy, many companies simply wrap experiences around their traditional offerings to sell them better. To realize the full benefit of staging experiences, however, businesses must deliberately design engaging experiences that command a fee. This transition from selling services to selling experiences will be no easier

for established companies to undertake and weather than the last great economic shift, from the industrial to the service economy. Unless companies want to be in a commoditized business, however, they will be compelled to upgrade their offerings to the next stage of economic value.[19]

The progression of economic value, then, is an issue of competitive advantage in a marketplace where imitation increasingly commodifies consumer goods. It is relatively easy to see how a business devoted to goods or services could first "wrap" these offerings inside an engaging experience and then, over time, focus on building experiences "from the ground up."

For example, since any coffee shop can brew coffee, a cup of coffee is relatively easily commodified. So coffee shops sell pastries, host art exhibits or poetry slams, or even go into the music business, as Starbucks did with their Hear Music stores.

Starbucks is a company that has always focused as much on their customer experience as on coffee. In 1999, for example, Starbucks bought a small record company, Hear Music. Their goal was to create special Hear Music stores where music and music purchases were part of the Starbucks experience. They even started a record label to sign new and established artists:

> "We believe strongly that we can transform the retail record industry," Starbucks chairman Howard Schultz said in 2004, and evidently others agreed. Paul McCartney ditched EMI to become Starbucks's first signee, saying that the coffee giant seemed more excited about the musical innovation than his record company did.

Other mainstream legends like Ray Charles and Joni Mitchell would soon come aboard, but so would younger, avant-garde acts. "Starbucks is the new record store, right?" Sonic Youth's Thurston Moore told a somewhat-horrified *Pitchfork* in 2007, and his colleague and then-wife Kim Gordon later said the band worked with the chain because it was "less evil" than their record-company parent, Universal.[20]

Obviously, not every experience-driven strategy will work. The Starbucks Hear Music stores were based on burning CDs for customers at the point of purchase. Unfortunately, this idea rolled out during the period when music customers had already begun to move away from CDs toward digital downloading—the iTunes music store was established in 2003. Subscription streaming access was also on the rise—early mover Listen.com/Rhapsody began in 2001, while Spotify launched in Sweden in 2008 and in the United States in 2011.

Their timing was against them, so both the Hear Music stores and the record label were discontinued by Starbucks in 2008.[21] Starbucks did not, however, stop using music to impact their customers' experience; they just "refined their entertainment strategy."[22] See "Further Consideration" topics at the end of the chapter for more on Starbucks and music.

On paper, the music industry has an inherent advantage in the experience economy. Music production is all about creating and providing access to musical experiences. Consequently, for a commercial music business there should be no need to "wrap" products/services in an experience. The end product is already "experience." In practice, this does not make a record label, for example, "bulletproof" from the effects of commodifying competition.

As noted above, music offerings comprise both a concept and a product. The conceptual content of a recording may be entirely original, but the product that embodies it—and provides the delivery mechanism, whether that is physical, downloaded, or streamed—is not. When companies were delivering "records" as vinyl LPs, everyone sold vinyl LPs. The same situation has prevailed with CDs, MP3s, and streams. Delivery mechanisms for musical products have been impossible to differentiate. In fact, each label having it's own product design would make playback and playback devices more complicated for consumers.

While producers are in the business of finding, developing, and providing access to musical experiences, monetizing that access has consistently depended on producing consumer goods (and services). Digital downloads and, later, streaming changed the parameters for recordings to act as private goods—and as a necessary precondition for accessing music. Instead, changes to the consumer experience—ease of access and discovery, free/illegal downloads, and virtually limitless and lossless copies becoming "perfect" substitutes—were immensely disruptive to mass production and distribution models because musical products began to behave as public goods.

Starbucks got a taste of this when they moved from layering music into their customer experience formula to becoming a music producer and retailer because they were seriously behind the curve with their emphasis on CDs and on-demand CD burning. The handwriting had been on the wall for physical products since 1999 when Napster demonstrated how efficiently MP3s distributed music. By 2007, when Starbucks formed a record label in collaboration with Concord Music Group, it was far too late. The music economy and musical culture had already pivoted.

PIVOTING TO THE FUTURE MUSIC ECONOMY

Over the first two decades of the 2000s, the music economy evolved to the point where demand for and access to recorded music had become almost limitless but the per unit value was approaching zero. In part, this was due to Napster and subsequently other file-sharing services that facilitated the sharing/piracy of commercial recordings. Even after the iTunes store was launched (in 2003 in the United States), soon followed by other online competitors, download sales remained fractional to drastically declining CD album sales. For example, in 1999 CD revenue was $14 billion in the United States. In 2004, the sale of digital singles was only $138 million, while that year's CD sales were $9.4 billion, representing a decline of 33% from 1999.[23]

The disruptive impact of digital downloads on twentieth-century music industry models was only the first wave. As CD sales continued to decline precipitously after 2004, download sales slowly increased until 2014, when the impact of streaming access began to become apparent. By 2017, the pivot to streaming, both advertising and subscription-based, was painfully obvious.

According to a review of RIAA data for 2017:

> More than 30 million people are now paying for a subscription streaming service in the U.S., which pushed streaming revenue up 48 percent, to $2.5 billion, in the first half of the year. Streaming now accounts for 62 percent of the U.S. music business.
>
> And that's pushing the overall music business back up again, after a fall that started in 1999, with the ascent of Napster, and didn't stop until a couple years ago. Retail sales were up 17 percent, to $4 billion, and wholesale shipments were up 14.6 percent, to $2.7 billion.
>
> Meanwhile, iTunes-style digital download sales continue to fall. They're down 24 percent. Because why buy songs for a dollar when you can legally stream (almost) anything you want for a price that ranges between zero and $10 a month?[24]

Much of the pressure on both legacy physical production and digital download models alike comes from the growth and influence of streaming giant Spotify. It wasn't the first (Listen.com/Rhapsody launched in 2001), nor is Spotify now the only international online streaming music service (there are also Apple Music, Deezer, Google Play Music, and Amazon Music Unlimited). Spotify is, however, an important case, not only because of the scale on which it operates, but also because it defines a new paradigm for the music economy. The company employs two interrelated yet distinct production process channels, using different inputs, producing distinct goods and services, and serving disparate customer bases. (See figure 4.)

On the *music production channel*, the commodities Spotify uses are the recorded output of both major and independent labels. The goods produced in this channel are its song database and on-demand streaming access to it. The services they provide listeners are—in addition to access—searchability, descriptive tags, and genre-based playlists. The experiential level includes the interface app, curated playlists, and recommendations for an almost limitlessly customizable listening experience.

On the *data production channel*, music listeners are the raw input and the goods produced are listener data.[25] The services they provide (to

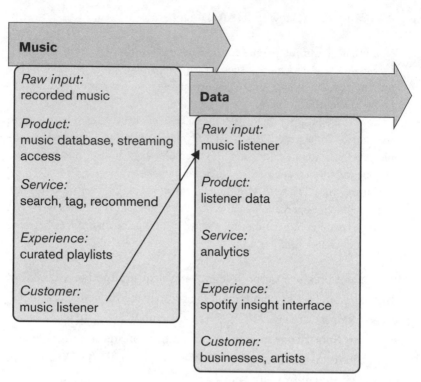

Figure 4. Spotify Economic Offering Model.

businesses) are the data analytics about a large customer database, and the experience is Spotify Insights (for artists, labels, and other brands), an interpretive analytics interface. In addition, Spotify partners with companies like Soundtrack Your Brand, "founded in 2013 to help businesses enhance the customer experience with music" by providing music access, playlist curation, and customer data.[26] For more on this partnership, see "Further Consideration."

The relationship between the Spotify music and data models is significant. On the production side, access to a curated musical experience attracts listeners on a global scale. As listeners use the service, the company collects a massive amount of information about them. User data then becomes the input for the data model. Their customers are also interrelated. Listeners take advantage of the low- or no-cost access to an extremely large music catalog and record labels take advantage of the access to listeners. Listener data is available to artists, to labels, and—since 2016—for sale to businesses that want to initiate targeted advertising based on user and playlist information.

Both of Spotify's models—music and data—put the company at the intersection of music experience, convenience of access, and listener data. In this position, the company not only has tremendous influence over music producers, listeners, and potential advertisers. Spotify has redefined how production and reception work.

Understanding and effectively responding to a market and musical culture increasingly defined on Spotify's terms have been a tremendous challenge for music producers of all kinds. Samuel Potts, Head of Radio for Columbia UK, looks at this landscape and recognizes that labels must change their culture—how they understand what they do, why they are doing it, and how they define and measure success.

One critical challenge that Potts identifies is a continuing reliance on sales figures:

> In our chart dominated culture, more volume = more success. But in a streaming first world where revenues are drawn out over time, are we concentrating too much on "vanity metrics"?[27]

Potts continues:

> The daily streams of a track seems to be becoming a default success metric for streaming probably because they're as close to the notion of conventional "sales" as we can get. But they aren't sales. They are more a hybrid of a licence and a sale, and the combination of discovery and consumption.[28]

As such Potts sees sales numbers and/or per-stream alternatives as not only a distraction but also a distortion of reality and an impediment to understanding how record labels, records, and listeners interact in the streaming era.

Instead, he recommends using a model taken from a company that originated in the digital era, *Buzzfeed,* "that has original creative content at the heart of its business—just like record labels."[29] Potts is intrigued by their proprietary metric, "viral lift," which is a measure not only of views or likes but of how often and how many times content is shared combined with views. A high share rate and moderate views are stronger than lots of views with few shares.

Potts sees this perspective—that "viral lift" is a critical measure of reader (or listener) engagement—as a vital one for record labels to understand in a production and reception climate driven by streaming. He concludes:

> Some labels are advancing very quickly in their ability to assess the new data that music streaming provides. It feels like the data "arms race" could be [led] by whoever gets closest to working out what our version of "viral lift" is, a way of accurately measuring the artist/fan experience across the multitude of touchpoints that now exist—probably some complex amalgamation of shareability, conversion, retention, and sentiment? This might end up being the most valuable metric of all in our connected music economy, helping us to build long term artist careers.[30]

Successfully pivoting to a changed and changing economic and social situation depends not only on practical implementation but also on conceptual shifts. Recommending new metrics is a perfect example of recognition that not only do the old solutions not work, but the old questions are no longer the right ones to be asking.

FROM MUSIC ECONOMY TO MUSIC CULTURE (AND BACK AGAIN)

As noted in chapter 3, the mass production and distribution of music that began and proliferated in the twentieth century was a source of concern for some. Social observers and scholars worried that music would become just as "standardized" as any other mass-produced product. And, if and when it did, the impact on listeners would almost certainly be a negative one.

But, as also discussed in the previous chapter, listeners and mass audiences do not necessarily respond or consume content passively. Not every mass-produced record is a hit. Styles change, sometimes disruptively. New technologies upset established patterns of consumption and production. But that said, repetitive—or, perhaps more accurately, replicable—production has been a consistent goal of the popular, commercial music industry. Thus the term "hit factory" for a music production business that produces consistently appealing and commercially successful records and artists.

Beginning in the late 1800s, print music publishing—epitomized by the Tin Pan Alley publishing district of New York—became the first music industry capable of mass producing and distributing musical products. As the scale of success for sheet music began to be routinely measured in the millions of units sold and millions of dollars made, the incentive to produce more hit songs increased.

Tin Pan Alley publishers routinely test marketed songs and lyrics. Songwriters would rework existing songs and publish them under a new title, with altered lyrics or music to replicate or enhance the success of the original. An example of this practice is in the various versions of the song "Oh, You Kid!," written in 1908.

The original version, much like the others, was a comedy song about courtship that included a slang term ("you kid") and a hint of infidelity: scandalous and shocking stuff in the 1900s. That particular song had sold one hundred thousand copies by early in 1909, making it modestly successful by the standards of the time, successful enough to encourage imitations.[31]

One of these, "I Love, I Love, I Love My Wife, But Oh! You Kid!" by Jimmy Lucas and Harry von Tilzer, outperformed the original. It not only became a hit song; by the summer of 1909 it was culturally pervasive. Clothing and novelty items appeared with "Oh! You Kid" imprinted on them. Sermons were preached against the song and serious-minded newspaper editorials warned of its dangers to society. Even so, the phrase appeared in novels, films, and comedy routines. And, of course, many "humorous infidelity" songs followed.

The "Oh! You Kid!" saga suggests that, on a large-enough scale, making popular music (or other entertainment) means shaping popular culture. Conversely, Tin Pan Alley recognized that making a song idea culturally pervasive made a lot of money. The interconnection of culture and economics in music was made clear over one hundred years ago.

In the years since then, many popular singer-songwriters—from Bob Dylan to Biggie Smalls to Taylor Swift to Declan McKenna—have been acclaimed as "the voice of a generation." It is an accolade connoting popularity and economic success as well as the cultural influence and meaning listeners find in experiencing the music. Opinions vary greatly about the authenticity or lack thereof of such designations. Nevertheless, whether arising from a marketing strategy, critical assessment, or grassroots sentiment, the title persists. See "Further Consideration" below for more.

Songs have raised millions for charity, challenged authority, and changed the world. At the same time, social and political protest songs made millions for the creators and producers. Marvin Gaye's "What's Going On," Bob Dylan's "Blowin' in the Wind," and Crosby, Stills, Nash, and Young's "Ohio" became iconic markers of protest in the 1960s and 1970s. As stated by musician and writer Danny Ross: "Not only did these songs influence the culture, but they also made money. Gaye's *What's Going On* album went gold, *The Freewheelin' Bob Dylan* went platinum, and CSNY's *So Far* went six-times platinum."[32]

The synergy of making music, making money, and shaping culture has been amplified by the expansion of Internet-based social media. Online audiences cocreate cultural meaning for their musical experiences even as they make or break economic offerings. In fact, an expectation of personalized, curated experience through on-demand access is what defines the twenty-first-century music listener and consumer.

From this perspective, Music Dealers founder Eric Sheinkop tells a story—about storytelling—to describe the new experience landscape. He recounts attending a pop-up live show in Chicago hosted by a Trip-Hop DJ for a millennial crowd. He observed the audience, connected to social media, even as they danced to a remixed version of Bob Dylan's "The Times They Are a Changin'," and had an insight about how younger music fans expect musical experience to be highly personalized (see chapter 9, "Connection," for more on this).

Sheinkop was describing one of Potts's "multitude of touchpoints" for the "artist/fan experience" and finds it to be purely experiential in nature: memorable, customizable, unfolding over time, and unique to each individual participant. In addition, Sheinkop sees this space as increasingly a lifestyle issue for music experience consumers:

> In August 2015, music analytics company Next Big Sound announced that it had tracked over one trillion plays across Pandora, Rdio, Spotify, Sound-Cloud, Vevo, Vimeo and YouTube since January of that year. Music is a key companion to the life experiences of the modern consumer, as the innumerable "Workout," "Dinner," and even "Sleep" playlists on Spotify demonstrate.
>
> No product, show or even video game has been invited into people's lives more than music has. People score their lives with soundtracks, and brands are learning to do the same with the stories they tell. The media industry is getting more musical. Synchronization—when music is licensed for media like TV shows, films, advertisements, video games, and more—is on the rise, according to IFPI's Digital Music Report 2015.[33]

Sheinkop's vision and business model are based on an understanding that the musical experience is more than playing/streaming a recording or attending a concert. In this view, music becomes a soundtrack for living and the musical experience becomes more pervasive, a critical component—but a component nonetheless—of a larger creative, experiential endeavor: life.[34]

Pott's view is equally revolutionary but he grounds it in both traditional and forward-looking thinking about record labels:

The lifeblood of our business—signing, developing, nurturing and guiding creative artists—will not change. But the way we translate this creativity into monetizable, digitally-mediated experiences requires a culture change.[35]

Where Potts and Sheinkop find common ground is in the recognition that consumer engagement and experience are critical to the success of music producing and "music including" business models. Both also assert that modern measures of success cannot be based on historical goods and services models or sales and volume models. Potts gets the last words here: "Our conventional measure of success: volume, could end up with us simply counting how good we are at generating discovery plays for a transient audience that don't care that much."[36]

CRITICAL CONCEPTS

- Music enterprise is an experience economy—and always has been.
- Once a technology has been invented that makes copying musical products possible, there has never been an effective method for preventing nonauthorized copies from being made.
- Realized on a large-enough scale, making and selling music become indistinguishable from shaping culture.

FURTHER CONSIDERATION

Starbucks: The Entertainment Strategy

Starbucks went beyond playing music in their retail stores to become music producers.

- Consider whether the music strategy worked for Starbucks: as customer experience, as retail coffee/music store, as record label.
- Did the company push too far into the music industry, past creating a music experience for its coffee customers? Why do you think so?

- What about the issue of timing for the company's rollout of their music service and product?
- See the following:
  - Starbucks History Lesson: Concept Music Stores
    www.starbucksmelody.com/2011/05/06/hear-music-a-memorable-piece-of-starbucks-history/
  - From Sonic Youth to Sia, the Surprising History of Starbucks' Record Label
    www.dazeddigital.com/music/article/38713/1/from-sonic-youth-to-sia-the-surprising-history-of-starbucks-record-label
  - Starbucks's Failed Music Revolution
    www.theatlantic.com/entertainment/archive/2015/02/starbuckss-failed-music-revolution/385937/
  - Starbucks Refines Its Entertainment Strategy
    https://web.archive.org/web/20130116172638/http://news.starbucks.com/article_display.cfm?article_id=48
- How did the company pivot from a CD-burning model of entertainment to what came next?
  - Spotify and Starbucks to Partner on Music Streaming Service
    https://news.starbucks.com/news/starbucks-spotify-partnership

Soundtrack Your Brand
- www.billboard.com/articles/business/8342072/soundtrack-your-brand-launch-licensing-deals-background-music

"Founded in 2013 by Beats Music co-founder *Ola Sars,* ex-Spotify executive *Andreas Liffgarden* and Beats veteran *Joel Brosjö, Soundtrack Your Brand* provides brick-and-mortar businesses with a modern solution for playing and curating licensed music in public. According to the company, it now has hundreds of direct deals with labels including Sony Music, Warner Music, the Beggars Group and the indie collective Merlin, as well as multi-territorial direct publishing arrangements with Sony/ATV Music, Warner/Chappell and Kobalt. The firm also has deals with various collecting societies around the globe, including ASCAP, SOCAN and the joint venture known as ICE (Sweden's STIM, Germany's GEMA, UK's PRS for Music).

"'For the first time,' said the company in its announcement, 'a background music service will license most of its music usage directly from labels and publishers, and the new deals include a pioneering per-stream-based compensation model that will make sure that all artists and composers get paid accurately.'"

Songs That Changed the World

- 20 of Your Songs That Changed the World

  www.bbc.com/news/magazine-21143345
- 10 Influential Songs That Changed the World

  https://theculturetrip.com/north-america/articles/the-10-influential-songs-that-changed-the-world/
- 8 Protest Songs since 2000 That Inspired Change (All The Way to the Bank)

  www.forbes.com/sites/dannyross1/2017/01/30/8-protest-songs-since-2000-that-inspired-change-all-the-way-to-the-bank/#c2afab41715c

Economics: Music as a Public Good

- Graham Hubbs, "Digital Music and Public Goods," in *21st Century Perspectives on Music, Technology, and Culture,* ed. Richard Purcell and Richard Randall, 134–152, Palgrave Macmillan (2016).
- Jens Leth Hougaard and Mich Tvede, "Selling Digital Music: Business Models for Public Goods," *NETNOMICS: Economic Research and Electronic Networking* 11, no. 1 (2010): 85–102.

Voices of a Generation

- Bob Dylan Doesn't Accept Being "The Voice of His Generation"

  www.npr.org/2016/10/14/497911840/bob-dylan-doesnt-accept-being-the-voice-of-his-generation

- Biggie Smalls: The Voice That Influenced a Generation
  www.npr.org/2010/08/02/128916682/biggie-smalls-the-voice-that-influenced-a-generation
- Taylor Swift Named "The Voice of A Generation" by the President of Her Label
  www.idolator.com/5395432/taylor-swift-named-the-voice-of-a-generation-by-president-of-her-label?safari=1
- The Generation That Grew Up with Taylor Swift
  www.theodysseyonline.com/the-generation-that-grew-up-with-taylor-swift
- Declan McKenna: "Voice of A Generation? It's Just Sensationalism"
  www.irishtimes.com/culture/music/declan-mckenna-voice-of-a-generation-it-s-just-sensationalism-1.3159051

CONCEPTUAL PROTOTYPE QUESTIONS

You're developing plans for a record label while considering the principles and concepts outlined here. How would you, following Samuel Potts (see discussion in chapter), apply his two-part analysis that states, "the life blood of our business—signing, developing, nurturing and guiding creative artists—will not change. But the way we translate this creativity into monetizable, digitally-mediated experiences requires a culture change."

Potts suggests that this has to do with how success is measured and what it means in a digital environment. Eric Sheinkop (also discussed in the chapter) sees the "experience" from a wider perspective. Are these views compatible, or not? How do you redefine success metrics, remap the consumer/listener experience, and protect the "lifeblood" of the recording industry? What would be a proof of concept? What would be a minimum viable product?

5

Monetization

Publishing, Performing, Recording

MAKING MONEY, MAKING MUSIC

Money is by no means the only or most important form of value created by music. If, however, you want music to be a business, then—regardless of whether it is producing goods, services, or experiences—someone has to make money and someone has to pay. Put another way, regardless of the primary motivation for making music—artistic, social, or commercial—there is always a need for a sustainable economic model for it to survive, let alone thrive.

While there are a number of support structures based on private or governmental sponsorship, the majority of music created in the industrialized world over the last one hundred plus years has been produced in a market framework. In the marketplace, monetization of music depends upon a balance between control and access. If access to a musical good has no limits—anyone can hear it anytime they want, for free—then its monetary value approaches zero. Conversely, if the access control approaches 100%—that is, almost no one can have the musical experience because it is too difficult to get or too expensive—artistic value, social value, and cultural value are minimized.

Regardless of era and style—from Beethoven to Bruno Mars—the dynamic tension between access and control of musical productivity has been constrained by copyright law. Whether we are talking about the twentieth-century model (based on a synergy of records, radio, print publishing, and live shows) or the twenty-first (downloads, streams, licensing, and live shows), there is a copyright statute and a body of case law that are applicable. Further, as new technologies, social behaviors, and economic conditions have emerged, copyright law was adapted or newly created in response.

In addition to legal considerations, this chapter also looks at practical operations—the different ways that money comes in (and goes out) of various kinds of music enterprise, especially the publishing, performing, and recording sectors. It also examines the interrelated distributive media—broadcasting, downloading, and streaming—as well as licensing opportunities not only for music and musical services, but also for brands and merchandise.

The modern music business was built on the interconnected creative and economic spheres of performance, publishing, and recording. Publishing depended upon performance, as did the sale of recordings. Live or broadcast performances helped sell sheet music and records. Popular products—or an appearance on a popular radio show—helped sell tickets to live performances. Although the types of activities, products, and services have changed in the intervening century, their interconnection remains as important in the 2010s as it was in the 1890s.

Let's begin with a look at how these sectors operate and make money.

REVENUE MECHANISMS

Across the publishing, performing, and recording sectors there are a number of monetization mechanisms. These are *sales, subscriptions, advertising,* and *licensing. Sales* are the most traditional and ongoing revenue source. This category includes printed music, recordings, concert tickets, and related merchandise—from headphones to concert T-shirts.

Subscription-based revenue models are a more recent development. They almost always involve access to recorded music and include streaming, satellite radio, and bundled products where access may be paired with mobile data or a shopping/shipping service like Amazon Prime.

Advertising-based models go back to the earliest days of broadcast radio and carry forward through YouTube and Spotify's freemium service. Advertising allows musical content to be "free" to consumers, who actually pay in two ways for this access: their time and attention during commercials and their data being collected and sold by the music distributing medium to other businesses for targeted advertising.

Licensing models add tremendous value to copyrighted (or trademarked) musical ideas, recordings, and artist brands.[1] As discussed below, when the publishing industry pivoted from a focus on producing printed music, they shifted to the administration of licenses: mechanical, synchronization, performance rights, and more. Licensing also includes the use of music, likenesses, and trademarks—and often more than one of these. Putting a song lyric on a T-shirt, for example, could involve copyright, trademarks (potentially), and contractual arrangements (if any) concerning profit percentages or royalties.

UNITS OF MEASUREMENT

Because sales have been—at least until relatively recently—the most important measure of success in the music industry, "units sold" has been a critical metric for assessing profit and loss within or across multiple ventures. Even in newer approaches, such as the sharing-based *viral lift* metric, "something" is being counted as a way to compare one venture and/or one fiscal period to another.[2] What that "something" is tells us quite a bit about how businesses understand themselves and what they are producing.

Sales units have often been labeled with the name of the thing being sold: tickets, "sheets" for sheet music, singles, albums, or streams. As technologies have created new kinds of consumer product—for example, from 45 singles to LP albums, to downloads, to streams—what constitutes a unit may change, but the need to sell them and count what has sold does not. Tracking sales is vital to understanding profit/loss for a given project or a label's performance over a financial period, to evaluate a trend over a longer time frame, or to make predictions about future projects.

For example, in the early 2000s, when downloaded singles began to displace CD sales, it became difficult to compare pre- and postdigital statistics. To do so, a new metric—the "track equivalent album" (TEA) was created. A TEA represents ten digital tracks as the equivalent of one traditional album. This made it possible to compare sales during the vinyl LP or physical CD eras with the singles-dominated sales figures from digital music stores.

In the second decade of the 2000s, the situation grew more complex. While ten digital tracks remained a TEA, streaming access required a new comparative metric: the stream equivalent album (SEA) in which fifteen hundred streams equal one album equivalent unit. In addition, since consumers have been able to access music via both downloading and streaming platforms as well as physical sales, revenue figures became a cumulative measure of equivalent albums across all delivery formats/platforms.[3]

ECONOMIC SCALE

Today, the economic scale of the music industry is measured in the tens of billions of dollars (US) every year. For example, by the end of 2016—from all sources, including recorded, live, publishing, merchandise, and branding/sponsorship—the global music industry had generated $59.8 billion in revenue.[4] In the United States alone, the revenue generated from live, recorded, and various licensed offerings totaled $17.2 billion that year.[5]

Looking at data on this scale has obvious advantages for music production businesses of all kinds.[6] For students of the industry, a broad understanding of the value being created illustrates the stakes involved in large musical ventures. There are also, however, potential drawbacks to this kind of "big data."

A particular challenge comes from combining sectors of music production—for example, saying that the global industry in 2016 produced nearly $60 billion in revenue. That aggregated information can be difficult to apply to any particular venture. In order to make such data more useful—and the data collection and analysis services themselves more profitable—these aggregate figures are typically broken down by types of economic offering and geographical location, as well as other identifiers.

Consider, for example, the US revenue figures from 2016 noted above.[7] The $17.2 billion total breaks down into live music ticket sales (43%), streaming (18%), and live music sponsorship (12%), with downloads, physical sales, performance rights, and synchronization rights comprising the balance. Note that tickets sold for live concerts represent by far the largest segment of revenue production and that streaming is the next largest. You can see how these data points suggest that the music industry in the second decade of the twenty-first century depends primarily on concerts and streaming to make money (73% of the total) along with a variety of significantly smaller revenue streams.

Let's take a step further. These data points facilitate year-to-year comparisons and can be used to both identify trends and make predictions. For example, from the same US music industry report: "Digital music streaming revenue was up a quite astonishing 99.1% year-on-year in 2016 to total $3.0 billion." And "music streaming revenue is now forecast to rise to $7.4 billion in 2021."[8]

Looking beyond that five-year prediction to a longer scale of comparison, the global report referenced above compares music industry revenues in 2000 and 2016.[9] This is a particularly significant period because it spans from the dawn of the digital era—immediately post-Napster, but pre-iTunes—through the rise (and fall) of digital downloads and the explosive growth of streaming.

Two metrics from this time frame suggest a significant trend: the value produced by recorded music fell from 53% of total revenue in 2000 to 38% in 2016. At the same time, live music grew from 33% to 43%. This supports a standard position of many industry insiders today—that live music is the cornerstone of revenue production in music.

From the same global study, predictions of economic growth for both streaming and live music (between 3% and 7% a year through 2021) suggest that the future of music commerce—at least in the short term—will be based on a *live show + streaming = revenue* equation. Music producers continue to plan accordingly.

There are, however, variables that impact how accurate such predictions can be, especially as applied to specific ventures. These include things like overall economic conditions, world events (violence at concert venues, for example), ticketing policies and strategies (see "slow ticketing," below), and technologies (ranging from live streaming concerts to virtual reality to radio frequency identification [RFID] wristbands to enhance the music festival experience [see chapter 9]).[10]

Consequently, while there is broad agreement that access to data and data analytics are important, what that means in practice is less clear. See chapter 11, "Aggregation," for a closer look.

Regardless of the analytical tools employed, revenue mechanisms must function or a venture fails. So the balance of the chapter looks at monetization practice by sector—publishing, performing, and recording—and the particular variables of each.

PUBLISHING ECONOMICS

Publishing revenue depends on relationships with songwriters and performers, record companies, and distributive media. In fact, the publishing sector controls the rights for most forms of copyright-based licensing and is connected to virtually every form of monetization in music.

This position of power is based primarily on copyright law, both within individual countries and through international agreements. Since copyright laws tend to follow economic developments, understanding the publishing industry requires looking not only at the legal framework, but also at the music marketplace and culture that shape it.

Music publishing began as a production system that monetized musical creativity via the sale of printed music. The early publisher-to-consumer business model was based on the sale of "sheets" or folios of music for either professional or amateur performance. As discussed in the previous chapter, music publishing became a successful large-scale business during the nineteenth and early twentieth centuries and, in the United States alone, sold millions of copies annually between 1910 and 1920.

As often happens in the music business, new technologies proved disruptive to the print music industry. By the mid-1920s, the sale of recordings surpassed that of sheet music, a situation amplified by the concurrent rise of network radio broadcasting. It became evident that, to survive, music publishing would have to change from an industry based on the production and sale of printed music to one based on managing and monetizing the rights of composers and publishers in live performance, recordings, and broadcast media.

Before the emergence of records and radio began to change the business, music publishers were aware of the importance of live performance to their business model. But when they paid performers to endorse (or "plug") their songs, they saw this as a promotional cost to improve the sale of printed music rather than as a revenue source to be licensed. This is similar to the mid-twentieth-century view that the cost of concert touring paid off in albums sold, rather than serving as the critical income generator concerts have become today.

Consequently, although the right to publicly perform music was included in US copyright law as early as 1897,[11] it was often ignored by publishers. Until the sale of recordings began to seriously damage the market for printed music in the mid-1920s, publishers were more concerned with pirated copies of printed music than with performance rights royalties.

But as the synergy between records and radio increasingly diminished demand for sheet music, publishers began to change their game. One of the first adjustments was the result of performance rights organizations (PROs) aggressively collecting royalties due for live performances.

PERFORMANCE RIGHTS ORGANIZATIONS AND LICENSING

Today, performance rights are administered in the United States by ASCAP, BMI, SESAC, and, since 2013, Global Music Rights (GMR). Rates are established by the organizations themselves based on complex formulas that include the mode of delivery—live, broadcast, satellite, or stream—and the size of venue or media organization as well as other factors.

According to National Music Publishers Association (NMPA) statistics, performance rights accounted for 54% of publishing revenues in 2016. In order to understand performance royalties today, we need to look at two critical aspects of performance rights that impact monetization: *blanket licenses,* a system created by PROs; and *consent decrees,* legal rulings imposed on ASCAP and BMI by the US Department of Justice.

Blanket Licenses

The first PRO in the United States was ASCAP, established six years after the Copyright Act of 1909 specified the right "to perform the copyrighted work publicly for profit if it be a musical composition and for the purpose of public performance for profit." ASCAP immediately began the process of collecting royalties for the compositions of its members from live performance venues. As this was a new practice, there was reluctance on the part of the owners of businesses where music was played—either by live musicians or mechanically, via piano rolls—to pay for what had previously been free. Some argued that, absent an admission fee for a musical performance, there was no basis for claiming that it was a "for-profit" use.

The issue was resolved in 1917 by the US Supreme Court in the case of *Herbert v. Shanley Co.* The defendant, the Shanley Company, arranged for a live performance of Victor Herbert's music in the dining room of the Vanderbilt Hotel "for the entertainment of guests during meal times."[12] The court overruled the circuit court of appeals, which had found that, because there was no admission charge, it was not a performance "for profit" and the copyright act did not apply. The higher-court ruling stated that (a) "If the rights under the copyright are infringed only by a performance where money is taken at the door, they are very imperfectly protected," and (b) that "If music did not pay, it would be given up. If it pays, it pays out of the public's pocket. Whether it pays or not, the purpose of employing it is profit, and that is enough."[13]

This was an extremely significant ruling that made it possible for ASCAP and eventually other PROs to charge businesses for all uses of music, whether as the primary focus or a secondary part of their business offerings. To simplify the rapidly growing licensing process, ASCAP developed a system that allowed a business to pay a single "blanket" fee to use any song in the company's catalog for a period of time.

There were benefits to all stakeholders in this system: songwriters, publishers, and businesses using music. Music buyers got "one stop shopping" for the entire ASCAP catalog of music and ASCAP members were assured compensation for the public performance of their works. As noted by Frederic Boucher, the blanket performance license was "at once a brilliant solution to a thorny problem and, as experience has shown, a potent tool of monopoly."[14]

Consent Decrees

Blanket licensing was in fact so powerful that ASCAP's practices were investigated by the US Department of Justice:

In 1941, the United States charged that the ASCAP blanket license was an illegal restraint of trade and that arbitrary prices were being charged as the result of an illegal copyright pool.... That case ultimately was settled by a consent decree, which placed various restrictions on ASCAP's licensing procedures.[15]

BMI was also sued by the DOJ in 1941 and entered into its own consent decree. Both decrees have been revised several times since their establishment, but in their current form they constrain ASCAP and BMI in similar ways. Both companies must allow their members to also negotiate directly with potential buyers, they must grant a license to anyone who requests one at a "reasonable fee" (see below), and, if the user and the PRO cannot agree on the fee, the issue goes to a "rate court" that will decide what the fee should be.

The terms of the consent decrees allow both ASCAP and BMI some latitude to establish licensing fees for the performance of the music they manage. But the "reasonable fee" language and the recourse of users to "rate court" create real constraints. As a consequence, the consent decrees have been and remain a source of frustration for publishers and composers who feel that they are at a disadvantage in terms of setting fees for their productivity that reflect their actual market value.

In fact, the DOJ reviewed the consent decrees beginning in 2014. The closing report (2016) states that since the music industry "developed in the context of, and in reliance on, these consent decrees," they should remain in effect for the present. But in addition, the report also "encourages the development of a comprehensive legislative solution that ensures a competitive marketplace and obviates the need for continued Division oversight of the PROs."[16]

Shortly after the release of the DOJ review findings, both ASCAP and BMI issued an open letter urging the replace of the consent decrees with a "free market" solution.[17] The debate about the decrees is thus ongoing and part of a larger discussion of music licensing, reflected (in late 2018) in the Music Modernization Act (see below).[18]

Mechanical Licensing

In addition to addressing performance rights, the Copyright Act of 1909 introduced the first "mechanical license," which at the time was intended to prevent any monopoly in the production of piano rolls. It was also applicable to the production of recordings, in which capacity it became foundational to the music industry. Thus, years before the recording industry superseded print publishing, a foundational connection between the two music sectors was established in copyright law.[19]

Perhaps the most significant aspect of the mechanical license provision of the Act of 1909 was that the license to make physical copies was designed to be compulsory—that is, physical copies could be made without permission of the copyright holder as long as payment was made. Further, the amount of the payment owed was set by Congress.

The impetus for this aspect of the law arose from arrangements made between a player piano manufacturer, the Aeolian Company, and eighty-seven members of the MPA. Under that agreement, in exchange for the exclusive right to manufacture piano rolls for all eighty-seven publishers for a term of thirty-five years, the company would pay a 10% royalty on sales. Because this was seen as a monopolistic practice, the US government stepped in to create the first compulsory license arrangement.[20]

Under the terms of the Copyright Act of 1909, the mechanical royalty was two cents per copy, which it remained until 1978. This static rate obviously did not reflect seventy years of massive growth in the recording industry. As a result, publisher and composer income lagged behind the increasing economic value of music production overall.

But the system had another, perhaps more serious flaw: it was inflexible. "Because the rate was set by statute, and because the user paid the owner directly, there was no need for a government agency either to set the mechanical rate or to engage in a distribution of the mechanical royalties."[21]

Both issues—the compulsory royalty rate and the responsiveness of the system—were addressed in the Copyright Act of 1976, which included the creation of "an administrative body to act as the distributor of the royalties collected from users in situations where there were many copyright owner claimants to the same funds and there were controversies as to how much each claimant was entitled to receive."[22]

After a number of unsuccessful attempts at creating a workable "administrative body," the Copyright Royalty Board (CRB) was established by the Copyright Royalty and Distribution Reform Act of 2004. Judges with specific expertise in copyright law were given "full independence in making determinations concerning adjustments and determinations of copyright royalty rates and terms, the distribution of copyright royalties, the acceptance or rejection of royalty claims, rate adjustment petitions, and petitions to participate, and in issuing other rulings under this title."[23]

The shift from arbitration to legal proceedings by the CRB has had a significant impact on mechanical licenses in the digital era. You might think that with the decline of physical product sales, followed by the eclipse of digital product downloads by streaming services, the value of mechanical licensing would be reduced or even eliminated. In fact, mechanical royalties still represented nearly 20% of the $2.7 billion music revenue for 2016, "because of the mechanical part of interactive streaming.[24]

DIGITAL LICENSING ISSUES & THE MUSIC MODERNIZATION ACT

Much of the challenge faced by contemporary writers, publishers, and licensing organizations arises from the rapid growth of and scale of access provided by digital music services. As predictions suggest that the streaming access business will continue to grow, it becomes increasingly apparent that the licensing system cannot keep up. As a result, as observed by David Israelite of the NMPA, even well-intentioned music distribution businesses often find themselves in legal difficulties.

Anyone who enters this space is going to get sued because it's practically impossible to license content properly. In the old days, when music was physically sold, the record labels would be the ones seeking the mechanical license. They'd come to us and say "We need these 10 songs." Today, I have Amazon in my office saying "How do we license 40 million songs tomorrow?"[25]

The solution advocated by the NMPA was to use data to make licensing more convenient and practical by creating "a transparent database paid for 100% by the digital companies that use it but managed by creative community."[26]

In a sense, this licensing database would be similar to the blanket licenses pioneered by ASCAP. Where it differs is that it transcends individual organizations and requires the participation of all PROs and the publishers/writers they represent. Consequently, if this database proves to be as effective as hoped, will it not raise further questions about monopolistic control of the market for music licensing? (See "Further Consideration" below.)

Sync Licensing

In addition to mechanical and performance licensing, the third economically valuable license refers to the use of music in a timed, or synchronized, relationship to visual elements in a multimedia work. This type of use appeared first in film, then television, and now across Internet-based media. Sync rights apply not only to film, television, YouTube-style videos, and video podcasts, but also to advertising, computer games, and virtually any other multimedia use of music.

The origins of synchronization licensing are surprisingly convoluted. Although they are not specifically mentioned in the copyright acts of 1909, 1976, or 1978, they were defined and upheld by court rulings, including in 1939 and 1952.[27] The history of licensing music for media synchronization is beyond the scope and purposes of this text. But the practical framework that supports the sync license is not.

In practice, synchronization requires permission from both the publisher and the owner of the master recording, typically a record label. The rights that support publisher and record label ownership are the right to make and distribute copies and the right to make a derivative work. The publisher has, in addition, the comprehensive right to public performance of a copyrighted work. This complex web of ownership and rights helps to make synchronization one of the most complex rights to manage and a not infrequent cause of litigation.

In addition, unlike mechanical and performance licenses, sync license fees are entirely market-based. Recent rulings from the US government have supported this market orientation and resisted calls from media producers to create a compulsory arrangement comparable to mechanical and performance rights. In addition, calls for so-called "bundled licensing" that would include mechanical, performance, and sync have met with disagreement among producers and the US Department of Justice.[28]

Sync licenses are an increasingly large percentage of music publishing revenues—21% in 2016 according to the NMPA.[29] The NMPA's engagement with licensing issues illustrates the historical importance of trade organizations to represent the interests of producers—in this case composers and publishers—in a multiplayer business environment. Trade and licensing organizations, like the NMPA, ASCAP, and BMI, to name a few, also play a significant role in the development and adaptations of copyright law. One such development is the Music Modernization Act.

MUSIC MODERNIZATION ACT AND PUBLISHING

The Musical Works Modernization Act (MMA) was passed by the House of Representatives on April 25, 2015 (H.R. 5447, 115th Congress, 2nd Session), and then unanimously by the Senate on September 18, 2018, and then signed into law by the president on October 11, 2018.[30]

After its passage, the MMA was acclaimed by most music industry professionals. For example, *Billboard* magazine reported,

"The Music Modernization Act is now the law of the land, and thousands of songwriters and artists are better for it," Recording Industry Association of America President Mitch Glazier said. "The result is a music market better founded on fair competition and fair pay. The enactment of this law demonstrates what music creators and digital services can do when we work together collaboratively to advance a mutually beneficial agenda. It's a great day for music."[31]

The Music Modernization Act has three areas of focus: a blanket license for digital uses available from a single source, a "music licensing collective"; pre-1972 sound recording licensing issues, which were included in the previously proposed Classics Act (see "Recording Economics" below); and a way to manage and distribute funds allocated for music producers and engineers (previously the Allocation for Music Producers [AMP] Act).

For publishers/composers the most significant element is the first: blanket licensing for digital use from a single source. The quid pro quo for that simplification is that digital services will adopt a different payment standard based on a "'willing seller, willing buyer' rate standard, meaning, what would happen if we were in a free market?"[32] While the full effects of the Music Modernization Act are yet to be realized, it represents a major step forward in music licensing for the digital era.

RECORDING & DISTRIBUTIVE MEDIA ECONOMICS

Records—both physical and digital downloads—are consumer goods, the sale of which was the primary economic driver of the music industry in the twentieth century. They continued to account for just over 31% of recorded music revenues in 2017 (streaming of all kinds represented 65%).[33] In addition, from its origins, the recording business has always been interconnected with media that increase public access to its products. So it is impossible to understand the economics of recorded music without also considering radio, television, and various digital distribution systems.

The rights and licenses managed by the publishing sector have a direct connection to productivity and revenue in the recording business and the distributive media. That said, the recording industry has opportunities and challenges distinct from publishing. These include, on the positive side, greater freedom to negotiate performance royalties without governmental and legal system constraints and, on the negative, that the recording industry must contend with the broadcast radio exemption from paying performance royalties.

Let's begin there.

Performance Rights Broadcast Exemption (PRBE)

Copyright for sound recordings includes the right to make and distribute copies, make derivative works, and publicly perform the work, which includes playing the recording via a public medium. While the performance rights controlled by publishing are comprehensive—both live and mediated—there are restrictions on the performance royalties due owners of recordings, typically record labels.

For example, the owner of a recording gets no payment from terrestrial radio broadcasts of the record. This means that record labels get no royalties from AM/FM radio play and, consequently, the recording artists signed to the label get no royalties for radio airplay of records on which they have performed. The only exception to this rule is a result of the Digital Performance Right in Sound Recordings Act of 1995 (see below.)

Essentially, the broadcast exemption is based on conflicting business models between broadcasters and record labels and the organizations that represent them. It is beyond the scope and purposes of this section to look at this century-old conflict in depth, but the "short" version is that the National Association of Broadcasters (NAB) lobbied successfully not to pay performance rights for sound recordings and the

Recording Industry Association of America (RIAA), to date, has not countered effectively.

Pre-1972 Recordings

In addition to issues surrounding the broadcast exemption, sound recordings were not, in fact, covered at all by US copyright statute until 1971. Revenue for the recording industry was based entirely on sales of physical products—45s, LPs, and so forth. The law of 1971 added the right "To reproduce and distribute to the public by sale or other transfer of ownership, or by rental, lease, or lending, reproductions of the copyrighted work if it be a sound recording."

That new protection applied, however, "only to those fixed, i.e., produced, on or after February 15, 1972."[34] For recordings made prior to that, the so-called "pre-1972 recordings," state laws were considered to be the basis for copyright coverage. In addition, this law did not change anything involving public performance or broadcast rights.

In 1995, the US Congress passed the Digital Performance Right in Sound Recordings Act (DPRA), which "granted owners of a copyright in sound recordings an exclusive right 'to perform the copyrighted work publicly by means of a digital audio transmission.'"[35] The act also laid out a framework of statutory, compulsory royalties for this use. Labels and recording artists welcomed this change, but it had no impact on terrestrial radio and in 1995 there were relatively few "Internet radio" businesses to object.

That was going to change.

In 1998, as Internet-based information/entertainment platforms expanded, Congress passed the Digital Millennium Copyright Act (DMCA). The DMCA was a comprehensive law that addressed issues from international treaties concerning intellectual property to the right to make backup copies of computer software. The most critical issue for the recording industry was the expansion of the "statutory license for subscription transmissions to include *webcasting* as a new category of 'eligible nonsubscription transmissions.'"[36]

To be eligible for the statutory license (and rates) under the DMCA, webcasters had to meet the requirements established under the DPRA: that their services were noninteractive (listeners could not pick which songs to hear) and that they paid the required rate. This is the framework in which companies like Pandora and SiriusXM do business.[37]

The statutory royalties for digital transmission laid out by the DPRA and expanded in the DMCA are paid to SoundExchange, "the only entity authorized by Congress to administer the statutory licenses described in sections 112 and 114."[38] By the end of 2017, SoundExchange had collected over $5 billion in royalties for the digital transmission of recordings.[39]

A great source of controversy between labels and webcasters has been the "gap" in copyright coverage for pre-1972 recordings. Even a passing familiarity with the history of commercially recorded music will make clear that there were many, many artistically and economically significant records made before 1972. A large percentage of the catalogs of incredibly popular artists is included in that group. These records are an important part of terrestrial, satellite, and Internet-based media content.

Because of the "gap," companies like Pandora and SiriusXM "take the position that they are not legally required to pay for pre-1972 recordings, because neither the DPRA nor DMCA apply to such recordings."[40] Record labels and recording artists disagree.

The resulting lawsuits over rights payment have resulted in multi-million dollar settlements over the pre-1972 repertoire. The expense of such and the difficulty of going to court under a complicated web of state jurisdictions have been motivating factors for updating the law to cover these earlier recordings. As noted above, the Music Modernization Act addresses this issue and its signing into law is expected to revolutionize and streamline licensing for composers, publishers, labels, recording artists, and digital services, while preserving the accessibility that music listeners have come to expect.

Sync Licensing

The issue of synchronization licensing was discussed in more detail above, under publishing economics, but it is a significant part of the revenue picture for sound recording producers as well. The main difference is that typically copy/distribute and sync licenses are bundled between record labels and multimedia producers.

The scale of the sync license market is limited, but significant in the recording economy. "According to the International Federation of the Phonographic Industry (IFPI) 2017 Digital Music report, sync maintained its 2% share of the global recorded music market in 2016, growing by 2.8% (compared to 7% in 2015). The US is the world's largest sync market, accounting for 57% of sync revenues in 2015."[41] In the United States alone, sync licensing accounted for $232 million in revenue (3% of the recording industry total).[42]

DIGITAL SERVICES ECONOMICS

While online music stores that provided legal music downloads represented a major shift in how recordings were sold and distributed, they were essentially an online version of the traditional record store. The businesses that followed iTunes with their own versions of online stores competed primarily on the basis of copy restrictiveness: how many computers could be authorized to play the MP3s, for example.

Likewise, webcasters, discussed above, represented an updated version of broadcast radio, providing users either free or subscription-based access without being able to choose specific music on demand. This became a significant development because of the DPRA and DMCA (see above), which provided for performance royalties to be paid to the rights holder of recordings.

By far the largest shift in production, monetization, and reception of recorded music, however, came from the rise of streaming services. The nearly universal, on-demand access for listeners combined with no-pay, advertising-based, and low-cost subscriptions has been a paradigm-smashing development.

Although it is by no means the only digital streaming service, as the largest Spotify has a major impact on the music economy. Some of this impact will be considered in chapter 8, "Disruption." But here, it is important to look at the implications of the purchase of Spotify equity by a significant number of record labels.

As part of the deal with the four major labels/music groups (and the independent label aggregator Merlin) to be able to license their catalogs for streaming, Spotify agreed to sell them 18% of the equity in the company in addition to paying royalties. In 2008–2009 it was reported by several sources that Spotify sold the shares at a fraction of market value, perhaps as low as $10,000 US, when the actual price was closer to one thousand times that much.[43] At the time, some analysts considered this a protective strategy for labels, in case Spotify sold out to another company—as YouTube did to Google in 2004—with no compensation for that sale coming to music copyright holders.

Although Spotify's paid memberships have grown slowly, the company has in fact paid out (as of March 2018) "some $10bn in royalties to artists, music labels, and publishers so far, according to the financial services company Hargreaves Lansdown, and it is obliged to pay at least $2bn in further royalty payments over the next three years."[44] While this growth has helped to make streaming revenue the largest individual segment of the music industry, more important for labels and the recording artists signed to them is Spotify's recent IPO.

Spotify's first day of trading on the New York Stock Exchange—as *Spotify Technology SA*—was April 3, 2018. The company was valued at just under $30 billon, an astonishing number considering that the company has never made a profit.[45]

For the major labels holding significant shares of Spotify stock—including Sony Music Entertainment, Warner Music Group, and Universal Music Group—it was an opportunity to realize significant revenue from the sale of those shares. Warner sold 75% of its stock for about $400 million and Sony sold 50% of its own for $750 million.[46]

All three major groups, along with independent group Merlin, have committed to sharing the revenue from Spotify stock sales with their artists as well as with the independent labels they distribute. The latter point is a result of advocacy by the Worldwide Independent Network (WIN)—an international independent music collective.[47] In response to concerns from the independent artist community, WIN developed their Fair Digital Deals Declaration, "a voluntary initiative promoting fair and transparent accounting to artists and music companies.[48]

The WIN Fair Digital Deals Declaration illustrates the tensions in the web of relationships among streaming services, major music groups, and the independent music community. As noted in the previous chapter, as Spotify (as well as the growing streaming sector in general) becomes more and more central to music reception, it increasingly aggregates the productivity of record labels, which, in turn, aggregate the productivity of composers and performers.

The larger music groups have demonstrated that they have enough leverage (due to the size and comprehensiveness of their catalogs) to make profitable streaming deals. But the artists signed to those labels complain about the extremely low per-stream payments they receive.

Independent labels and artists that are unable to apply the same leverage do not do as well. Merlin, for example, received only 1% of Spotify's stock, as compared to four to seven times as much for Sony, Warner, UMG, and Universal.[49] In addition, Merlin's royalty rate has been reported as less than what was paid to the large music groups. But a new contract negotiated between the independent group and Spotify in April 2017 has been unofficially reported to put Merlin on a comparable footing to Universal.[50]

The innovative disruptions to music production, distribution, and reception in the decade and a half at the beginning of the twenty-first century not only reframed the industry on a large scale, but also impacted the DIY music sector. Overall, though music production generally was disrupted, large-scale operators were more able to adjust and benefit—though the situation remains volatile, and further disruptions are sure to come.

For individual artists, the disruption has been more profound and the necessary adjustments have been more challenging. The responses of the independent music community to the digital marketplace are discussed more fully in chapter 8, "Disruption."

PERFORMING ECONOMICS

Live performance is the oldest economic offering in music, and is the most important so far in the twenty-first century. As noted previously, concerts, tours, and festivals accounted for 43% of the $17.2 billion music industry in the United States in 2016. Corporate sponsorship of live music events added another 12%, which raises another point. Performance has a synergistic relationship with every other revenue stream in music, from publishing to media and merchandise licensing. In this section we examine two primary ways that live performance is monetized: concert tickets and merchandise.

The primary focus here is performance in commercial, popular music genres. Legacy and/or "art music" sectors, like jazz and the classical symphony orchestra, are also highly dependent upon ticket sales. Each has its own particular challenges, which include limited potential audience size and aging demographics. In the case of the symphony orchestra there are also the problems of high operating costs, fixed location, and a history of dependence on funding from nonperformance sources.

CONCERTS, TOURS, AND FESTIVALS

In the commercial music business, concerts have been long presented in touring format, moving the show from city to city, in order to reach a larger, aggregate audience. In addition, there are also location-based live music events designed to bring audiences to the venue and performer.

These range from solo engagements in destination locales, such as Las Vegas Casinos, to massive festival events, like Lollapalooza.

Whether we are considering location-based festivals or a multicity (or multicountry) tour, the fundamental issues are scale and scalability. Performing careers typically start small (in their venues and audiences) and grow over time. The essential question for emerging artists is how to optimize their current, typically limited performance opportunities to support growth to the next stage:

> At that level, says Gary Bongiovanni, the editor-in-chief of *Pollstar,* a publication that tracks the concert industry, "Everything depends on an act's ability to attract paying fans. At club level, many [bands] can't even generate enough to cover basic expenses," Bongiovanni wrote. "From a club or promoter perspective, the act is only worth part of what it can dependably bring in the door. The stronger the draw, the safer the risk, and thus the artist can command more of the money. At this level it really is eat what you kill."[51]

From the artist perspective, early stage "success" may mean being able to quit your part-time, nonmusic job. Indie manager Dawn Barger (from small club acts to the National and the Antlers) points out: "I mean, if you're selling out every night, you're probably supporting yourself and you're able to quit your job, but you certainly have roommates, you're barely getting by, you're watching how many hotel rooms you get each night."

When artists move up, or more accurately, when an artist has the listener relationships to support moving up, the formula changes and "the infrastructure that surrounds a particular venue, or the tour as a whole," matters as much to revenue creation as the number of tickets sold, or more.[52]

Barger provides an example of the options available to a band touring medium-sized cities "at the level of the National," who were on the road to support their first album in 2002, the date of Barger's interview.

> "Usually … you can choose between two rooms, one of which is an older, gorgeous theater that sometimes has union help, or you can choose a venue

that's sometimes owned by a promoter. And your earnings potential in those two rooms is incredibly different," she says.[53]

The differences are the result of a number of factors that include issues such as union stagehands, and any costs associated with lights, sound systems, and security. A venue that is otherwise extremely attractive—larger, acoustically superior, or in a better location—can cost the artist a much greater percentage of ticket sales. In contrast, in a venue owned by a promoter, it can be more profitable to sell fewer tickets at a much higher return per ticket.

Infrastructure costs are only one aspect of the equation for the mid-level artist, particularly when considering a move to larger venues. In terms of this stage, when artists are considering playing an amphitheater, for example, Barger states:

> "If you are able to sell the full 18 to 20,000 tickets and fill the lawn, ... the earning potential is off the scale," she says. "But when you're looking at a band where you think you're going to do somewhere around 8 to 10,000 tickets, ... you're not making that much more by going there than you are by going to the theater in town that has a 3,000 person capacity. A lot of the earnings for the band are in those last 2 to 3,000 tickets sold in a big space like that. You don't really hit the profit until you sell out or get close to selling out."[54]

At the upper end of the concert tour scale, national and international tours of twenty-thousand-plus-seat venues become the norm. Obviously at this scale costs also increase and the artist's brand, the depth of audience relationships, the timing, and the ticketing strategies are factors with huge money implications. Even at the highest levels, however—with perennial top-performing artists like Taylor Swift or U2—concert tours are affected by not only venue and ticketing logistics, but also larger market conditions. Again, as artists move up, the equation becomes more complex.

The Jay-Z and Beyoncé On the Run tours (2014 and 2018) are good examples of this complexity. In June 2014, after completing individual tours that began in 2013 and ended early in 2014, the two artists launched a joint tour that presented nineteen events in North America and two in Europe. The tour reached nearly a million people and generated $109 million in ticket sales. More critically, for reasons we will discuss below, because concerts sold out in just minutes in some locations, additional dates were added to the tour. Selling all tickets for concert dates, particularly when they sell out very quickly, is considered to be an indicator of not only consumer demand, but the value of the artist's brand in that moment.

In addition, two of the final concerts of the tour were filmed and shown on HBO the week after the tour concluded. On the day it aired on HBO, the concert film was seen by just under one million viewers and was nominated for Best Music Film at the fifty-seventh Grammy Awards (2015). Various clips from the film were used online, including a video of Beyoncé's live performance of her song "Flawless" on her Vevo channel.

Both the HBO special and the tour itself were critically well received and the tour was a commercial success, ranked by Billboard's Boxscore as the eighth highest grossing tour in North America (at $96 million) and by PollStar as the fifth highest worldwide. Each of the shows played to forty thousand to fifty thousand people and grossed close to $5 million at an average ticket price of $111 (the cheapest seats were $40).

Despite some robust early sales, in line with the predictions of success for the tour, there were rumors of poor and/or slow sales in the music press in the late spring of 2014, just weeks before the tour began. The final numbers for the tour as reported by PollStar, Billboard Boxscore, and other sources support the anticipated success (with a slightly lower per-night box office). Live Nation also informed Billboard that the tour was generating "unprecedented VIP and Platinum ticket sales."[55]

The reports of slow sales and unsold seats were not, however, pure fabrications. Billboard also reported that in mid-June "a fair amount of tickets are still available for sale in some cities on both the primary and secondary markets."[56] They also pointed out that secondary market tickets, purchased by speculators hoping to resell at a profit, are a poor predictor of demand. Fans have learned that, if patient, they will be able to purchase tickets closer to the date of the event as ticket resellers cut prices in an attempt to minimize their losses.[57]

Billboard additionally observed that given seating capacities of up to sixty thousand in some venues on the tour, selling 90% of capacity would still produce highly successful numbers. Further, by using the infrastructure of stadiums, Jay-Z and Beyoncé would be able to optimize their planning and performing schedule. Thus, a stadium slightly undersold at fifty thousand tickets can be more efficient and cost-effective than two amphitheaters sold out at twenty-five thousand each.

The bottom line, despite concerns about the timing of sales and other factors, such as both artists being on tour (albeit separately) in the preceding months, was that On the Run was a highly successful tour in a strong year for touring. But, as Billboard concluded, "concert promotion is a risky business by its very nature. Though in this case it appears as though the risk/reward quotient will play out positively. The end results will show up in the Boxscore charts—and whether they opt to do it again."[58]

In fact, Jay Z and Beyoncé did decide to tour again, launching an On the Run II (OTRII) tour beginning on June 6, 2018. Predictions for this second joint tour were extremely positive. In part based on the strong numbers of their first combined tour and on predictions of growth for concerts in general (anywhere from 3% to 7% per year through 2021, see "Economic Scale," above), Billboard predicted that the artists could sell $200 million in tickets, doubling their revenue from their previous joint tour.[59]

This prediction was based on more dates, higher ticket prices, and stadiums built since the tour in 2014. In addition, new ticket-pricing strategies are an important part of scaling and selling concerts in 2018 and are expected to positively impact both financial results and, theoretically, concert-goer satisfaction because they allow for cheaper upper-level seats to still be available closer to concert dates.[60]

A major concert tour, however, is not only a matter of the logistics of delivering and selling music. The press and social media conversation about an upcoming and/or ongoing tour have a significant impact on the results. So promotional strategies are extremely important. In addition to the reputations of Jay-Z and Beyoncé individually, as well as the buzz from another duo tour, they also had the resource of streaming service TIDAL, purchased by Jay-Z in 2015, to help them on their second joint tour.

Most of the pretour publicity was, like the Billboard article cited above, extremely optimistic. Soon after the tour announcement on March 12, however, fans on social media weighed in—negatively—on the ticket pricing, which ranged from $371 to almost $2000 for VIP options. By mid-June it appeared that ticketing prices and presale allocations that limited public availability had negatively impacted sales.

On the UK leg of the tour—where the couple had not performed in OTR 2014—sales were slow enough that tickets were given away for the Glasgow performance and fans with tickets received free upgrades. Tickets remained unsold for most of the OTRII UK dates. As noted by one media report, "As the tour launched, one of the myriad of presale options was for members of Jay-Z's Tidal music service. Now, the script has flipped, and many tour dates are offering those who purchase tickets free memberships to Tidal for six months."

In addition, the two artists did a surprise release of a new, collaborative album, *Everything Is Love,* on June 16 and announced that CDs would be on sale on July 6. The timing of the release—and an accompanying music video—seemed calibrated to support and promote the tour. And the support may have been necessary. As of July 5, 2018, Ticketmaster showed thousands of tickets still available for the Cleveland, Ohio, show on July 15, ranging from the forty-nine dollar upper-level seats to many VIP seats at different price levels. But despite such concerns expressed on social and professional media, the OTRII closed with $235.5 million in sales, exceeding the early predictions and more than doubling the figures for attendance and sales set by OTRI.[61]

The question in evaluating an unfolding event like this is whether "slow" sales are the result of low demand, an artifact of a pricing strategy designed to impede ticket resale (slow ticketing), or something else. As noted in both 2014 and 2018, reports of poor sales were not reflected in the final tour numbers for Jay-Z and Beyoncé.

But there is also the ongoing issue of how ticket pricing and release strategies can balance revenue production with fan access while limiting the profits siphoned off by second- and third-party resellers. The practice of "slow ticketing" was used by Jay-Z for his *4:40 Tour* in 2017 and by Taylor Swift for the December 2017 release of tickets for her *2018 Reputation Tour*. In Swift's case, her tour in 2018 grossed $277 million, an increase of nearly 40% from her previous tour, despite performing twenty-two fewer shows.[62]

While some in the music press and media see "slow ticketing" as a way to hide the fact of soft demand for concert tickets, others consider it a groundbreaking strategy. As David Marcus, Executive Vice President and Head of Music at Ticketmaster, stated of the sales strategy for the Taylor Swift tour, "We'd like to sell the last ticket to her concert when she takes the stage each night. We're not trying to sell all of her tickets in one minute; we're trying to figure out how to sell tickets in a more modern way."[63]

Unlike concert tours, music festivals are destination-based. The idea is that by offering a larger, more comprehensive experience based on both music and location, fans can be tempted to travel farther and spend more money than they would for a conventional stop on a concert tour. Other than being place-bound, the primary defining feature of the festival is the diversity and number of acts, consisting of multiple headliners (and sometimes middle-tier groups, often on an additional, smaller stage) all spread over a day or more.

There are a number of practical advantages to festivals: one setup for staging, lighting, and sound; security and logistics don't change from night to night; and travel time and stress for artists and production crews are drastically reduced. In addition, staying in one location from one year to the next facilitates developing better facilities and interactive experiences for the fans. While the old joke is that Woodstock was three days of peace, love, music, and mud, modern festivals offer modern fans what they expect: music, social engagement, and amenities.

For well-established festivals like Coachella, Lollapalooza, and Bonnaroo, revenue is in the tens of millions of dollars and attendance reaches well into the hundred thousands. These events, with their established brands, regularly sell out and often early. But stories about how much money these major festivals make can be deceiving:

> "One of the obvious reasons music festivals have taken off is a lot of people think they can make a lot of money with them, and it's not that easy," says Grayson Currin, who co-founded the Hopscotch Festival in Chapel Hill, North Carolina, now entering its fourth year. "The margins are pretty small."[64]

In that regard, the history of Coachella is instructive. Festival founder Paul Tollet began by booking local bands in bars and clubs. In college he made a connection with the founder of the promotion company Goldenvoice, Gary Tovar. Tollet, Tovar, and his partner Rick Van Santen began booking bands in Los Angeles. They were successful in that they booked a lot of shows, but in practice, their business was losing money. The Coachella festival was supposed to fix that.[65]

By the end of the first Coachella, however, the partners were $1 million in debt. Due to long-term relationships with artists, Tollet was able to get headliners to wait for payment. Staff employees had to accept the same conditions. Finally, they sold Goldenvoice to AEG Live to pay their debts. Tollet retains 50% ownership in Coachella and AEG Live/Goldenvoice manages it.

Of this story, the founder of the Warped Tour, Kevin Lyman, said:

> Guys like us, we didn't make any money. Paul and myself, we had to bring in partners to make it work. Paul put his heart and soul into it, but it was his heart and soul, so he had to bring in AEG to share his whole business

because he believed so much in it. I had to bring in Vans as a partner to kind of keep me going until we gained traction. I know that it takes a while to be successful.[66]

If sponsorship has become increasingly important to the business model of concert tours, it is now absolutely essential to the festival business. As noted above, live performance of all kinds becomes ever more entwined with targeted advertising, and this trend will certainly continue and likely increase. With the advent of RFID technology—which nominally is used to simplify ticketing and site access—targeted ad experiences on festival grounds are already a reality.[67]

MERCHANDISE

Selling merchandise at concerts, or "merch," has long been a significant source of supplemental revenue for tours and festivals. The idea of artist T-shirts and a business to sell them began in the 1950s with Elvis Presley. Elvis Presley Enterprises was set up in 1954 to generate profit from Elvis-branded merchandise. Although a fan club apparently produced an Elvis T-shirt in the later 1950s, no connection between the two groups was made. There is a tremendous amount of Elvis Presley merchandise today, but that revenue stream was not realized during his lifetime.[68]

Like many other trends in commercial popular music, artist merchandise got a jump-start from the Beatles in the 1960s. Brian Epstein had a feel for the band's music and an intuitive understanding of their relationship to their fans. He saw to it that there was a great deal of Beatles-themed merchandise on the market in the early 1960s. Unfortunately, Epstein's business acumen rarely matched his intuition. Most of the money disappeared into the hands of unscrupulous vendors and bootleg producers. It wasn't until the merchandise arm of the Beatles enterprise was turned over to someone who understood the business—Nicky Byrne—that things began to change.

Byrne moved to a royalty model where the Beatles name and like-nesses were licensed for a 10% royalty. The response was, to say the least, overwhelming:

> In 1964, a factory in the US was manufacturing 35,000 Beatle wigs per day, a Liverpool bakery sold 100,000 Ringo dolls in two days, and a Blackpool company received an order for 10 million sticks of liquorice with the Beatles' name on it. Beatles chewing gum made millions of dollars within a few months.[69]

Although the Beatles still saw little of this revenue, Beatles-related merchandise established the monetary value of artist and tour-related merchandise. Imitators soon followed. One of the first companies to design and market concert T-shirts—soon to become the staple of touring merchandise—was founded by iconic music promoter Bill Graham in the 1970s. That company, Winterland Productions, remains in business today and is still a producer of concert merchandise.

As a producer, Graham was adept at monetizing and profiting from the shared artist–audience experience at live events, including merchandise. Other artists, like the Beatles, tried to manage merchandise themselves. Still others, like the Grateful Dead, took a DIY approach to merchandise, but unlike the Beatles merchandise, Dead merch generated significant revenue for the band while they were active and for decades after their careers ended.[70] But clearly, most artists benefit from licensing merchandise to independent professional manufacturing and sales companies.

Concert merchandise not only continues to be a significant source of revenue today, but goes even further than that. Merchandise can be an extension of the artist's identity and creativity. It can become a tangible connection between the audience member and the artist or a commercial portal for advertisers and festival consumers to connect.

At the cutting edge of merchandise, enter Manhead Merch, a company that "is looking to shake up the very old ways of how artist-merchandise is created, marketed, and sold."[71] Eric Jones, a musician who joined the company in 2012, wondered, "why can't fans see what bands are selling before the show starts? When you have 20,000 fans at a show, technology should be able to be used to identify those fans and to know who's buying what."[72]

He quickly came up with an idea. Called Sidestep, it was a business model that allows

> merchandise companies, ticket suppliers, or record labels to ping ticketed fans before a show. They'd be able to browse available t-shirts and other merchandise, and pre-order it for pick-up at the show. They could have first dibs—and skip the massive line of sweaty concertgoers mobbing the merch stand after the show.[73]

Sidestep is an innovative and adaptive response to the changed marketplace and culture of musical experience. Even as music listeners and consumers are drawn to the social connection—with one another and the performing artists—of the concert or festival, their individual experience is tailored to their preferences. They are afforded the convenience of online shopping in the context of being an audience member at a large, immersive multimedia event.

The artist–audience connection remains paramount to all forms of value creation through music. But the means of making that connection—and monetizing it—evolve continuously.

CRITICAL CONCEPTS

- The music business depends on the interconnected creative and economic spheres of performance, publishing, recording, and distributive media.
- In assessing and predicting economic performance, it is critical both to look at the big picture, aggregate numbers, and to "drill down" into specific sectors and ventures.
- The artist-audience connection remains paramount to all forms of value creation through music. But the means of facilitating that connection evolve continuously.

FURTHER CONSIDERATION

Digital Licensing Database: Monopolistic Practice, Again?

As noted in the chapter, the NMPA is advocating for the creation of a database to facilitate music licensing, regardless of PRO, publisher, or individual representation. While this appears to be a solution built for the scale and speed of modern music streaming, it may also raise similar questions and concerns about monopolistic practice as the blanket licenses pioneered by ASCAP in the early twentieth century did.

First, read these articles:

- Bill Rosenblatt, "The Big Push To Reform Music Copyright For The Digital Age," *Forbes,* February 25, 2018, www.forbes.com /sites/billrosenblatt/2018/02/25/the-big-push-to-reform-music-copyright-for-the-digital-age/#639dd6612d6d.

  This is an excellent summary of music licensing legislation in early 2018. Of particular importance for this discussion is the section on the Music Modernization Act.

- Thomas M. Lenard and Lawrence White, "Music Licensing Reform Is Singing the Same Old Song," *Technology Policy Institute,* April 2, 2018, https://techpolicyinstitute.org/commentary /music-licensing-reform-is-singing-the-same-old-song/.

Then consider these issues:

Rosenblatt states: "The MMA calls for a single agency—a monopoly— to take over this task, and requires that the agency be a nonprofit entity. The agency would have little accountability or oversight, and minimal incentive to improve."

- Is this like or unlike conditions surrounding the original lawsuits by the US Department of Justice Antitrust Division against ASCAP and BMI. Why or why not?
- If so, does this not inevitably lead to more antitrust litigation? Why or why not?

Festivals and Communities

The margins may be small for festivals, but the impact on local and regional economies can be significant. Consider the following quotation from the LA Weekly article "The Economics of Music Festivals: Who's Getting Rich, Who's Going Broke?," www.laweekly.com/music/the-economics-of-music-festivals-whos-getting-rich-whos-going-broke-4167927:

> When you consider the $254 million Coachella brought to the desert region around Indio (and $90 million to the city itself), you can see why a city would do whatever it can to help. Apparently that only holds until a festival's established itself, at which point you grab for more. (See, Indio proposed, then ultimately withdrew, a $4–$6 million ticket tax.)

Do you agree that this is a "grab" by the city of Indio of the festival's revenue? What about the infrastructure costs that the community must bear with the increase of traffic on the roads, public accommodations, and businesses? In other words, is it somehow "wrong" to tax a successful business, or is it a matter of finding an appropriate balance between costs and benefits to the community, the festival, and the attendees?

CONCEPTUAL PROTOTYPE QUESTIONS

Consider the disastrous 2017 startup of the "immersive music festival," Fyre Fest.

- See, for example Mary Hanbury's 1–19–2019 article in *Business Insider,* www.businessinsider.com/fyre-festival-expectations-vs-reality-2017–4 or the documentaries *Fyre: The Greatest Party That Never Happened* and *Fyre Fraud.*
- What was the fundamental concept?
- Who were the intended customers and audience members?
- What went wrong? Consider flaws in the fundamental concept, understanding of (and empathy for) the intended customers, as

well as poor or unethical management. What about in terms of the principles of Design Theory (see chapter 1)?

· Discuss the public reaction to the failure of the festival. Among other things, what do you make of the negativity expressed toward the "millennial" customers involved?

· Is there anything constructive you can learn from this event in terms of the process of starting a music festival?

6

Location

Scenes, Venues, Labels

Music happens somewhere.

Knowing the place where a particular musical expression was initially created and shared is essential to understanding how and why it "works," both creatively and economically. On the simplest level, "location" refers to the place—from street corner to concert hall—where performer and listener meet. But it's not just the room, the hall—the immediate physical space. It is also where it stands, in a city, region, and community. That is to say, it's geography—economic geography, to be more precise.

Economic geography is not a term often used in the music business. More often, a locus of musical creation, production, and public reception is referred to as a "music scene." A scene is where artists and audiences come together around shared musical experience that has a particular meaning in their common local experience. And, even though the places where artists and audiences "meet" are increasingly mediated by technology, in-person relationships are as important today as they ever were, if not more. So location still matters. There are still music scenes.

You could argue with some confidence that music almost always begins personally and then develops locally, in a place shared by both performers and listeners. Music scenes are typically associated with cities that provide the resources for production and consumption along with other necessities and amenities of living. While these resources vary by location—and the music produced varies accordingly—one common feature of all music scenes is that they attract and nurture both the creators and the consumers of music, as well as the various kinds of facilitators who bring them together.

Economist Richard Florida explains that the term "was originally used to describe the geographic concentrations of specific kinds of musical genres that evolved in mid-20th century musical centers like New Orleans jazz, Nashville country, Memphis soul, Detroit Motown, or Chicago blues."[1] Further, regardless of their specific geographic location, all of these scenes brought together "musical and business talent (e.g., agents, managers, taste-makers, gate-keepers, critics, and sophisticated consumers) across social networks and physical space (neighborhoods, communities, clubs, venues, recording studios and venues)."[2]

In addition to providing necessary infrastructure for production—also according to Florida—successful music scenes support a vibrant environment for reception and monetization through "the diversity of people and the institutional and social infrastructure required to commercialize cultural products like music."[3] As a result, by bringing together creators, producers, and consumers, music scenes can support musical productivity and, sometimes, nurture the emergence of a musical genre that reflects the particular values and experience of that place.

But it is not enough to say that there is, for example, an "Akron Sound." (There is, by the way.)[4] Although the musicians and listeners who created and supported the music unique to that city (and region) were essential to its development, if we don't also talk about the Crypt, the Market Street bar where so many people played and heard this music, we miss something essential about the Akron scene. So, music scenes are about the city (and region), the musicians and listeners who live there, and the specific venues—sometimes a single business—where they come together.

Music scenes not only foster local musical culture and experience; some have also launched national and even global musical careers and trends. One important reason that local scenes become incubators for large-scale developments in music is that independent record labels have so often been the first step in scaling from the local to the global. Consequently, understanding how and why music scenes work also involves understanding the independent record labels associated with them.

Although, as we will discuss below, record labels tend to come later in the process of scene development—after there is already an identifiable style of music to record—they are often among the highest-profile and best-known aspects of a given scene. So we will start there—at the end of the local processes, at the pivot point to a larger world—before unpacking the elements that make a scene productive, and that build it in the first place.

Below we examine a few representative labels that (a) were closely associated with a particular city, (b) were instrumental in nurturing the creation of new musical genres, and (c) launched them to national prominence.

SUN RECORDS—MEMPHIS

Sun Records was launched by Sam Phillips in 1952 in a small storefront building in Memphis, Tennessee. Phillips's dream was to make records that brought the power and beauty of Southern Gospel music to larger audiences, regardless of their racial identity. He soon learned that a dream is not necessarily a business model and found himself—as did many small studio owners in the 1950s—renting out his facilities to semiprofessional and amateur musicians, to anyone willing to pay to make a vanity record.

Phillips did not abandon his dream; he adapted it. He accepted that the market for Gospel records was not what he had hoped, but he held on to the underlying idea that musical experience need not be constrained by race. He intended to demonstrate—via the right artists and songs—that music could transcend the social constraints of the music and broadcasting businesses of the day to reach audiences of all ethnicities.

In this belief and intention, Phillips was well served by the city of Memphis. Located in northwestern Tennessee on the Mississippi River, the city had long been a transportation hub and both a destination and a pass-through for people traveling from the southern to the northern United States. It was a place where people and products from the North and South and from both rural and urban settings met, mingled, and went to market.

As such, 1950s Memphis was a crossroads city that provided the people and resources necessary to become a music scene. Though it was not evident at the time, Sam Phillips's arrival and establishment of Sun Records were to be the catalyst for the emergence of an incredibly powerful and influential musical style that would both reflect and transcend its Memphis origins.

Sun began as a small rented studio at 706 Union in Memphis. Though it was launched at a time when there were a number of record label startups in the city, "in a short while Sun gained the reputation throughout Memphis as a label that treated local artists with respect and honesty. Sam provided a non-critical, spontaneous environment that invited creativity and vision."[5]

Sun Records came to be known for giving previously unknown performers their first recording contracts and then helping them define and develop their creative identity and commercial brand. Sun artists included Elvis Presley, Carl Perkins, Roy Orbison, and Johnny Cash. They and other Sun artists went on to sign with major labels and have international careers. But it was Phillips's vision, as well as his musical and business acumen (aided by now-legendary engineer producer Jack Clement), that not only launched those careers, but also supported the creation of a new musical genre, "Rockabilly," and, to no small degree, launched the transformative cultural and economic force of Rock and Roll into the world.

Creativity and vision were what drove Phillips. His patience (being willing to listen to everyone who came through his door) and insight (the capacity to elicit amazing performances from musicians of all genres and backgrounds) came from his deeply held belief that "there was a type of music that could transcend divisions of black and white and appeal to everyone."[6]

The artist that provided the "proof of concept" for Phillips's vision—and certainly the best-recognized Sun artist today—is Elvis Presley. Presley was a local Memphis teen whose family had relocated there from Mississippi in search of better work opportunities. Presley shared with Phillips a love for Gospel music. He began hanging around Sun studios, hoping to be discovered by Phillips—an obvious example of how a local independent label is more accessible than a major. After some time and a period of uncertainty about his talents, Phillips helped Presley record a version of the previously recorded song "That's All Right."

The Presley recording, based on an R & B classic made by Arthur "Big Boy" Crudup, recast the song in a Country style. It was "backed with" the song "Blue Moon of Kentucky," a Bluegrass hit by the then huge star Bill Monroe. The Monroe cover was also stylistically reframed, into an uptempo Rockabilly number. Both A- and B-sides of this 45-rpm release were successful, appearing on the R & B, Country, and Pop charts. As a result, not only did Phillips launch Elvis Presley's career; he demonstrated the crossover potential of Rockabilly, as well as the tactic of treating both sides of a 45 as potential hits that targeted distinct market demographics.

This early effort produced an immediate buzz in the Memphis radio market, first accessed by Phillips through his network of connections. The success of "That's Alright, Mama" (as it was retitled for the Sun release) was followed by other successful singles by Presley. Soon Phillips's small operation and limited capital were unable to service the demand for product and distribution. As a result, Phillips ultimately sold Presley's recording contract to RCA Records for $35,000 in 1956. Phillips did so because he recognized that he did not have the promotion or distribution resources that Presley's career was soon going to need.

In addition, Phillips planned to use those funds to develop new artists, which was always his primary motivation. In many ways these decisions by Phillips define the strengths and limitations of Sun Records in particular and of independent labels generally:

Strengths

- Connection and accessibility to local artists;
- Connections to local/regional media;
- Commitment to artist discovery and development;
- Commitment to specific musical/social/cultural values.

Limitations

- Supporting artists who fall outside the specific musical frame of reference;
- Resources for large-scale promotion and distribution.

As Sun's reputation grew, Phillips's particular strengths—artist discovery and stylistic development—attracted aspiring artists to Memphis to work with him and drew the attention of larger labels. Ultimately, Phillips recognized that the resources of the majors were just too much for him to compete with effectively and saw it as part of a larger trend:

> When I saw the big companies were going to eat me alive—I didn't want to face that fact, but I saw what was coming. Not that they could out-produce me, but they were buying all the artists from the independent companies. I knew this was going to make the structure of distribution very unhealthy. They had the ability to do it. They had that glamour over you. And artists had felt for many years that if you weren't on a major label, you just weren't very good. And that's sad, because there should be room for the majors, room for the independents, but the independents are just about extinct now.[7]

Finally, Phillips sold Sun in 1969:

> So I saw the writing on the wall. I knew it was time to sell, and Shelby Singleton [who had once been the head of production for Mercury Records]

approached me on buying. Shelby loved the old Sun records, and I just wanted the Sun label to be bought by somebody who would take it under his wing and love it like I had loved it. I sold to Shelby for way less than half of what I could have gotten.[8]

The story of Sam Phillips and Sun Records embodies many of the factors common to independent labels: they start with the vision of an individual or small team and become part of the musical culture of a particular place. But under the right conditions, their success can change what music sounds like on a global scale. When that happens, it typically leads to artist defections to larger labels. This can lead to the end of the independent label—at least as a personal vision—as larger labels and music groups buy them out. Independent labels, like the local music scenes with which they are associated, have a developmental arc: they rise and fall, or are absorbed into a larger, corporate production process.

MOTOWN RECORDS—DETROIT

The origins and historic achievements of Motown are discussed in more detail in chapter 2, but here are additional factors worth exploring. First is that the existing music scene in Detroit was a critical resource for the establishment of TAMLA Records, which subsequently became Motown. Second, when songwriter-entrepreneur Berry Gordy, Jr., launched TAMLA in 1959, he was seeking a way to make his involvement in music more profitable. His initial strategy was to establish a position from which he could control publishing and the recording process using the rich resources of Detroit performers, songwriters, and producers as inputs.

Where Motown and Sun differ most is in the intended outputs of their labels. Phillips used Sun to focus on the discovery of artists and the development of a sound—values that Gordy shared. But Phillips was far less concerned with the development of a national brand for the label, the control of publishing, and the mass distribution and promotion of his artists. Gordy, on the other hand, recognized from the beginning that musical, economic, and artistic quality could be blended to optimize their impact musically and commercially on a national or even international scale.

Both Phillips and Gordy were skilled entrepreneurs with a musical and cultural agenda. Records by Sun artists defined Rockabilly and pioneered early Rock and Roll. Through that early work, Sun redefined the sound and the look of popular music. The impact of Motown, however, was indisputably larger commercially and arguably had an even deeper cultural impact.

Motown recording star Smokey Robinson described his experience of Motown—and its social and cultural significance—this way:

> Never in my wildest dreams did I ever dare to dream that it would become what it has become—to the world, not just to the United States, but to the world. Into the '60s, I was still not of a frame of mind that we were not only making music, we were making history. But I did recognize the impact because acts were going all over the world at that time. I recognized the bridges that we crossed, the racial problems and the barriers that we broke down with music.[9]

As discussed in chapter 2, production at Motown was a highly organized, even systematic process, with many participants on the creative and promotional sides of the house. It was a strong business in terms of artist discovery and the development process was extremely effective. Ultimately, Gordy and Motown did not escape some of the issues that Phillips and Sun faced, especially artists that became frustrated with the label and, particularly, the level of control exercised by Gordy and who consequently sought creative and economic opportunities elsewhere.

Like Phillips with Sun, Gordy sold Motown (to MCA in 1988 for $61 million).[10] Unlike Sun, Motown is an ongoing concern, signing artists and producing records, although now as a part of the Universal Music Group.

SUB POP RECORDS—SEATTLE

Sub Pop did not begin with a vision for music as a means to transcend racial identity or to create a national brand. In the early 1980s, Bruce Pavitt started a newsletter to talk about independent bands in the Olympia, Washington, area in order to complete a college assignment. His project, *Subterranean Pop,* became a monthly "fanzine" that periodically included compilation tapes of unsigned and underground bands. In 1983, he relocated to Seattle and began writing a monthly column of critical reviews for *The Rocket,* a local music newspaper.[11]

By 1986, Pavitt, still writing for *The Rocket,* released his first compilation LP, *Sub Pop 100.* The album featured many acts that would define the Seattle sound in the coming years, including Sonic Youth and Green River. Pavitt's approach differed in many ways from Phillips's with Sun and drastically diverged from Gordy's at Motown. But there was at least one critical similarity to Sun and Phillips: Pavitt didn't have enough money to release individual albums or even singles for the artists recorded on the compilation tape. Like Sun in the late 1950s, Pavitt's still-nascent label was already artist-rich and distribution-poor.

Enter Jonathan Poneman. In 1987 he invested $19,000 to support the release of the first Soundgarden single. By 1988, Poneman was a full partner with Pavitt and they both quit their "day jobs" and began to work full-time on Sub Pop.[12] They established a goal of bringing the Seattle sound—which came to be known in the national press as "Grunge"—to national attention.

Further, they studied Motown's branding strategy: "We were trying to be very consistent in our packaging, very consistent in our sound, really putting focus on the region, in the same way that Motown put focus on Detroit Soul."[13]

They recognized—in no small part due to Pavitt's experience working in the press—that getting attention for local labels on a national scale was extremely difficult. As students of the business, they decided to use a tactic made popular by established alternative bands: seek the attention of the British music press.[14] In contrast to this relatively sophisticated approach to media promotion, Sub Pop had to cut corners in production by using low-tech, low-cost recording methods. Guided by local producer Jack Endino, they recorded cheaply and fast, and in so doing, some of the characteristics of the Seattle/Grunge sound were established—not so much from a vision like that of Sam Phillips, but as a result of economic necessity.

These strategies were effective for Sub Pop bands, perhaps most notably for Nirvana, Sub Pop's proof of concept artist. Their eponymous first album turned out to be very big indeed. But Sub Pop was more than Nirvana. It was the result of many factors converging in a particular time and place.

Poneman explained the success and impact of Sub Pop synergistically:

> It could have happened anywhere, but there was a lucky set of coincidences. Charles Peterson was here to document the scene, Jack Endino was here to record the scene. Bruce and I were here to exploit the scene.[15]

Poneman uses "exploit" in a particular way, in a sense that underscores how the creation-production-reception cycle works commercially. In order to create value, culturally or economically, musical creativity must be exploited. The question of how such exploitation occurs and by whom is important, but still less critical than understanding whether or not the exploitive phase of a creative enterprise adds value or merely extracts it. It would be hard to argue that Poneman and Pavitt did not add value to the Seattle music scene in the late 1980s and 1990s (or Phillips and Gordy in their respective places and times). Or, that through that local/regional success, all of these record label entrepreneurs did not fundamentally change and enrich popular music on a global scale.

The three independent labels discussed above are compared in table 4. Each label is evaluated in categories that reflect situational/contextual issues, critical events and choices, relationship to the local scene,

TABLE 4

Comparison of Three Independent Labels and Their Local Scenes

Location	Critical Years	Key Agent(s)	Platform	Contextual Resources	Pivotal Choices	Pivotal Outputs	Relationship to Local Scene	Means of Mass Distribution	Extended Outcomes
Memphis	1952–1960	Sam Phillips	Recording studio, record label	Confluence city, White/Black culture, Elvis Presley walks into studio	Establish Sun Records; move from Gospel to R & B Records; goal of racial transcendence through music; cracking "code" for Elvis Presley's musical style; revised a-/b-side marketing for 45s	Elvis Presley et al.; signature sound	Live performance locally and then regionally; hand-delivered records; local DJ relationships	Radio play, records; live show, touring	Sale of Presley contract to RCA; reinvest in Sun artists; sell label in 1962
Detroit	1959–1972	Berry Gordy	Recording studio, record label	Confluence city, White/Black culture, active jazz community as pool of studio performers and arrangers	Recognition: race-based issues in Soul music market; define new genre bridging Pop to Soul; establish TAMLA Records, then Motown Records; incorporate jazz musicians into house band for all	Defined new crossover genre; signature sound; 100s of Top 10 hits; dozens of major careers	Focus on mass distribution from beginning led to limited involvement in and influence on Detroit scene	Radio play, records; live show, touring; print media; television	Massive economic success and cultural influence; defined R & B for a generation; relocated Motown to LA in 1972; sell Motown to MCA in 1988

(continued)

TABLE 4

(continued)

Location	Critical Years	Key Agent(s)	Platform	Contextual Resources	Pivotal Choices	Pivotal Outputs	Relationship to Local Scene	Means of Mass Distribution	Extended Outcomes
					artists; professional songwriting/production teams for all artists; control of all aspects of artist music and brand				
Seattle	1986–1996	Bruce Pavitt and Jonathan Poneman	Music newsletter, newspaper article; compilation tapes and LPs; record label	Major regional city; major university; strong local music scene; multigenerational support for original music	Start a Seattle-based music newsletter for a community college class: *Subterranean Pop*; distribute compilation tapes of local bands; studied earlier independent labels: all successful movements have a regional basis; SubPop mission take Seattle music to a national audience w/o compromising its unique character	Nirvana, *Bleach*; Grunge: signature sound & style	Print media; live performance; SubPop Singles Club subscription list; regional distribution of records; regional radio play	International music press; regional, then national radio; national print media; national distribution deals: Geffen/Warner	Nirvana moves to Geffen; SubPop royalties from *Nevermind*; SubPop continues niche brand; partnership with Warner; Pavitt leaves label; downsize to Internet-based distribution

pivotal productivity/outputs, and—looking forward to the next chapter ("Diffusion")—mass distribution and outcomes.

Despite differences in location, era, and musical focus, there are obvious parallels and similarities between these labels, particularly in terms of relationships with local musicians and fans and the demonstrated potential for radio and records to extend, expand, and ultimately transcend the local scene.

All of this may be interesting from a historical perspective, but it also has a practical value. That is, it is useful to be able to identify persistent issues, things that work in—or that can be adapted to—a variety of contexts. And the issue of context raises an additional consideration: How do music scenes impact and interact with cultural and economic conditions in the cities where they flourish?

SONIC CITIES

In 2007, economist Richard Florida examined three contemporaneous music scenes in Canada: Toronto, Montreal, and Vancouver. All three were home to artists with major careers (Feist, Arcade Fire, and New Pornographers, respectively). Florida wondered whether this indicated that these three large Canadian cities were "on the verge of becoming music meccas" and what that might suggest "about their economic potential."[16]

To answer those questions, Florida began a project to study the "evolution of popular music scenes and what they mean for regional economies."[17] In 2008, Richard Florida and Scott Jackson's study *Sonic City* applied economic metrics and social demography to illustrate how traditional twentieth-century music scenes differed from those emerging in the early twenty-first century in North America.

Their findings suggest that innovation and economic activity continue to cluster geographically even in an increasingly globalized, digitized economy. Florida and his research partners found this puzzling, "because music-making requires little, if anything, in the way of physical input (such as iron ore or coal) to succeed, and they don't generate economies of scale."[18]

Further:

> Because musical and artistic endeavours require little more than small groups to make their final products, you would think that musicians should be able to live anywhere they want. Music scenes have every reason to "fly apart" and spread our geographically, especially in this age of the Internet and social media. But they don't. Instead, they concentrate and cluster in specific cities and regions.[19]

In a sense, Florida's and Jackson's research underscores the analysis (some sixty years earlier) of Theodor Adorno, who saw music as not truly an industry but rather as a "handcrafted" activity (see chapter 2). But Florida was looking at the musical experience more broadly and, by including production, consumption, and optimization with the creative process, found that music scenes are about creating experience: that they represent "modes of organizing cultural production and consumption."[20] The creation and early, local performances may be personalized, but the production of that experience—even on a local level—is the result of a relatively complex organizational system.

Such systems/scenes may be understood, according to Florida and Jackson, as comparable to what Silicon Valley represents to the tech industry:

> A vehicle for bringing together highly skilled talent, sophisticated consumers, cultural gatekeepers who identify new trends, economic infrastructure such as state-of-the-art recording studios and leading venues, and business moguls who take those trends to market in a concentrated physical and geographic space.[21]

In order to move from understanding the particular details of specific music scenes to general principles, Florida tracked the movement of musicians in the United States from 1970 to 2004. In doing so, he identified three trends. First, there was an increasing concentration of musicians living in thirty-one metro regions. For example, in 1970 Nashville was already a center for Country music, but the musical population grew dramatically until, by 2004, only New York and Los Angeles (both much larger cities) were home to more musicians. Florida and Jackson believe that a key factor for this growth was the expansion of Nashville productivity into other musical genres besides Country, including Rock and Pop music.

The second trend was the decline of traditional crossroad city musical scenes, including New Orleans, Memphis, and Detroit. This is likely due to some extent to the increasing "gravity" of the three major US musical cities. Examples include Memphis native Justin Timberlake making Los Angeles his base of operations and Jack White relocating from Detroit to Nashville.

There is, however, a countertrend—the third identified by Florida. According to his research, "smaller, more specialized music scenes were also flourishing in other locations such as college towns and even in some smaller, less urban places."[22] What is not clear from the *Sonic City* research is whether this is an example of the periodic rise of new scenes and independent labels that defined the popular music business throughout much of the twentieth century, or something different, resulting from technological, social, and cultural shifts in the twenty-first century.

A place where Florida and Jackson identify a phenomenon that may reflect uniquely contemporary issues is in the relationship between independent music scenes and high-tech industry locations. They use San Francisco (Google and Silicon Valley), Seattle (Microsoft), and Austin (Dell Computers) as exemplars. Florida also acknowledges that the music scenes in those cities predate by decades the evolution of high-tech industries. So causation is difficult to infer, let alone prove.

But Florida and Jackson are concerned less about defining a causal relationship between music scenes and tech, and more about identifying a synergy between and among music, technology, and business innovation. In that light, the authors see ambitious up-and-coming musicians as entrepreneurs who are particularly open to "new ideas, new people, and new sounds." He further suggests that the qualities and resources that make music scenes flourish also appeal to other innovative entrepreneurs. They explain: "Creative people don't like marketing slogans. But they do identify with a city's sound—[its] audio identity."[23]

It seems clear that Florida and Jackson have discovered a number co-factors that together make a city an attractive location for the young and innovative that drive thriving economic and vital cultural systems (see below for more). While interesting and perhaps useful in terms of deciding whether or not to bring a musical venture (band, label, festival, or something else) to a given location, these criteria do not offer much insight into how or even whether a music scene can be created intentionally in such a place.

If an entrepreneur wants to make a music scene happen, is it simply a matter of "right time, right place," or can it be made to happen by design? If so, what would the music scene process model look like?

MUSIC SCENE MECHANICS: ESSENTIAL COMPONENTS

Following the publication of the seminal work *Rise of the Creative Class* (2002), Richard Florida became a top consultant for cities and regions seeking to become "creative," attract "creatives," and reap the apparent benefits of hosting a "creative economy." More often than not, however, cities found that they could not "seed" this development. In fact, even Florida admitted that the benefits of courting young creatives accrue mostly to the members of such groups. The economic impact does not necessarily spread to other sectors of a community.

Perhaps a fundamental consideration about the validity and utility of Florida's creative class theory for music scenes is whether one uses it to describe an existing (or emerging) scene or as a blueprint for building one "from scratch." In terms of description, Florida and Jackson (in *Sonic City*) provide a list of elements common to almost every music scene and note some trends that explain how they have changed and are changing.

Let's begin there.

The key features of Florida's list of music scene elements are that they are located in large cities that have a diverse population and culture and a tradition of artistic innovation, are crossroads cities (historically), have one or more large universities (more recently), and are tech-friendly (even more recently). These are the elements you can reasonably expect to find in a city with a robust musical culture.

But in order to use this list to understand the process by which a music scene emerges, there are two broad questions to answer. First, is this list complete, and if not, what are the other critical components that foster a music scene? Second, to what extent must the listed elements appear "organically," that is, be preexisting? Conversely, can they be created intentionally? The first question—is the list complete?—is an analytical one. The second is operational: Which elements can be affected by the agency of one or more individual entrepreneurs?

In terms of completeness, everything Florida and Jackson mention has been present in music scenes over the past sixty-plus years. The independent label/music scene comparison table above shows that Memphis, Detroit, and Seattle were all large cities with diverse populations and a good cultural mix. Each had an established music and arts community of producers and consumers and the first two were crossroads/confluence cities, while Seattle is home the University of Washington and nearby Redmond is the home to computer technology and software giant Microsoft. Applying those criteria to Austin in the 1960s, Athens (Georgia) in the 1970s, and other hubs of musical productivity shows comparable factors.

In fact, the *Sonic City* list describes everything about the listed music scenes except the specific enterprises and people who made them. This is not so much an oversight as it is a reflection of the intention of the research, which is to produce an "abstracted" model of economic behaviors, something that optimizes comparisons across a wide variety of contexts. It also, however, creates blind spots. It does not take into account the impact of the agency of Sam Phillips, Berry Gordy, or the Bruce Pavitt–Jonathan Poneman collaboration. Further, without considering what these people did, we cannot fully appreciate the network of individuals, businesses, institutions, or ideas that caused pre-existing ingredients to yield a music scene.

It is the position of this text that we must consider the people and their actions—agents and agency—in order to operationalize music scenes. If we don't do that, we can't truly understand how and why they work. It is also agency in context—how individuals used the resources and relationships available to them at a specific place and time to implement their musical, cultural, and economic vision. As we begin to "wrap our arms around" this larger context, we start to understand whether music scenes are replicable in any sense.

Let's look at elements of the criteria identified in *Sonic City* from the perspective of how they come about and how they can be exploited.

Size and Demography

Changing the size of a community and character of the citizens takes time and is beyond the scope of individual action. So, whether or not a city is "large enough" is a precondition. What that means—how large is "large enough"—is actually a variable with a wide range of possible values. In 1950, two years before Phillips established his recording studio, the population of Memphis was 396,000 people. In the 1970s, the years the music scene exploded in Athens, Georgia, the population rose slowly from eighty thousand to just under one hundred thousand residents. Despite having only 20% to 25% of the population of Memphis, Athens was productive of new artists and a new genre of music, much as Memphis (and Sun Records) had done twenty years earlier. Consequently, population size is not, in and of itself, definitive of whether or not a music scene will emerge or thrive.

Mobility and Churn

Although being able to move readily across a city is a significant factor, the more critical issue is people moving in and out of the city, or *churn*. The turnover of the population—particularly of the segments most relevant to music production and reception—is a critical factor. In the 1950s, in Memphis (or most any city) the presence of a university was not yet significant in defining the success of music scenes. The population/audience churn in Memphis, Detroit, New Orleans, and other music hubs was the result of economically driven social migration and/or tourism.

In Athens, like Seattle and Austin, churn was the result of university student enrollment. In 1977, for example, the year the B-52s formed in Athens, the enrollment at UGA was just under twenty-four thousand students, over 25% of the city's total population.[24] Just as with earlier economic and/or tourism-based churn, university students add numbers, changeability, and diversity relative to the permanent residents.

Local Networks and Community

One of the most significant values created by music is its capacity to form communities. This is a key feature of local music scenes that both supports and transcends the economic value created. On the most basic level, musicians need to be able to connect with potential listeners as well as with one another. Since venues depend upon audience turnout to keep the lights on—let alone make money—being able to promote shows and connect artists with audiences is critical for that piece of the local, live music business as well.

Consequently, connectivity across the (relevant) community is vital to the ongoing health of a music scene. This kind of social networking ranges from word of mouth—fans talking to fans—to direct promotional activities ranging from handing out flyers or putting them on car windshields, local music friendly radio PSAs, and, in the past decade or so, the use of digitally mediated social platforms such as Twitter, Instagram, and, for traditionalists, Facebook.

Regardless of the medium, connectivity must be present in the scene and it must include robust listener-to-listener, musician-to-musician, and audience-to-artist components. Without them, especially without a group of music lovers that supports specific artists and local music generally, there is no community. No community equals no music scene.

Support for Original Music

Having a tradition of artistic innovation in music implies that there are musicians motivated to create original music and audiences who want to hear it. For this to be possible, producers and consumers must obviously be present in the population. In this, churn has an obvious impact and, more specifically, a population of college-age students provides a demographic that is particularly important to the creation and appreciation of popular music in its many forms. Social connectivity among this most critical demographic is also vital. It is important to note that having many college students who enjoy musical experiences for both aesthetic and social reasons does not necessarily translate into support for original music. This is a big variable.

Recording Resources

As discussed above, having a local recording studio or record label was a characteristic of music scenes throughout the twentieth century. The option of making a demo recording—locally—to promote live shows and shop for a recording contract has been a key ingredient to keeping musicians local as opposed to motivating them to move to another music market. With a local label that also supports original local music, the process could go a step further and the necessity of "leaving town" could be deferred until demand began to spread beyond the region.

Since the advent of digital audio in the 1980s, recording and distribution processes have been fundamentally transformed. It is now entirely possible to make a high-quality recording using digital audio tools for a fraction of the cost of professional studios of the past. And as a result of the digital distribution of music—in terms of both piracy/sharing and modern music streaming services—the profitability of the traditional label role has been substantially reduced. In this sense, Sub Pop was the first of the modern, digital-era record labels: dependent more on sophisticated use of media, direct connections to fans, and low-tech production methods.

In terms of sparking a scene, however, a label is almost certainly not the first business to launch. Labels are critical optimizers of a developing scene with rising artists, but do not necessarily catalyze one that is unformed or dormant.

Capitalization Opportunities

Traditional means of capitalizing a rising venture, whether that is a band or a label, have included self- and family-funded models: Sun, Motown, and Sub Pop all started this way. At a certain point, however—usually when a label becomes talent-rich but distribution-poor—outside capitalization becomes necessary. For Sun, this came from the sale of Elvis Presley's contract to a major label, followed by several successful singles from other Sun artists. For Motown it was a result of Gordy's early recognition of the importance of controlling the publishing for the songs that he wrote personally as well as for what his label staff produced collectively. For Sub Pop it was initially via Poneman's $19,000 to release a Soundgarden single, followed by a gradual, cost-conscious brand development strategy, until Nirvana's success (before they left the label to sign with a major) helped Sub Pop reach a tipping point of funding.[25]

For artists, it is a good news–bad news situation. Digital recording tools have streamlined and facilitated DIY recording, so expensive studio time is no longer a necessity for making a quality demo recording. On the other hand, a modern recording contract is not necessarily a pathway to funding. As noted in the previous chapter, record labels no longer provide financial support for emerging artists at anything resembling twentieth-century levels. Today, artists are not only self-producing; they are self-capitalizing.

The best-established way for musical artists to fund themselves is by playing live shows. In a local scene, there has to be a robust "gig economy" for this to happen. This is dependent on all of the factors in Florida's list. But, as important as it is to have lots of places to play, not every club or bar or coffee shop—or their customers/audiences—will support the performance of original music. Not having such a place will mean that a music scene capable of creating something new will not form. On the other hand, there are a fair number of scenes that developed and thrived on the basis of a single venue.

Venue

In any city with aspirations of being a "music city," there must be places where performers and listeners can come together: music venues. These can be municipal buildings—city-owned amphitheaters, for example. Most often, though, places where people go for musical entertainment are private businesses. As such, there is almost certainly a profit motive in their operation. If venue owners cannot make money and pay their employees, operational costs, and music costs, they cannot remain open.

When live music is part of that economic equation, the return on the investment—whether that is PRO licensing or live performers—must be a net positive for the business. How music generates revenue for businesses ranges from charging for admission to encouraging customers to stay longer, dance more, drink more, and—if offered—consume more food. So the question of the value of music to a business boils down to how many people it brings in and how they spend money once there.

For example, bar sales are typically crucial to a music venue's business model. Obviously, more people mean greater potential sales. Demographics also matter. Older audiences may spend more money than younger ones, but drink different beverages with differing profit margins. Music directly impacts not only size but also identity characteristics in crowds. Obviously bands that draw more people are good for business. But who they are, what they drink, and how much the total "customer spend" is for particular artists are also significant factors in determining whether that act is a good "investment" or not for the venue.

An Eventbrite guide for small music venue owners recommends that they also consider seasonal factors in forecasting bar sales. These include upcoming holidays, students returning to campus in the fall, outdoor drinking spaces and weather, as well as weekdays versus weekends.[26]

Since small music venues typically do not have large profit margins, every decision—including what music to offer—is a critical choice. For many, this leads to reluctance (or straight-up refusal) to give local musicians playing original music stage time. If a band has a proven record of success drawing customers, that's one thing, but for artists who are just starting out, whose skills and musical point of view are by definition unproven, there is a risk. The business owner has costs that remain relatively constant regardless of whether the audience draw is two hundred or two.

This creates a tendency toward business models that are economic, even consumerist, in orientation. In terms of vibrant entertainment options—not to mention economic impact on the community—this type of music scene is unquestionably important. But for the purposes of this discussion, it is necessary to make a distinction between music scenes that work because they are filled with ongoing musical performances, enthusiastic audiences, and a viable economic model (that depends at least in part upon touring acts and cover artists) and those that emphasize original music that is rooted in the place where it is performed and heard.

How-to advice on running a music venue is beyond the scope of this book. The broad principles for presenting and monetizing live performance were addressed in the previous chapter. Venues that support and nurture original music that reflects local/regional identity are examined in the next section with a view toward understanding not only what they are but how and why they work.

MUSIC CITIES, SCENES, AND VENUES: PROCESS MODEL

Whether they are oriented primarily toward financial success, supporting original music, or a combination of the two, music venues depend upon city and regional infrastructure and community resources. This is a big picture/small picture situation and we can't understand why a venue does or doesn't work, spark a scene, stay in business, or go under without also considering the civic and even regional perspectives.

Florida and Jackson's *Sonic City*, as discussed above, looks at big picture issues: geographic mobility, demography, and economics. They also identify three essential trends that defined music scenes on the cusp of the twenty-first century: a concentration of musicians in a given place, a decline in the importance of cities that were transportation and manufacturing centers as music scenes, and an increase in those that were home to large universities and/or high-tech industries.

While providing a detailed, descriptive, and comparative framework, the *Sonic Cities* model suffers the same limitation that Florida's earlier *Creative Class* model did: it is not a reliable predictor of success. As already noted, communities that worked to attract the "creatives" of the creative class with appropriate infrastructure and amenities often found that doing so did not necessarily enhance local economies in general. So too have cities attempting to foster a local music scene—with, for example, city-based music commissions, whitepaper studies, and so on—found that neither creativity nor opportunities for monetization increase. Thus, while the *Sonic Cities* model makes it possible for many of the elements of success to be precisely defined, the process for achieving it is not.

In 2015 Dell introduced the Future Ready Economies Model, based on the Strategic Innovation Summit: Enabling Economies for the Future at Harvard University.[27] The Dell model uses three primary indicators: human capital, commerce, and infrastructure. In a broad sense, these align with the *Sonic Cities* description of music scenes as places that "provide the diversity of people and the institutional and social infrastructure required to commercialize cultural products like music." But, while comparable to the *Sonic Cities* framework, the Dell model is a specifically predictive tool, designed to use the three broad indicators (plus twenty-three subindicators) to assess cities in terms of "how closely they are structured to optimal future readiness."

This section explores how Florida's *Sonic Cities* framework can be combined with Dell's Future Ready model to move beyond descriptive analysis to develop an adaptive (useful in multiple settings) and predictive model for emerging music scenes and to create prototypes for ones yet to be established. Let's begin with a comparison of the three "essential trends" from *Sonic City* and the "primary indicators" from Future Ready Cities.

Dell's model suggests that in terms of human capital, "future ready cities are where people want to be" and the *Sonic City* data suggest that music cities attract innovative and creative people. The Dell model states that collaborative entrepreneurship drives growth. *Sonic Cities* identifies ambitious up-and-coming musicians as entrepreneurs who are particularly open to "new ideas, new people, and new sounds."[28]

In terms of infrastructure, Dell finds the adoption of advanced technologies to be a predictor of growth. This correlates with Florida's assertion in *Rise of the Creative Class* that high-tech cities foster creative economies. But the *Sonic City* data suggest an additional element. Technology infrastructures are central to the music cities and scenes that Florida and Jackson identify. They also point out, however, that the specific impact of technology on the music industry has facilitated not only lower-cost recording but also democratized distribution to an unprecedented degree. This has impacted not only the well-established cities/scenes like Nashville, but also, per Florida and Jackson,

> the persistence of significant music clusters in places like Billings, Montana, and smaller urban and even exurban counties. At the same time that powerful forces push toward economic consolidation and geographic concentration of music talent, enterprise and infrastructure, significant counterforces are shaping some degree of geographic diffusion. It is important to note that this diffusion does not take the form of a random or ubiquitous spread of musicians, but rather takes shape around specific music scenes in particular places frequently organized around a critical mass of talent in a particular genre or even subgenre.[29]

From a predictive perspective, is a city with most or all of the elements identified by Florida and Jackson in *Sonic City* and that also meets the Future Ready Cities criteria likely to be a good place for a music scene to develop? Let's compare Dell's Future Ready Cities rankings from 2015[30] to Eventbrite's "5 Unexpected Cities Experiencing a Live Music Renaissance" (2017)[31] and see if there are any correlations.

The five "unexpected" cities listed by Eventbrite are Sacramento, Pittsburgh, Memphis, St. Louis, and Oakland. They are not, obviously, all new music scenes. They were included on this list due to recent developments, particularly in media and venues, along with music festivals and free events. Of these cities, only Pittsburgh is in Dell's top twenty-five future-ready cities, at number twenty-two. Other lists about music scenes show a similarly low level of correspondence between the Dell model and music scene activity.

Why?

First of all, this is a nonsystematic comparison. There could be correlations found by drilling down more deeply into the data. Second, these comparisons may reflect an issue raised in chapter 5 about the difficulty in applying broadly collected data to specific initiatives. Just as the overall economy and the climate for live touring do not necessarily provide a valid projection about how a given tour will perform, so too may the *Sonic Cities* and Future Ready Cities models be unable to predict—or even explain—the emergence of a new scene in music, unexpected or otherwise.

Further, it is possible that while the factors by Florida/Jackson and Dell are in fact necessary requirements for a music scene, they may not be sufficient for one to develop. As noted in the first two chapters, there are variables in the music creation, production, and reception cycle that depend upon complex interactions among many agents. In reference to a given music scene, there are highly specific roles that must be filled. It may be that they can't converge to produce a scene without the larger elements—as defined by Dell and Florida/Jackson—but without those critical people, the music doesn't happen.

There must be, for example, musicians who have a talent for original music. This is a very specific subset. There must also be fans willing to listen and support it. This is probably the most predictable demographic via the Dell and Florida/Jackson models. But in addition, there must also be venues of a certain kind with owners of a certain mind-set: willing to present and subsidize music to the public for creative and social reasons rather than for (or at least in addition to) commercial ones.

So let's look at the people and relationships of musical experience inside the context of Future Ready Cities and *Sonic Cities*.

Figure 5 represents the connection/transaction between artist and audience at the heart of the musical experience. In this case we are considering a live performance, where the musician and listeners interact within the same space, which means the venue, which is the box around the circles and arrows.

We can also put a series of larger boxes around the first one to represent the neighborhood, the city, and the region in which the venue sits (see figure 6).

The largest, outer box represents the geographic location of the scene: the city and region. The next box inward is the larger community and the people who comprise it: not all of them are producers or

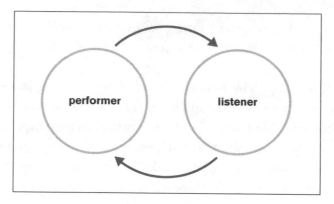

Figure 5. Performer–Listener Transaction.

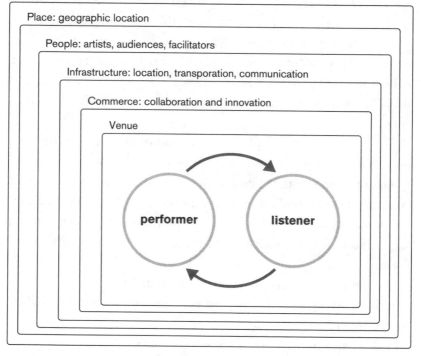

Figure 6. Music Scene Frames.

consumers of a music scene, but those who are come from this group. The next box represents the infrastructure of the community and city. This level is a major attractor for people to the city/community and essential to commerce in general and music making specifically. Collaborative entrepreneurship and innovation sits inside this, facilitated by the right people and the right resources. This frames the venue (or venues) in which musical experience occurs, the places where artists and audiences, facilitated by venue owners, come together.

In this conceptual model, the three primary indicators of the Dell research—people, infrastructure, and commerce—sit inside the geographic space and provide a progressively focused frame in which a music scene, based on at least one music venue, can develop. It is critical to note that this model does not indicate that the presence of the outer frames is predictive or productive of the central one. Nor would the central frame likely flourish or even develop without the framing human and infrastructure resources. Consequently, this is both an outside-in and inside-out model.

Returning to the question of whether or not a music scene is something that can be intentionally created and developed, in the context of this model, certain things are worth considering. First, if all of the outer elements are present, it would suggest that the inner square could flourish. But, as noted above, there are essential subsets of the population, from adventurous audiences, to creative artists, to facilitative presenters who must be present, connected, and engaged.

But, if enough of the outer elements/frames are present, is there a way to facilitate that connection and engagement? It is the position of this text that there is. One of the most important roles of a pivotal venue in original music scenes is that it provides a place in which like-minded musicians and listeners meet, interact, and cocreate musical experiences. Such a place can become the *essential venue* for a nascent music scene and the intersection of artist, audience, and presenter that it supports, its *critical nucleus*. This is the minimum viable condition for the emergence of a music scene (see figure 7).

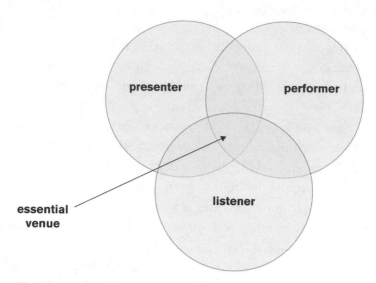

Figure 7. Music Scene—Critical Nucleus.

This would also represent the likeliest opportunity for entrepreneurship: to start a business with the potential to launch a music scene. This kind of venue, though it could be relatively low-cost to start (see "Essential Music Clubs and Dives" below), still represents a high-risk investment. The full payoff for music scene development, if there is one, only begins to be realized after an artist gets picked up and promoted by a record label.

Make no mistake, that is also a high-risk, often low-reward venture. Local independent labels are also mission-driven and the result of a particular kind of agency and entrepreneurial mind-set. Often, if there is to be "big money," it comes after the artist(s) have also moved from the independent to a major label, at which point they are almost certainly no longer available to play in the venue where they began.

The essential dilemma of music scenes is that the things that make them grow and nurture musical artists are the things that artists are driven to escape. The tension between the desire to tell authentic, personal artistic truth to people who know and understand us and the drive to have an impact on the larger cultural and economic stage has defined music enterprise throughout the last century and so far in this one.

The Beatles were not, for example, just motivated by a desire to be the best band in Liverpool or even in Britain. As their ambitions and artistic expertise both grew, they began to think more globally, seeking success in Europe and the United States. Likewise, though Sub Pop was committed to the Seattle "sound" of the early 1990s, they also wanted to take that sound to the world, without giving up on the things—the local character—that gave it value in the first place. Nevertheless, Sub Pop's first big success, Nirvana, quickly signed to a major label and, though remaining nominally connected to their original scene, became a mass-produced version of who and what they were when they were at home playing at the Crocodile in Seattle.

Thus, "making it big" means leaving behind the places and people who made you and your music valuable enough to reach a larger, broader audience. In a sense, this inevitable departure from the local scene is the geographic face of commodification in music, the musical experience, and the musician personally. And, as with other costs related to mass production and consumption, Cobain, Lennon, Presley, Smalls, and others have found that, by achieving the success that allowed them to break free of the confines of local economic geography (and personal history), they got what they wanted, but also lost what they had and where they had come from.

CRITICAL CONCEPTS

- In order to create value, culturally or economically, musical creativity must be exploited. The question of how such exploitation occurs and by whom is important, but still less critical than understanding whether or not the exploitive phase of a creative enterprise adds value or merely extracts it.

- It is important to note that having many college students who enjoy musical experiences for both aesthetic and social reasons does not necessarily translate into support for original music. This is a big variable in music scene viability.

· The essential venue of a scene is the point of optimum intersection between like-minded presenters, musicians, and listeners. This is what we will call the *critical nucleus,* which is the minimum viable condition for the emergence of a music scene.

FURTHER CONSIDERATION

Internet and the Death of Scenes

· Has the Internet Killed Music Scenes?
www.theguardian.com/music/2010/jun/10/local-music-scenes-internet

· The Internet Didn't Kill Music Scenes—We Did
http://diffuser.fm/the-internet-didnt-kill-music-scenes-we-did/

Science of Scenes

· Can City Hall Make a Music Scene?
www.citylab.com/life/2017/09/can-city-hall-make-a-music-scene/539436/

Essential Music Clubs and Dives

· www.laweekly.com/music/the-20-best-la-music-venues-that-are-gone-but-not-forgotten-7588407

CONCEPTUAL PROTOTYPE QUESTIONS

Using the process model/abstraction for Def Jam Recordings found in chapter 1 as a template, create models for Sun, Motown, and Sub Pop. Develop a comparison chart (like the one that compares Def Jam and the Beatles, also in the first chapter) for all four labels. Identify critical similarities and differences. What do they mean? Are they more about local time/place issues or something more structural and strategic?

Build a model—the fifth one in this sequence—for your local music scene. What has to be there? What will your proof of concept be?

For the prototype you developed above for the time/place/setting of your local scene, what is the "critical nucleus"? Is it a venue? Something else? Does it already exist? (If not, that's another prototype.)

7

Diffusion

Here, There, Everywhere

One of the critical constraints on live performance is the number of people who can hear and, secondarily, see the performers. This is the result of acoustics, venue size and configuration, and the characteristic volume of the performance medium: whether amplified, acoustic, a brass band, or a string quartet. These factors impact the musical experience for performers and listeners and the extent to which it can be monetized.

In order to optimize revenue from performance, the number of paying listeners must increase, either by increasing the size of the venue and the number of tickets sold, or by performing to fewer listeners in smaller spaces, but more often. Either way, whether the strategy is to attract as many people as possible to a given event, or perform a series of events for smaller audiences, the challenge is to attract enough people who are willing to pay for the experience.

In the broadest sense—for performance as well as other platforms for monetization—it is a question of aggregation. Performers must aggregate listeners (who they hope will become customers) and venue owners must aggregate performers as well as listeners. Failure to do so leads to careers failing to develop and venues closing or having to change programming format.

FROM LOCAL TO GLOBAL (AND VICE VERSA)

In a local music scene, as discussed in the previous chapter, public performances typically depend upon performing in smaller spaces, for smaller crowds, often comprising the same subset of the population interested in original music generally or particular performers. If there are only four hundred potential customers for a given musical offering in the population, having a venue that holds one thousand is no advantage. Nor is it an advantage to perform for one hundred people, seven nights per week. In that case, between Monday and Thursday, every potential listener has heard the band. Getting people to come back again on Friday and/or Saturday is difficult, particularly if there are other entertainment options.

For live performers, there are only two options for aggregating listeners. Either they must work in a market with sufficient population churn that new audiences regularly appear, or they must travel to different localities to find new listeners. These two approaches are what we can describe as *tourism* and *touring* models.[1] Either way, scale is the issue. Without sufficient scale, revenue potential is limited. If a community resource includes population churn, then venue owners and performers can benefit. If it does not, music talent buyers must seek new and varied musical offerings to keep the available pool of listeners/customers coming back. Either way, performers have to be cognizant of the risk of overexposure.

This circumstance creates a dual incentive for musicians to tour. Every musician must survive—at least at first and sometimes throughout a career—in a gig economy: a series of single or short-term engagements. A band or solo act plays as often as possible locally and then begins to perform in nearby communities, venturing further afield as opportunities present themselves. Musicians in other communities are doing the same, seeking audiences, coming into "your" town, and playing for "your" audience.

This is not a how-to book about making it in the music business, but it is worth noting that opinions vary about how soon a band or solo artist should begin touring. Everyone understands, however, that sooner or later, you will have to travel to find audiences or accept whatever share of the local market you can get and sustain. For a discussion of how technologies have disrupted traditional touring practices and encouraged the development of new DIY touring models, see chapter 8, "Disruption." (See also "The Deli: Emerging Music from Your Local Scene," under "Further Consideration" below.)

In a vibrant musical market/scene, although there may be lots of local venues and nights where live music is offered, there is local competition for those opportunities. There are also touring musicians. This means not only performers from other local scenes, who are trying to bridge to a regional identity. There are also middle- and upper-tier performers who come through to fulfill their own touring and career development plans. Money is being spent on musical experiences, but the local share is reduced in a lively music city that books lots of "outside" acts.

LESS SUCCESSFUL NUMBERS: THE MONEY OF LOCAL MUSIC

In addition to the market implications of touring acts for local musicians, there is also the impact of locally based events and festivals. At the highest levels, these draw national and international attention and create global brands. As discussed in chapter 5, "Monetization," festivals do in fact boost local economies and not only serve local fans but attract people from other places. While this benefits hotels, restaurants, and other businesses, it typically does not benefit a local music scene. In spite of being a spark for a tourism model—lots of new people coming in who, by definition, are interested in and willing to spend money on music—the structure of festivals most often excludes local venues and acts. High prices—especially the increasingly popular VIP ticket options—can also exclude local fans of original music.

Ultimately, scaling music ventures is a matter of distribution and access. Concert tours are the performance analog to the distribution of musical products. For most of the twentieth century musicians toured in support of an album and to encourage sales. Distribution of that album meant printing enough copies and physically shipping them to retail stores all over the country (ultimately the world) for people to be able to buy them.

Distributive media—like radio and television—also provide access by broadcasting audio/video versions of either live performances or recorded product. Just as musicians sooner or later need to get out of their hometown and scene and travel to other communities, so do they need to use available media to reach new potential audiences.

In the broadest sense, the diffusion of music today (the second decade of the twenty-first century) still depends on touring live performance, distributive media, and the sales potential of recorded music. The mechanisms and media technology change, but the multipronged approach remains relatively consistent.

One mechanism that has changed is that, with the decline in economic importance of physical recordings, "distribution" now means the digital distribution of content and access. As noted in chapter 2, twenty-first-century media have caused a convergence of discovery and consumption via digital, social media. This convergence applies across the board. Today all forms of access to music must also be points of discovery, engagement, and—if possible—consumption.

As digital audio and media have eliminated or drastically reduced the monetization potential of recordings, the diffusion equation has changed. The good news is that it has never been easier for millions of listeners across the globe to hear your music—even while you are still an unsigned, local artist. The bad news is that the tools that make this possible dramatically reduce the revenue potential represented by those listeners. This has led to an increasing emphasis on live performing and on touring, which both encourages every local band to go global and pressures every local band (and venue) into competition with an almost unlimited number of performers from across the world, both in media and on tour.

In a very real sense, digital media, including web-based video plat-forms like YouTube, make everything both global and local. A live gig video can put a music fan in Maine in a club in Albuquerque hearing a just-starting-out band from Lubbock, Texas, on tour. Location still matters and the amenities that support daily life, music making, and shared experience are still relevant. But the ease with which the musi-cal experience can be extended—including by live streaming a local event—is unprecedented. How musical artists can leverage this tech-nology is also discussed in more detail in the next chapter.

But mechanics and tactics aside, it should be clear that music fans are the big winners in this climate. Never has more music been available with a mouse click or a tap on a multitouch screen than today and with such low-cost (or no-cost) options. If there is a drawback for fans, it may simply be that in the sheer mass of music available, it is difficult to find the right song for you. Curated playlists are one response to this chal-lenge (see chapter 3, "Reception," for more). But in fact, producers have always had to work to develop strategies that facilitate discovery and consumption. Understanding how information and innovation spread helps us to understand the way diffusion strategies in music work.

DIFFUSION OF INNOVATION: THEORY

The study of how new things spread across society must begin with the work of Everett Rogers. Rogers, a sociologist, published the first edition of *The Diffusion of Innovations* (DOI) in 1962. Now in its fifth edition (2003), it is one of the most influential studies in the adoption of new products, services, or ideas.

Rogers found that the social diffusion of new things has a defined process consisting of five steps: knowledge, persuasion, decision, imple-mentation, and confirmation. These steps align with the process of moving from discovery to engagement to purchasing to—ultimately—becoming a committed fan. (See Samuel Potts in chapter 2.)

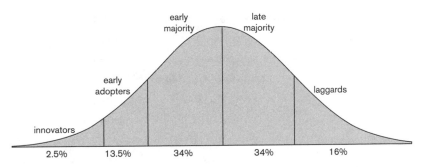

Figure 8. Diffusion of Innovation Curve Landscape.

Another critical concept from Rogers's work is that people who "adopt" innovations can be grouped and displayed along a distribution curve. Rogers categorizes these groups as *innovators, early adopters, early majority, late majority,* and *laggards* (see figure 8). This idea has been accepted and applied across many fields and has inspired or influenced many more recent works, most notably Malcolm Gladwell's best-seller *The Tipping Point.*

Rogers's work, as well as that of Gladwell and others, has become a major influence on contemporary marketing. This pattern of adoption and the role of the different kinds of adopters have shaped the development of contemporary marketing strategies designed to increase the impact of exposure to a new product, influence purchasing decisions, and optimize social confirmation.

DIFFUSION OF INNOVATION: APPLIED

Rogers's diffusion theory can be used to explain strategies for breaking new music to the public. For example, when Pavitt and Poneman recognized the difficulty of getting the mainstream media to pay attention to a small independent label, they opted to focus on the underground music press in Britain. From a diffusion theory perspective, this was a choice to try to first persuade innovators (the people who wrote the journals, columns, newsletters, and the like) to influence the early adopters of new music with their coverage of Sub Pop artists.

This approach uses the few to eventually influence the many: specifically, using the status and influence of innovators and early adopters (together roughly 16% of the population) to eventually persuade the early majority (34%) to buy and buy-in (confirmation). This strategy requires a smaller initial investment in promotion than, for example, the kind of media campaign a major label might engineer for a major artist (or a film studio for a movie they want to be a blockbuster). It also takes time to become effective. This is a pivotal factor—and one that explains why Sub Pop remained artist-rich and sales-poor even after becoming critical favorites.

More broadly, Rogers's description of how people react to new things explains the fundamental relationship between small independents and larger labels. Labels embedded in a local scene are well positioned to understand and reach the more innovative and early-adopting members of that community. Obviously this is interconnected with local venues that feature original music and draw the listeners interested in new and innovative music to connect with performers. Local music scenes are arguably all about innovators and early adopters.

Past a certain point of adoption, as noted previously, limited and local resources of an independent label can neither drive nor meet rising demand. From the perspective of the DOI curve, once the innovators and early adopters are on board with a new artist and the early majority has begun to respond, decisions must be made.

Thus, Nirvana left Sub Pop to move to Geffen after the success of *Nirvana*. Likewise, Phillips agreed to sell Presley's contract to RCA. Motown exemplifies the same challenge from a different perspective. Gordy recognized, from the beginning, the importance of being able to contract national promotion and distribution. For a diffusion theory perspective, Sun and Sub Pop were aimed at acquiring early adopters by development new artists, while Motown always had the early and late majorities in mind and the label's product development, branding, marketing, and distribution strategies reflect that.

Beyond comparison of label strategies and scene characteristics there is another factor in the diffusion of local, original music: the artists themselves. Why did Nirvana spark national recognition and adoption while other Sub Pop bands—Mudhoney and Green River, for example—did not. It is not purely a Seattle phenomenon either. The Athens scene some ten years earlier showed the same tendencies. Other bands—not R.E.M. and the B-52s—were not only popular in Athens; many were considered "better" than the bands that went on to achieve national and international success.

What factors explain what happened and why? Is it a matter of the scene itself and its potential to influence listeners in other regions? In other words, can a scene serve as an innovator/early adopter for a national early majority? Or is it a matter of starting the cycle again on a broader scale, reaching early adopters in a larger market who can influence the later adopters in their cities and regions?

These questions can be answered in a variety of ways. First of all, an artist or band that resonates strongly in a given local context may simply not travel well. Audiences in different areas may not share enough contextual and cultural values with the "home" audience for the connection to happen. R.E.M. was successful in Athens and even more so in other contexts. Love Tractor, even more beloved in Athens, did not connect with other audiences. Is it that simple?

Is it also an issue of how new music is rolled out onto a national platform, of how and where new audiences experience regionally based performers? For most of the twentieth century, expanded promotion depended upon radio play of records, touring, and key media appearances. For Presley this began with the popular music broadcasts *The Grand Ole Opry* and *The Louisiana Hayride*. These programs were followed by millions across many regions and put Presley on the same stage as far more established artists. In other words, it put him in front of a majority (early and late) audience.

It was more than exposure to the majority, however. Performing on a widely recognized platform with established artists provided a kind of validation—a critical factor in moving from early adopters to early majority. Part of the reason why music fans are early majority rather than early adopters is that they are waiting to see if emerging music has a proven value. This is even more true of late majority adopters. Phillips could have leveraged this exposure to foster the wider adoption of Presley's music, but he did not have the operational structure or resources to do so. Later in Presley's career, "Colonel" Tom Parker made sure that his films, records, and live shows were calibrated for maximal public accessibility and acceptance rather than the edginess of the once-controversial performer.

The capacity of an artist/label to build from innovators to laggards on the diffusion curve has significant implications for business decisions and business model longevity. If you commit to discovery and innovation and the segment of the audience that prefers these things, at a certain level of success, artists will inevitably move on to larger businesses. Yet when done correctly, the early profitability and label credibility can be used to develop new artists—a strategy shared by Sun, Sub Pop, and many more.

In this model, having a sustainable long-term strategy depends upon the continuing discovery of new music more than the value of multiple albums by the same artist and the "back catalog" sales this can generate. Conversely, adopting a strategy that moves more directly to the early majority and then on to late majority and laggards involves a different kind of resources and the ability to maintain them over time. This is where Motown was the exception as an independent and is, in fact, the approach where major labels have traditionally dominated.

The diffusion curve thus explains other features that define record industry business models. First there is the relative advantage independent labels have had in identifying and producing the innovative and even genre-disrupting artists. Rock and Roll, Punk, and Rap, to name three, did not appear first on major labels.

Further, because of the importance of back catalog sales to major labels—which gives them a larger capital reserve than independents—it made them far more vulnerable to the impact of file sharing and piracy. It is one thing to have a new release pirated, but entirely another to have popular albums from the past—say forty years worth of Rolling Stones albums—appear entirely for free on a file-sharing site. This has a particularly negative impact on well-established bands that no longer wish or no longer are able to tour to create revenue.

These differences aside, both major and independent labels must meet the challenge of diffusion. For most of the twentieth century, this was achieved primarily via radio. While radio stations tended to favor major labels (and the "gifts" from their record promoters), there is ample evidence that independents were able to crack this market. In fact, from one perspective the payola scandals in the 1950s were driven by major label (and publisher) concern about the capacity of the independents producing Rock and Roll records to get airtime on important regional stations.

Since the advent of file-sharing technologies and Internet-based social media, music diffusion has changed remarkably. While radio play continues to play a role in distributing music, primarily on a local basis, the Internet and, in particular, video sites like YouTube drive far more music discovery and facilitate more transferring of files—legally and illegally—than anything before. This topic will be discussed in more detail in the next chapter.

CONSEQUENCES OF DOI: CONTROL, ACCESS, ECONOMICS

It is difficult to dispute the importance of access—particularly in terms of convenience—as a factor in driving the decisions of music consumers about which artists to follow, or what music to share or to purchase. It is entirely possible to posit that the music industry on its largest scale is not so much in the business of creating content as of providing access to content.

For example, for the sale of LPs to be the revenue driver for the music industry for so many decades of the twentieth century, certainly there needed to be artists who made records that people enjoyed. But we should not ignore the control wielded by record labels. Labels were able to decide who got a contract and who got an album produced. Their established distribution and retailing relationships determined what records got into the stores and at what price they were sold. At each step along the distribution and sales cycle, labels were in a dominant position.

What Napster disrupted more than anything else was diffusion: the distribution phase of the record industry business model. Napster was innovative not because it was digital, but rather because distribution moved online and rendered retailers obsolete. Certainly, older studios and labels were marginalized by digital audio, but "record stores" were demolished as a market sector. Those that remain depend upon both laggards—those who refuse to give up vinyl—and extreme innovators and early adopters who wish to capture the cachet of being so far behind the adoption curve of digital music, they are ahead of the next one.

Ultimately, three factors that govern the capacity of a diffusion model to create value are the degree of exclusivity of the distribution/sales process, the capacity to establish price and bundle content, and the extent to which a distributor can aggregate the productivity of content creators.

When labels held the means by which records could be produced, promoted, and distributed on a large scale, it permitted an extremely high degree of control over access. As mass production, distribution, and sales became increasingly concentrated under the control of a diminishing number of major labels, the ability to set the price for an LP or a CD was also increased. The "average" price of a CD became a significant point of contention in the 1990s and was a factor that amplified consumer discontent and willingness to adopt illegal music file-sharing options.

Perhaps even more significant than controlling production and distribution of recorded product is the practice of bundling that content. In the early days of the recording era and until the later 1960s, the standard product of the record industry was the 45 single. The A-side of a 45 was the "hit" or the song that the consumer wanted and the B-side was a song that—with few exceptions—the label considered unable to drive purchases on its own.

When albums began to replace singles, at first they were simply compilations of previously released singles. The early US releases of Beatles albums fell into this category, for example. Later, as albums became the primary format for releasing new music, they afforded both new creative and expanded economic opportunities.

Creatively, albums allowed artists to explore relationships between and among songs and to treat an LP as an extended musical form. Once the Beatles received critical and popular recognition for *Sgt. Pepper's Lonely Hearts Club Band* in 1967, many other artists and labels followed suit. By the end of the 1960s, the concept album had become a benchmark of creative significance and maturity for artists.

The economic impact of bundling singles into album format cannot be underestimated either. While there were albums that produced multiple number one or top ten singles, for the most part, even one successful single could make an album sell five hundred thousand or more copies (gold record status or better). Thus, a single—already a central component of a large-scale diffusion strategy for new music—could not only sell as a single, but also drive album sales.

If, for example, an LP cost $4 to $5 (prices varied a great deal by region, but call this a rough average for the 1960s) and a 45 was $1, then an album that produced two singles could have generated $2 per customer based on 45s or twice that for the LP. In addition, LPs only gradually impacted the sale of 45s. In fact both LPs and 45s continued to be produced and sold well into the CD era in the 1990s. Regardless, it should be apparent that the LP, even priced at the low end of the possible retail average, could produce double the revenue—at least—of a 45. In addition, the increased musical content, expanded artwork, lyrics, and biographical information on LP covers and inserts made it possible to deepen artist–audience relationships and extend the value of the brand.

The impact of digitization and file sharing as diffusive tools was obviously disruptive to distribution models based on physical product. But because MP3s were shared and sold as singles on a massive scale, the effect of unbundling albums was even greater.[2] In fact, the idea that fans could once again—as they had in the prealbum days of the 1940s and 1950s—buy or download their favorite song as a single was powerful. In addition, the idea that fans could choose one or all but one song from an album created a previously nonexistent à la carte market for music.

So, on the one hand, file sharing, paid digital downloads, and streaming services have made access easier, more pervasive, and cheaper than ever before. But, in aggregate, they have drastically reduced label control and unbundled product to a point where the profitability of an individual song cannot be measured in dollars or even cents, but rather in fractional cents per stream. Further, the idea of a "hit" has changed. Songs can be massively heard and liked—by millions globally—but not purchased. The economic implication of the DOI—that getting to the early/late majority meant big money—is no longer absolute.

BLOCKBUSTERS AND THE LONG TAIL

As the per-product income has diminished for single songs, the importance of aggregation has increased. Traditionally, record labels have been able to benefit from the productivity of multiple artists. There are advantages to this position beyond simply having more product on the market than could be produced by a single artist or group, beyond even the value of being able to offer a variety of music for different musical tastes. Perhaps the most critical advantage of having multiple artists/ products entering the market at the same time is the opportunity to use extremely successful entries to offset the costs of the less popular.

As noted in earlier chapters (2 and 5), for most of the twentieth century, the economic model for record labels was based on the reality that many commercially released records never recoup the cost of making them. Because of that, the sustainability of the model depended upon producing hits that were large enough or frequent enough to essentially subsidize the discovery and development of new and rising artists with the by-no-means-certain potential to become successful. "Hit" records and "blockbuster" sales were thus vital to the music industry.[3]

They still are. But what the terms mean and imply about revenue has changed. For example, in 1994 the top-selling album for the year, *The Sign* by the Ace of Base sold 3.8 million records. In 2014, the top-selling album, the soundtrack from the film *Frozen,* sold over three million as well. At first glance, this appears to indicate that albums continued to produce value, even if the numbers show no growth.

When looking below those top albums, however, the actual trend becomes much more apparent. In 2014, the second strongest-selling album, Beyoncé's self-titled release, sold fewer than one million copies all year, while in 1994, thirty-eight albums had sold over a million by the beginning of September.[4] In fact, no artist had a platinum album in the first nine months of 2014.[5] By the end of the year only four albums had sold more than a million copies.[6]

The declining effectiveness of the blockbuster model is paralleled by another effect of the digital marketplace. In 2004, Chris Anderson discussed the long tail distribution curve of product sales in an article for *Wired* magazine. In a long tail distribution, the few top-selling products are in the "head" and the rest in a long-declining tail. He used examples of online businesses like Amazon and Apple that were able to profit from products that did not sell well individually but in aggregate produced significant revenue. The idea was that a company could in fact sell many different items in small quantities to extremely large numbers of customers without (or in addition to) the vital few big sellers.

From a diffusion perspective, even selling to the 2.5% of the population that are innovators could become profitable, in theory, if you sold millions of distinct products to this small group over and over. Long-tail economic models obviously can only work (and there is dispute about whether they work at all) for companies that are in a position to aggregate a great deal of product and for which there are minimal stocking, warehousing, and distribution costs. These factors are all present in the digital products environment and thus the electronic books of Amazon and the digital song downloads at the iTunes store positioned those companies perfectly to be long-tail "winners."

On the one hand, long-tail business models not only optimize the diffusion of product; they do so on a scale never before achieved in publishing or recording. From the perspective of the aggregating company (rather than the creator or producer), the advantages are apparent. If something is a hit they can sell many copies. If not, and the overhead costs are fractional, even a few copies sold produce a profit.

The model breaks down for creators and producers. Record labels are in the business of distributing and providing access, but their role in discovering and developing talent is antithetical to long-tail models in that the cost per discovery is very high. Without a blockbuster, producing one hundred modestly selling records (say, fewer than ten thousand copies) would be economically disastrous. For artists, the situation is even worse. The per-stream payoffs by streaming services—often in single-digit dollars per song per year—starkly illustrate the problem (see chapter 8 for more).

Regardless of the economic model in play—blockbuster or long tail—the capacity to aggregate customers is key. But diffusion of content, experience, and access is not only about sending it "out there." Much as performers have the option of going out on tour or working in a setting that draws new customers in significant numbers on a regular basis, location can also be used to diffuse a brand that draws experience seekers from a wider world to a specific location.

FESTIVALS AS DIFFUSERS AND AGGREGATORS

One thing that happens as a city becomes known as the home of a music scene is that a sonic brand identity develops. This brand can support more than local, original music. It can also do more than host touring acts at all levels and sell tickets on a recurring basis. Unique music scenes create a cachet of their own, an identity that can be diffused in order to attract customers on a national or even global scale to local events.

Two examples of this phenomenon are South by Southwest (SXSW) in Austin and the Forecastle Festival in Louisville. Austin is the more famous music scene and the self-styled "Live Music Capital of the World." Louisville is less widely recognized outside the region, though it has a long and rich tradition of supporting local, original music and launching a number of national careers. Both Austin/SXSW and Louisville/Forecastle exemplify how a local identity and resources can be leveraged to bring the world home.

They also illustrate the tensions between global diffusion and local productivity. In Austin, the local music scene and the live music business are struggling to support the artistic community that made the city famous. Forecastle revitalizes the music brand of Louisville, while at the same time alienating local fans who are "priced out" of the festival. In Austin the Music and Entertainment Office represents a governmental response to the issue. In Louisville, the Poorcastle Festival is a grassroots response. In both cases, the tensions and reactions are both cultural and economic in nature.

Austin: Working for Tips in a High-Tech World

On August 29, 1991, Austin declared itself the Live Music Capital of the World. By that time the city already had a decades-long history of supporting live music. But in 1988, the city, recognizing the economic impact of music, established the Austin Music Commission.[7] The *Austin City Limits* television show was already on the air and SXSW held its first conference in 1987. The commission's job was not to create or even nurture the Austin scene as much as it was to extend its brand.

SXSW grew from a discussion among local Austin residents "about the future of entertainment and media.... A fundamental opinion shared by the group was that the local creative and music communities were as talented as anywhere else on the planet, but were severely limited by a lack of exposure outside of Austin."[8]

This idea, that the talent native to Austin deserved recognition outside the city, differs from the traditional strategies of local bands and independent record labels that toured and distributed beyond the region to demonstrate their value. The visionary and ambitious leadership of SXSW sought "an event that would bring the outside world to Austin for a close-up view."[9]

The motivation for developing that solution included pride in the community and its creative artists, as well as economic opportunism. Obviously, for business owners—live music venues and otherwise—touring is not an option. The tourism model was the only way to increase cultural status and economic opportunity for place-bound businesses.

The history of SXSW since then has been one of steady growth in attendance, direct and indirect income, international recognition, and corporate sponsorship. In 2016, the festival generated $325 million (USD), up 2.5% from the previous year. The indirect income to Austin area business was estimated to be an additional $576 million. Official participants totaled nearly eighty-five thousand and attendees were well over one-quarter of a million people.[10] They came from all over the United States and 22% came from more than twenty countries in North and South America, Asia, and Europe.[11]

SXSW illustrates how a festival can diffuse the reputation and brand of a locality around the world while, at the same time, aggregating international businesses and consumers and bringing them to the point of origin, the place whose local scene is the genesis of the "buzz." The results of succeeding in this initiative have been mixed. According to a 2017 NPR report,

> The business underlying "The Live Music Capital of the World" stands bifurcated between its lucrative festivals (SXSW principally, but Austin City Limits, Fun Fun Fun Fest and others, too) and, as studies have found, a dwindling local music scene. Austin didn't become the self-styled

"Capital" solely by hosting a handful of gargantuan events, which were first born from and since have capitalized handsomely on Austin's brand to increase their now-global footprints, which have drawn outsized attention to the city. These large events and a rapidly expanding population have put an unintended strain on the infrastructure of the local music scene which helped create them and on which they still rely—it's hard to throw innumerable shows, as during SXSW, in a city with fewer and fewer venues to put them in.[12]

This is another facet of the dynamic tension between local music scenes and economic and cultural impulses toward a wider world and market. It also exemplifies how the issue flows both ways—talent and competition coming into the scene and talent "draining" out of it, as local artists strive to "make it big." This type of large-scale festival, with a global footprint and increasingly substantial sponsorship from corporate brands, represents a more extreme example of the impact of the global on the local and some unintended consequences of success.

In 2015, the Austin Music Census was released. It was commissioned by the Austin Music and Entertainment Commission, part of Austin's city government, under the leadership of director Don Pitt. The census looked at three sectors of the city's music economy: live performance venues, individual musicians, and music industry workers across private, nonprofit, and city-run business and institutions.

Despite overall growth in the music sector, the census revealed some critical issues for the health of the local music scene including that rises in cost of living combined with stagnant incomes created an "affordability" crisis for local, working musicians, that cover charges were frozen, decreased, or "disappeared entirely" as local patrons became unwilling to pay covers for local musicians, and that changes to consumer behavior, regulatory constraints, and narrow profit margins (6% to 15% for small to mid-size establishments) created negative pressures on small venues.[13]

Jennifer Houlihan, "former executive director of a local music industry advocacy group, Austin Music People, and now the director of business development of a local music business, Nomad Sound," describes the situation this way:

> We were seeing a real decline across the board in what we called our primary music economy. At the same time, we were seeing an uptick in revenue from the festival economy. SXSW, Austin City Limits—those folks were doing really well. As Austin has become more expensive and attractive—particularly to tech companies, a lot of our folks [members of the local music industry] that work for tips and minimum wage can't afford it anymore.[14]

For any local music scene it is an existential crisis if local creative artists can no longer make a living or afford to live there. Ironically, the thing that makes a scene "cool" and desirable enough to attract touring artists and launch large festivals also attracts entrepreneurs. In Austin's case these come from the high-tech industries and they have driven the value of property and the cost of living beyond the reach of the working musician. In addition, the newly arrived residents, although they may well have an interest in music and the financial resources to patronize it, do not have a historical, grounded interest in the local scene and its music.

All of these pressures lead venue owners to book an increasing number of touring acts, rather than local ones. It also pulls investment money from local creation and presentation into large-scale festivals. This strategy may provide short-term relief for venue owners and opportunities for entrepreneurs, but it only exacerbates the problem from the perspective of the "on-the-ground" creatives who sparked and sustained the content of the scene: working musicians.

As noted by *NPR* music writer Andrew Flanagan, "Technology isn't going anywhere, but without a focus on grassroots creation and local vibrancy, much of its distributive value may wither, as creators are barred from growing into their own."[15]

What to do about it? According to Austin Music and Entertainment Commission director Don Pitt:

We're no different than Seattle, or Chicago, even Nashville for that matter, if you focus on that local scene. If the industry is globalized, if technology has globalized the ecosystem, then you've got to think globally in return. I think that's where a lot of cities, including Austin, fall short.

The potentially negative impact of touring and large-scale festivals on local music scenes is both inherent and inevitable. If a scene is capable of creating, in the words of Andrew Flanagan "distributive value," then musicians who can will leave to go on tour. That means musicians from elsewhere will come into the scene. Further, if a scene develops an established reputation, like Austin, Memphis, or Seattle, because of the productivity of its native music and musicians, that will lead to efforts to expand and exploit that brand, which gets us to large-scale festivals and declining opportunities for local musicians and venues.

If those are the dynamic features in play, then it seems possible to develop a strategy to counter them, to protect the value of the expanding brand on the larger stage and market while still nurturing local opportunity and creativity. But what if there is a more fundamental issue? Another Austin music entrepreneur and leader, Bobby Garza, has this to say: "Music is such an integral part of the cultural fabric here that people assume it's just always going to be here. Part of our challenge as music advocates is to say actually, it might not be."

Whether a situation like Austin's can be mended with an adaptive strategy remains to be seen. An alternative—hinted at by Garza—is that scenes have a life cycle and Austin's, like others', may come to an end, or mutate into a tour- and festival-based economic system, more than a creative one. For more on the idea of "life cycles" for music enterprises, see chapter 10, "Incorporation."

Austin and its national/global presence through SXSW (and other events and institutions) represent—perhaps—a cautionary tale about the limits of diffusion. How far afield can you spread an identity rooted in a vibrant local scene before it kills the roots of that scene? A contrasting example follows.

Louisville: A National Happening and
A Festival for the Rest of Us

Louisville, as the location for a music scene, checks all the boxes: river city, strong economy based on tobacco, bourbon, and manufacturing, with a tradition of businesses, socially prominent families, and citizens supportive of the arts. While the city's economic base suffered with the decline of tobacco sales and the general reduction in American-based manufacturing, the city still supports a vibrant arts community, including touring and locally based musicians.

In addition, in the second decade of the 2000s, Louisville government and civic leaders have made a coordinated effort to attract high-tech businesses and jobs to the region—with some success. The city has invested in computer programming training—Code Louisville— free to anyone with a library card and secured a deal for Google to install their Google Fiber infrastructure throughout the city. These strategies align well with the Dell Future Ready Cities model (see the previous chapter).

Louisville has also recognized that music and the arts will play some role—per the Richard Florida, *Creative Class* model—in attracting a creative, entrepreneurial work force.[16] Consequently, by both traditional and twenty-first-century standards, Louisville appears to have the structural components to host a contemporary music scene.

An event that blends the creative/visionary side of local music advocacy, the impact on the regional economy, and increased global recognition for a community is the Forecastle Festival. In the summer of 2002, Louisville native J.K. McKnight parlayed $200 into a free music event in a park near his parents' home:

> When the sun ascended on the morning of July 20th, several hundred people gathered to see live performances by The Vixen Red, Fire The Saddle, Blue Goat War, and other local favorites. The atmosphere was progressive and positive, and encouraged 21-year-old festival founder JK McKnight to build upon it the following year.[17]

For that next year, McKnight worked with members of the Louis-ville arts community and "socially conscious" organizations to create a festival that was "a distinct, equal representation of Louisville music, arts, and activism."[18]

McKnight talks about what happened next:

> The audience size tripled. It was also more diverse: young people, older people, families.... Of course I was open to *any* audience. The first year the bands comprised half of the crowd. The music, art, activism blend really resonated with people. Plus Louisville is close to a number of major markets: Cincinnati, Indianapolis, Nashville.... We invited people from those communities. And they loved it.[19]

Forecastle audiences continued to increase, as did the size of the shows. In the third year, McKnight was able to attract corporate sponsorships for the event, including Patagonia and Red Bull, as well as local financial support. With the help of volunteer workers and the cash from sponsors, the event expanded again. The cash also enabled McKnight to "build real stages, attract touring acts ... and that year we had over 5,000 people attend."[20]

Even with a volunteer work force and sponsorship money, the festival lost money again in year four, because it was still free to attend. On the advice of his family, McKnight decided to move to a paid attendance model, book more successful artists, and move to a larger venue (but still in a public park). He also incorporated the name "Forecastle Festival" and "won a federal trademark for music, art, and activism programming because the model was unique."[21]

These changes expanded the scope and revenue-generating potential of the event, but did not solve all problems. Presenting live shows (as discussed in chapter 5) is a relatively high-risk undertaking. As the locally oriented, free event moved toward touring artists and a paid attendance model, local support was affected. Locals came, but not in the same numbers or in the same "mood" as before. Attendance depended increasingly on tourism from other regional cities. The dynamic tension between local and global became more apparent and significant.

McKnight talks about this period of the festival this way:

> The next three years were incredibly tough from a growth standpoint because I had to learn everything as I went along. And then we got really lucky. We had partnered with a local promoter, Billy Hardison, who really helped us build the scene. We were deciding whether to book Sleater-Kinney or Yo La Tengo and Billy said, "Yo La play here every year, they're a known quantity, I can tell you how much they'll sell . . . that's the safe play. On the flip side, Sleater-Kinney is relatively unknown but could be big because they get tons of national press, etc."
>
> I chose Sleater-Kinney. Ticket sales were going okay . . . but not great. Then one night I start getting all these messages from people. "Congrats!" "We're flying in from Portland!" "We're coming in from Texas!"
>
> It turns out the band had decided to break up and Forecastle was one of the last events they would play. We sold thousands of tickets overnight. We got national press coverage. *Spin* magazine named us one of their Top 101 Things to Do. It was huge.

"Huge" is where the opportunities expand dramatically: for revenue, for brand recognition, for cultural influence, and for bringing the world home to—in this case—Louisville. Local artists leave the scene where they grew to get "huge." But "huge" is the opposite of what makes a local scene grow and thrive. Like other festivals, including SXSW, Forecastle has become increasingly integrated with corporate brands, while striving to keep in mind how outside visitors experience Louisville and Kentucky:

> We put an emphasis on the consumer experience. People come not just for the music and art and activism but also for the micro experiences we build in. We focus on the DNA of Kentucky—if you're traveling in from one of the 2,400 cities people come from, you want an authentic Kentucky experience. So we roll out that red carpet. We build in those micro experiences in a way that is authentic and unique . . . but also convenient and easily digestible.[22]

Make no mistake, however. This is about the non-Louisvillian and non-Kentuckian experience of the event and the place. Like SXSW and every other large-scale festival, Forecastle only works when the brand is widely diffused and the customers are broadly aggregated from many places.

So what about the impact on the local music scene, the community of fans and performers?

Enter the Poorcastle Festival, the "festival for the rest of us," which began in 2012, "literally as a joke":[23]

> [Musicians and radio hosts] Kevin Gibson and Butch Bays were hosting their Flies on the Wall show on Crescent Hill Radio, talking about how tickets to the Forecastle Festival had gotten too expensive. Louisville needed a cheap alternative showcasing nothing but local music—a festival for the rest of us, they called it. Friends [also Crescent Hill radio hosts] Shaina Wagner, Adam Crowhorn and James Ryan Bohr were hanging out with them in the studio. They took the joke a bit more seriously. "We mentioned it on the air and when the show was over, they said 'You know we're going to do this, right?'," Gibson said. "That's how it started."[24]

As hosts of a local radio music show with deep connections in the community, this formative group recognized that they could leverage those resources to do something that would be important for the local artists and fans. In an interview in 2015, Shaina Wagner described it this way: "We think of Poorcastle now as a precursor, or a local gateway building up to the big Forecastle weekend."[25]

Timed not to compete with Forecastle, Poorcastle differs in focus and philosophy. According to Butch Bays, "The spirit of Poorcastle is uniting artists with music fans in an idealized and uncomplicated atmosphere. Low cost, friendly and fun. 'Where the have nots shall have and the unfortunate shall indeed find fortune,' as we say at the beginning of each festival."

The first year the festival presented twelve local bands over the course of a single day. By the third year it was thirty-three bands over three days. Speaking of that year, Wagner stated:

> We were astounded by the number of bands submitting to play this year. It's the first year we have had too many submissions and could not fit them all into three days. It saddens us to have to turn any of them down, but the surplus of fantastic musicians makes us feel so lucky to live in this city.[26]

The festival's sixth year, 2018, featured thirty-six artists in a lineup described as both eclectic and stylistically diverse, "plus food trucks, beers, and more." Insider Lousiville writer Sara Havens also observed that

> The biggest catch of the event is the extremely low admission fee— $5 a day, or $10 for the entire weekend—and all proceeds go to local non-profits like AMPED, Louisville Leopard Percussionists, MERF and WCHQ-FM. Last year, Poorcastle raised more than $11,000 for the charities.[27]

In Austin, the value of the music scene to the local economy was recognized in the 1970s and 1980s. A city commission was established to optimize and exploit its potential. Successfully. The growth of media and festival events like *Austin City Limits,* SXSW, and others illustrates the effectiveness of that initiative and the generative power of the original scene.

Tensions between local and global initiatives developed and tended to favor the growth of the global brand diffusion and global audience aggregation model. This tendency, combined with decades-old high tech industry growth and worker influx combined to compress opportunities for the local scene. Since the Austin scene operates within a city-driven commission model, solutions that are proposed—following the commissioned Austin Music Census also tend to be city-driven.

In Louisville, the situation differs in some significant ways. Although the Forecastle Festival's success follows the brand-diffusion/audience-aggregation model, the city itself has only recently engaged with what the government can do to optimize the local music economy. This corresponds to relatively recent initiatives to attract high-tech industries and "creative class" workers and entrepreneurs.

Both Forecastle and Poorcastle are operating in an environment in which there is far less government-driven support or input than in Austin. Because of this, the Louisville "solution" for global versus local optimization of the music scene is a grassroots phenomenon.

Poorcastle is both an "answer to" and a "buildup for" Forecastle. Local artists and their supporters are given an opportunity to appreciate and support a stylistically diverse lineup at a modest cost. The event both benefits from and contributes to the media and community discussion of summer music festivals in Louisville. This synergistic relationship may be a model for the coexistence of both diffusion and localization within a music scene.

LIMITS OF DIFFUSION

Diffusion is about maximizing access, monetization, cultural influence, and status. Music moves from the personal to the social, is fostered in local venues, distributed via local/regional media and record labels, and augmented by touring and then larger-scale distribution and promotion of recordings.

For most of the twentieth century, the idea of mass distribution—diffusion on the largest possible scale—was the basis of the music industry. Today the music industry sits inside a sociotechnological framework based on Internet connectivity and mediated social platforms. This makes local and global presence, productivity, and interconnection more pervasive and develop more rapidly than ever before.

Local scenes can be leveraged widely, not only by touring, recording, and broadcasting local music and musicians, but by branding a scene in a global market and aggregating audiences from around the country and the world to come and have a "local vibe" experience.

At the same time, the economic value of music—taken in the form of individual songs and performances—has never been less even as it is spread by digital streaming media into virtually every facet of daily life. The idea of the universal jukebox, where every song is available anywhere and any time, has become a reality. And, for the first time, access is not a reliable predictor of capturable value, particularly when delivered via distributive media.

As a result, enhanced diffusion tools and techniques have become disruptive innovations in the production and distribution cycles. The next chapter explores how disruption works and why it is both inevitable and necessary for creative and economic growth.

CRITICAL CONCEPTS

- Scaling music ventures is largely a matter of distribution and access.
- Local music scenes can be expanded in two ways. (1) Through touring, recording, and media distribution of music and musicians. (2) By diffusing the local brand globally to promote festival events and aggregating global audiences to come to festivals to have a "local scene experience."

FURTHER CONSIDERATION

- The Deli: Emerging Music from Your Local Scene
  - http://national.thedelimagazine.com/homepage
- Adele Rejects Streaming for 25
  - www.nytimes.com/2015/11/20/business/media/adele-music-album-25.html

- How does Adele's resistance to streaming her album relate to diffusion theory in music? Have diffusive technologies reached a point where there are no economic opportunities or has the current synergy between creation, diffusion, and value simply changed and thus requires new business models to optimize it?

CONCEPTUAL PROTOTYPE QUESTIONS

Diffusion Theory Models

In terms of practical entrepreneurship, the comparisons between Sun, Motown, and Sub Pop (discussed in chapter 6) raise a question. Why do independent labels have such widely varying degrees of influence over the marketplace and culture, both large and small? Diffusion theory suggests that differences will be a result of which segments of the adopter curve are targeted. That targeting also has implications for production cost, as well as promotion and distribution logistics.

If you are prototyping a label (or other production company) startup, which part or parts of the distribution curve will you target? Why? What correlations are there between the service you intend to provide to your intended customers, the resources of your company, community infrastructure, and your personal mission? Which phase of the music creation-production reception cycle matters most to you and your customers: artist discovery and stylistic development, establishing a local or regional brand and following, or scaling upward to wider distribution?

Given your answers above, how do Rogers's five steps of adoption—knowledge, persuasion, decision, implementation, and confirmation—impact your model? Remember these are about the public and the individual adoption decisions each prospective customer makes.

Local–Global Tension

Consider the discussion of the music scenes in Austin and Louisville in this chapter. If you were trying to build a response to a growing festival trend in your home city, which path would you try to take? Work with, or form, a local music commission to support, constrain, or optimize large and small initiatives in the environment? Or develop an independent response that is neither directly competitive nor collaborative with the larger festival(s)? For whichever model you find appealing, consider the standard prototype questions, most particularly including who you are intending to serve—local audiences, local musicians, local artists, or global ones. What value are you attempting to create for them that matters to them?

8

Disruption

Pattern, Deviation, Adaptation

A fundamental reality of social, cultural, and economic conditions is that there is an ongoing shift from stable states to disruptive ones. Sometimes things change because tastes and social behaviors change. Sometimes the impetus is a relatively slow generational shift while at other times change is sudden, due to a new, popular technology. Whether we consider music as either art/entertainment or a business, its changing nature is obvious.

From the creative perspective, musical tastes change (at least) generationally and, as time passes, musical styles—let alone individual songs or compositions—move from cutting-edge to passé and are replaced with a "new" sound. And the more music is tailored to appeal to a youthful audience—as is most of commercial music—the more changeable it must be as listeners move from their pre- to early to late teenage years and beyond.

In addition, as performers inevitably age and move through the phases of life, their creative perspective inevitably evolves. Their capacity to connect with a younger (and increasingly much younger) fan base may well diminish. They can then reinvent their music and brand to chase trends or follow the musical preferences and consumption patterns of their aging fans. All in all, it makes for a volatile environment in which to create and sell music.

Over the past one hundred plus years, musical experience—particularly in terms of access and ways to monetize it—has been thoroughly and repeatedly transformed. Every system of production, distribution, and consumption has been disrupted, replaced, and disrupted again. As new technologies, social behaviors, and economic conditions emerged, these systemic frameworks—whether based on records, radio, print publishing, and live shows or downloads, streams, licensing, and live shows— have been inevitably affected. In response, the institutions of music production and the people who guide them have either adapted to changing circumstances or collapsed into irrelevance, insolvency, or both.[1]

There are periods of relative stability based on established production and consumption conditions and behaviors. The period between the late 1960s and the late 1990s was—from a broad music industry perspective—relatively stable. Even though recording/playback media and musical styles changed, sales climbed and major labels got bigger. But stable conditions in the music business, during which everyone understands "how it works," are temporary at best. In reality, the perception of any "business as usual" stability is often a matter of being unaware of an emerging disruptive force.

Disruptions to any status quo are inevitable. In fact, cultural, social, and economic conditions cycle from disruptive to stable states over and over. In music this process impacts the individual elements of creation-production-reception and the cycle collectively. In this chapter we look primarily at production and reception, however noting where changes impact creative processes.

In this discussion, the term "production" includes performance, publishing, and recording, as well as their mechanisms for access/distribution and monetization. "Reception" refers to all ways of accessing musical experience, including live/mediated, type of content, options for customization or curation, and—of course—cost. Although chapter 5 examines monetization in some detail, here we take a closer look at the disruption of revenue sources, changing revenue management practices, and new technologies that directly impact monetization.

Understanding the causes and consequences of disruption requires more than an examination of specific events. It is critically important to look also at patterns and the cycle of change between disruptive and stable states. In the next section, we look at several theoretical perspectives that can shed light on disruptive processes.

Joseph Schumpeter's concept of *creative destruction* looks at the nature of disruption and regeneration in the business environment. The *innovation wave* concept helps to explain how technology drives change and even large-scale disruption when it is combined with "socially primed economic opportunity." Finally, the interrelated concepts of *adaptive expertise* and *complex adaptive systems* illustrate how, in disruptive conditions, there are opportunities for entrepreneurship and new structures/ processes to emerge.

STABILITY AND DISRUPTION CYCLES

The invention of sound recording and playback technology was obviously revolutionary. Radio, film with sound, television, digital audio, the Internet, P2P file sharing, and streaming have all driven changes in the consumption, production, and creation of music. The emergence of these technologies and their social adoption ushered in disruptive cycles that brought an end to some established practices and, at the same time, provided the opportunity for new business models to emerge and become successful and stable.

Though change is inevitable, it is tempting—from both emotional and operational perspectives—to seek steady states. Knowing "how things work" reduces feelings of uncertainty and relieves us from the necessity of having to constantly invest in discovery and development— which are both cost- and risk-intensive. Instead, stable conditions make it possible to accrue benefits from known processes and products that can be replicated as needed. The impulse toward stability and replicability encourages the growth of major record labels, for example, and the proliferation of similar musical "product" inside an established genre. Once it becomes apparent, for example, that EDM—whatever that means in a given context—sells, much more EDM will be produced.

This "stable state" approach works best when there are significant constraints on a system—control over who gets to access resources and create musical products, when there are "gatekeepers" with the power to say who gets a record deal, what gets played on the radio, is available from a digital store, or is streamed by an online/mobile service. This was the situation for most of the twentieth century and the framework upon which the mass production, distribution, and consumption model of the "music industry" was based.

A critical limitation to business models based on stable conditions and gatekeeper structures is that there will always be an emerging "threat," always someone following an impulse toward innovation. Whether in the form of new technology, forms of musical expression, methods of delivery, or simply improved access at reduced cost, creative innovations destabilize and destroy established business models. Organizations that remain aligned with the old model collapse. Institutions aligned with the emergent model prosper and, through their success, a new stable state emerges.

DISRUPTION THEORIES

Technology is often tagged as a trigger for disruptive social and economic change. And it would be hard to claim that new technology is not sometimes destabilizing. One can argue, however, that a new tech product is rarely disruptive in and of itself. In virtually any case we can examine, it is the widespread social adoption of a technology (and what it offers) that is far more disruptive than its invention or entry into the marketplace.

This phenomenon is clearly explained by the "innovation wave" concept introduced by Andrew Lippmann and David Reed in a paper published in 2003 from the Media Laboratory Research program at MIT:

Innovation often comes in waves when the social and economic environments synchronize around a technologically primed opportunity. This happened in the 1930s with the telephone, in the 1950s with the automobile and in the 1980s with the personal computer. The communication industry is facing a similar disruption. As in the past, vertically integrated giants tied to centralized or mainframe technologies and services are being eclipsed by newcomers with new ideas about individual ownership, incremental adoption and instant turnover. Technology enables the change by making local intelligence affordable; society transforms that power into something useful to them, and the potential for diffuse economic investment fuels new options.[2]

Although Lippmann and Reed are specifically discussing the communications industry, it is clear that they see how the "innovation wave" concept can apply to other large, "vertically integrated" companies that depend upon central control systems and services. When these businesses encounter "newcomers with new ideas" about ownership, scalability, and speed they can be disrupted, or "eclipsed."

This is not a bad description of the recording industry at the end of the twentieth century faced with businesses, like Napster, that exploited decentralized, rapidly scalable communications structures that emphasized "sharing" as opposed to "buying." As music listeners flocked to file-sharing sites and collectively made millions of downloads, it first appeared that this would destroy the revenue model of the traditional music industry. Instead, it generated many "new options" for investment: digital download "stores" and streaming services, most prominently.

From another perspective, the process by which listeners/consumers move from awareness of a new technology to broadly adopting it and, ultimately, considering it to be an essential part of life is addressed by the Diffusion of Innovation (DOI) concepts discussed in the previous chapter.

Taken together, both DOI and "innovation wave" concepts underscore the complexity and volatility of the creation-production-consumption cycle. Complex systems theory (discussed below) can be used to explain the interconnected and adaptive processes that come into play at any given point when stable conditions give way to disruptive ones. But before we explore specific examples that illustrate complexity, we need to look at the larger, recurring cycle of change itself.

The most influential theory about periodic disruption comes from German economist Joseph Schumpeter, who applied the term "creative destruction" to cycles of change in business in his seminal work, *Capitalism, Socialism, and Democracy*.[3] Schumpeter emphasized the importance of innovation and entrepreneurship in capitalist systems and stated that innovation inevitably disrupts existing business structures, paving the way for the creation of newer, better, less expensive, and/or more efficient ones.

In commercial sectors that are technology dependent, such volatility may occur more often and develop more quickly. In commercial sectors that involve popular tastes and/or entertainment for a "youth" market, cyclic volatility increases. Enterprise in music—particularly popular music—is therefore a "perfect storm" of disruption and instability. In fact, disruptions to twentieth-century music business models since the advent of Napster et al. have been predictive of issues facing most other creative content providers in the twenty-first century, including film, television, print journalism, software, and so on.

Schumpeter's economic analysis is often referenced as a descriptor and analytical lens through which to view economic conditions broadly. For example:

> In a paper presented at a recent Fed retreat, former treasury secretary Lawrence Summers and his ex-deputy Bradford DeLong observed that "the economy of the future is likely to be 'Schumpeterian,'" with creative destruction the norm and innovation the main driver of wealth. Products based on ideas—music, software, pharmaceuticals—require an enormous investment to develop but very little to keep making. And they're often subject to network effects, which reward those that achieve critical mass. Together, these factors—high cost to create, minimal cost to produce, and a winner-take-all environment—tend to generate natural monopolies, at least until the next innovation comes along. How regulators should respond is debatable, but clearly the rules that governed manufacturing economies don't apply.[4]

Though a full discussion of Schumpeter's work is beyond the scope and purpose of this text, it is worth going a bit deeper than simply to note his "creative destruction" concept. More recent economic studies have, for example, explored the three major types of economic evolution outlined by Schumpeter:

> The appreciation of Schumpeter's works is eased if we distinguish between his three different models of evolutionary processes. The Mark I model describes economic evolution as the outcome of the interaction between individual innovative entrepreneurs and routine-based incumbent firms. The Mark II model describes economic evolution as the outcome of the innovative oligopolistic competition between incumbent firms. The Mark SC model describes socioeconomic evolution as a coevolutionary process between the major sectors of society.[5]

The "major sectors of society" in the SC model are economic, political, family, and science.

Schumpeter's perspective on these "sectors" is

> that every sector of social life has an evolutionary process in which innovators interact with agents who merely adapt. Given such sectoral processes, we can study the coevolutionary processes between the sectors. However, the overall process of socioeconomic evolution is characterized by the different speeds of the individual sectoral processes. The consequence of these asynchronous sectoral processes is that the outcomes of overall societal evolution are highly indeterminate.[6]

Because Schumpeter considered that all of the sectors evolved not only individually but also collectively, at varying rates, the resulting complexity was "hardly analytically manageable" without limiting the number of interactions considered.[7]

This hard-to-manage complexity and uncertainty are evocative of the music industry. The multiple economic offerings, processes, and stakeholders across the creative, production, and reception sectors are indeed complex and the results often uncertain. We will look at complex systems theory below, but here it is worth recognizing that all three of Schumpeter's economic models have been in play in the music industry over the past century and up to the present day—sometimes at the same time.

For example, Napster (and other digital file-sharing technologies) brought a disruptive evolution led by visionary entrepreneurs. Napster and other file-sharing platforms surpassed standard music industry offerings in 1999. In the Schumpeterian sense, that's a Mark I model. When Apple created the iTunes store (using and expanding existing products and technology), they did so in collaboration with major labels (who adapted their established licensing practices for digital delivery). This was all done at a high level of corporate leadership. The arrangements were made among a financially elite and powerful group in both the technology and the recording sectors of the economy. That's Mark II.

Because Napster and file sharing—or piracy, depending on your perspective—were related to social and legal issues and developed in response to evolving technologies, this corresponds to the family, legal, and science sectors of the Mark SC model.

If Schumpeter is correct, that (a) there is an inevitable cycling between stable and disruptive conditions in business and that (b) evolutionary processes can take multiple forms and cross social and economic sectors, what does that tell us about institutions designed to optimize stable conditions?

There are three main points to consider. *Point 1* is that, while the "rules" of stable conditions work, they work very well. For much of the twentieth century, major labels were the most important source of investment and income for rising artists. They were also the "deciders" for what constituted the music of mainstream culture. For decades, disruptive influences came in the form of new playback technologies (LPs, 8-Tracks, Cassettes, and CDs) and in the appearance of new musical genres (1950s Rock and Roll, 1960s British Invasion, 1970s Punk, and so forth). Playback technologies did not disrupt the production of music very much, if at all, and adjustments were made. The emergence of new styles benefits independent labels—Sub Pop with "Grunge" in the

1990s, for example—but did so without fundamentally disrupting the business model of the majors.

In contrast, the creative destruction of the mainstream music industry model of the twentieth century came as the result of a synergy between and among technologies (digital audio, MP3s, P2P file-sharing platforms), the expanded availability and social adoption of personal computers, accelerating data connection speeds, and mediated social networks. In that complex and interrelated context (Mark SC), the emergence of Napster in 1999 had a devastating effect on "business as usual" for the music industry.

According to the theory and principles of creative destruction, this should not have been in any way a surprise. In fact, one could argue that, because it represented an inevitable development, the most strategic response would have been to reposition, redesign, or reinvent music distribution to optimize for changing circumstances, in other words for the major players to make a Mark I adjustment at the highest corporate levels. That is not, however, what immediately happened in 1999 or for several years after.

That brings us to *Point 2* about stable state enterprise: the fundamental reaction to disruption is to act aggressively to stop it. Thus, the Recording Industry Association of America (RIAA), the band Metallica, and ultimately many individual record labels sued Napster and its users to force them to stop destroying the paradigm. That reveals *Point 3*: that interdiction of a "destructive" creativity does not work and, in fact, often accelerates the ultimate failure of the nonadaptive business model.

These patterns play out again and again throughout the history of the music industry. Success emerges and the innovation/disruption that produced it is imitated and codified into standard practice. Then some emergent creative force—technological, economic, artistic, and/or social—appears and destabilizes this new normal. Some of its institutions attack the emergent creative force, losing social support and accelerating economic losses. Business institutions aligned with the old model collapse. Institutions aligned with the emergent model prosper. The next, new stable state emerges, temporarily.

In disruptive environments, businesses fully aligned with emergent processes and products tend to rise above the competition (for example, Spotify in terms of streaming and data management). Established businesses that can optimize and/or aggregate innovative processes and products and/or adapt established ones also gain competitive advantage (iTunes, for example, or Pandora's purchase of Next Big Sound).

Lessons from a disruptive view of cycles in music include (a) invention and innovation without exploitation and social adoption don't go anywhere, (b) optimizers almost always outperform inventors in the marketplace, (c) aggregators trump everyone else, and above all (d) taking a position in a cycle of change that new social behaviors must be "stopped" is a losing position.

Understanding these concepts and lessons is all well and good, but applying them requires—in addition to being aware of them in the first place—a particular skill set, one based on knowledge of historical patterns and contemporary conditions and a capacity to transfer and adapt knowledge from one context to another. It is one thing to recognize, for example, that a particular strategy has not worked in the past. But determining what would work in the present, whether a previous strategy is adaptable or whether an entirely new one must be developed, is another thing entirely.

ADAPTIVITY & COMPLEXITY

The relevant skill set for that kind of problem solving is found in the realm of adaptive expertise. In the educational sense, there are two ways to learn how to become an expert: "routine" and "adaptive." Educational theorists define

> "routine expertise" as the mastery of known procedures and having the goal of developing increased speed and efficiency in their application. In contrast, while "adaptive experts" acquire the same practical knowledge,

they do so in order to develop a conceptual understanding of how and why a given process works. Routine experts operate at peak efficiency in the world of known problems. Adaptive experts excel in their ability to analyze problems and re-purpose existing solutions or create new ones as needed.[8]

How might this be relevant to actual conditions in the music economy?

Consider, for example, the year 1999, when Napster brought file sharing and piracy to the forefront of music industry concerns. It was routine expertise that guided major label decisions to act against Napster (and others) through the legal system. That's lesson (d), above. Trying to stop/outlaw the innovation/disruption is always a losing proposition.

But it's also an example of routine expertise. Illegal file sharing is just that: illegal. Copyright infringement calls for lawyers. The difficulty, however, was that the routine definition of the problem—file-"sharing" infringements on copyright—was incomplete. Consequently, the response was inadequate, even counterproductive.

A more adaptive perspective at the labels could have led to the recognition that the problem as presented—file "sharing" where nobody pays—did not fully describe the larger social situation. Or, that on the scale represented by Napster, a massive shift in the mechanisms of the distribution and consumption of recorded music represented an unprecedented opportunity.

Ultimately, an adaptive solution for the digital music era did emerge in the form of Apple's iTunes store. The products and processes Steve Jobs used to create and implement iTunes on a scale that transformed business practices and social behaviors alike exemplify the potential of adaptive expertise to impact the marketplace and society by synthesizing existing, adapted, and innovative approaches.[9]

Since then, the emergence of competitors in the digital download sector did not prove significantly disruptive to Apple's business model. The emergence of streaming services, like Spotify, had greater impact due to the widespread social adoption of streaming access. In response

Apple adapted by introducing Apple Music and other businesses did the same, rolling out their own streaming music options.

Depending on whether we are looking at the example of individual entrepreneurs—who drive Schumpeter's Mark I evolutionary model—or the complexly adaptive adjustments across multiple sectors of the music industry as a whole (Mark SC), we see different things and, as a result, different theoretical perspectives are valuable. For example, one of the reasons that the adaptive expertise of a Steve Jobs worked so well is that he acted, skillfully, within a complex adaptive system.

The "complexity" of systems, as noted in the first chapter, means in the most basic sense that there are a lot of processes, rules and regulations, roles, and stakeholders. One of the earliest and most influential writers about complexity, physicist Murray Gell-Mann calls this "effective complexity":

> It would take a great many different concepts—or quantities—to capture all of our notions of what is meant by complexity (or its opposite, simplicity). However, the notion that corresponds most closely to what we mean by complexity in ordinary conversation and in most scientific discourse is "effective complexity." In nontechnical language, we can define the effective complexity (EC) of an entity as the length of a highly compressed description of its regularities....
>
> We can illustrate with a number of examples how EC corresponds to our intuitive notion of complexity. We may call a novel complex if it has a great many different characters, scenes, subplots, and so on, so that the regularities of the novel require a long description. The United States tax code is complex, since it is very long and each rule in it is a regularity. Neckties may be simple, like those with regimental stripes, or complex, like some of those designed by Jerry Garcia.[10]

It is no stretch to use "complexity" as a descriptor for the music industry in this "effective" sense. As discussed in chapters 1, 2, and 3, the creation-production-reception process depends upon the actions of individuals across all three sectors. A hit song cannot exist until "someone" writes it, performs it, records it, and makes it available, hears it, likes it, and buys it.

The people involved in doing all of these things bridge all three segments of the cycle. When a change (technology-driven or otherwise) affects any of those interlocking areas, the others will be impacted as well.

Gell-Man also advances the concept of the *complex adaptive system* (CAS). A CAS is complicated; it has effective complexity. But it is also a system that is capable of monitoring data about itself, the environment in which it operates, and its interaction with that environment. This systemic "self-awareness" is connected to a capacity to change itself—to adapt—in response to changing conditions.

The data monitored by a CAS are sorted into "regularities" and "random features." Information identified as a "regularity" is incorporated into a set of operating principles—the business-as-usual perspective—that Gell-Mann calls a "schema." He further explains that "Each schema provides, in its own way, some combination of description, predictions, and (where behavior is concerned) prescriptions for action."[11]

Gell-Mann further states that the prescriptions of the schema of a given system "may be provided even in cases that have not been encountered before, and then not only by interpolation and extrapolation, but often by much more sophisticated extensions of experience." The practical, real world results of actions prescribed by a CAS schema feed back into the CAS. Adjustments, ranging from changing short-term tactics to replacing one schema with another, are made.

There are also three levels of adaptation in Gell-Mann's CAS framework. The first is *direct adaptation*. In music this would be the decision of a record label to change a promotional strategy for an artist whose debut album (or concert tour) is selling poorly. If sales are too low (data monitored), increase the number of media appearances to generate "buzz" (adjustment), continue to monitor sales, and see if the media tactics worked. This response is based on a schematic understanding that poor sales may be an indication that the intended audience is unaware of the album/tour.

The second level is *schematic adaptation*, where some aspects of the "business-as-usual" view are questioned and changed. If we are talking about a tour in which ticket sales are slow and we have already increased media appearances and advertising to no effect, we must consider whether lack of public awareness is the problem, or something else.

A schematic adjustment calls into question a basic premise. In this hypothetical, we could question whether media strategies effectively drive sales, there is a structural problem with the tour, or the artist's brand value is in decline. We might even reconsider fundamental assumptions about what constitutes "success" in a tour. Do we have to sell out to be successful? Are some empty seats OK, if the high-value VIP sales are robust? Will touring continue to be a viable revenue model in music? If not, what will replace it?

Gell-Mann's third level of adaptation is what he calls "Darwinian." He states that "At this level the successful schemata are the ones that permit the societies using them to survive."[12] As applied to business— replacing "societies" with "record labels," for example—Darwinian adaptation refers to situations that represent a threat to the existence of not only particular businesses but also entire sectors.

So far we have not yet seen a Darwinian adaptation in live touring— although historically it was feared that, first, recordings and, later, broadcast media would kill the performance business. We have, how- ever, seen adaptation at this level in recording production and distribu- tion. It was not an uncommon view in 1999, and for a few years thereaf- ter, that MP3s and file-sharing sites represented the death of the music industry.[13]

Although there was—and continues to be—debate about the actual impact of digital "sharing" on music revenues, concerns about the dam- age to established businesses were not merely perception. The iTunes online music store was, for example, the first Darwinian adaptation of this cycle. Between the time it launched (2003) and 2010, it became the top music retailer in the world and longtime brick and mortar record stores, including giants like Tower Records, went out of business (spe- cifically, in 2006) as consumers moved away from the purchase of phys- ical recordings.

According to the RIAA, in 2002, US CD sales were $13.2 billion, but by 2017, they had dropped to $1.1 billion. Some of that change was the result of consumers buying and downloading music instead of buying CDs, but illegal downloads/shares continued to have an impact on sales, both physical and digital. Further, the decline of downloaded single sales from a high of $1.6 billion in 2013 to $650.8 million in 2017 shows another adaption in process—this one triggered by the emergence of streaming services. For an exploration of whether this shift from downloads to streams is adaptive, schematic, or Darwinian, see "Further Consideration" below.

Applying concepts drawn from theories of innovation, stability/disruption, and complex adaptive systems (and expertise) yields a more complete and adaptable understanding of the complex system that is music production and reception. It also supports the development of an ability to recognize critical points of stability and disruptive opportunity. Those points are the places where agency can happen, where a creative entrepreneur may be able to make a system work in a particular way, even if—or *especially* if—it has never worked in exactly that way before.

DIY DISRUPTIONS AND RESPONSES

As human beings we tend to see "disruption" as a bad thing. But in nature, society, culture, and business it is both inevitable and valuable. In music, for example, the disruption of production systems has often produced enhancements to reception in terms of access, convenience, cost, scale of choice, and customization. Perspective also matters. If your business is successful and deeply invested in the status quo, then any disruption is a threat. If you are an aspiring entrepreneur, disruptive states represent opportunity.

In addition to the large-scale, corporation-level responses cited previously (iTunes, Spotify, and many more), it is important to examine individual actions. Not only is this the sphere from which disruptive entrepreneurs often emerge; the adaptivity of a CAS is dependent, according to Gell-Mann, upon "a collectivity of interacting adaptive agents," rather than a centralized control structure.[14] This creates the field of opportunity in which individual innovators and independent entrepreneurs act.

Revenue and Capitalization

In the post-Napster climate, the reduction of income from album sales has had a major impact on recording artists in two ways. First, in terms of income, per-stream compensation is a small fraction of what an artist used to make for the sale of a record.[15] As noted in chapter 1, in the streaming era, fifteen hundred streams equals ten downloads, which equals one album equivalent unit. The per-stream payment varies by platform, but ranges from $0.0006 per play on YouTube to $.0038 on Spotify to $.016 per stream on top-paying Napster.[16]

Because streaming payments must be split among the label (or whoever owns master rights), performers, and writers/publishers the amount an artist actually clears can range from the lucrative (rarely) to the miniscule (quite often).

> For example, Taylor Swift earned between $280,000 and $390,000 for her song "Shake It Off" which garnered 46.3 million streams, according to one report. But that's for one of the world's biggest pop stars. Most musicians won't generate that many streams in their lifetime. Another calculation shows that 1 million plays on Spotify translates to around $7,000, and one million plays on Pandora generates $1,650.[17]

Other than for exceptionally popular artists and songs, streaming does not generate enough revenue for artists to make a living, even at one million streams. On the other hand, for labels, the numbers look quite a bit better. The three majors—Universal, Sony, and Warner—made $14.2 million per day in the second quarter of 2017. Merlin, the independent label collective, made $358 million from March 2016 to March 2017.[18] According to MIDiA research, global streaming revenues for 2017 were $7.2 billion, or 43% of all recorded music revenue.[19]

The difference between the per-stream, artist-level numbers and those for major labels and the recording sector in general illustrates the advantages of aggregation. Despite the fact that recording artists (and songwriters) provide the essential ingredient of the streaming music experience—music—individuals are not in a position to benefit from the scale of streaming or the negotiating position of major music groups that control significant catalogs.

Artists are, nevertheless, a significant element of the complex adaptive system that is the music industry. In fact, per Gell-Mann, artists collectively constitute a CAS in their own right. When the artist CAS receives data that include unfavorable album equivalent streaming numbers and reduced capitalization from record labels for development, they can be expected to make a schematic adaptation—rethink the rules of the game—before an existential crisis develops. The schematic changes for artists in the post-Napster era include self-capitalization and self-aggregation strategies.

In addition to revenue, another difficulty for musical artists in the digital marketplace is significantly reduced record label support. New artists are particularly vulnerable to the loss of the development capital that labels traditionally provided. Along with that capital also came access to studio time and production expertise. While technology has facilitated DIY audio recording to a large extent, you still have to know how to write and arrange a song and capture it on the recording medium.

Money can solve those expertise concerns, as well as promotional ones. But if record labels aren't funding rising artists and neither are the streaming giants, what is the adaptive response? A shift in the schema from label funding to artist self-funding has become one path forward. This can take the form of personal savings and/or resources from family and friends. Or, capital can be raised from the public.

The idea of going directly to the public to fund individual music projects has a long history, dating back well over two hundred years. The early model depended largely on the patronage of wealthy individuals and church institutions. The mediated social networking of the digital era, however, amplifies the speed, scale, and accessibility of public funding dramatically. It is, for example, possible to aggregate thousands of small financial gifts into a significant amount of capital using a web page. In addition, since production, promotion, distribution, sales, and noncommercial consumption are also threaded through social media, online fund sourcing—or "crowdfunding"—can help artists raise money for a project, as well as publicize and build a following for it.

Although there are hundreds of crowdfunding services today, one of the best known in the United States is Kickstarter, founded in 2008. Between then and 2012, the company raised over $775 million for some forty-eight thousand projects.[20] Between 2012 and April 2018, the total was $3.6 billion. In 2018, most projects were funded at a level between $1000 and $10,000. Of the total number of funded projects over twenty-seven thousand included music, with a total approaching $200 million.

Like all aggregated figures, the total is impressive, but even the per-project average is not insignificant—roughly $7,000. It does not approach the level of funding a label might have provided to a promising yet unproven band or artist to make a first album, but neither is it restricted by industry gatekeepers. Anyone can use Kickstarter or the many other crowdfunding sites to capitalize an album, a tour, or another musical venture.

In addition to Kickstarter, Indiegogo, and similar platforms, there is also a more entertainment and music-specific site: Patreon. Launched by Jack Conte of the DIY band Pomplamoose, Patreon was specifically designed to improve monetization opportunities for creators of digital media, including music. Beginning in 2013, Patreon began connecting musicians and others with a public interested and willing to provide financial support for creative projects—including doing so on an ongoing basis.

In just over a year, the company had distributed over $1 million to artists comprising fifteen thousand content creators and fifty thousand patrons with an average monthly contribution of $9.80 or $117.60 annually. Some earned as much as $100,000 during that period. In 2014, using those numbers, an artist with a following of three hundred patrons making the minimum contribution could realize about $35,000 a year from Patreon alone.[21]

Not everyone does that well with Patreon, but some do better. In 2017, Patreon had more than fifty thousand content creators that earned over $150 million from one million plus patrons. According to a *Bloomberg Technology* profile, while some creators "pull in tens of thousands of dollars a month, most make less than $100 and have only a handful of supporters."[22]

Patreon is not only a crowdfunding business. It is a network that connects artist to artist, support business to artist, patron to patron, and all of the members who fit more than one category. It is a networked community of resources that shares (aggregates) social, cultural, creative, and economic capital. Taken together, Patreon and other music-friendly crowdfunding sites and the musicians and listeners they serve are themselves a complex system, one that is a reaction to the disruption of twentieth-century music industry models and an expression of twenty-first-century adaptations.

While some things have changed for creators as a result of Patreon (and other crowdfunding models), others have not. Patreon is much less of a gatekeeper than traditional record labels, for example. Within the restrictions of the company's terms of service, anyone can create an account and solicit support for their creative work.[23] That's a remarkably innovative and potentially empowering development for creatives.

But Patreon is not a "nurturer" of talent, another role of the traditional label system. There are, for instance, no producers to guide song structure, arrangements, or recording methods for rising musicians. There is no promotion and branding team to help create unique products that engage the potential customers/patrons. The company does provide data analysis for creators and some tools for managing patrons, but creatively, artists are on their own. This is a feature and a bug.

There are few restrictions based on commercial/corporate aesthetics or expectations. You can create exactly what you want and reach directly to the public with it. But the project has to catch the eyes and ears of potential supporters. If it doesn't, they won't support it. In direct-to-the-public funding models, just as in record label guided and financed ones, the audience is part of the complex adaptive system.

In addition to the tradeoff of increased freedom of access and creativity for no professional guidance or support, the relationship between creatives and a business like Patreon has a traditional economic component. Like labels, publishers, and other production businesses, Patreon is in a position to aggregate the creativity of tens of thousands of creators and millions of patrons. The 5% fee Patreon collects on the money raised across all artists and projects amounts to millions of dollars in revenue per year for the company. That is not a criticism. The value provided by connecting creatives with those who wish to support their work is self-evident.

Being able to aggregate creative productivity and those who support it financially is a position of advantage from the perspectives of both economics and cultural influence. This has been an unchanging truth of the music industry since the mass production of printed music became practical. Artists are constrained by the limits of their own creative capacity and the logistics of producing songs, recordings, and live performances. Aggregators are not. Consequently, emerging aggregative technologies and strategies have the potential to be extremely disruptive to the status quo.

The recognition of this aggregative advantage did not begin in the post-Napster adaption era. Associations of independent artists and small record labels and publishers were first created in the earliest years of the twentieth century. Some such organizations genuinely represent the interests of smaller organizations—Merlin and WIN, for example. Others function as trade organizations for sectors dominated by large corporate interests—RIAA and NMPA, to name two.

Artist-oriented groups have been more rare. Perhaps the best early example, discussed in chapter 5, are the PROs—particularly ASCAP in the United States. ASCAP was launched by prominent composers to advocate for and collect performance rights payments. In a sense, ASCAP was a schematic adaptation to the growing mass production of music around 1900. More and more venues used music to improve their business opportunities without paying for the right to do so; ASCAP was formed to provide a collective resource for individual composers. But because it also included publishers—themselves aggregators of composer creativity—it must be considered a hybrid creation/production organization. In addition, ASCAP itself was aggregative of composers and publishers.

Disintermediation and Self-Aggregation

We may call the impulse that led to the creation of ASCAP one of self-aggregation. This kind of organization has typically developed in response to disruptions in production and reception patterns and structures that impact access, control, and monetization opportunities for creatives. This type of organization can also be intended to disrupt practices—established or emerging—that favor producers, who—as businesses—are better resourced to create processes and legal structures that protect their interests than are creatives.

Obviously, producers have advantages relative to independent artists in terms of aggregation, distribution, access to scale, and commensurate monetization. Even so, producers must adapt to changing distribution, reception, and consumption conditions. As they do so, the advantages they hold relative to creatives are often amplified and the cost of doing business the new way may seem, or literally be, disproportionately borne by artists.

It is in these conditions that artist frustrations about producers tend to spike. Even though they provide essential connectivity in the creation-production-and consumption cycle, with producers functioning as intermediaries between creatives and consumers, distrust and dislike for the "middlemen" in the music business is long-standing. When times are hard, these feelings become more intense and alternatives become more attractive.

It is important to distinguish between two related but fundamentally disparate responses to such conditions. On the one hand, companies like Patreon and many other DIY artist-supporting ventures both facilitate and exploit independent creators. While the business terms are different from traditional labels and publishers, the fundamental relationship between company and client is one of aggregation and distribution for a percentage of the revenue generated. In this category we can also list organizations like TuneCore, Music Audience Exchange, and others.

Thus, these organizations whose stated purpose is to empower individual artists do so, in effect, by exploiting them. This "exploitation" is not by definition negative because it creates value for the artist, for society, and for the business itself. In one sense, however, the difference between a Patreon and an Atlantic Records is simply one of who collects the percentage fee for making it possible for audience and artist to come together. We can see this as an adaptive shift—a change of tactics within an aggregative and exploitive schema.

On the other hand, there are organizations created for and run by creative artists. They must also find a way to aggregate audiences, customers, and patrons by finding effective ways to make the creative productivity of their members accessible. But perhaps the more fundamental question is, if you are successful in building such an organization, how do you avoid creating another "middleman" entity between creator and receiver?

The concurrent development of digital audio technologies and media along with the Internet and web-based social platforms caused many to think that the era of the middleman in music was over. Artists could reach listeners/consumers directly.

Let's look at that idea.

On the most fundamental level, any music business is based upon the artist-to-audience relationship as a transaction. The musician provides music and the audience, in exchange for musical experience,

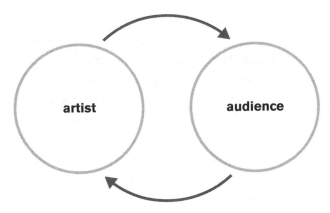

Figure 9. Artist–Audience Transaction.

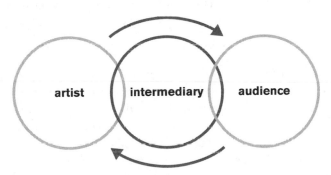

Figure 10. Intermediary Business Model.

provides feedback to the artist in the form of acknowledgment, recognition, and—among other things—money (see figure 9).

In practice, and particularly in the context of large-scale music enterprise, intermediary business models "live" in the space between the circles and comprise the delivery and feed back arrows (see figure 10). These businesses range from record labels to radio to concert venues to publishers to streaming services.

Disintermediation became a central consideration in discussions of "the future of music (business)" relatively early in the Internet era. This discussion took two basic paths: The first path discusses which businesses were being disintermediated but replaced (usually traditional record labels by download stores or streaming services). This is a relabeling of the intermediary circle, including adjustments to the processes represented by the arrows. The other path discusses how intermediaries are eliminated altogether by using the Internet to facilitate direct artist-to-audience connection—returning to the first diagram.

The first of these could be described in CAS terminology as an adaptive shift. As noted above, the aggregative-exploitive role of the intermediary business remains, even as the names and tools change. The second is a schematic adaptation—one that could, potentially, become an existential Darwinian shift for intermediary businesses—in which artists are able to directly reach their audience via the Internet. A research paper published in 2014 provides this overview:

> In the aftermath of the digital revolution, business models are changing and disintermediation is impacting the music economy. In these circumstances, we observe the widespread claim that music artists are able to successfully reach the market on their own, leveraging access to networked global communications and the use of digital network media as a means of production. This paper argues such arguments feed on the ideals of independence in the context of an experimental and transitional stage that the music industry is currently undergoing, and that may be part of a recurrent cycle leading to the establishment of a new generation of intermediaries.[24]

This view is in line with the concepts cited above: that disruptive conditions lay the groundwork for new stability as innovative entrepreneurs inevitably seize the opportunities within disruption to introduce an adaptive model for doing business, in this case facilitating artist–audience connections. In the period when old models have been destabilized but before new ones have become dominant, opportunities for disruption—not only for new business models, but for more fundamental thinking about "how things work"—continue.

DISRUPTING MONETIZATION AND MONEY

Electronic currency has been around for quite some time. Or more precisely, using electronic means to buy things instead of cash has. The main challenge for electronic payments is one of verification. When you were paying for a vinyl album with money—in 1980, for example, you couldn't spend the same $10 more than once. The bill left your wallet and entered the Tower Records cash register. In order to pay with a credit card someone must verify that the purchase actually happened and that money moves from (or is charged to) your account and moves to the account of the vendor.

The monitoring of that purchase transaction is handled by third parties: credit card companies and banks. Whatever the mechanism—debit card, credit card, PayPal, Amazon Payments, Google Wallet, or something else—money is moved from your account to someone else's. Electronic payment is not a disruption of physical currency or traditional banking. It is an extension of it.

As more and more commerce moved onto the Internet, interest in truly digital currency began to grow. In 2008, a research paper by the pseudonymous Satoshi Nakamoto stated:

> Commerce on the Internet has come to rely almost exclusively on financial institutions serving as trusted third parties to process electronic payments. While the system works well enough for most transactions, it still suffers from the inherent weaknesses of the trust based model.

The weaknesses cited by Nakamoto center on being unable to insure "non-reversible transactions" in online purchases, which leads to an increasing need for "trust." As Nakamoto stated:

> Merchants must be wary of their customers, hassling them for more information than they would otherwise need. A certain percentage of fraud is accepted as unavoidable. These costs and payment uncertainties can be avoided in person by using physical currency, but no mechanism exists to make payments over a communications channel without a trusted party.[25]

The implications of this for music business in the post-Napster era are obvious. Even assuming that listeners want to be purchasers rather than sharers, there is a significant need for trust in the exchange. Labels and publishers must license download stores and streaming services to use their musical property. The iTunes store, early in the era, acted as a go-between for labels, publishers, and customers, facilitating access, tracking sales, collecting payment from consumers, and paying labels and publishers. Part of the genius of the setup was the use of an "Apple ID" with an associated credit card account to "verify" payment. But since both the payment and the product sold and purchased (MP3s) were digital and ephemeral, the "need for trust" was very great indeed.

Nakamoto's solution, the one that launched the cryptocurrency era, was Bitcoin. According to a whitepaper published in 2008, Bitcoin is "a purely peer-to-peer version of electronic cash [that] would allow online payments to be sent directly from one party to another without going through a financial institution."[26]

There are two essential elements to Bitcoin that are critical to its potential to disrupt monetization in the music industry (and perhaps, as some argue, banking as a whole). The first is that, because it is a cryptocurrency and based on a complex, time-stamped code, it replaces trust in third-party institutions like banks with verifiable transactions. The underlying verification technology—the blockchain—creates a sequential record of every time the Bitcoin has been used and by whom. That transaction becomes part of the permanent record/identity of the coin, which is stored and publicly available across the Bitcoin (or other cryptocurrency) network.

As explained by David Gerard, author of *Attack of the 50 Foot Block Chain,* "What Bitcoin does is make possible a tamper-evident public ledger of transactions, without any central authority declaring whose ledger is the official one."[27] The lack of central authority and the complexity of validating the "public ledger" are the other essential element of Bitcoin. The "proof of work" methodology behind this validation is well beyond the scope of this discussion. But it supports the second essential aspect of cryptocurrency: it provides secure transactions between individuals, hence its description by its inventor, as a peer-to-peer currency.

In terms of the music industry in the post-Napster era, the first element, the potential of cryptocurrencies to take third-party banks out of the online transaction process, is less important than the second: verifiable peer-to-peer transactions. This is, in fact, essential to the potential disintermediation of the creator-to-listener connection. As reported by Matthew Ingraham in an article about cryptocurrency and blockchain technologies in relation to music:

> Singer Imogen Heap and violinist Zoe Keating say using the blockchain—along with Bitcoin or some other payment method—gives them an opportunity to go directly to their fans for support. Instead of having to use a record label or a platform like iTunes or Spotify, they can sell their work to individual users.
>
> "I thought, wouldn't it be nice if I could decide what I wanted to do with my music?" Heap said at a recent Guardian Live event. "I might decide, today's my birthday, I'm going to give all of my music to everyone for free today. At the moment, I can't do that. Because it's out there, and once it's out there, I don't really have a say in it any more."[28]

The extended implications of blockchain go beyond such transactional uses. For example, part of the purpose of Imogen Heap's organization, Mycelia (discussed in chapter 11), is

> to create a system of identifying everyone who was involved in a piece of music, along with how they would be compensated for the finished song—as well as rules around how and where and when the music could be used, either for free or in return for a fee.... I can imagine instant, frictionless micropayments and the ability to pay collaborators and investors in future earnings without it being an accounting nightmare.[29]

Heap is working, through her collaborations with Ethereum (a cryptocurrency) and Ujo Music, to realize a platform that revolutionizes and automates not only payment structures but also collaborations and licensing agreements. Others, like Bittunes, for example, use block-chain and Bitcoin technologies to pay musicians when their music is purchased as well as rewarding the fans that purchase and share it. Bittunes is inherently disruptive and is in fact built upon ongoing disruption of music distribution and monetization rules. For more, see "Further Consideration," below.

Whether or not the mechanics of blockchain technology or cryptocurrency platforms like Ethereum or "smart contract" platforms like Ujo Music (see chapter 11) are disruptive to the extent imagined by Imogen Heap and other advocates, the efforts made to implement them are revealing. Mycelia, for example, is not only reactive to change. It aspires to be a change driver. In that sense, we can see it not only as an optimizing force in a disruptive cycle. It is built specifically to function in the current disruptive state.

That is not to say that Heap and others don't want to see conditions stabilize in music creation, production, and consumption. Clearly they do. But what the Mycelia idea and startup represent are more than an acceptance of the nature of change. They are a commitment to change for the better, for music makers, listeners, and the business structures that connect them.

Whether or not artists and entrepreneurs embrace or reject it, disruption is inevitable. Theoretical frameworks from Schumpeter's creative destruction to Gell-Mann's complex adaptive systems underscore the process and describe a range of possible responses.

Overall, history shows that disruptive conditions favor innovative and adaptive individuals and approaches. Successful adaptions—from the tactical (adaptive) to the structural (schematic) to the business-ending Darwinian—tend to produce models that define a new stability and new business-as-usual conditions.

That said, in disruptive cycles it is critical to distinguish between what has profoundly changed and needs to be adapted or replaced entirely and the things that are relatively unchanging and require only relatively minor adjustments. In the next chapter we look at one of the most persistent and essential principles of music enterprise: the relationship between artist and audience. There is no scenario—technologically driven or otherwise—in which a weaker or more diffuse connection between the performer and listener is better than a closer one. Or as stated by Imogen Heap, music *"belongs to the two collective parties who solely make music complete. The music makers and their audience."*[30]

How that connection is created, implemented, and sustained may change in terms of tools or even in the definition of what "connection" means and what value(s) it produces. But, as we will see in the next chapter, disrupting the connection itself is not an effective strategy.

CRITICAL CONCEPTS

- Disruption of production systems has often produced enhancements to reception in terms of access, convenience, cost, scale of choice, and customization.

- (a) Invention and innovation without exploitation and social adoption don't go anywhere; (b) optimizers almost always outperform inventors in the marketplace; (c) aggregators trump everyone else; and above all (d) taking the position in a cycle of change that new social behaviors must be "stopped" is a losing proposition.

FURTHER CONSIDERATION

Disintermediation—Music Audience Exchange

- www.musicaudienceexchange.com
- https://techcrunch.com/2017/03/02/music-audience-exchange-wants-to-get-musicians-paid/

Disrupting Publishing and Licensing

- 22 Ways That We Are Looking to Alter the Traditional Approach to Media Rights https://medium.com/dotblockchainmusic/traditional-music-industry-approach-vs-whats-coming-155db689a408

· Merck Mercuriadis, Hipgnosis Songs Fund LTD

https://variety.com/2018/biz/news/hipgnosis-songs-pays-23-million-for-stake-in-the-dream-catalog-lists-on-london-stock-exchange-1202870792/

"It's critical for us to set the highest standards with our first acquisition," Mercuriadis said. "The-Dream is not only arguably the culturally most important songwriter of his generation but he has written the marquee songs for the culturally most significant artists of our time including Beyoncé, Rihanna, Justin Bieber, Jay Z and Kanye West. It's an honor for this to not only be our first order of business but also to welcome Dream to our Advisory Board future."

The-Dream said, "I'm proud to be part of this beautiful venture. Merck is a music titan who began his career well before I ever imagined having one. His futuristic views captured my attention and instantly made an impact. Merck sees me as I see myself. I sought out to be my generation's Babyface and Dr. Dre, he sees the same. In making this decision I said to Merck, 'I need a Jimmy Iovine in my life,' not just to nurture my songs but to also help solidify the legacy I seek for myself and my songs even after I'm gone, for my children and beyond. His reply was simply 'I Got it!,' and after [that] came action like the one you see playing out today in real time."

Also:

· www.sharesmagazine.co.uk/article/hipgnosis-songs-fund-to-tap-into-popular-songs-for-attractive-returns
· www.cnbc.com/2018/07/11/investment-fund-backed-by-song-royalties-signs-up-hits-from-major-star.html
· www.hipgnosissongs.com

Disrupting Distribution

Bittunes

- Nothing to Do with Money, but Everything to Do with Monetization
- www.bittunes.com
- https://medium.com/@Bittunes/why-we-started-bittunes-3ab0b63bfad4

CONCEPTUAL PROTOTYPE QUESTIONS

Disruption as Foundation

What if we look at the long-term cycle between stability and disruption as not only inevitable but generative? And not just of the next stable state and best-practice business model? What if you embraced disruption and sought to deliver the value it can create for musicians and the public on an ongoing basis (a rolling disruption, if you will)?

If we look at the restaurant business we see a sector that is volatile, relatively high-risk, and highly dependent on public tastes and preferences. A phenomenon that embraces the risk and complexity of bringing a food experience to the public is the pop-up restaurant.

Pop-Up Restaurants

- www.gq.com/story/pop-ups-america-restaurants
- www.popuprestaurants.com/what-is-a-popup/
- www.restaurant.org/Manage-My-Restaurant/Operations/Alternative-venues/Test-new-ideas-with-pop-up-restaurants

Pop-Up Restaurants & Music

- www.fastcompany.com/3069163/will-pop-up-hotels-become-a-permanent-fixture-of-the-millennial-tr
- www.dailymail.co.uk/tvshowbiz/article-4674798/Callan-Smith-details-plans-pop-musical-restaurant.html

- www.amazon.com/PopUp-Republic-Successful-Pop-Up-Restaurant/dp/1119145910

Pop-Up Music Shows and Venues
- From The Beatles on the Roof...
- www.rollingstone.com/music/music-news/beatles-famous-rooftop-concert-15-things-you-didnt-know-58342/
- www.nydailynews.com/entertainment/music/beatles-bruce-springsteen-pop-up-concerts-article-1.2378648

9

Connection

Artists, Audiences, Networks

The relationship between musical artists and listeners is obviously an essential element of musical expression and experience. As previously noted, while music creation and performance can be intensely personal or even private, it is only when the performer-listener relationship is put into a social context that music's full potential for creating value can be realized. And, although a musical performance and the shared musical experience between performer and listener can be very small-scale, in order for music experience to be effectively monetized audience sizes must increase.

From this perspective, connecting artists to audiences has the goal of aggregating as many people as possible into a given audience, or into a series of performances, or both. This listener-aggregation model is based on the idea of finding and collecting listeners and then turning them into consumers. An absolutely direct artist-to-audience connection has always been and continues to be available. Anyone so inclined can perform on a street corner as people pass. Variants include the impromptu, or "pop-up" concert for a small, unsuspecting audience either in a local venue or in something like the Beatles' rooftop concert in 1969.[1]

But in order to optimize revenue potential, audiences need to be larger and consistently willing to by tickets. This has been achieved by touring, by tourism, and via various kinds of media. But success in this endeavor—larger and more consistent audiences—brings other challenges to artist–audience connectivity. The greater the size and the geographic spread of the audience base, the more remote the connection to the performer. It is not just that, as venues get bigger, the stage is higher and farther away from the fans. It is a distancing effect based on fame, status, economic resources, and accessibility.

Technologies—first recording, then broadcasting, and later Internet-based—amplify both the potential size of the audience and, in terms of physical reality, distance from the artist. Consequently, fully understanding the artist–audience connection at scale requires us to consider not only how that is accomplished, and the resulting distancing effects, but also how connection is maintained in spite of size and distance.

Music's potential to connect people is not limited to the performer–listener relationship, or to the producer–consumer relationship (see chapters 2 and 3). Music supports the development of all kinds of collaborative relationships on creative and professional levels. Music also supports the formation of communities (and see chapter 6 for a discussion of community-based music scenes).

In this chapter we look at various forms of connectivity that support music, musicians, and music enterprises. These include artist-to-audience, audience-to-audience, and business-to-audience relationships. Along the way, we also take concepts from marketing, audience, and network theories to bring these relationships and how they work into focus.

In addition to those listed above, there are some other relational issues to consider. Music makers may or may not create music as a solitary or small-team practice. But music production—whether of live shows or recordings—is inherently collaborative. In recording production, for example, musician-to-musician as well as musician-to-producer (and engineer) relationships are critical to realize the creative product.

In reference to live performance production, we have examined the professional relationship "pool" as a component of music scenes and how access to creative collaborators is a critical resource afforded by music cities. These issues were discussed in some detail in chapter 6, "Location," and, in reference to more recent developments, chapter 8, "Disruption."

Business-to-artist relationships are typically contractual in nature and historically have often been characterized by disagreement and accusations of exploitation or failures to produce. While, in some cases, modern business-to-artist relationships continue the gatekeeper/nurturer and creator/exploiter roles of the past, a number of new options have emerged that are based on DIY practices and disruptions of the traditional structures (as discussed in the previous chapter).

Business-to-business relationships can be collaborative, competitive, or, in the case of complex adaptive system (CAS) elements, both concurrently. For more on this feature of CAS, see chapter 10, "Incorporation."

We begin here with a closer look at the artist-to-audience relationship. It is widely recognized in the music business that building a relationship between musical artists and their audience is not simply a matter of making the music available, or even leading people to discover it for the first time. The relationship of listener to performer is more complex and based not only on musical content but also on personal attributes and the perception of a human connection between artists and fans. We examined this connection from the perspective of music production and the management of reception by music producers in chapters 2 and 3. Here we look at marketing theory (and practice) to explore how musical artists and the production/distribution businesses that monetize them shape customer feelings and connections to the performer and their music.

MARKETS AND COMMUNITIES

As noted in chapter 6, music happens somewhere and the people who make it and listen to it come together in order for that to happen. The thing that both markets and communities have in common is that they are places where people come together. Where a community meeting space may be public property and the events there are accessible to every member of the community, markets are based on ownership and the buying and selling of things that people own or want to own.

Historically, this distinction has played out in the social and legal differences between marketplaces and commons. In intellectual property law for music, the comparable concept is the difference between a song that is copyrighted and one that is in the public domain. In the former, someone owns a song and can monetize access to it. In the latter, there is common ownership and anyone is free to play, listen to, record, revise, sample, and/or otherwise reframe and publicly present a public domain song.

For the most part, any student of music enterprise—or active music entrepreneur—is going to be primarily concerned with owned musical resources and using access as a tool for monetization. But saying "access as a tool for monetization" does not mean that all you need to do is put your song on a "shelf" in the music marketplace and wait for listeners to line up and buy it.

Marketing is a series of actions intended to let potential consumers know about your product, how/where to access it, how much it costs, and what you do to promote awareness and desire for it. Music is—as noted in the chapter 4, "Commodification"—both a good and a service. One of the key features that distinguish music from other economic offerings is that a potential customer cannot realistically make a decision about purchasing music without hearing it. So, in the case of marketing music, access and promotion are essentially the same thing. Or at least tend to happen using the same material: whatever music you are trying to promote.

Historically, both access and promotion of music have depended upon giving the public a "preview" of the music on offer. The history of music promotion is beyond the scope of this discussion, but early promotional activities included having musicians play in parades when, for example, a circus came to town to give people a "taste" of the entertainment being presented. For most of the twentieth century, broadcast media, in playing records and live performances on radio and television, served a similar purpose. Listeners/viewers and potential customers could hear and see the music and performers before deciding to buy a ticket to a concert or a record.

Broadcast promotion of music and musicians also included interviews in addition to performances. The interview and performance combination was particularly effective because it promoted both the music and the musician as a person and a personality. Typically compensation for this kind of mediated appearance was small or even nonexistent, but it was seen as contributing to the marketing and promotion of the music/musician and as advertising for upcoming concert appearances and/or record sales. They also strengthened the performer–listener connection, making the artist more personable, more human, and seemingly more accessible. All of these connective activities were designed to improve business opportunities both in the immediate and in the longer term.

MARKETING: FINDING LISTENERS, MAKING CONSUMERS

Today, people in the music business talk about bands or solo artists developing a "following": people who will come to a club specifically to hear an artist perform, track their activities on social media, stream their music, and perhaps even buy some product. But the journey from discovering an artist to becoming a committed fan and customer does not "just happen." How it happens and the tools used to make it so vary by era and to some extent by musical genre. Digital technologies and the utilities on the Internet have introduced new means of making connections, but contemporary practice is still a combination of traditional and innovative thinking.

The fundamental principles of product, price, placement, promotions, and people remain valid. But digital technologies have changed production, distribution, reception, and consumption mechanisms for music. As a consequence, twenty-first-century music marketing includes additional considerations designed to foster connection and engagement between modern listeners, musicians, and their music. These include, most critically, approaches that are *interactive, personalized, authentic,* and *conversational.*[2]

One reason why these four elements are important to contemporary marketing in music has to do with reactions to standard twentieth-century music industry practices. For example, the mass production, mass distribution model for music last century was based on a one-to-many model of production and communication. That is to say, the creative work of a small group of artists, produced by a single label, was distributed to millions, potentially around the world. By definition, mass production is not "personalized," nor are mass media "conversational." Hit songs were calibrated to reach the maximum slice of the listening and music-buying public, not the individual or even a select few. When successful on a large-enough scale, artists were criticized as having "sold out"—the opposite of "authenticity." And mass consumption models were based on an idea that consumers would consume, not interact. Fan interaction was limited to concerts and, in some cases, fan clubs (see below).

Today, however, social media platforms have created an expectation for digital experiences of all kinds—from shopping to watching a movie to listening to music—to be inherently interactive and personalized. We can consider the marketing strategies and practices of the digital era from the perspective of Samuel Potts and his consideration of record label culture today (see chapter 2). Potts believes that what consumers are seeking is digital experience in which discovery, engagement, and consumption of music have converged into a single service.

One of the authors cited by Potts in his assessment of the recording industry in the digital era is Mark Milligan. Milligan states:

> The power of music discovery used to lie in the hands of the radio DJ, now it lies in the hands of the playlist curator. And because streaming has melded discovery and consumption into a single whole, that means their power is becoming absolute.[3]

That power comes from control of both the listener's access and the listener's relationship to the music—how it is integrated into and used in their daily lives. In addition, curated playlists guide the process of moving from a first-time listener to a consumer (or not). The control exercised by music curation is thus both connective and economic. It also raises a question about the location and roles of the relationship. That is, is the listener developing a relationship with the musical artists who created the content of a playlist, or with the curation service that put it together and made it available and customizable?

Some have already answered this question. According to Jonathan Good, a Spotify user and amateur playlist maker:

> I've always enjoyed sharing my musical discoveries, and Spotify gives me the ability to do that on a larger scale. Playlists are now the way we listen to music, and I can see a time coming when the playlist creator becomes just as important an element in the process as the artists being featured.[4]

But for additional perspective, see "Further Consideration," below.

In a very real sense, playlists are not just about access, recommendations, and discovery. Playlists facilitate personalized uses of songs that become a soundtrack for daily activities. They provide a new kind of relationship between a business and the music audience in which, perhaps, the artist is less critical to the listener experience than the list curator:

> The strong connection between music and the gym isn't lost on streaming companies. Working out and playlists are joined, if not at the hip, then at the foot, and the link between the two is emblematic of playlists' importance more broadly. In May, Spotify introduced its *Running* feature, which is designed to detect and complement a user's running pace. Google Play Music offers a *Working Out* category of playlists, with subcategories from "Hillbilly Bodybuilding" to "Girl Hold My Earrings."[5]

In addition to convenient access and customized guidance, the digital landscape of social media provides a space for conversation. Eric

Sheinkop, founder of Music Dealers (previously cited in chapters 2 and 4), had an epiphany about "Instagramming millenials" as music fans:

> Last weekend I was at a pop-up trip-hop party in a remodelled apartment on Chicago's west side to check out a glitch-grime DJ whose SoundCloud a friend had DM'd me on the preceding Friday.
>
> I stood beside a precariously stacked column of speakers, watching my fellow trap lords Snap the Technicolor stage, and I thought to myself, "The times they are a-changin'." No, literally. To the carnivorous delight of the surprisingly cultured crowd, the DJ remixed Bob Dylan's iconic "The Times They Are a-Changing'" with an overdub of drum and synth with violent, dramatic bass drops.
>
> That moment ... represented something much greater than just another ordinance violation and neighbourhood nuisance. It is the new face of the media industry.[6]

This experience speaks to a number of issues. First of all it is an example of a music scene or subcultural community forming round a music event. Sheinkop relates how he found out about the "pop-up" event—he was "DM'd" by a friend. His interpretation of that experience and how the participants engaged with it is significant:

> Consumers are virally sharing the stories of their real-life experiences. Content is repurposed and personalised to fit individual tastes. Places of engagement and interaction (whether that's online like social media or offline like the migratory Trap House of last weekend) are blossoming where consumers can cultivate their own experience without the intrusion of advertisements.[7]

Second, this demonstrates the importance of the idea of "authenticity" in communication about musical offerings. Freedom from advertising with expanded opportunities for engagement is important. But beyond that, Sheinkop talks about the content of the consumer conversation as being "stories" and says that "storytelling is changing the landscape of marketing."[8] And when the storytelling space is online, there is no real limit to its impact on production and distribution strategies in music designed to convince casual listeners to become customers. As a result, "media brands of all kinds have been forced to evolve from traditional product-marketing practices to open and creative conversation with consumers."[9]

This storytelling perspective aligns with Beckerman's and Gray's observations (see chapter 3) about the power of music to create meaning for brands:

> Effective use of sound means building a strategy to pick and create music that helps people understand the brand's place in their world. With the right foundation, sound and music can help transform a business or a message by communicating a clear emotional story and helping people feel the brand.[10]

Songwriters and performers use music to tell their own stories. Any given listener may or may not connect to the specifics of that message. If many do not, the music doesn't go anywhere in terms of popularity or commercial success. When you try to blend the story of an artist with the story of a car, there is an even greater chance that a listener will not make that secondary connection. In fact, listeners may reject the entire construct as manipulative and inauthentic. Hence, Sheinkop's observation about the "intrusion of advertisements."

It is also more than a matter of avoiding intrusive elements. Music, correctly deployed, enhances experience. Beckerman and Gray discuss how sound and music shape the viewer experience of, for example, the Super Bowl television broadcast. They explain that it's not enough to see the game; you have to hear it. "That's why you hear the sounds of helmets crunching, quarterbacks yelling signals, and bodies hitting the turf. Sounds bring the game to life. But music turns it into a story—it's the emotional engine."[11]

The game, like a movie, has a soundtrack that guides the viewer, holds their attention, triggers their emotions and memories. As noted above, this also appears to explain the nature and importance of curated playlists for specific lifestyle activities.

The principles of marketing—both the well-established "five Ps" and those introduced in the digital era—are designed to be practically applicable. But, in order to understand what happens when people become part of an audience—whether that is a literal concert audience or a conglomeration of fans via recordings and media—it will be worthwhile to take a look at audience theory. Much as ideas about production and distribution changed in the course of the twentieth century, so did thinking about communication and audience behaviors.

AUDIENCE THEORY

As noted above, the music "industry" developed to produce and sell musical products and experiences to the largest number of people possible. Critical to this model is the principle that listener/consumer behavior can be managed: that music can be intentionally and systematically produced to appeal to a mass audience and that the members of that audience can be motivated to consistently consume it.

This idea of a consumption model—as opposed, for example, to a participatory one—was a characteristic of virtually all forms of commercial enterprise in the twentieth century. In music, the rise of recorded sound products and broadcast technologies paralleled a decline in amateur music performance. The idea of passive consumption as an economic positive and a sociocultural negative certainly applied to music (discussed in chapter 3).

In audience theory, the idea of a passive, mass audience developed in response to the rise of broadcast media and mass distribution of cultural products during the twentieth century. Because of the pervasiveness of mass media, particularly television, many scholars came to the conclusion that the message conveyed by network programs and advertising, for example, would be so overwhelming that viewers and listeners would have little choice but to accept them as reality.

Thus in music, a "hot" new artist was promoted as someone that any "true" music fan would want, or need, to experience. The latest release of an established star was represented as a significant event in musical culture and society. And, by many measures, this approach produced results that appeared to validate the principles: people lined up to buy new albums by popular artists, tours sold out, phenomena like "Beatle-mania" underscored the cultural influence and stature of popular music and musicians.

Although the idea of passive consumers for goods/services and passive audiences for media and experiences became a norm for discussing audiences and massed consumer behavior, more recent audience theory has diverged from that perspective. It has, for example, recognized that audiences are often active cocreators of experience and meaning—so-called "active audiences." Further, audiences become resistant if the content of a message is unwelcome.

In a review of audience theory research from 2008, John Abercrombie and Nicholas Longhurst posited the existence of three distinct types of audiences: *simple, mass,* and *diffused.*[12] The simple type describes the concert audience in attendance at a concert open to the public, with an in-person performance in front of the crowd. The mass audience refers not so much to size, but rather to whether or not a performance is mediated, is dispersed across large geographic space, and is perhaps experienced in private via a medium like television.

The diffused audience is an effect of generations of mediated experience, particularly including the digital era. Abercrombie and Longhurst describe this audience and their experience of performative content as

> strongly dispersed and fragmented, yet at the same time embedded in or fused with all aspects of daily life; characterised by routine and casual inattention and yet always present—as in the "always on" internet connection, multitasked with television, conversation and working from home.[13]

This describes the users of curated playlists rather well. In fact, Abercrombie and Longhurst see the diffused audience as understandable not just in terms of modern, increasingly pervasive media and services like Spotify—to extend their logic to a business that did not yet exist when they wrote *Audiences*. They consider this type of audience and content consumption also as an effect of what they call the *spectacle/performance paradigm*. This describes the condition of a society in which "the qualities and experiences of being a member of an audience have begun to leak out from specific performance events which previously contained them, into the wider realms of everyday life."[14]

The implications of this perspective are discussed in more detail in chapter 12, "Simulation." But here it is worth noting that marketing to a diffused audience whose expectations are based on on-demand access to infinitely customizable digital experiences will certainly differ from the strategies used for other or older audience types. Even in what would nominally be "simple audience" conditions—a live concert setting—today there is increasing demand for personalized, interactive experience. See, for example, the discussion of festivals in chapter 5.

Another way to look at audiences and their collective behaviors is in terms of their consumption patterns. Traditionally, data analysis in the music industry has been based upon correlating sales (tickets or recordings) with buyer demographics. Even when researchers began to dig deeper to find out how listeners value various musical experiences, the "audience" in question is grouped demographically. While data analysis is discussed in more detail in chapter 11, "Aggregation," in this context it is worth noting that being able to categorize listener and consumer activities in terms of having either a "passive" or an "active" motivation has become increasingly important.

Nielsen, the data analytics company, produced the *Audio Demand Landscape* study in 2014. The study created six categories to describe audio listeners, the ways they use audio content, and the technology they use to access it: *music loving personalizers, discriminating audiophiles, convenience seeking traditionalists, information seeking loyalists, background driving defaulters,* and *techie audio enthusiasts.*[15]

In this framework, *music loving personalizers* "are passionate music listeners who are mainly seeking an emotional benefit by listening. They prefer free services and often play music in the background." Though this is the category that is most interested in music, these listeners are not necessarily deeply involved with any particular artist or even genre of music. Related categories include the *background driving defaulters* who "typically have the radio on in the car for background entertainment or occasionally news and information"[16] and *convenience seeking traditionalists* that "prefer broadcast radio, listening to their favorite stations and hosts; and they routinely listen in the car."[17]

In contrast, *discriminating audiophiles* are "highly engaged consumers ... willing to pay for specific content" (not necessarily music). This category pairs with the *techie audio enthusiast*, which also comprises "avid consumers" with a particular interest in new technologies. Again, however, this is not an exclusively musically oriented group.

In a review of the Nielsen study, music industry blogger Kyle Coroneos observed:

> Though some of these categories deal with how people listen to audio instead of what, or deal more with the sports/news/talk realm, the categories of "Discriminating Audiophiles" and "Background Driving Defaulters" make near perfect definitions between fans who might find appeal in music that really speaks to them and has something to say, and fans who simply want to bob their heads to something catchy on the way home.[18]

To pursue the idea of distinguishing between active and passive music listeners a bit further, we can draw on a framework developed by Abercrombie and Longhurst to describe engagement with media content on a continuum from least to most engaged: casual consumer, fan, cultist, enthusiast, and petty producer. For those authors, the consumer category aligns with the type of fans described by Coroneos as those that want "to bob their heads to something catchy on the way home."

The criteria for the other types are also worth considering in terms of how connections are made between artists and audiences and among audience members themselves. *Fans* move from casual consumption of media—in this case music—generally to an interest in specific performers and or musical styles, hence the description of someone as a trip hop or Massive Attack fan. This is the point on the continuum where a listener moves into a position of engagement with an artist and their music and begins to become a reliable consumer of it. You could argue that a fundamental purpose of music industry marketing and promotion practices is to move people from being casual consumers to enthusiastic fans.

The *cultist* category is like the fan, but more so. Cultists may, for example, travel to other cities to see an artist perform. They may engage in social activities centering on an artist, from traditional fan clubs to Internet communities. There is the implicit assumption that a cultist will spend more money on specific musical experiences than a fan. This category aligns with the "discriminating audiophiles" in Nielsen's *Audio Demand Landscape* study.

The *enthusiast* type is more engaged still than the cultist, but their focus broadens. Where a cultist focuses attention on a particular artist and engages with the community around them, the enthusiast delves more deeply into an entire genre. This may include formal or informal study of a musical style or period, systematic reading, attending conferences such as SXSW, and going to workshops of interest. The enthusiast obviously spends money on musical experience and related activities and this level of engagement is often a precursor to the last step on the continuum.

The final type, *petty producer,* brings us to the domain of the individual who is both a consumer and a producer of music. Where an enthusiast reads blogs and books about a musical genre, the petty producer creates a blog. Where a cultist knows everything about Maroon 5, the petty producer starts a tribute band or creates "lyric videos" and posts them online. See also chapter 11 for a more aggregative take on listener types and chapter 12 on the phenomenon of audience members becoming artists.

AUDIENCE AS COMMUNITY

The cultist category, with its emphasis on social engagement in relationship to a passionate interest in a particular artist, brings us to the idea of audiences as communities. The term "community" is apt both as a metaphor and as a literal description. Historically, as groups of people have migrated from one part of the world to another, they have brought their cultural traditions with them, including music.

In the centuries before broadcast media and recordings, by traveling with the music of their homelands, musicians exposed people from other places and other communities to new sounds. Germans emigrating to Texas, for example, brought polka music with them. Their interaction with local musicians led to the creation *conjunto,* an amazing hybrid of polka-driven and accordion-performed music with roots in both Bavaria and Jalisco. This reveals another literal truth about music as a community-defining force: it can transcend traditional relationships and make new ones.

These effects are not just the result of social migration. Certainly, broadcasting and other distributive media have brought music from one place to listeners in many others. In that sense, the community of fans of *conjunto* virtuoso Flaco Jimenez extend far beyond San Antonio, south Texas, and even the United States.

But in addition to artist- or genre-driven communities, another kind of community forms when people come together at a concert. Nathan Hanks, the CEO of Audience Exchange, describes it this way:

> Concerts are communal focal points, where strangers gather because they share a powerful bond. Yes, they like the same music, but the bond is actually much deeper. We sing along to share common emotions. We move to the same beat. We buy t-shirts and souvenirs of the band we love, but what we're really doing is participating in one of the civilization's oldest rituals—forging community through music.[19]

The formation of such communities is not exclusively dependent on what happens onstage at concerts. Certainly, the performers and the music are the motivating factor for people being at the event. And "common emotions," as noted by Hanks, are critical to the experience. But there is also something to be said about artists and audiences physically sharing the same space at the same time.

As part of her Reputation Tour in 2018, Taylor swift performed on July 21 at MetLife Stadium in New Jersey. Prior to the show, weather forecasts predicted heavy rain and that is exactly what happened. It was raining before the show began, and when Swift took the stage, the audience was already drenched, despite many wearing ponchos, branded with the artist's lyrics, some homemade and some purchased at the event.[20]

Before the concert from backstage, Swift used Instagram to post a video to her followers about the impending weather and how much she enjoyed the rain. She was as good as her word. Swift completed the full set list—over two hours—including choreography and technical effects. The fans were also contributors to this event, remaining in the arena, fully engaged with the performance, and aware of their unique opportunity to share this experience.

That engagement, the fan recognition of the significance of the lyrics to her hit song "Come in with the Rain" in the context of a concert in a rainstorm, and the customized ponchos are all evidence of this being a "skilled audience," already connected to the artist and her music before the event.[21] In addition, many people came to the concert with friends who shared this connection. But the experience of the storm, of standing in the rain and seeing a favorite performer singing and dancing in it, falling and getting up with a smile—those things intensified the bond.

Swift was cognizant of this opportunity as well as being determined to share that with those attending, announcing to the audience that evening:

> The thing about rain shows is they're very, very, very rare, as far as I've experienced. And this sounds a little weird, but I think a rain show happens to a crowd for a reason. It happens to a crowd that is ready to take it to the next level.[22]

Skilled audiences not only know what to expect, but help make the event have meaning, for one another, and for the performer. If they are "skilled" enough, have enough history with the artist, both in past concert settings and "fueled by the media," they have enough relationship to the artist and the event to "construct particular identities," to bring those with them to the event, because they are already part of what Abercrombie and Longhurst call an "imagined community."[23] The Swifties, for example, knew who they were long before they entered MetLife Stadium.

Swift's comments to the crowd at the "rain concert" on July 21 are not only the artist's recognition of the unusual nature of the event, based on weather. They demonstrate that she understood that it was an opportunity to deepen the connection with her fans. Just as music shared has the potential to create artistic, social, and economic value, Swift's remarks were both social and commercial in motivation. Concert experience and concert communities don't just happen. They are made.

MANAGING THE CONCERT COMMUNITY

Perhaps the most basic challenge of the concert setting is the tension between scale and intimacy. As success leads to larger audiences and venues, the literal distance between most of the audiences and the performers increases. In an interview with NPR, Nirvana and Foo Fighters drummer Dave Grohl describes his first two concert experiences this way:

> I went to this club called The Cubby Bear—it's right across the street from the baseball stadium—and a band called Naked Raygun were playing, and they're this legendary Chicago punk rock band. But I'd never seen live music. So my introduction to rock and roll was in a club that held about 150 people that was half full and I was belly up against the stage watching this incredible live band, like, sweat and spit and bleed in front of me.[24]

Grohl's first professional concert created a set of expectations about immediacy and intensity that were frustrated by his first arena experience:

> "The first time I ever went to a big concert it freaked me out," Grohl says. "It was a monsters of rock tour featuring Dokken, The Scorpions, and Van Halen." The first thing he noticed, from the cheap seats, was the lag between the action he had to squint to see on stage and what his ears were telling him. "I was watching the drummer and the sound [was] taking three seconds to get to me. [I thought,] 'This is insane.'"[25]

Some of those discrepancies were technological. Visibility is now routinely enhanced with giant video screens. Increasingly sophisticated sound reinforcement eliminates delays, dead spots, and other audio problems. But some of the issues Grohl cites are simply inherent in the two different settings. Small venues afford intimacy for the audience and artist, but lower revenue potential. Large ones are more distant and require more mediation, but can generate much greater income.

In addition to technological solutions to large-venue, large-audience problems there are also means to optimize the concert experience—and revenue potential—by offering special VIP amenities for those willing to pay for them. Typical VIP features include reserved, closer-to-the-stage seating, reserved parking, separate entrance to the stadium, VIP receptions including food, drink, and—sometimes—the chance to meet the performers, souvenir merchandise, and/or VIP merch shopping.[26]

The price of VIP tickets can be anywhere from twice to ten times the price of regular admission. VIPs are identified by wristbands that given them access to the amenities and, when equipped with RFID chips (see chapter 5), allow for faster—and cashless—admission, food, drink, and merchandise purchases. From the producer's perspective, this technology also increases the capacity to collect real-time onsite data about attendees and allows sponsors to interact and customize advertising for them. In addition, bracelets can be upgraded in real time and/or coded to provide special opportunities.

In the "Tipsheet" on "The Top 10 Benefits of Using RFID for Events," Eventbrite notes that

> Once attendees receive their RFID badge or wristbands, there are endless ways to engage on-site. One of the most popular is RFID-enabled photo booths. By simply tapping their wristband or badge at the photo booth, attendees can automatically email themselves their pictures. This option is especially popular for sponsor activations, as a way to engage attendees and collect their contact information for lead generation.[27]

Obviously, technological mediation is an increasingly critical factor for managing the audience experience at concerts and festivals, both in terms of every audience member seeing and hearing the performance and for the amenities offered to VIP customers.

Technology is also critical to broader definitions of "audience," as applied to fans across all means of access to music. Of particular importance are technologies that support communications networks and their capacity to connect producers to consumers, artists to audiences, and fans to fans.

NETWORKS

The above exploration of "audience as community" is based on literal audiences and their experience of being together at the same place at the same time to hear and see a performance. And as noted previously, "audience" can also apply to fans across media, including distributive forms (radio, satellite radio, download stores, streaming services). But it is important to look more deeply at fan networks, in which audience members talk to one another away from the concert setting. It is particularly critical to examine how digital media, especially the social media platforms of the Internet, not only expand fan communities, but empower them to go far beyond what has previously been possible in terms of affecting sales, production, and even creativity.

Social networks can be understood in a basic sense as relationships between and among people. In addition to the emotional value of such connections, we can also consider other resources that social networks can provide, ranging from references and recommendations to tangible resources that others are willing to make available to you. It is in this sense that people often advise others about the importance of professional "networking," or express the cliché, "it's not what you know, but who you know."

When communications media expand the size and geographic scale of a social network, the resources available and the scope of their impact potentially increase as well. In addition, while most twentieth-century media were "mass" in the sense that radio and television could reach millions of listeners and viewers with a single broadcast, they were also one-way communications. The audience could not "talk back" to the producers or performers. Nor could they talk to one another unless they were in the same room or used a different medium such as the telephone, for example, to do so.

This one-way, one-to-many model worked very well for a music industry dominated by large record labels and music groups who periodically released and promoted products intended to sell to the largest customer pool possible. But when Internet-based communications began to proliferate late in the twentieth century and combine with digital music, it was not just the control and distribution structures of the music industry that were disrupted. The lines of communication were redrawn entirely.

In discussing the "communications architecture" of the Internet, researchers at MIT's Media Laboratory describe how "innovation and the potential for growth are coincident with major architectural shifts in the design of systems where the intelligence or adaptability is moved from the center to the ends."[28] This shift has empowered those who would have only been able to consume via mass media in the last century not only to talk back to producers and to one another, but also to create and distribute their own messaging and content globally.

For music creators, as we have already discussed (chapter 7, "Diffusion"), this has meant expanded opportunity to distribute original music without the support of record labels or traditional broadcast media. For consumers, this has led to dramatically increased opportunities not only to "share" music on a very large scale (see "Sharing Economy" below), but also to engage in forming interactive fan communities. These communities not only allow for social outlets and shared interpretations of music. They have also empowered such groups to shape music production.

There are (at least) two ways to consider music fan communities online. The first is by media platform. In 2015 Instagram, already aware that much of its content involved music and musicians, created launched@ music, "an account dedicated to exploring music on our platform—those who create it, and the community around it."[29]

From that perspective, the company found that

> More and more, we're seeing the music industry look to Instagram as an authentic storytelling tool and indispensable resource for fan engagement and content promotion. Major and emerging artists are eager to break native content on Instagram, and they're using the platform to personally connect with a global audience of fans through visual storytelling.[30]

In order to clarify how Instagram was creating value for music creators, producers, and fans in 2016, the company commissioned Nielsen to study "the habits and lifestyles of U.S. music listeners on Instagram."[31] They found that Instagram users spent 42% more money and 30% more time on music than the general population.

In addition, Instagram users were found more likely to stream music and twice as likely to pay for streaming as the public generally. These numbers suggest that Instagram music users are more in line with the *fan* or even *cultist* categories of Abercrombie and Longhurst's engagement continuum than more casual consumers.

Finally, Instagram users were found to be twice as likely to attend live music events—both concert tours and clubs—and 83% used Instagram during live events. This obviously has a business value, but it also facilitates the social dimension of fandom and the communities that form around particular artists and their music.

Today, fan communities centered on individual artists—called "Internet fandoms" or "fan armies"—include Taylor Swift's "Swifties," Beyoncé's BeyHive, Ed Sheeran's Sheerios, the Directioners of One Direction, and many more. In one sense, these groups are like the fan clubs of past eras in that they represent a network of people who share a passion for particular performers and their music and who enjoy talking/writing about their enthusiasms, sharing information and gossip about the performer, and discussing upcoming tours and releases with like-minded people. In another sense, contemporary groups are quite different in terms of organization and function.

Prior to the web, to early Internet Usenet groups, and even to email, the logistics of finding and connecting with like-minded music enthusiasts were more challenging and more likely to be based on a particular location, an aspect of a local music scene. From around the mid-twentieth century forward, such groups included "both 'official' fan clubs, run by an artist's management, and 'unofficial,' run by fans out of their homes."[32] Obviously, the "official" groups gathered and maintained mailing lists and used them to promote tours and record releases. Clearly there was a promotional advantage in maintaining an official club as well as a financial incentive. On the other hand, the "unofficial" groups were a combination of passionate hobby and obsession.

In an article about *The Fan Club Directory* (designed to help fans connect), American Studies scholar Daniel Cavicchi explains early unofficial groups this way:

> Nevertheless, fans' intense feelings of connection motivated them to seek one another out and attempt to build a sense of community, something that they did mostly with regular face-to-face meetings (at conventions, performances, and parties) and print communication (fanzines, newsletters, and private letters). Much of this activity, especially for fans of lesser-known stars and art forms, was DIY, and it required an amazing amount of labor and love. You really need a certain level of devotion to work at a job all day, manage a family, and then also spend your remaining time, night after night, doing the rather isolated work of collecting clippings, writing articles, compiling fan art, and mailing out photos and tapes to fellow fans.[33]

As with so many other aspects of twentieth-century life, the Internet thoroughly changed how fan clubs worked. Not only did the tools to connect and engage with others evolve, but also the potential uses of such connections drastically expanded. Today, fan groups not only share news and discuss music; they capitalize tours and projects, and they impact and manipulate critical industry metrics.

It has been suggested that the modern Internet-based fandom began with Lady Gaga and her Little Monsters. By 2009, Joanne Stefani Germanotta had fully established her Lady Gaga stage persona, had a hit record (*The Fame*, 2008), charted two number one singles ("Just Dance" and "Poker Face"), and launched a major international tour—her first as a headliner (*The Fame Ball Tour*, March–August 2009).

During the summer phase of that tour, Lady Gaga began addressing those attending her concerts as "little monsters." As observed by music critic Jake Hall:

> Giving a whole fandom a nickname of sorts was already commonplace in K-pop, but Gaga was the first to do it on such a grand scale in a western context—using it to describe the way fans would writhe, scream and dance in the pits of her high-octane performances. Naming her fans did two things. First, it created an "us" and "them" narrative. You were either a true Gaga fan, or you weren't. And second, it grouped them all together in a way that made sense online. For a generation of kids who existed on the internet, being a Little Monster meant more than going to a few gigs. It meant having a support network of like-minded people from around the world that you could interact with, like an extended family. Finally, there was a name for all the people who spent their waking hours immersed in the online world of Lady Gaga; one that was getting bigger by the year.[34]

Soon other stars began naming their fans: Beliebers, the Rihanna Navy, and Swifties. It was more than branding, however. It was using social media to create community with an immediacy and relative ease of interactivity that earlier fan groups did not have.

Mathieu Deflem, professor of sociology and author of *Lady Gaga and the Sociology of Fame*, analyzed the impact of modern fandoms this way:

"Gaga and her team understood the creation of a hardcore fanbase via social networking sites, and her approach to fans has always been very personal and direct," says Deflem, explaining how and why the Little Monsters ultimately thrived on the internet. "She established a culture where it seems there's a symmetry between her and her fans, as they can communicate with one another. You can tweet Lady Gaga, and who knows? She might respond. That sense of horizontal interaction, however illusory it may be, works to create that sense of community."[35]

This illustration of "horizontal interaction" through which fans talk to fans and possibly with the artist is a particularly significant effect of the Internet fandom. One effect of such direct artist–audience connectivity is that audiences became engaged with discussions about where artists tour and, by raising funds to cover costs of tours or projects, directly engaged in production.

A very early example of this effect came in the 1990s, as described by Nancy Baym in *Playing to the Crowd: Musicians, Audiences and the Intimate Work of Connection* (2018). After a show, Marillion keyboard player Mark Kelly was given printouts of an online fan group for the band. Surprisingly, although Marillion had not toured in the United States at that point, that is where most of the subscribers to the group lived. What happened next was even more surprising.

Kelly spent the first couple of years reading without posting, watching the discussion in secret. But the internet is the internet, and finally, someone said something so wrong that Kelly couldn't stop himself from jumping in to correct him. His cover was blown.

Immediately North Americans asked why they didn't tour in America.

"We don't have a record deal in the States," he told them, "and every time we toured in the past it's always been with money from the record company." "Oh, well," a Canadian fan wrote, "why don't we raise the money for you to come and tour?" Others quickly agreed that this was a good plan.[36]

Though Kelly was dubious, the fans raised more than the $50,000 he had told them it would take to fund a North American tour without record label support. Long before Kickstarter and other crowdfunding sites were launched, something amazing had happened:

> Marillion did the tour in 1997. The fans who had fronted the money also bought tickets. Being fan-funded generated publicity. "Each gig that we were playing, there'd be a little local newspaper that would run the story about the tour fund and how the American fans had raised the money for us to tour." It was exciting, a moment of transition, and a master class in "the power of the internet, and how rabid fans can change things, make things happen."[37]

In addition to capitalization, chart rankings also shape production and touring decisions. While reaching number one was a relatively straightforward process for most of the twentieth century, by leveraging record sales, radio play, and touring, Internet-based distribution and P2P file sharing changed things. Strategies now include using fan groups to spread the word about new releases and tours as well as—especially for emerging artists—the use of viral memes (Rae Sremmurd's "Black Beatles," for example, or Baauer's "Harlem Shake") to capture, however briefly, public attention.

But there is no widely recognized process for success on the Internet, though there is no shortage of music industry professionals attempting to develop one. But, as discussed in previous chapters, if music creation, production, and reception are a complex adaptive system, then we can't leave the listeners/fans out of the equation. Music critic Britanny Spanos analyzes the current state of chart rankings:

> Internet-based fandoms are still figuring out the formula, and many are trying to take matters into their own hands, creating grassroots promotional campaigns. Fan accounts that aren't affiliated officially with the artist go to great lengths to ensure that everyone is on the same page, taking a keen interest in statistics and sales and offering specific instructions on how to maximize streams and change IP addresses for fans who live outside the United States.[38]

Spanos cites the work of Will Cosme, blogger at Pop Crave, who has "been charting the movements of fan Twitter and passionate promotional campaigns initiated via social media for years":[39]

> For Cosme, the first and best examples of when fan Twitter became an effective promotional tool [were] with the rise of One Direction and later Fifth Harmony, whose fans and label mimicked the promotional campaigns of Directioners to give the girl group a public boost following *The X-Factor.*
>
> "[Directioners] were the first fandom to use radio requests as a weapon," Cosme details, noting the specific organizational tactics that set them apart from other fandoms and also made them effective. "Other fandoms began using the same strategies—Katy fans, Nicki fans, Taylor Swift fans. It wasn't as well-organized though."[40]

Online strategies involving Twitter, Shazam, and streams have proven effective because, as Spanos states, "Fans have found a way to reach the industry on more logical, data-driven terms that can help give their artists more attention from the inside."[41] As a result, companies whose business models depend on data analytics have responded with "fraud-detection measures." As a "Spotify spokesperson" told Spanos, "The Spotify Content Operations team regularly monitors consumption on the service to look for fraud and any possible fraudulent activity is investigated and dealt with immediately."[42]

While some see Internet fandom initiatives as an inevitable part of marketing, promotion, and data management, others question their effectiveness over the longer term of a career. Nevertheless, two things are clear. First, fan communities on the Internet are a significant factor in music production, reception, and monetization. Second, the more effectively these communities act to support the artists around whom they are organized, the more data-driven companies can find themselves in opposition to them. Like other points of conflict in the past, such as file sharers/pirates versus the recording industry, resisting a technologically fueled social development is likely to be a losing proposition.

Interactive fan communities are not just the result of Internet-based communications architecture and utilities. The people who comprise them are members of a generation that is networked across both professional and personal life, and whose experience is "networked, curated, publicized, fetishized, tweeted, catered, and anything but solitary, anything but private."[43]

Because of the values and expectations of this population, empowered by viral network technologies, never has so much music been experienced with an expectation that it be free. While some research may suggest that the negative impact of piracy/sharing has been overestimated, it is clear that the large-scale shift from "ownership" to "sharing" has had a significant impact on musicians and their capacity to monetize their creativity.

SHARING CULTURE AND
PEER-TO-PEER ECONOMY

Long before the term became trendy, there was a sharing economy, or at least sharing. As noted in a recent post at Knowledge@Wharton: "Carpooling, for instance, has long been a way of sharing both the cost of commuting and leveraging an expensive asset—the private automobile (which sits idle more than 90% of the time)."[44]

The same posting continues:

Few observers in the last few decades recognized carpooling as a vanguard phenomenon, but that's what it was. The same basic concept, technologically assisted, has been applied to nearly every aspect of modern life. And it's enabled cost savings, convenience and environmental benefits on a large scale. As a result, the peer-to-peer story is one of stellar growth. From modest roots, the international sharing economy reached about $15 billion in 2014, reports PricewaterhouseCoopers (PwC), and it is on track to reach $335 billion by 2025.[45]

Two characteristics of the sharing economy are critical to its potential impact on music production and consumption. As defined by Yochai

Benkler, these are "lumpiness" and "technology."[46] Lumpy goods are defined as being goods whose cost exceeds the buyer's immediate need and capacity; homes and cars would be examples. Car pools serve to realize the unused capacity of a car by distributing both the cost and the transportation capacity necessary for a given trip, or regular daily trip, among several riders.

Excess capacity is thus what makes a sharing economy possible and explains not only carpooling, but also web- and app-driven car services like Uber. But what makes it possible to talk about a "sharing economy" (as opposed to just "sharing") are the technologies that drive twenty-first-century social media.

> "In the collaborative economy it's not the idea of sharing that's new; people have been doing that for eons," notes H. O. Maycotte, founder and CEO of data rights management company Umbel in an article published on Dell. com. "What's different now is the introduction of technology into the concept—particularly easy-to-use digital technologies like location-based GPS that allow people to quickly make and respond to requests for goods and services."[47]

As a description of what has happened and why, this makes sense. But some analysts argue that the sharing economy is no economy at all or, conversely, that it is actually a business model masquerading as "sharing." As stated, for example, in a Harvard Business Review article from 2015:

> Sharing is a form of social exchange that takes place among people known to each other, without any profit. Sharing is an established practice, and dominates particular aspects of our life, such as within the family. By sharing and collectively consuming the household space of the home, family members establish a communal identity. When "sharing" is market-mediated—when a company is an intermediary between consumers who don't know each other—it is no longer sharing at all. Rather, consumers are paying to access someone else's goods or services for a particular period of time. It is an economic exchange, and consumers are after utilitarian, rather than social, value.[48]

From this perspective, the so-called sharing economy is more about using social networking to reduce the cost of doing business. As such, the widespread practice of sharing and/or businesses based on the sharing concept has become "a disruptive force in a slew of industries, particularly travel, consumer goods, services, taxis, bicycles and car rental, finance, music, employment and waste."[49]

One additional point of discussion among analysts of the sharing economy is the idea that access has "become the new ownership." For example, researchers Eckhardt and Bardhi state that "Consumers simply want to make savvy purchases, and access economy companies allow them to achieve this, by offering more convenience at lower price."[50] And, if this can become an effective practice in such tangible goods as automobiles and power tools, how much easier is it for the intangible products of the arts and entertainment sector to be shared?

Convenience of access is obviously a critical factor in the music industry and so it is easy to see why music file sharing—without an economic incentive—was so quickly adopted by so many listeners. In addition, because online file sharing was based on connections between and among music fans, it reflects another feature of sharing-economy entities: an emphasis on the recommendation and validation provided by crowd sourcing. Thus the elements of cost, convenient access, community, and trust are key ingredients of the sharing-economy model for music.

The particular challenge that the sharing economy represents to larger businesses in the music industry and independent artists alike is that there are (and have long been) companies that mediate music "sharing"—for example, you don't own music you hear on Spotify, you simply pay for temporary access to it. This is the role that broadcast radio played for most of the twentieth century. Beyond that, a great deal of what is called "sharing" is actually "stealing" from a copyright law perspective. Music "piracy" and "bootleg" copies have been around since the late 1800s and each new technology that facilitates copying also creates opportunities for this kind of usage to expand.[51]

The essence of the problem is that the music experience—the access to which is what all music businesses sell—is intangible intellectual property. It would be one thing, for example, to "share" music that you actually own, but almost without exception, people don't own music. They have only purchased a right to personally access it.

Nor can you share a concert ticket like you can share a ride in a car pool. Lending someone a CD as you might a power tool is legal, but making copies to distribute is not. This issue—distribution of illegal copies—is aggravated by the ease of making copies—even millions of copies—in the digital era and then using the Internet to distribute them globally. There is no practical way to do that with a power tool, but in the digital era, amplified by the Internet and social media, music is the ideal digital good for large-scale and widespread "sharing."

Given this, it is no coincidence that profitability in music today is derived most from those aspects of musical experience that are difficult for consumers to share: live performances. Because live concerts work from an economic perspective and selling physical product doesn't and because streaming revenues are so small, the business of live performance is booming for the present. In addition, licensing music to multimedia projects ranging from entertainment to advertising provides the only other viable balance between access and control that allows for musicians and listeners to connect culturally and economically.

In the next chapter we look at some of the business models designed to optimize and exploit this highly networked, sharing-intensive market and culture.

CRITICAL CONCEPTS

- Understanding the artist–audience connection requires us to consider not only aggregation and how that is accomplished, but also the resulting distancing effects and how connection is maintained in spite of them.

- Contemporary music marketing techniques use social media to foster connection and engagement between and among listeners, musicians, and their music by using approaches that are *interactive, personalized, authentic,* and *conversational.*
- In using playlists, listeners may develop relationships in which the curator of the list is more important than the musical artists who created the content.
- A concert "community" is not merely the inevitable result of a planned event and/or environmental factors. It is also constructed.
- The Internet thoroughly changed how fan clubs work. Not only did the tools to connect and engage fellow fans evolve, but the uses to which they could be put drastically expanded. Today, fan groups not only share news and discuss music; they capitalize tours and projects, and they impact and manipulate critical industry metrics.
- Given the rise of a P2P sharing economy and culture, it is no coincidence that today profitability in music is derived from those aspects of musical experience that are the most difficult for consumers to "share"—live performances.

FURTHER CONSIDERATION

Music Curation: Playlist–Audience Relationships

Historically, distributive media like radio were intermediaries between performers and listeners.

- As playlists have become more and more important to music fans and consumers, is it purely a "middle-man" relationship, or something more?
- Consider whether a listener of a SiriusXM channel has a more meaningful relationship with that "brand" than with the artists whose music constitutes what it plays?

- Is it different when the artists whose music is featured host a channel, perhaps in anticipation of a tour or product release? Is this any different than the role of DJs in the twentieth century? Why?

From another perspective consider songwriter Clarence Clarity and his 2018 album, *THINK: PEACE*, and his project, *LEAVE EARTH*, which he describes as a "long form body of work—an anthology perhaps—made up of tracks from the last two years." Not only is *LEAVE EARTH* a kind of artist-curated playlist; Clarity encourages followers to "mix and match from the playlist material—curate the album you want to hear." See https://twitter.com/clarenceclarity/status/1047818604845158401.

- Do you think this may be a response to the increasing importance of playlists and curators?
- Do you think it will be effective?
- Who might benefit?

Resistant Audiences/Consumers

Consider the following article:

- Ben Sisario, "A Stream of Music, Not Revenue," *New York Times*, December 13, 2013, www.nytimes.com/2013/12/13/business/media /a-stream-of-music-not-revenue.html

As stated in the article:

"There is this irrational resistance for people to actually plunk down their credit card for streaming services," said Ted Cohen, a digital music consultant with the firm TAG Strategic. "We're 13 years into the Napster phenomenon of 'music is free,' and it's hard to get people back into the idea that music is at least worth the value of a cup of Starbucks coffee a week."

- Why do you think this is the case?
- Are music fans really "resistant"?
- Or is something else going on?

CONCEPTUAL PROTOTYPE QUESTIONS

Can fan campaigns reinvent the music industry? Or should companies depend on data analytics to reduce their impact through "fraud detection" measures? Are coordinated efforts by fans to send a message via engagement with critical metrics like Shazam actually "fraudulent"? Why or why not?

Your answers to the questions above can provide a framework for entrepreneurial possibilities. Are you solving a problem (for whom?) by using data to create better-targeted and more useable playlists? Or should you be looking at something like a twenty-first-century version of *The Fan Club Directory* of thirty years ago to facilitate more engagement and advocacy by online fan communities? Do you think one is a better choice than the other? Why? Is there an alternative that better serves musicians, producers, and listeners?

Before you begin to sketch a prototype consider this:

"Through online campaigns and crowdfunding, music projects that labels and promoters wouldn't touch have managed to get off the ground. But is the fan-driven revolution in music really as utopian as it seems?"

From:

- Ben Beaumont Thomas, "Can Fan Campaigns Reinvent the Music Industry?," *Guardian,* June 17, 2014, www.theguardian.com /music/2014/jun/17/can-fan-campaigns-reinvent-the-music-industry-kickstarter-crowdfunding

Does this change your thinking about where an entrepreneurial opportunity lies today? If so, why?

10

Incorporation

Production, Monetization, Affiliation

The idea of a "corporation" in business is fundamental. Beginning with a literal definition derived from the Latin "corpus," a corporation is a "body" that can function in many ways as a person: own property, take legal action, and make contracts. Corporations also pay taxes and can be sued. Corporations are established under the laws of the state (in the United States) in which they are founded.

In one sense, corporations are like other business arrangements that pool the efforts and resources of owners, partners, backers, and employees. In the broadest terms, the reasons for establishing such collective and collaborative arrangements are a matter of expanding resources, expertise, and effort. You can start a talent agency, recording studio, or streaming service as an individual effort, using only your own capital and know-how. But it is difficult to do so unless you have lots of money and an extremely diverse skill set. Division of labor and pooled resources confer advantages. And, even if you start small, with a lean organization, enough success will require an expansion of personnel and materials.

The legal decision to incorporate brings several advantages relative to other collaborative business structures and these are as valid for music ventures as for any other. First, a corporation protects its owners from personal liability from corporate debts and obligations. If the venue you and your college roommate bought goes under, if you simply signed a contract or established a legal partnership other than a corporation, you are personally liable for the debts incurred. There are limits to this, of course, but it is one of the primary advantages of incorporation.

Additional advantages include unlimited life, not dependent on the life of a sole proprietor or partners; ownership of a corporation is transferrable; and it is relatively easy to attract capital investment to an incorporated business. The final point is a crucial one, particularly for any venture that has a high risk of failure, such a starting a record label, or hosting live shows in a purchased or rented venue. The limited liability of the corporation also protects investors and shares purchased in a corporation by investors can be sold or transferred.

There are disadvantages to incorporation as well. It costs more to set up than a sole proprietorship or partnership, the tax code is more complicated, and there are procedural rules about filing paperwork, annual meetings, and so on. The ins and outs of filing for corporate status are beyond the scope of this chapter, but how corporations operate and the advantages they confer illuminate both traditional and evolutionary business structures in music.

Because establishing a corporation is more complicated and expensive, many startup ventures do not begin that way. In music, the most common type of startup "organization" is a band or even a solo act. If you are a coffee shop singer/guitarist in Des Moines or a cover band in Albuquerque, you probably don't think about sole proprietorship or partnership structures and contracts, let alone filing corporate paperwork. In fact, many musicians starting out don't think much about fiscal matters at all. One of the challenges of building a venture based on musical creativity—songwriting and performance—that has long-term viability is a general lack of organizational, contractual, and financial expertise or awareness at the beginning and, sometimes, as an ongoing issue.

On the other hand, businesses designed to function as intermediaries between performers and listeners—including record labels, concert promoters, publishers, broadcasters, digital download stores, and streaming services—are much more likely to have a business orientation from the beginning. This is not because the principals of such businesses don't care about music. Often, that is not at all the case. Many intermediary businesses are launched by people inspired by music and who are often musicians themselves. But when you start a business that is designed to bring artists and audiences together and monetize the connection, your frame of reference for planning will differ fundamentally from when your primary goal is making music.

The things that make intermediary business structures so scalable (aggregation of creative productivity of multiple artists and optimizing distribution and sales) make the advantages of incorporation (limited liability, transferability, and capitalization, to name three) more evident. This makes it more worthwhile to take the steps necessary to incorporate and to acquire the financial and knowledge resources to do so.

As we look at collaborative associations that are designed to facilitate creation, production, and monetization, we will make a number of distinctions among the reasons for creating them and structures employed to do so. Most broadly, we will distinguish between organizations created by artists to support making music and taking it to the public with the intention—or at least the hope—of popular recognition and monetization. These artist-oriented affiliations are the garage bands and talent show singers (today, including YouTube posters) of the world. These are the organizations more centered on the creation-to-production segment of the creation-production-reception cycle. They are more likely to begin as informal arrangements rather than legally created entities.

The other broad segment includes organizations that center on the production-to-reception segment—the intermediary businesses that discover and promote the creative productivity of multiple artists (or even—at the level of a streaming service like Spotify—record labels) to the largest audience/customer base possible. At one end of the spectrum are smaller entities, like independent labels (Sun, Def Jam, Sub

Pop, and XL Recordings, for example, or more recently Mixpack, Ghostly International, and Mind of a Genius).[1] At the larger end are major labels and music groups in the traditional marketplace and download stores and streaming services in the postdigital contemporary one.

The further we move away from small independents to complex, vertically integrated structures, the greater the likelihood that the business will formally incorporate. It is no accident that this progression of scale from small to large and from informal affiliation to legal incorporation also increases the distance of the core business from the creative artist. These issues are also discussed from different perspectives in previous chapters (4, "Commodification," and 9, "Connection").

The progression of an organization is an important factor in studying how businesses work. And, while not every band becomes wealthy and world famous, there is almost always some development from simple social connection to professional networks and associations. If, for example, your cover band starts working for a booking agency and not just playing the gigs you can find, you have added a layer of complexity to your operation. In this chapter we look at those layers, particularly as they develop from the startup phase to the next steps of more extensive distribution, promotion, and monetization.

In addition to the distinction between informal, music-oriented startups versus more formally structured intermediary businesses, we need to look at the creation-production-reception cycle through several lenses, some already introduced: as a complex adaptive system; as the result of reactions to a series of inevitable disruptions; or as an economic sector dominated by mass production–inspired "hit factories."

Across all of these perspectives, a fundamental intention of a business always includes monetizing reception, that is, consumption. Whether or not it is in the business of creating or producing music, or it takes already produced music as an input, at some point providing and selling access to musical experiences must become a factor for a business. You can't have a band that is more than a hobby if you never play a public gig. You can't start a record label unless you make and sell

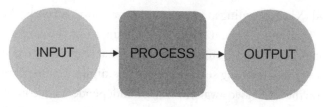

Figure 11. Music Production Model.

some records, even if it's out of your dorm room, like Rick Rubin's first efforts.

So in this chapter, we take several things as given. People want to make music. They and/or other people may seek to sell it. In the process of making and selling music, people will form collaborative relationships in support of those goals. To understand this in greater depth, we will examine theories and organizing concepts, structural models, and specific cases. Since a number of twentieth-century business models are discussed in earlier chapters, here we focus on businesses that have adapted earlier models and/or adopted entirely new approaches for the musical culture and markets of the twenty-first century.

MUSICAL AFFILIATION AND VALUE

In chapter 2 we discussed three types of production models for music businesses: those that produce performance, distribution/access, or curation. As part of that discussion, a model was offered, shown in figure 11.

This model applies to any venture for which musical creativity of some kind is the input and a marketable product/experience is the output. In earlier chapters we have examined how some twentieth-century businesses—record labels, for example—filled a "middle-man" role in the discovery of developing artists and promoting and distributing recorded product to the public. Distributive media from radio to streaming services take recorded output as their input and provide access to even larger audiences. Guided discovery and listening experiences—curation—have been provided by radio disc jockeys and continue today via the playlists of Spotify and other streaming services.

In every case of an intermediary business—a connector between creation/performance and reception/consumption—the question of added value must be considered. For example, if the primary meaning and value of musical experience rest in the direct relationship between artist and audience, what does an intermediary "bring to the table" to justify their share of the revenue for doing so?

A booking agent provides performers contacts with presenters. A record label provides (or used to provide) guidance about repertoire, recording expertise and resources, marketing, promotion, distribution, merchandising, and so on. A radio station provides free access unrestrained by location. File-sharing sites offer free access on demand to a vast catalog of music. Digital download stores did the same at a cost as close to "free" as practicable. Streaming services also provide free or low-cost access to vast music catalogs and, as an additional value, provide a curated experience, with recommendations for "other songs you'd like" and playlists for a variety of purposes.

Much closer to the core artist-to audience "transaction," as noted above, bands and solo artists are also musical ventures. People come together to pool the performing, songwriting, and arranging resources of the group and refine them—adding value—in the context of public performance. This is not just true of the modern era with its emphasis on artist entrepreneurship and DIY production. No band of any era was ever discovered before they were able to play a gig.

Where a twentieth-century A & R process might put a group under contract on the basis of its potential for development, contemporary businesses are looking for a more completely realized, already viable product before signing artists. As a consequence, as we look at contemporary business models, we will consider several that are driven by, or at least created to facilitate, independent artists and their growth from the startup phase to an "investable" economic brand.

Brand and Franchise

In terms of branding in music, the conventional view is that the brand identity of an artist is colocated in their music and personality—the hit songs and stars model of traditional A & R development. Record labels may also be brands, as can producers. And, as noted in the previous chapter, playlist curators can become more important to listeners than the artists who created the music they curate. But in terms of cultural significance and economic impact it is the relationship of the audience to the artist and their music that seems most impactful, so the artist's brand is, for the present at least, most significant.

Musicians also work to extend the values of their personal and musical brand beyond live performances and recordings. They do so by licensing music to other media, for example, or attaching their name and/or image to products. Such products may be those produced by other companies, or they may be products purpose-built for the artist to promote and sell under their own label.

It is worth noting here that for a long time, the concept of a "brand" was primarily associated with products and services, rather than with people. It wasn't until the 1990s that the concept of personal branding was developed and popularized. In music, for as long as we can look at musical ventures, there has always been an interconnection for listeners between the music and the person making it, even if it wasn't called a personal brand.

The fundamental function of developing a brand is differentiation from other products and services—in the context of this discussion, to be distinct from other music and musicians. In the broadest of terms, the goal of brand development in music is to go from being a cover band to being a band with a unique musical identity that people recognize and value. The idea is that, once established, a musical brand can be extended from recorded release to recorded release and from tour to tour.

Since one of the established principles for effective brands is consistency, in music this means that one Imagine Dragons record, for example, must have a recognizable similarity to previous offerings. This correlates to the importance of repetition and familiarity discussed in chapter 3, "Reception." But it also can become a challenge if the artists want to move in a new direction creatively, or if popular tastes change and listeners move to new sounds from new performers.

Still, familiarity and consistency are important as a platform for generating value. The development of collaborative processes that support a brand follows its establishment. In other words, once you know how to make, produce, promote, and sell a One Direction album, for example, it is a natural tendency to build a process that makes it easier to do so.

In the film industry, there is a great deal of discussion, planning, and production centering on the idea of a "franchise." A franchise takes the idea of brand across multiple creative projects. For example, the *Fast and Furious* films (really any movie generative of sequels) are considered a franchise. Moreover, a franchise typically extends not only from film to film, but to other media. Often books and films are interrelated, as are soundtracks and computer games.

In popular commercial music, one can argue that every successful band and artist engages in a form of brand franchising. Producing a successful album has historically been leveraged into promoting a successful tour and vice versa. Next year's album and tour leverage the popularity and notoriety of this year's—see Beyoncé and Jay-Z's *On The Run I* and *On The Run II* tours, discussed in chapter 5. As also evidenced during the OTRII tour, music videos not only promote a tour, and/or product release, but also extend the franchise: the tour, affiliated products, the artists individually and, in this case, as a married couple.

Some recording artists have explicitly packaged their serial album releases as a franchise, by simply using the band's name and a number to describe each release. The band Chicago, for example, established in the late 1960s, was up to *Chicago XXXVI* in 2014.

Even more literal franchise initiatives exist, such as a band touring under its original name and performing the music that made their name famous, but with new performers involved. In part, this is the result of the necessary replacement of band members for a variety of reasons. It is typically not so difficult to replace a "side" musician, but lead singers are more difficult as they are literally the "voice" of a group and, since they "front" the band, are the face as well. Still, successful groups from previous decades do go on tour from time to time under their original name, but with few or even none of the original members.

A relatively "pure" example of a music franchise is the Trans-Siberian Orchestra, which puts two distinct "companies," including two different sets of onstage performers, on tour each year in order to fill the demand for their music during the holiday season (see "Further Consideration"). In addition, since the brand is based on the group name and seasonal music offerings, the individual performers are largely interchangeable, a relatively rare situation, but one comparable to film franchises in which even a principal character (Batman, for example) can be cast with a series of different actors.

FACTORIES, LEAN STARTUPS, AND COMPLEX ADAPTORS

Regardless of the placement on the creation-production-reception continuum, brand/franchise strategy, operating structure, or philosophical model, a fundamental question for every music business is, what kind of value is being created? While making money is always a factor—though what that means can vary widely in terms of how much and how important it is to the people involved—it is rarely the only motivation for making music. Or even for starting a business based on bringing music to the public. When considering the question of value, one way to look at it is to ask whether the motivation for a business is to create economic value, artistic value, or social value.

As discussed in chapter 2, Bill Ivey, former head of both the Country Music Foundation and the National Endowment for the Arts, posited that every venture involving the arts was engaged in three forms of productivity: making great art, serving the public good, and having a viable economic basis to continue doing so. The relative importance of the three factors can change, not only from business to business, but also from project to project within an organization. But the overall balance among art, social benefit, and economics must be present for a business to succeed and thrive. In this sense, you can argue that any music business must be built to create and balance multiple forms of value, even when the processes required are different and the goals are sometimes contradict one another.

In addition to balancing multiple forms of value, music businesses must also be capable of managing risk. Because music is a volatile economic offering, dependent on changing tastes and technologies, as well as larger social and economic conditions, predicting success for a given project is difficult at best and the risks associated with launching a new artist and/or project are relatively high. As also noted in chapter 2, as poor as the odds are using conventional thinking like the 80/20 rule, in which 20% of the music produced earns 80% of the financial return, the reality is much worse. In 2011, the ratio was closer to 80/2 for albums and, for digital singles, more like 80/.8.[2]

Streaming tilts the percentages even further as paid streaming subscriptions pass 40% of revenue and digital singles represent less than 8%. As discussed in chapter 5, predictions about industry-wide aggregate numbers are tricky to use for planning purposes. The long and short of it is that a relatively small number of artists, albums, and singles generate the overwhelming majority of revenue from recorded music. That means the majority of creative products generate very little. Consequently, there is a tendency in music business organizations to create processes that minimize risk and increase the odds of repeat success, whether by brand consistency or imitation of successful examples.

This thinking is what leads to the use of a mass production/distribution model to create a "hit factory." One of the inherent difficulties in establishing such an organization is that it requires a significant infrastructure. As discussed in chapter 2, Motown Records began as a startup—the vision of one person. Relatively quickly, it accumulated a staff of writers, producers, house musicians, and an increasingly large pool of vocal performers. The combined effort of these people and others moved songs and singers through a hit and star development process.

While this worked it was incredibly effective. But eventually changes in popular taste, cultural reference points, and a market shaped in no small part by earlier Motown successes afforded artists and listeners other opportunities. The company was unable to successfully adapt to being based in Los Angeles rather than in Detroit. This exemplifies how the stable processes that facilitate a factory-style business can become the very things that make it less adaptive in the face of changing circumstances.

It is not unreasonable to conclude that businesses using a factory model are particularly vulnerable to disruption and less able to react quickly and effectively to evolutionary impulses of a complex adaptive system (CAS). Consequently it is not surprising that traditional business structures like record labels have been in decline since the disruptions of the digital era began circa 1999. But in addition, other large, vertically integrated structures have emerged. They differ from labels in terms of what they produce, but not so much in their attempts to minimize risk and change. The iTunes music store is one example. Adaptive and innovative when it appeared, it was disrupted some years after it was founded by the emergence of streaming services.

Thanks to the vision and leadership of Steve Jobs, Apple was a very early mover in the digital single download market. The iTunes store was genuinely groundbreaking when it opened in 2003. But the fact that it was a stability-oriented model—a kind of factory—was soon made clear by Jobs and his opinion of streaming music services:

> People have told us over and over and over again, they don't want to rent their music. Just to make that perfectly clear: Music's not like a video. Your favorite movie you may watch 10 times in your life; your favorite song you're going to listen to a thousand times in your life. If it costs you $10 a month, or over $100 a year, for a subscription fee to rent that song, that

means for me to listen to my favorite song in 10 years I paid over $1,000 in subscription fees to listen to my favorite song 10 years from now, and that just doesn't fly with customers. They don't want subscriptions.[3]

Over a decade later, in an interview with Billboard (2014), Spotify CEO Daniel Ek was asked about Apple's then-planned purchase of Beats Electronics and the implications for the streaming music sector.

The one thing I can say—we know streaming is the better model in music and we've said that for over 5 years—when everyone else said it wasn't the case. I've always assumed Apple would offer a streaming service at some point—but we're focusing on building the best possible product and feel pretty good about that.[4]

It is clear from Ek's remarks that he saw (and had seen) streaming as the superior delivery/access mechanism to downloading. There is also an implication that he was surprised at how long it had taken Apple (to that point in 2014) to establish its own streaming service. It is likely that Jobs's negative attitude toward streaming contributed to Apple's relatively slow reaction to the emergence of Spotify and other such services. Whatever the reason, because of Apple's delay in developing an adaptive strategy for streaming once they had established a stable and stability-oriented business model based on downloads, the roles of disruptor and disrupted flipped. This is clearly a risk for established companies, even those that begin in disruptive positions relative to other business models. (See the discussion of Ed Catmull and Pixar, under "Further Consideration.")

So, obviously, there are challenges and vulnerabilities inherent in building a "factory" model that emphasizes replicable, high-volume success, whether in the sense of a Motown or that of an iTunes store. One of these is, as noted, a lack of adaptability or a slowness to react to changing conditions. One way to avoid this is to build a business from a more adaptive position from the startup phase. We will examine this from the perspective of the Lean Startup Model, below, and how it can be applied to ventures in music.

Adaptive Organizing Principles: Lean Startup

As already noted, it is important to recognize whether a business emphasizes creation and creative productivity as an input, or is working to distribute and/or curate already produced content. On the creative end of the spectrum—the artist or band as startup business—we find that the principles of the Lean Startup (introduced in chapter 1) align extremely well both with the inherent challenges of producing one's own creative output and with the emphasis on DIY production and promotion in the contemporary marketplace. In particular, both the idea of quickly getting to a minimum viable product (MVP) and learning to "fail quickly and fail cheaply" have a tremendous value for self-funding musicians early in their careers.

Examples of how the MVP applies to music ventures include demo recordings and low-stakes gigs in small, local venues (see chapter 1). More significant, however, is how often bands just starting out almost unavoidably (though usually unconsciously) adopt the Lean Startup method of connecting with "actual or potential customers" very early in the process, before they are necessarily very good at what they do.

Entrepreneur and author Brinkley Warren describes it this way:

> Starting lean is all about putting together what might best be described as a shitty, buggy and generally worthless tech product, and releasing it to potential customers as soon as possible, and constantly updating the product and releasing it in short batches over and over and over again until you find a sustainable business model. To me this is similar to punk rock. They make a shitty song, and then they take it to the clubs and tour with it over and over and over, playing night after night until they start nailing it and it becomes a fan favorite.[5]

This is a story that could be told about virtually any musical artist from any era. There is the de facto assumption that before an intermediary business signs an artist to a recording, publishing, or promotional deal, this early phase will have already been completed. It may in fact have already cycled through a series of startups, pivots, and adaptive changes before that happens. From the perspective of Lean Startup theory, this is the build-measure-learn cycle (see chapter 1 for more).

Given that this is how most artist careers/businesses get started, a question to ask is, to what extent is this applicable to other production businesses in music that don't begin with music making? That is, what about those that start further along the production chain in music?

One of the key issues has to do with the closeness of the relationship between the business and the listeners and/or customers. Music-oriented businesses that are thriving today place a heavy emphasis on presenting live performances. That is, they put a musical product/experience in front of people who then demonstrate how much or how little they like it in a direct way. Either they buy tickets or they don't.

A festival like Coachella, for example, thrives by selling tickets (as well as other things, see chapter 5). It is by no means "lean" at this point in its development. But there are other concert experience options that could be.

Lean Startup Concert Production: House Concerts

One way to look for Lean Startup potential in an entrepreneurial idea is from the perspective of the minimum viable product (MVP). As noted, a "lean" approach to concert promotion is difficult to see, particularly if you are using an established festival as a template. In an earlier era, high schools hosted weekly dances for their students and hired local bands to perform. Small bars—then and now—pay minimal amounts to musicians to provide entertainment for their patrons. In the case of the high school dances, though bands used the "high school dance circuit" to launch and promote careers, the high school was not in the promotion business. For bars, music was also an ancillary activity. A bar is in the business of selling drinks.

But what if you wanted to apply Lean Startup thinking to concert promotion, not as an ancillary activity to another business, but as the primary focus? What would the MVP look like for that?

Obviously you need someone performing music live and someone listening to it at a given place and time. So the first question to be answered is, where will this happen? For an increasing number of aspiring presenters, the answer is at home.

Presenting a concert at your house affords one particular advantage. Your home is a space that you control, either by ownership or by an existing rental agreement. There is little to no overhead for venue location or acquisition. In addition, amenities like food and drink can be relatively easily provided. In fact, in a number of ways presenting a house concert is a great deal like hosting a party. If you have ever thrown a party at your house for a few dozen friends, you already have done a good bit of the basic work for hosting a concert.

Consider this experience of Frank Sullivan and Maribeth Sayers, described in 2013 as "newcomers to the house concert model":

> About 40 people are due to arrive, most[ly] friends and family, at "Chez Saysull," as those regular visitors dubbed it many get-togethers ago. ("We just call it home," Frank says.) But as promising the aroma of jambalaya, they're coming for something else than good food and drink. A sign on the back door reveals the nature of this evening's festivities: "Performing Tonite: Callaghan. Cover: $20."
>
> This isn't just a party for Frank and Maribeth. They're putting on a concert. The kitchen will double as a record store, with the window sill as a makeshift merch table. One of the house's three bedrooms does double duty as a green room, and the stage will be in the living room near the picture window. Later, when it's all over, the kitchen will become the post-show meet and greet area for those holding a VIP pass, which in this case will be everyone.[6]

In one sense, this kind of event works because it is exactly the kind of low-stakes, local audience–connected venture that has sparked music scenes in clubs from Austin to New York.

But for house presenters, the stakes are even lower, in that the venue is "home" and the connection, both to the audience and to the artists, is more personal.

As noted, if you've hosted a party with food and music and friends, you have a proof of concept for a house concert. Just adding a live performer to that party instead of a recorded playlist produces your MVP. The build-measure-learn loop of your parties—people didn't eat the deviled eggs, but loved hummus—applies also to the music and amenities of concerts.

The house concert phenomenon emerged early in the 2000s and was largely driven by artists seeking low-stakes, intimate opportunities to connect with existing fans and make new ones:

> In 2001, Pat DiNizio of the Smithereens logged 70 shows (and more than 65,000 miles) in his five-month "Living Room Tour." Emerging bands like Brooklyn septet Ava Luna supplement club dates with shows in quasi-professional DIY performance spaces and private homes, veteran artists like Pere Ubu's David Thomas offer fans the chance to book living room shows and current acts like Atlantic's Scars on 45 perform house dates, as well.[7]

As more and more people got involved with hosting shows—with motivations ranging from just liking them to thinking of it as a secondary revenue source—a "side hustle"—it became an increasingly standard part of live performance strategies, particularly for singer-songwriters.

This is an important fact, because it reflects the inherent constraints on presenting a concert in a private home: limited space for attendees, limited space to perform, and volume limits based on room size and neighbors. An acoustic performance with a single performer self-accompanying on guitar fits all those parameters. Not only is this kind of performance a good fit logistically and appealing to people who like music and parties; presenters like Sullivan and Sayers "are helping reshape the business of touring, if not music consumption entirely."[8]

That statement about reshaping touring and music consumption is not hyperbole. The fact that house concerts represent a synergy between presenters and performers that connects performers to audiences, monetizes the connection (in multiple ways, including selling merchandise), and reduces cost of touring (house concert hosts typically provide bed and breakfast amenities to artists) is powerful. The world of house concerts and house concert tours, the hosts, and the audiences who like to attend them represents a complex adaptive system that operates both independently and collaboratively—or at least noncompetitively—with larger-scale, commercial concert activities.

In addition to adaptivity, there is also the issue of how a company treats the interrelated issues of innovation and risk avoidance. When you are just beginning a venture, there are of course risks in terms of time, energy, and capital. But in this phase, when there is everything to gain from finding the right approach, it is easier to be adaptive and open to new ideas. In the case of a failed house concert, however, it's not that much worse than throwing a bad party.

It cost money and was no fun. You move on.

But once an approach is established and you've had some success, there is a natural and almost unavoidable tendency to shift to replicating success and avoiding failure (see, for example, the discussion of Ed Catmull and Pixar under "Further Consideration").

This tendency is amplified as the activities of a business scale upward. If, for example, Frank Sullivan and Maribeth Sayers wanted to franchise their house concerts across the northeastern United States, their activities would be less like a party and more like a business, with attendant increases in costs and risks. At the same time, the impulse to take house concerts to scale is inevitable. And, as with any other business model based on expanded production, distribution, and monetization, growing the house concert model favors formal corporate rather than informal individual structures.

Airbnb is an excellent example:

Many people think of Airbnb as the poster child for disruption: leveraging the sharing economy to democratize participation in the travel & hospitality marketplace, turning those industries on their heads. Now, the $31 billion startup is building a similar business case for music—and no one in the traditional music industry seems to be looking.

In November 2016, Airbnb expanded beyond its core Homes business
with the launch of Experiences, a highly-curated platform through which
travelers can book single- and multi-day activities and excursions with
locals. At the 2018 Code Conference last month, Airbnb CEO Brian Chesky
revealed that the Experiences product is growing 10 times faster than
Homes, with the former reaching 1.5 million bookings a year.

Music, one of the most powerful barometers of local culture and identity, naturally took prominence in Experiences, and Airbnb decided to
honor the trend with the launch of a separate Concerts page in February
2018. As of press time, Airbnb Concerts has a relatively small footprint—17
cities across Europe, North America and Asia—but the company antici-
pates that number climbing to between 50 and 100 cities by the end of 2018,
with the flow of concert guests growing to 20,000 per month.[9]

This is a classic example of the advantages of scale and resource management that corporate entities provide. At the same time, it also exemplifies the distancing effect of scale and incorporation. While house concerts driven by artist and host connections are personal and intimate,
the relationship between Airbnb the corporation and any given host or
artist is considerably more formal and remote. While the company "is
banking on intimacy,"[10] they plan to leverage the scale of their connections to optimize their impact on the small live concert sector.

Despite the presence of businesses like Sofar Sounds (launched
2009), Groupmuse (2013), Little Concert (2016), and Side Door (2017) in
what we may call the house concert aggregation market, the resources
of "a gargantuan travel platform like Airbnb" will obviously be significant. While this will have an obvious impact on independent presenters
and artists

> it's not only independent and DIY acts who are jumping on the opportunity:
> John Legend is hosting a sold-out Airbnb show for 48 lucky fans at a secret
> location in Downtown LA this Thursday, donating 100% of the ticket prices
> to his own criminal justice reform initiative FREEAMERICA.[11]

Airbnb's entry into the concert sector is, in a sense, an inevitable
result of changing circumstances in the music industry, the (sharing)

economy, and society at large. It exploits a number of factors that are changing music production-consumption, including an increasing reliance on live shows as a revenue source for the industry and the recognition that personalized and customizable experiences are increasingly important to music fans. As a result, the impact of Airbnb Concerts on the major venues and presenters may be even greater than for independents.

In the view of author and musician Cherie Hu:

> For the live events industry—which is currently dominated by corporate behemoths like Live Nation and AEG—the ramifications of a race towards intimacy are significant. [In a] recent online survey that Airbnb Concerts conducted among 2,000 Americans, not only did 69% of respondents agree or strongly agree that they are more likely to discover a new favorite artist in an intimate venue than in a large venue, but 78% of frequent concert-goers (five or more concerts a year) also agreed that intimate concert venues make for a better experience overall than large stadiums.[12]

From an aggregation perspective, this trend means different things, depending on where you stand in the marketplace. For Airbnb and other connecting aggregators, this is a clear win, in that it is a way to take advantage of the "long tail" of the live performance economy (see chapter 4, for more on this economic theory). For independent artists and promoters, this kind of aggregation affords more opportunity to tour and less time spent on the discovery and logistics of individual house concerts. For listeners, this situation increases the number of opportunities to see musicians in an intimate setting and to use the global reach of an Airbnb to connect music to curated tourism.

For presenters, venues, and touring artists using the mass audience, global stadium tour model, this may be a less encouraging development. Institutionalized house concerts have the potential to "steal" attendees from big-ticket tours and capture them with intimate, customized experiences.

Finally, whether a business adopts a strategy that emphasizes replicable success or is designed to be inherently adaptive and, if necessary, self-disrupting, it inevitably operates within a complex adaptive system that includes the entire creation-production-reception continuum. In order to consider all production and reception factors of music enterprise in their many interactions, we return to complexity theory as it is applied to business.

COMPLEX SYSTEM—BUSINESS

In an article from 2011, Tim Sullivan, Editorial Director at *Harvard Business Review Press,* described complex adaptive systems as having three characteristics:

> The first is that the system consists of a number of heterogeneous agents, and each of those agents makes decisions about how to behave. The most important dimension here is that those decisions will evolve over time. The second characteristic is that the agents interact with one another. That interaction leads to the third—something that scientists call emergence: In a very real way, the whole becomes greater than the sum of the parts. The key issue is that you can't really understand the whole system by simply looking at its individual parts.[13]

We have looked at numerous examples of the interactions of agents across the domains of creation, production, and reception and how new patterns emerge and the system evolves. But a critical issue, cited by Sullivan, is that understanding the actions and interactions of individuals does not necessarily explain the global system. As noted previously, creating a "hit record" is more than the sum of the individual actions of artist, record label, media, and consumer. The aggregate result "emerges" or it doesn't.

That doesn't prevent individuals and business from trying to understand what works and manipulate the system to increase opportunities for success. In fact, Gell-Mann describes a process of monitoring results, adjusting actions accordingly, and making adaptive changes of varying levels of intensity, depending on the results observed. But, per Sullivan, since the individual rarely understands or even sees the complexity from a global perspective, it is difficult to correctly interpret cause and effect (for nonlinear analysis of CAS, see the discussion of Edgar Morin, below). The antidote for this tendency, Sullivan suggests, includes having diverse points of view in an organization that challenge the consensus (the schema), paying attention to the data/results, and empowering people to make decisions in line with the broad goals of the company.

The key factors in this framework are consensus-challenging thinking, paying attention to incoming data, and making local decisions that align with the global goals of the organization. These operational concepts are defined more specifically by Edgar Morin, who developed three principles to describe them: *dialogic, recursive,* and *holographic.*[14] Let's examine these in more detail and test their relevance to musical ventures.

The *dialogic principle* describes the capacity of a complex system to be both cooperative and competitive at the same time. As applied to the music industry, this principle can be seen in the fact that unpaid music file-sharing and legal purchases—physical and downloads—coexisted throughout the first two decades (so far) of the twenty-first century, despite legal actions and multiple rights management strategies. In this sense, we can view the development of the iTunes store as a mechanism that optimized the dialog/conflict between traditional record label and the online music community. The rise of Spotify, followed by record labels buying stock in the company, was a further optimization of competition/cooperation.

The *recursive principle* refers to the capacity of a complex business system to adapt to environmental factors. In some complexity theories this is also referred to as "emergent" behavior. Recursion is the key factor that makes it difficult to distinguish causes from effects, since "the products and the effects are at the same time causes and producers" in a system. Thus shared files, a product of the file-sharing structure of Napster, became a primary cause for the emergence of paid downloads. The effect of the iTunes store—convenient digital downloads on demand—became a cause for the increased convenience of streaming.

Finally, the *holographic principle* holds that each element of a complex system expresses the characteristics of the entire system. In business, this is evidenced by macro- and microeconomic relationships. In the beginning, the key to making the iTunes store work was for the convenience of on-demand delivery of individual songs afforded by Napster to be maintained in each transaction with individual iTunes users.

At the macro level, the deals Steve Jobs struck with major labels required the same elements: on-demand access to individual songs, the convenience of a large database of digital music, and increased copyright protection. This aligned well, except at the micro level, copyright restrictions were the source of the greatest customer dissatisfaction with the early version of the iTunes experience. This misaligned "holography" was adjusted in later releases of the iTunes software.

In reference to the complex adaptive system of house concerts, at the micro level all the relationships are personal; artists connect with individuals, come to their home, and perform for friends and family of the host. Even when the concept is scaled upward to include a corporate entity like Airbnb, the artist-to-host-to-audience intimacy and connection must be maintained for the system to remain appealing and workable. Despite the expanded scale, the importance of local promotion by hosts is an explicit part of the macro Airbnb plan—a holographic expression of the personal values at the macro level of the system.

Businesses that embody all three of these principles tend to be more sustainable than those that do not, particularly during periods of disruption and change. It is clear, for example, that Airbnb must coexist and compete both with smaller, independent house concert presenters and artists, as well as with large-scale tours, venues, and festivals. Their model is based on artists needing more than one scale on which to tour and larger promoters benefiting from seeing the results of smaller, locally based tours. The Airbnb model is thus fully dialogic.

In terms of recursion, the successes of the small house concert model and independent "living room" tours are both the product of the DIY house concert movement and a cause for scaling the model upward using corporate resources. The company correctly recognizes that they must both respect the small- and large-scale competition (dialogic) and protect the intimate, personal connectivity of the original DIY versions even on a mass scale (holographic).

One way to look at prototyping a new initiative—in presenting or some other aspect of music production—is to look at it from the perspective of Morin's three principles. See "Conceptual Prototype Question" below.

SUCCESSFUL COMPLEX ADAPTIVE STRUCTURES

As discussed in a number of places in this text, the conditions that prevailed in the music industry following the introduction of digital audio and online access to music were both disruptive to existing business models and favorable to innovative ones. In the context of this chapter, we looked at innovation in the live performance sector from both ends of the spectrum, from the small and informal to the massive and corporate: from Frank and Maribeth's living room concert to Airbnb Concerts.

There are many other innovators who have created organizations for the complex twenty-first-century music economy. These include Tidal (see chapter 1), Mycelia (discussed in some detail in chapter 11), and the artist-oriented record label Mind of a Genius (see below). Despite significant differences in means and methods, a characteristic shared by all of these ventures is that they are adaptive and purpose-built to function in the complex adaptive system that is the postdigital music industry.

Mind of a Genius

Mind of a Genius (MOAG) is a Los Angeles–based record label founded in 2013. According to a review in 2018 of "independent labels you show know," MOAG "is built for the modern age of music, but they're not catering to the fast-food approach of quantity over quality."[15]

In a very real sense, the label is not only "modern"; they are also cognizant of and inspired by iconic independent labels XL Recordings and Motown. "We're all about nurturing artists in their own creative habitat," Dann says, "and not changing or altering their initial vision of where they want to go."[16]

Providing that "creative habitat" depends upon managing the physical plant of the label and studio and aligning it with the artists' and label's mystique. Thus, coming to the label to interview founder David Dann is like coming there to record a track or streaming a song by a relatively unknown MOAG artist: holographic.

> An unassuming one-story grey house serves as the home of rising record label *Mind of a Genius* and its enigmatic artists. An open lounge area drowned in natural light opens up to three dimly lit production rooms where all four artists signed to the label create. Step outside, walk three steps to the neighboring building, and you're in the office of David Dann, the 26-year-old founder and CEO of MOAG who opened up shop in 2013 in the same space that reportedly served as David Geffen's old studio in the '80s.
>
> ZHU, Gallant, THEY, and Klangstof all call this studio on South Robertson Boulevard their musical home. As a collective, Mind of a Genius' sound is organic and emotionally piercing. Each artist takes cues from respective influencers and lands in a place where the nostalgia of cult favorites like Radiohead meets the innovation of transcendent electronics. They're united in their ambiguity; you're as likely to hear the artists descending the depths of an abandoned warehouse party in Brooklyn—which ZHU did back in 2014—as you are to hear them on Beats 1 these days.
>
> All of these artists have singles to their name that have earned them much-deserved buzz along with swelling fan bases. However, none of them have released full albums just yet and remain well below the showy surface of their Instagram-dominating counterparts. For Mind of a Genius, being invisible is not a problem—it's the solution.[17]

Where an organization like Mycelia is consciously concerned with working with the largest database of music connecting all the music makers and their audiences, MOAG is collaborating with a few artists at a time to reach a tightly focused group of listeners. Both are in a competitive/complementary relationship with the production/distribution sector of the music industry. Mycelia aggregates artists to bring the resources of the macro corporations like Spotify to the micro level. MOAG seeks to make the intensely personal musical experiences of its founder, David Dann, available to the world.

He describes the journey to founding MOAG this way:

"I'm going to quit the DJ thing and I'm going to start this vision for a label that was going to reflect all of my favorite taste of music growing up," he says. "I didn't grow up in a traditional fatherly and motherly home, so music was my guide through life. I want to be able to give the fans and listeners that same outlet if they're growing up in a similar setting as I did."[18]

There are other successful business models built for complex adaptivity in music today. Some have been out for a while, some have just emerged, and some are still being prototyped. Some of them are listed in the "Further Consideration" section below.

Regardless of the scale and legal formality of the structure, collaborative relationships are an essential part of the creation-production-reception/consumption cycle. For those who begin on the creative end of the continuum—like forming a band—early arrangements are based on musical skill and social compatibility, and not necessarily in that order. Others may begin with partners who know one another and share common experiences. Often, it is only when success happens that business decisions must be made and legal relationships established. It's harder then.

Because of that, it is worth considering one final aspect of the holographic principle. The simplest, smallest unit of a complex system contains the essence of the entire system. At the most informal stage, give some thought to the kind of corporation you would need to form to fulfill your long-term goals. Bands and artists that have done so have tended to last a long time.

That's worth considering.

CRITICAL CONCEPTS

· People want to make music. They and/or other people will seek to sell it. In the process of making and selling music, people will form collaborative relationships in support of those goals.

· To succeed and thrive any music business must be built to create and balance multiple forms of value, even when the processes are different, and the goals sometimes contradict one another.

· In disruptive times, organizations built for adaptivity and that align with the principles of complex adaptive systems (dialogic, recursive, and holographic) tend to survive and thrive.

FURTHER CONSIDERATION

Musical Franchise: Trans-Siberian Orchestra

· Marah Eakin, "105 Shows, 61 Cities, 1 Holiday Season: How Does Trans-Siberian Orchestra's Tour Work?," *A.V. Club,* November 28, 2016, https://music.avclub.com/105-shows-61-cities-1-holiday-season-how-does-trans-1798255053

Building A Creative Culture and Organization

One consequence of failure avoidance is that the brilliant and unprecedented thinking that launched the business can all too easily become something that is "managed away," constrained by the routine operating practices that emerge following early success. One way of dealing with this tendency is expressed in the "core principles" for "building a creative culture" developed by Ed Catmull at Pixar.

See:

· www.creativityincbook.com/7-core-principles/
· https://hbr.org/2008/09/how-pixar-fosters-collective-creativity

Then consider the Disney/Pixar merger and the impact of sequels and franchise-oriented thinking on the studio.

- www.theringer.com/movies/2018/6/15/17466820/pixar-sequels-incredibles-2-disney-toy-story-finding-nemo-dory

Complex Adaptive Business Models
- Audience Experience Exchange
  - https://techcrunch.com/2017/03/02/music-audience-exchange-wants-to-get-musicians-paid/
- Ujo Music (see also chapter 11)
  - https://ujomusic.com
  - http://musically.com/2017/08/04/ujo-music-blockchain-uphill-battle-existing-companies/
- SingularDTV (see also chapter 11)
  - https://stocksgazette.com/2018/04/11/singulardtv-sngls-is-the-new-bizarre-cryptocurrency-on-the-market/
  - https://bitcoinmagazine.com/articles/singulardtv-a-decentralized-netflix-on-ethereum-1472760808/
- Bittunes (also briefly discussed in chapter 8)
  - http://music.bittunes.com/micro-earnings/
- Musical.ly (see also chapter 12)
  - http://musically.com
  - www.usatoday.com/story/tech/news/2017/04/21/musically-what-is-it-parents-guide-lip-syncing-app/100694200/
- Lean and Scalable Concert Promotion
  - Cherie Hu, "Why Airbnb Is a Dark Horse in Live Music's Intimate Future," www.forbes.com/sites/cheriehu/2018/06/19/why-airbnb-is-a-dark-horse-in-live-musics-intimate-future/#2dbde04b4c16

CONCEPTUAL PROTOTYPE QUESTIONS

Let's say you want to explore the idea of hosting a house concert. Let's also take it as a given that in the community where you live there is support for this idea. You are aware that some people are doing it already, but not too many, and not in the music sector that interests you.

You've thrown parties and people like them. They like your party play-lists. You are ready to take the next step.

In addition to the established prototyping steps we've applied in previous chapters, once you are sure you understand your customers (guests and performers) and what they want, you have a minimum viable product, and are prepared to carefully examine the data you get from putting your idea into action, let's take another step.

Apply Morin's three principles to your conceptual prototype.

- *Is it dialogic?* What is the competition and what are the complementary resources? How does what you intend to offer add to the scene? What can you leverage or optimize when you do so? Do you have a friend that does studio art or fashion? Can you combine graphic design, an art gallery, or a fashion show with your event? Is someone in culinary school? Is there a local pop-up restaurant or food cart that would like to cross promote with your event?

- *Is it recursive?* Do other local events naturally connect to yours? What has happened that leads inevitably to the creation of your product? Did a local studio open and throw a party to which people came, but they didn't like the food? Did you meet people there who complained about the lack of small-scale performance opportunities that were supportive of creativity and social connection? What will the successful launch of your MVP event cause elsewhere in the scene? Will your success be the result and/or cause of the success of others? How so?

- *Is it holographic?* What is the overall purpose and guiding philosophy of your event? Good music, good people, good food? All of the above? Will that overall purpose be clear in everything you do, from publicity to execution? Will every guest, every artist, and every neighbor have the same experience?

II

Aggregation

Consumption, Production, Prediction

At its simplest the music business is about bringing listeners together and playing music for them. When the number of listeners increases, the opportunities for musicians to expand their reputation and grow their income increase as well. From another perspective, once a musician has music to play, the next job is to gather an audience. Much of what we can talk about in terms of enterprise in music—theories, conceptual models, processes, organizations, laws, and case studies—relates to aggregation, of audiences, of artists, and of the music they create.

The aggregation of production and consumption on a mass scale is the function of the music industry. As we have seen in earlier chapters, one of the big lessons of the twentieth-century music marketplace is that "big" is better. At the same time, everyone has learned that the artist-to-audience connection remains at the heart of the music experience and is essential to the creation of value and meaning. Despite that, artists consistently find themselves "squeezed" between the limitations of their individual productivity and the ever-expanding corporations and structures of Big Labels, Big Concert Promotion, Big Licensing, Big Downloading, and Big Streaming.

In this chapter we consider the tools of aggregation. We will begin with the methods by which producers aggregate information about listeners and consumers and how those methods have evolved and continue to change. We will look at the aggregation of producers by distributive media and how data—about listeners, listening habits, recorded product, and curated playlists—have created a new web of aggregative possibilities. In this framework artists, producers, and listeners are all both consumers and product.

Describing companies like Pandora, Spotify, Google, Amazon, and Apple—to name a few "bigs"—as driven by data is now commonplace, but the significance of that description is, if anything, an understatement of the increasing importance of data. The digitization of music production, distribution, and consumption has provided an amazingly rich trove of information about who listens and to what. As a result, the music production sector—both live and recorded—is increasingly guided by analyzing and applying data. The publishing sector—particularly in the management of mechanical, performance, and synchronization rights—is looking to data systems to make it easier for customers to license music and to equitably collect and distribute royalties to creators/producers.

Beyond operational concerns, a significant part of how "Big Data" is transforming music is in the realm of prediction. As noted in the previous chapter and in several other places in this book, risk assessment and reduction are a major factor for decision-making in the music business. As data collection and analysis become more pervasive and the interpretation of data becomes more sophisticated, businesses are emerging whose primary productivity is prediction about future production and consumption.

The impact of data analytics is, of course, extending well beyond the music industry. For example, money and financial transactions may be disrupted by cryptocurrencies like Bitcoin and established payment and contractual practices by blockchain technologies. Everyone is now aware that "data" are something vital and that "data analytics" are a critical tool for success.

And it's not just the other "bigs" who are venturing into the world of big data. We will also look at data-based tools designed to empower independent artists that also aggregate them as customers and products.

AGGREGATING AUDIENCES/CONSUMERS

The chart system that has been the basis of record sales data for a century—beginning with Billboard's Pop, R & B, and Country categories—was always a rough guide intended to describe, first, the demographics of customers (wealthy/working class, Black/White, and urban/rural, for example) and, second, the music.

Both the approximate nature the chart categories and their after-the-fact quality (based on record sales from the previous week) made the Billboard charts reactive at best. This is one reason why the emergence of new musical genres has so often surprised the established industry, why new artists failed, and why imitation of established musical formulas proved to be such a persistent characteristic of major label thinking.

Among the independent labels, whose geographic and stylistic scope tended to be much more limited, decisions about artists to be signed and records produced were more often based on direct observation of the reactions of local audiences to live performances of rising bands (see chapter 6, "Location"). Once such local music was distributed to larger areas, specific information about what people were going to buy was more difficult to get and made the larger distribution strategy more speculative.

One of the advantages that broadcast radio provided to the twentieth-century recording industry was the information that local stations could get from their listeners about songs on the air. Call-in request shows were one direct measure of popularity for a specific group of listeners at a given time and place. As the century came to an end, younger listeners began to move from commercial radio, first to college radio in the 1980s and then to the Internet in the late 1990s and early 2000s. This meant that radio became less reliable as a gauge of the listening marketplace, let alone the larger listening culture.

This declining influence of broadcast radio for music discovery and the shift to digital audio were context for Parker and Fanning as they developed Napster. They believed that the capacity of web-based sharing platforms to collect individual data about users and the music they "shared" could be invaluable both to artists and to labels. The idea was not, however, appealing to most representatives of the music industry circa 2000. It was forward-looking, anticipating the rise of data-driven decisions in the music industry some years in the future. But it held little interest at the time for labels that couldn't yet imagine how important data and data analytics would become.

That reactionary thinking did not last. In the second decade of the twentieth century, data and data analytics have an unprecedented influence on popular commercial music. But years before Napster, the Billboard charts made a shift to a data-driven model that was almost as disruptive as P2P file sharing itself.

SoundScan, From Anecdote to Data

Billboard began as a magazine for the billboard advertising business in 1894. It shifted relatively quickly to focus on entertainment, both live performances and emerging technologies (the record player, for example). In 1936, "Billboard published the first pop chart based on record sales."[1] In fact, it published three of them, one for each of the three leading record labels of the time: Columbia, Brunswick, and RCA-Victor. By 1940, "Billboard was producing its own unified chart by asking what was selling well at 50 stores."[2]

It was the "asking" part that became the problem.

For the next fifty years, "the magazine used a survey method, in which staff members called record stores and retail outlets all over the

U.S. and took the managers' word on what had been selling during the past week."[3]

This was not a perfect system.

Stores could pass along inaccurate information based on poor record keeping, lapses of memory, or a desire to "hype" a record for which they had a lot of inventory. Or a store might actively try to game the system, encouraged by "gifts" from record label promotions staff:

> "In the past, the major labels gave away refrigerators and microwaves to retailers in exchange for store reports," Tom Silverman, then the chairman of the Tommy Boy indie label, told the *New York Times* in 1992. The allegations weren't sour grapes from an indie guy who couldn't compete. In the same article, the president of Tower Records confirmed the practice among his employees, despite decrying it.[4]

All of that changed on May 25, 1991, when Billboard introduced a new method for ranking the 200 Top Albums by using a data-driven method created by a company called SoundScan. The company began in 1987 as a system designed by former radio DJ and marketing expert Mike Shalett and his partner, Mike Fine. Their goal was to have a way to accurately track record sales using computerized records of every in-store transaction in the country:

> "The TV and movie and clothing and grocery industries have taken this kind of information for granted for years," Fine told the *Los Angeles Times* in 1991. "We realized that there had never been an accurate method in the music business to track actual sales and we figured the time was ripe for change."[5]

Their target customers were individual record labels, but comparable to the response accorded to Napster nine years later, no labels were interested in 1990. Billboard, however, was. As soon as the first chart using the system appeared, objections were raised by record labels because the new numbers differed significantly from the previous method based on record store self-reporting.

Shalett found that ironic.

"The chart is not the primary advantage of SoundScan," Shalett said. "The chart is a byproduct of the entire information management system. We designed the system so that it would provide information for the record business that is standard in almost every other industry."[6]

Ultimately, SoundScan—today, Nielsen SoundScan—became the benchmark for tracking record sales and soon labels were all subscribing to the service. They had little choice as the new system revealed what was truly popular as opposed to what the labels assumed (and had, along with retail personnel, gamed the old system) to be. This was not just a business issue either. The broad understanding of musical taste was impacted as well. As listeners followed popular trends as revealed by the actual sales data, producers inevitably followed:

> The best example of the changing musical landscape forged by SoundScan is Nirvana and the band's blockbuster album *Nevermind*. Would it have been a blockbuster before SoundScan? A 1992 article in *Spin* magazine deemed a No. 1 album by Nirvana "unthinkable" before the new era, suggesting that the "charts don't just report tastes; they amplify and shape them."[7]

The SoundScan era provided a boost for alternative and genre music generally, and for Hip Hop in particular. The impact of this first data-driven sales tracking system did not end in the 1990s. Nielsen SoundScan began tracking downloaded music and adding those numbers into the charts. Billboard became one of the first places to see the actual numbers as downloaded singles and albums began to catch up to and then pass physical sales. Even bigger changes followed in 2014 when Nielsen SoundScan began to incorporate on-demand streaming data into the sales charts using TEA (ten downloaded tracks or singles equals one album) and SEA (fifteen hundred streams equals one album) equivalences (see chapter 5).

While Billboard's charts are still widely used and are updated to reflect new patterns of access and consumption, there are ongoing challenges to interpreting the data that the system collects. Part of the difficulty is the rate of change. New technologies appear and are adopted by a significant slice of the listening public, but not every one of them produces sales, certainly not in the sense of that word during the physical product era. The SEA/TEA metrics are an attempt to create a point of comparison but it is an imperfect system. Companies like Pandora, Spotify, and Shazam—to name only three—collect much more data than simple sales figures. This information impacts listeners and their decisions about music listening and/or purchasing, but is difficult to meaningfully incorporate into the charts.

Recommendations and Predictions

One of the added-value dimensions of online streaming services is the recommendation function, which is also data-driven. The Music Genome Project, the algorithm behind Pandora, sifts through 450 pieces of information about the sound of a recording. For example, a song might feature the drums as being one of the loudest components of the sound, compared to other elements. That measurement is a piece of data that can be incorporated into the larger model. Pandora then uses that and other data to help listeners find music that is similar in sound to what they have enjoyed in the past.[8]

In a practical sense, the Music Genome Project transcends traditional definitions of genre. According to musicologist and American music scholar Brian Moon, "Genre is only one of 450 pieces of information that's being used to classify a song, so if it sounds like 75 percent of rock songs, then it likely counts as rock."[9]

Shazam takes the idea of songs as data a step further. The app was designed to identify songs when users hold a phone to a sound source. Shazam began as a startup—founded in 2000 by Avery Wang and some college friends—to develop a smartphone app "that could identify any song within a few seconds, using only a cellphone, even in a crowded bar or coffee shop."[10]

According to a profile in the *Atlantic* (2014):

At first, Wang, who had studied audio analysis and was responsible for building the software, feared it might be an impossible task. No technology existed that could distinguish music from background noise, and cataloging songs note for note would require authorization from the labels. But then he made a breakthrough: rather than trying to capture whole songs, he built an algorithm that would create a unique acoustic fingerprint for each track. The trick, he discovered, was to turn a song into a piece of data.[11]

But the real value of Shazam was to collect information about the listening habits of 150 million active users per month. When Apple acquired the company in December 2017 (see the discussion of the aggregation of producers and roles, below), Shazam was estimated to serve three hundred to four hundred million people annually.[12] But the app is more than a popular tool to attach a title and an artist to a heard song. By tracking the number, timing, and location of queries about a particular song, Shazam becomes predictive. According to Jason Titus, former Chief Technology Officer of Shazam, "Sometimes we can see when a song is going to break out months before most people have even heard of it."[13]

Using such data, record executives and tour promoters could make decisions about how to market an artist, in terms of both products and activities. Because the data is collected in real time, as listeners experience music and want to know what it is and who's performing it, it shifts the influence of public opinion earlier in the production-reception process. Instead of being anecdotal like early Billboard charts or accurate but after-the-fact like the SoundScan data, collected on already completed record sales, Shazam accurately tracks interest in a song, as it happens.

As reported by Derek Thompson, who writes about media and economics and who has followed the impact of data on music and entertainment:

> "We know where a song's popularity starts, and we can watch it spread," Titus told me. Take, for example, Lorde, the out-of-nowhere sensation of 2013. Shazam's engineers can rewind time to trace the international

contagion of her first single, "Royals," watching the pings of Shazam searches spread from New Zealand, her home country, to Nashville (a major music hub, even for noncountry songs), to the American coasts, pinpointing the exact day it peaked in each of nearly 3,000 U.S. cities.[14]

Shazam is a leader in a business sector that focuses on data collection and analysis not only to understand music listener choices but also to predict future behavior. For some, like Shazam, HitPredictor, and Next Big Sound (now a part of Pandora), this is a core business. Others like Spotify and Pandora, for example, use data predictively both internally and for the benefit of clients (Spotify for Artists, Pandora for Brands, and so on), as well as for song recommendations and playlists. Companies like Apple with their acquisition of Shazam continue to position themselves to incorporate all aspects of data aggregation—recommendations, playlists, prediction, and discovery (see below)—into their business models.

For more on competition in the chart and data analytics business, see "Further Consideration," at the end of the chapter.

AGGREGATING PRODUCERS

The key competitive advantage for twentieth-century aggregators of musical creativity—publishers, record labels, and broadcast media—was to accumulate listeners and generate sales on a mass scale. As labels merged into large, international music groups, publishers combined along similar lines, and media networks and conglomerates formed, these producers continued to control their production and distribution processes, and thus their musical and economic destinies.

With the advent of the online delivery of digital entertainment products, first through "sharing" sites like Napster in music and BitTorrent for visual media, record and film producers found themselves in a new and—from their perspective—undesirable position. Records—whether made by Atlantic Records, indie Sub Pop, or massive Sony Music Entertainment—all became raw material, first for the "pirates," then the iTunes store, and finally streaming services. As the importance of digital access became evident, record labels (like movie studios) lost any ability to hold out against it. They had to come to terms with such service providers.

We've already discussed Steve Job's role in the development of the Apple iTunes store at some length, so we won't go any further with that here. The relationship between record labels and Spotify has been discussed as well, particularly in terms of labels becoming Spotify investors and the Spotify IPO in 2018 and what that meant in terms of revenue for companies like Sony Music Entertainment, Warner Music Group, and Universal Music Group (see chapter 5). Here, we are not so much interested in the value of Spotify stock as in the power relationship between labels and the streaming service.

The study of music business history makes it clear that being in a position that allows your business to aggregate the productivity of others is a significant advantage. But at the beginning, as for Steve Jobs, who needed to persuade record labels to opt in to his digital download store, Spotify needed the labels more than the labels needed them:

> When Spotify launched in 2008, it had no power in the relationship since it had so few listeners. It needed to raise over $180 million in its first few years and pay the labels a huge upfront advance on royalty payments to convince them to let it launch in the US. Spotify also had to sell the labels equity so even if it succeeded, they'd be financially protected.[15]

One key to changing the power dynamic between labels and Spotify was for the streaming service to get more listeners, both paid subscribers and advertising-supported free service listeners. As of January 2018, the company had more than seventy million paid subscribers worldwide. Adding in Spotify's top competitors—Pandora, Apple Music, Google Play Music, Amazon Music Unlimited, and Tidal—there are over 245 million people listening to streaming music every month in the United States alone.[16] According the RIAA, in 2017 streaming accounted for 65% of all music revenue. While some individual (and very well-established) artists opted out (at least temporarily) of streaming, or joined to launch artist-oriented streaming services (like Tidal), streaming represents too much of the music marketplace for producers to ignore.

In addition, Spotify (along with other streaming services) drives discovery. The company's *Discovery Weekly* and *Release Radar* playlists generate personalized recommendations for its users based on past listening and algorithm-based recommendations. These are more than convenient features for listeners:

> They give Spotify newfound power to choose what artists and songs a large swath of its listeners hear. Instead of focusing on peer-to-peer sharing or direct channels between the artists and the fans, it's prioritized music discovery methods that put it in control. Spotify wants to take the place of the thousands of radio stations that record labels typically kiss up to.[17]

While the company denies that they weight recommendation playlists in favor of more cooperative labels, their influence over discovery clearly creates leverage. Although royalty payments represented nearly 80% of its 2017 revenue ($4.9 billion),[18] as Spotify diversifies into original content, including video and podcasts, their financial position will continue to improve.[19] In addition, Spotify could become—in effect—a record label and produce its own musical content. The entity that owns the content gets the royalties, so this would obviously be a great advantage for the company—and a real threat to record labels and music groups.

There are other initiatives that also have potential to marginalize the record production business. For example:

> Apple already offers up-front financial compensation in exchange for exclusivity, as Chance The Rapper just revealed he was paid $500,000 and given a commercial to make his album *Coloring Book* an Apple Music exclusive for the first two weeks.[20]

Tidal has offered similar exclusive deals and both companies have used such arrangements as a way to push back against Spotify's reach in the streaming sector. Apple has, in addition, provided funding for creative projects as part of such deals, including funding for songs and videos and providing promotional advertising support.[21]

Partly in response to such competition, Spotify is reportedly planning to go further and has explored making traditional label-style deals with artists to provide upfront financial support in exchange for streaming rights. In June 2018, Billboard reported that "Spotify has offered advances to a number of managers and indie acts in exchange for licensing their music directly to the streaming service."[22]

The report continues:

> Under the terms of some of the deals, management firms can receive several hundred thousand dollars as an advance fee for agreeing to license a certain number of tracks by their independent acts directly to Spotify. Then, in at least some cases, the managers and acts stand to earn 50 percent of the revenue per stream on those songs on Spotify. That's slightly less than the 54 percent of revenue the major record labels in the U.S. get per stream, on average, according to *Billboard*'s calculations, but major-label artists and their managers typically receive only 20 percent to 50 percent of the label's share, depending on an act's individual royalty rates, and don't usually get to own their master recordings.[23]

This type of deal, if true, falls short of the traditional contractual relationship between labels and artists. First, Spotify does not buy the copyrights to the recordings outright for the term of the contract, as labels have typically done. In addition, per Billboard, "the advances Spotify is offering are significantly smaller than the $1 million-plus sums that labels and independent distributors have been dangling lately to sign promising new acts."[24]

These Spotify artist/management deals are attractive. First, they permit separately licensing the same music to other streaming services at the same time and artists retain all of the revenue from such deals. In addition, although the royalty percentages are lower in these deals than under the arrangements with labels, independent artists will keep all of the revenue percentages here, where they typically get only a portion of the label share under the old structure.

In short, it is—for now—a limited launch into music content production for Spotify. They are, for one thing, limited in how far they can go by the terms of their deals with labels. But this does establish a scenario under which artists could remain independent of record labels altogether and license Spotify to distribute their music (as well as cutting separate deals with other services) in lieu of a traditional contract.

In that framework, the advance money is less, but retaining ownership of core copyrights is a significant value. Also, under this scenario, Spotify cuts its royalty costs and empowers independent artists to deal directly with them. Where the first phase of streaming was to aggregate labels as producers, this next stage could disintermediate them entirely.[25]

As important as the streaming sector is for access, for data analysis, and—potentially—for content creation and/or licensing, the issue of discovery is critical. As noted above, playlists are an important tool for connecting listeners to new music that, based on listening habits, streaming service users are predicted to like. But discovery in the digital era is more than that.

DATA-DRIVEN DISCOVERY

Getting people to discover music and engage with it is the essence of customer aggregation. Today, releasing new music online via YouTube, Bandcamp, SoundCloud, and many other platforms large and small has become a standard method for helping fans to find music. While understanding how to drive discovery of music has always been a pillar of the music industry, it was for most of the twentieth century based on broad strokes: radio promotion, appearances in other media (including print), and touring to ensure fan awareness of physical recordings. As noted above, information about those fans and transactions was often approximate, almost always well after the fact, and occasionally entirely made up.

Contemporary data access has changed all this and music entrepreneurs have come to look at discovery less as an art than as a science. But there are still questions about how best to use the new information that music apps and online discovery tools are designed to answer. According to an article in the *Guardian* in 2014, there are (or were then) five main tools for music discovery, "all of which have close ties to your smartphone and/or tablet" and rely upon insights provided by *friends, the "crowd," curators, algorithms,* and *serendipity.*[26] All of these, except the first and last, are inherent in twenty-first-century music services and they are doing their best to leverage your friends and serendipity, or luck, as well.

Friend-based discovery is certainly the oldest of the discovery methods. So using the mediated social platforms of the digital era seems like a logical extension. But early efforts—such as connecting your Facebook page to your streaming service plays in a continuous feed to your timeline—annoyed users, despite early optimism about its potential:

> You're connecting the app and your timeline together, adding all of the activity and history in the app to your timeline, and keeping them in sync going forward," said Zuckerberg at the time. "Being able to click on someone's music and play it is a great experience, but knowing that you helped a friend discover something new, and that you have the same taste in music, is awesome.[27]

But the unfiltered song lists proved unappealing and the company was forced to make it possible to disable the feature. The problem was simply that your Facebook friends do not necessarily share your musical tastes. The larger the list, the more problematic that became.

Soon services developed that allowed for a greater degree of discrimination. Spotify introduced its own "ticker-style feed" to show your friends—and only the ones you selected—what you were streaming with an option to email specific recommendations. Beyond that, Spotify's "Discover" option began to include recommendations based on what your designated friends were streaming as well.

Other music discovery apps, such as Soundwave Music Discovery and SoundTracking, provide feeds of what friends are listening to along with charts, playlists, and options for commentary, as well as the capacity to create "packages" of what you are listening to or viewing to push out to your friends. Shazam has also increased its options for social reference and recommendation (the "crowd"). Beyond the big streaming companies and others already mentioned, discovery-facilitating apps available in 2018 included Hype Machine, Jango Radio, ReverbNation Discover, 8tracks, SoundHound, TuneIn, Discovr, Clammer Radio, and Deezer.[28]

The tools to "tag" music in such a way that a meaningful recommendation along the lines of "if you like Artist A, you will probably like artist B" continue to be refined. Early attempts, such as the Music Genome pioneered by Pandora have been followed by others. Following its purchase in 2014 by Spotify, the Echo Nest's "director of developer platform Paul Lemere" stated:

> "Technology can really affect how we as listeners interact with music, and we are in the middle of this incredible digital music revolution where any song is just a few taps away," he said. "I think the next step in the music revolution is changing how we interact with music."[29]

Lemere continued to explain that "the future of listening" would be based on a deeper understanding of listeners and their habits than had previously been possible. He describes four categories of listeners: *savants, enthusiasts/engaged, casuals,* and *indifferents.* The savants spend more money on music per year and represent 10% of the listening public, the enthusiasts (20%) enjoy music but spend less (by a factor of 10), the casuals (30%) are not very engaged with music and spend little to nothing on it, and the indifferents (40%) rarely listen to or spend anything on music. (See chapter 9 for more on listener/audience types.)

In the Echo's Nest model as applied to Spotify, the savant and enthusiast listeners are considered to be already engaged and, therefore, the other 70% are the target group. This group of casual and indifferent listeners will be pursued with strategies that combine extremely low- or no-cost options along with greater ease of discovery. This is where the ability to predict musical taste becomes critical: for people who are unwilling to define their own playlists.

The strategy for making discovery easier was, first, to better understand listener's potential likes—which is a traditional music-marketing approach, updated by the available data provided by streaming services. Then, music must be aligned with what the Echo's Nest calls "taste profiles" based on personalized information (your smartphone indicating whether you are walking or sitting still while listening, for example), specific music characteristics, and apps that afford listeners an opportunity to engage interactively with songs.

More broadly, the Echo's Nest schema represents the potential for data analytics to understand consumers, artists, songs, and playlists across multiple service platforms. As of April 2019, the company's website (the.echonest.com) indicated that it had over 1.3 trillion data points about nearly forty million songs and four-plus million artists, serving over four hundred music applications, including, Spotify, Vevo, and MOG.

Crowd-referenced music is provided by essentially every aggregator of downloads and streams as are curated lists—whether done by humans or algorithms. In fact as curatorship in music is democratized by social media, anyone can publish their playlists to the world. Naturally, there are also apps to aggregate curators. As noted by the *Guardian:*

> Finding them [the many playlists] will be the challenge. Which is why there are already people curating the curators. The Playlists.net website—also available as an app—specialises in surfacing the best Spotify playlists.
>
> Meanwhile, for music blogs there are aggregators like Hype Machine and Shuffler.fm, which both have apps, including for the latter a new quarterly magazine app called Pause. If the thrust of modern technology is to make anyone—potentially—a curator, it's good that there are also tools to help identify the best ones.[30]

In summary, the most data-driven option for music discovery—and the one most appealing from a prediction/control perspective—is the development of algorithms that analyze music and individual listening habits and then combine the two. Despite the growing popularity of this approach and its impact on music production, the use of algorithms has also produced significant backlash. Music fans and professionals alike have expressed concerns about the potential for a dehumanizing effect on creation and reception. For more on that, see "AI and Music Creation," below.

ARTISTS AND AGGREGATION

As noted above, artists have often been marginalized in the decision-making processes of large producers and aggregators. Overall, this is one result of how the power of aggregation and analytics is of greater benefit to major labels and music groups than to independent artists and smaller labels.

There are, however, tools created specifically for or applicable to the needs of the independent music creator. This is a critical development for a number of reasons. One of the most significant is the impact of massively scaled streaming services on musical innovation generally:

> Some records can be made in a laptop, but some need musicians and skilled technicians. These things cost money. Pink Floyd's catalogue has already generated billions of dollars for someone (not necessarily the band), so putting it on a streaming site makes total sense. But if people had been listening to *Spotify* instead of buying records in 1973, I doubt very much if "Dark Side" would have been made. It would just be too expensive.[31]

Streaming music services have—to date—invested little into new artist and music development and production. Since label support for artist development and production has drastically decreased, that function has increasingly devolved outward and downward to individual artists. Increasingly, capitalization, production, promotion, and discovery have become DIY issues.

While a discussion of the full spectrum of "DIY aggregation" options is beyond the purposes of this discussion, it is worthwhile to take a closer look at the proliferation of data analytics services available to the individual.

An excellent example is Next Big Sound (NBS), a company established in 2009 by a group of musicians and fans. The creators of Next Big Sound were "inspired by a desire to figure out how bands and artists became famous. Then they realized that what they really wanted was to be able to identify 'the next Lady Gaga.'"[32]

According to one of the founders, Alex White:

> "The idea is that lying in these massive, massive data sets are untapped correlations and value that can be harnessed," says White. "If you can sift through and track and filter this data in meaningful ways, there is a huge opportunity in identifying the next big sound and understanding how markets and bands grow in popularity and spread."[33]

In its early business model, the company mined twenty social media sources for data related to individual bands, artists, and songs. In aggregate, these metrics formed a composite picture of online fan engagement—social, listening, and purchases—for every artist in the NBS database. Since Pandora acquired NBS, the Pandora Trendsetters chart has incorporated the

> Taxonomy of Artists research developed by the Next Big Sound team Based on a combination of social and streaming activity, artists are categorized into one of five stages: Undiscovered, Promising, Established, Mainstream, and Epic. In order to ensure that the artists captured on the Pandora Trendsetters chart can be considered emerging, artists are no longer eligible to appear once they have passed the Established stage.[34]

There are other music analytics services providing comparable information at varying price points, including Buzzdeck, Chartmetric, Gracenote, Music Fibre, and Musicmetric (purchased by Apple in 2015).

Despite this apparent democratization of the tools of music analytics for small-scale and individual music ventures, artists remain in a position of disadvantage vis-à-vis aggregation. In fact, "the network of businesses supporting DIY production, promotion, and monetization by independent artist-entrepreneurs also aggregates and exploits them."[35]

ARTIST-ORIENTED AGGREGATORS

Artists have not universally accepted marginal or consumerist roles. In an interview in 2015, singer/songwriter Imogen Heap and audio engineer and producer George Howard, founder of disruptive intermediaries TuneCore[36] and Music Audience Exchange,[37] explore the "wholesale reinvention" of the music industry. According to Imogen Heap:

> We need to begin again. With the artists and their music at the start and heart of their industries' future landscape. It's the only way. There is little to be kept, yet a lot to learn from the hotchpotch of services present today—from labels to distribution mechanisms. *We need to cut out the middlemen, of which, in the music industry, there are way more of them than there are artists; one reason perhaps why it is such a struggle to create a fair platform for artists from within the current landscape.* Music needs to breathe and so do the music makers.[38]

Heap further observed that despite reaching an unprecedented number of people with her music—which she values—"music, in itself, doesn't generate a fair income and reflect this growth. I'm more popular than ever but I'm earning less cash from the music itself."[39] She also notes that other revenue streams are available—synchronization, live performance, merchandise, and personal appearances:

> But not everyone is going to be able to sustain themselves with these alone (and you'd have to be an established artist to do so on the most part). Shouldn't we just at the very least, simply be able to make music and derive a fair amount of pay, directly linked to that? It also always feels as if there always has to be a clever business plan or marketing strategy to earn money from the music we make.
>
> So I thought: I'll put myself in the shoes of an unsigned act with no management and reimagine things a bit.... And when I do, I dream of a

kind of Fair Trade for music environment with a simple one-stop-shop-portal to upload my freshly recorded music, verified and stamped, into the world, with the confidence I'm getting the best deal out there, without having to get lawyers involved.[40]

Heap's response to this "dream" was to create Mycelia,[41] whose mission is

- To empower a fair, sustainable and vibrant music industry ecosystem involving all online music interaction services;
- To unlock the huge potential for creators and their music related metadata so an entirely new commercial marketplace may flourish;
- To ensure all involved are paid and acknowledged fully;
- To see that commercial, ethical and technical standards are set to exponentially increase innovation for the music services of the future;
- To connect the dots with all those involved in this shift from our current outdated music industry models, exploring new technological solutions to enliven and positively impact the music ecosystem.[42]

The final point in the mission statement is of particular significance. Essential to Heap's vision for Mycelia is how new technologies hold the potential to transform and disintermediate the artist-to-audience connection.

> It dawned on me a few months ago that the mechanism to create and sustain a place like Mycelia exists now with the help of blockchain technology and crypto-currencies. I am for the first time EVER, really excited and positive for the future of music and its industry; for artists old and (more importantly) new, along with the hyper enriched feedback loops that could exist with their listeners, collaborators and flag wavers.[43]

For Heap, the potential of blockchain technology as leveraged by an organization of artists like Mycelia is to connect "millions of music lovers" with a "grand library of all music forming the basis upon which all music businesses from digital radio to tour bookings can then grow and thrive from. Empowering the artists, turning and landing the industry finally on its feet."[44]

The key to this empowerment, according to Heap and others, rests in the capacity of "blockchain" technology to decentralize the exchange of currency for direct sale of music (and other things) and make "smart contracts" that potentially eliminate intermediaries currently necessary to manage rights and collect fees. Opinions vary about the significance of this technology for the future of the music industry, but if the potential is realized to any significant degree, it will be a massive, schematic disruption (see chapter 8 for a more complete discussion of these concepts).

Other companies are working to build a structure that supports the individual artist with blockchain technologies (including cryptocurrencies) that support secure transactions and contracts. One such is Ujo Music—a partner of Imogen Heap on her "Tiny Human" project. In an interview in 2017, Heap explained the project this way:

> Soon after discovering Ethereum, I dreamt up a music industry ecosystem that I called Mycelia, and used my next musical release—the song *"Tiny Human"*—as an excuse to explore the potential of blockchain further. I began by posting everything about that track on my website for anyone to experiment with and for fans to enjoy. Phil Barry at the Ujo Music platform joined in, which resulted in *"Tiny Human"* being the first song ever to automatically distribute payments via a smart contract to all creatives involved in the making and recording of the song. It was very basic—no licensing terms were exhibited—and it raised little money, due in part to the fact that you had to have an Ether wallet with Ether in it (the crypto-currency used on the Ethereum platform) before you could purchase the track, which lost some people along the way. But it nonetheless was a first step forward that generated a lot of steam for those in the business of music and blockchain.[45]

Artists like Heap and entrepreneurs like Phil Barry are committed to the transformative power of blockchain platforms to reframe the music industry through the aggregation and management of digital currencies, contracts, and direct artist-to-audience transactions. Others remain unconvinced either because (a) they think that the technical difficulties will be extremely difficult to overcome for producers and listeners, or (b) the culture of the music industry will be resistant to the innovation.

The Ujo Music and Imogen Heap partnership on "Tiny Human" is a particular concern to David Gerard, music and technology author, because he sees it as an example of "magical thinking" about the usefulness of blockchain technologies for the music industry:

> With widespread publicity and hundreds of articles in the blockchain, music and general press, it ["Tiny Human"] sold a grand total of 222 copies, for a gross take of $133.20—not $133,200, but one hundred and thirty-three dollars and twenty cents. The book details the many points at which the initiative stumbled, most involving the primitive state of the Ethereum ecosystem at the time.[46]

Those numbers fall short of the hopes of artists like Heap for blockchain-supported platforms, like Mycelia, of which she stated:

> Its success will come from the adoption of millions of music lovers. A grand scale ongoing, collective project like no-other. To document, protect and share that which we love and build a place for it to grow, enabling future generations of artists to blossom as well as honouring those of the past.[47]

Gerard sees this result as a combination of unrealistic expectations, a lack of expertise in the complexities of building such a system, and a fundamental misunderstanding about data and its application. According to Gerard:

> The way Blockchain hype works is that advocates promise all sorts of unlikely outcomes—money directly deposited in artists' accounts directly upon an iTunes purchase or Spotify play, transactions that occur "nearly instantaneously" ("in less than one second"—an unworkably short block time, but that's the least of the idea's problems) and directly, without intermediaries. All you need to do is clean up the data, and you get all the magical stuff![48]

A detailed discussion of the blockchain and cryptocurrency is beyond the scope of this discussion. Even a summary of David Gerard's analysis of the technology and its practical applications is too much. For the purposes of this chapter, we will focus on one technical and one cultural aspect of his critique of current thinking and practice involving blockchain technology and music.

Gerard finds that the outcomes that most blockchain advocates enthuse about are impossible using current technology. He cites the data demands of the music industry, complex contractual arrangements, and how copyright infringement lawsuits could potentially change contractual details and/or ownership of music. Gerard summarizes as follows:

- No single blockchain can possibly scale to the whole music industry. Spotify played a billion streams a day by mid-2015.
- Apart from the metadata itself being huge, there's the encoded details of all the hundred-page contracts. And who will pay for the computing resources to execute all the smart contracts for each song played?
- "Where there's a hit, there's a writ." You sue and win. How is the "immutable" blockchain corrected?[49]

As serious as these technical/practical issues are to Gerard, he finds record label culture to be of even greater concern. First, there is the by now well-established tendency of labels to be resistant to change and to "treat technological change as a threat and resist it as bitterly as they have every other technology."[50] The other issue is the practice of keeping contractual arrangements secret and compartmentalized from artist to artist (see George Howard's comments below).

Finally, Gerard points out that the businesses that are promoting blockchain as a solution for artists are engaged in "resentment-based" marketing and thus inherently exploitative:

If you can get people feeling resentful and then claim you have a solution, you can sell them anything, whether or not it's feasible, usable or even functional. But it's heartwarming to see how keen all these "blockchain" people are to helpfully intermediate between you, *the artist*—their eternal and only concern!—and the prospect of money.[51]

Although George Howard is more optimistic than Gerard about the potential for cryptocurrencies and blockchain technology to "save the music industry," he shares some of the same concerns about record label culture: that labels will not want greater transparency or equitable access to comprehensive data:

Of course, the parties who benefit the most from lack of transparency in the music industry are the labels, publishers, and streaming services. The record industry was built upon a firmament of information asymmetry—that is, the labels/publishers have more knowledge than those signing the contracts. Given this, they are able to exploit this information imbalance to their benefit. At the extreme end, this meant blatantly lying to artists who were under-educated, under-represented, under-experienced (or all of the above) to strip them often, forever—of their rights. At a slightly more benign level, these labels and others create agreements and "reporting" so byzantine in nature that only the most experienced (and expensive) lawyers can parse them, which forces many artists who don't have the resources for such representation to accept the deals/reports *prima facie*.[52]

Thus, as access to data and increasingly sophisticated tools for analysis have reshaped music industry practices, they have also highlighted some of the inherent inequities of aggregative systems. Control over creative content was the primary source of revenue and power in the twentieth-century music industry model. This put labels and publishers in a powerful position relative to individual composers and recording artists.

As digital music access providers have increasingly aggregated the output of labels and publishers, they have developed an advantage over them on the basis of controlling both necessary access to listeners and data about them. For artists, the difficulty now rests in three layers of control "above" them in the vertical system: their deal with their label, their label's deal with Spotify, and Spotify's control of its own data. This situation is comparable for every streaming and online access provider.

Finally, businesses claiming to empower artists to have access to data and analytical tools, as well as data-driven technologies like blockchain, have an inherent conflict of interest. The technologies do not necessarily perform as marketed and artists are very possibly being manipulated through a combination of resentment and "magical thinking." And, at the very bottom line, blockchain businesses "for artists" must inevitably aggregate and exploit them to be economically viable in the music marketplace.

PREDICTION AS PRODUCT

Speculation about the future of blockchain technology and the music industry fits inside the larger issue of prediction generally. Understanding the future has always been a critical factor in a high-risk endeavor like the music business. Traditionally this played out in the realm of the A & R representative, who would identify new artists based on an intuitive understanding of what listeners were going to like in the near future. The development and production of records depended on the capacity of the producer and artists working collaboratively to create a potential hit single.

Data and data analytics have sparked the idea that such predictions can become more science than art. But it is one thing for an algorithm to be able to predict what song a listener wants to hear next on a given streaming service and entirely another to predict what songs should be released in the first place.

Data researchers at the University of Antwerp took a big step toward making such a prediction a reality by examining Billboard dance single charts from 1985 through 2014.[53] The research team used data from the

Echo's Nest and from Spotify's recommendation function. An article (in 2015) about the research describes it this way:

> They looked at 139 different musical aspects to analyze songs. This includes basic features like length, tempo (measured in beats per minute or bpm), time signature, key, and loudness; more subjective features like beat, energy, and danceability; and even more intangible qualities like a song's timbre or tone color, or what we might think of as its general *feel*.
>
> Timbre is measured by 13 different features related to the basic components of the audio spectrum, and how each changes over time. For example, the number of high or low frequencies in a sound determines its perceived "brightness." "It seems that brightness has a big influence and how the time between beats evolves throughout a song," said [one of the study's authors, Dorien] Herremans.[54]

Applying this standard to Billboard's "Hot Dance/Electronic Songs" for 2015 revealed that all of the top ten would have produced a 65% to 70% probability of being a hit record.

Though "hit science" is clearly in the primitive stages and makes some artists and fans uncomfortable, the potential impact of this technology on the music business is profound. As noted in chapter 2, even after the industrialization of many aspects of entertainment culture in the twentieth century, the creation of music remained individual and "handcrafted." If predictive means are refined, it opens the door for the incremental industrialization of the creative component of the creation-production-reception cycle.

Aggregative tools and practices in the twenty-first century are not merely the next step in managing and monetizing music. These trends go beyond collecting songs and artists and labels under the umbrella of massive streaming services. Or even of data as a product, as a tool to manage reception, production, and creative decisions, or to predict the Next Big Thing. They are artifacts of a larger cultural transformation.

As media become increasingly available and pervasive in daily life, the fundamental relationship between and among artist, audience, entertainment "spectacle," and lived experience is changing. That shift and its implications for the creation, production, and consumption of music are the focus of the final chapter.

CRITICAL CONCEPTS

- In the twenty-first-century, music business, artists, producers, and listeners are all both consumers and product. Artists, audiences, music, and media are also all data.
- Data-based tools designed to empower independent artists also aggregate them as customers and products.
- Control over creative content and distribution were the primary sources of revenue and power in the twentieth-century music industry model. In the twenty-first century it is the control of access, discovery, and data.
- It is one thing for an algorithm to be able to predict what song a listener wants to hear next and entirely another to predict what songs should be released in the first place.

FURTHER CONSIDERATION

Next Wave Aggregation

What happens when expanding global markets meet rapidly growing media and entertainment conglomerates such as China's Tencent?

- http://www.tencent.com/en-us/index.html
- https://www.fool.com/investing/2019/04/07/why-tencent-music-is-poised-for-growth.aspx
- https://www.reuters.com/article/us-tencent-music-ipo/tencent-music-presses-play-on-12-billion-us-ipo-idUSKBN1O218V

What are the implications of businesses that connect multiple sectors of the entertainment market: music, video, gaming, and social networking?

- https://www.sfchronicle.com/business/article/Online-video-game-powerhouse-Twitch-the-future-12999233.php

- https://www.wired.com/story/fortnite-marshmello-concert-vr-ar-multiverse/

Chart Wars
- https://www.billboard.com/articles/business/8510461/rolling-stone-magazine-music-charts
- https://pitchfork.com/news/rolling-stone-to-challenge-billboard-with-new-music-charts/

CONCEPTUAL PROTOTYPE QUESTIONS

- Let's return to the idea of hosting house concerts as a business prototype (chapter 10). Obviously you must know and understand who your prospective customers are and what matters to them. But, from an aggregative perspective, how might you find enough of them to make it worthwhile to build the venture?
- Or do you want to create a booking agency for performers who want to do house tours? Who are your clients now? Touring and local bands? Or other people who need talent for their own house concerts. How might you find and aggregate those prospective clients?
- Or do you want to create a web resource that does it all for aspiring presenters and aspiring touring artists? You would need to aggregate artists for hosts, hosts for artists. In so doing, what data about hosts and artists could you collect? Would this be for your own use or can you envision external clients for that house concert artist and host data? How far can you aggregate that model?
- After you come up with a rough conceptual design take another look at this:
  - "Airbnb Expands Music Offering with Launch of Dedicated Concerts Platform," www.billboard.com/articles/business/8216223/airbnb-expands-music-offering-concerts-platform
- Then ask yourself, how do I compete with an aggregator like that?

Simulation

Creation, Production, Consumption

The idea of spectacle is quite old. Spectacular entertainment goes back—at least—to the Roman Empire and the violent displays that featured fighting gladiators, wild animals, and racing chariots. But the concept of spectacle is associated with more than visually interesting or even extravagantly staged events. Spectacle is also about society, control, and power. And, historically, music has always been threaded through virtually every form of spectacle.

The philosophical and political ramifications of spectacle theory are beyond the scope of this book. But the impact of spectacle on music production and reception is indisputable—particularly in performance, whether live or mediated. The spectacular element in performance ranges from presenting "things to look at" during a performance—a sequined jacket and stage lighting—to creating immersive multimedia experiences—stage sets, smoke, fire, giant screens, lasers, holographic projections, and more. Regardless of the technology employed or the production budget available, the purpose of adding spectacle to performance is to intensify the experience, engage and gratify the audience, and justify the cost of attending an event.

At one time—particularly prior to television and other visual media—spectacular experience was separate from daily experience. In fact, a central part of its value to the entertainment consumer was precisely that separation, because spectacles provided escape from mundane reality. In addition, the fact that spectacular entertainment was separate from daily life made it possible for access to be controlled and, therefore, for spectacle to become an economic offering.

Because presenters discovered that making a music event "spectacular" attracted audiences and sold tickets, spectacle became more common. A concert without any visual elements was distinctly unusual— virtually unheard of in commercial popular music in the twentieth century. As the means to experience the spectacular became increasingly available via film and then television, one might have expected the spectacular to lose its value to attract audiences and make money.

That's not what happened.

Certainly, the fact that spectacular presentation became a normal expectation of tours encouraged competition to find increasingly striking effects. Periodically, an artist might elect to do a deliberately simplified presentation, which became a novelty in the context of ever more elaborate shows. But on the whole, even smaller tours and local bands adopted the basic vocabulary of lights, costuming, visual and audio effects, and so on.

As spectacular experiences became more common and more commonly threaded through everyday life via visual media, more and more businesses adopted an entertainment mind-set in delivering products and services to their customers. As the twentieth century drew to a close, the influence of spectacle and its ability to create value of all kinds increased.

According to business scholar and professor David Boje writing in 2002:

> The Spectacle is an entertainment force that has a major impact on the economy, our business models, and societal culture. Business is becoming entertainment, more theatrical, and we live in the Society of Entertainment.[1]

That idea—that "we live in the Society of Entertainment"—is particularly important. For Boje and others, it was clear that society in the twentieth century not only produced and consumed spectacular entertainments. Their view was that social experience was increasingly defined by spectacle. There are two implications of this to consider. First, that spectacular experience would increasingly replace "actual" experience and people would begin to lose the capacity to tell the difference. Second, people would demand spectacular experiences, not just in their music and other entertainments, but also in the transactions of daily life.

This chapter argues that this is no exaggeration. Spectacle is everywhere. Going to a movie, buying coffee, or having a musical experience are increasingly expected to be spectacular and businesses, including music production in its various forms, are eager to oblige.

FORMS OF SPECTACLE

As noted above, David Boje explores the relationship of spectacle theory and business in his research. He identifies four types of spectacle— *concentrated, integrated, diffuse,* and *megaspectacle*—and places them in both social and economic contexts. The most comprehensive form— *concentrated spectacle*—refers to the overarching spectacle that defines an entire culture. This is the most difficult to recognize because it is so pervasive. We can get a glimpse of concentrated spectacle if we consider the entire Super Bowl experience: the NFL season that leads up to it, the weeks of interviews and predictions, the television ads, the halftime entertainment, and the game itself. For football fans (even those who only watch the big game and not the rest of the season) it is a consuming experience.

The Super Bowl phenomenon goes beyond that, however, generating many millions of dollars of ad revenue and shaping traditional, online, and social media conversations for weeks. As such it becomes a snapshot of American culture and society and, carried across a decades-long tradition, spans generations. The entire culture that produces all of that is concentrated spectacle. The Super Bowl is only one manifestation and any given television commercial and even the half-time show—which is typically a miniconcert "spectacular"—represent small pieces of that bigger piece.

The *diffuse spectacle* is more illustrative of the impact of particular products and events. This form is reflective of societies where commercial activities and consumerism are important. The public is intended to take, for example, the Super Bowl, individual ads, and the halftime show at face value, rather than see them as examples of larger forces at work. But according to theorists, this quality of diffuse spectacle is not necessarily an intentional effect, but simply a result of how much spectacular entertainment and commodification are present. This brings people to a point, for example, at which it is hard to distinguish between entertainment content and advertising. Thus, for many, the Super Bowl ads are what they watch and care about rather than the game itself.

In order to explain how businesses can use spectacle to influence consumer behavior in specific ways, we come to the concept of *integrated spectacle*. The integrated form combines elements of both the concentrated and the diffuse forms. According to Boje, this is where "the concentrated mask of corporate theater diffuses onto a global stage."[2]

Put another way, we might talk about the importance of a brand, whether of the music itself or a celebrity performer. The music business, for well over a hundred years, has used integrated spectacle—the music, the performer, and the performance experience—to sell tickets and products and build fan loyalties. It is the model of music and other entertainment industries that provided the inspiration for experiential branding in the 1990s and spectacle-oriented business models in other sectors.

Finally, there is the *megaspectacle*. This describes spectacular events that both are spread by globalized communications media like the Internet and allow a degree of interactivity on the part of the audience. This would include, for example, the reposting of Super Bowl commercials on YouTube as well as extended opportunities to "buy in" to experiences that extend beyond the event itself.

EMINEM, CHRYSLER, AND THE SUPER BOWL

A television commercial featuring the music of (and an appearance by) Detroit rapper Eminem first aired during the 2011 Super Bowl broadcast. Nominally an advertisement for the Chrysler 200 and Chrysler's new advertising concept, "Imported from Detroit," it is also a two-minute-and-three-second story, told in words, images, and music, about a city that has been "to hell and back." The broadcast on February 25 was seen by 111 million people—the most watched program in television history. Afterward, the commercial was available on Chrysler's YouTube channel and had been seen (as of April 11, 2011) by over ten million viewers, as well as voted Best Commercial in YouTube's "Ad Blitz" gallery of Super Bowl commercials.[3]

Accord to a press release from Chrysler in March 2011:

> The new 2011 Chrysler 200 mid-size sedan continues to build momentum in the marketplace in the wake of Chrysler brand's Super Bowl ad. Sales of the 200 increased 191 percent in March, compared with sales in February. Hot on the heels of the new 200, the all-new 2011 Chrysler 300 sedan began hitting dealership showrooms in March.
>
> Chrysler brand's car sales in March increased 38 percent, compared with the same month a year ago. The Chrysler brand introduced the new "Imported from Detroit" merchandise in March. The new collection features an array of products with the "Imported from Detroit" logo, which represents the hardworking spirit captured and celebrated in the brand's Super Bowl commercial, "Born of Fire."

Beyond sales, the "Imported from Detroit" initiative produced a significant "buzz" among consumers. According to the Detroit News, "The commercial, created by Wieden + Kennedy, of Portland, Ore., was crafted to help re-build Chrysler's luxury image, but it soon became apparent it was much more than that, stoking water cooler buzz and generating more than a million hits on YouTube."[4]

In addition, Chrysler created an opportunity for fans of the commercial to engage via the sale of "Imported from Detroit" T-shirts and merchandise, with a portion of the proceeds going to local Detroit charities, including Eminem's Marshall Mathers Foundation.

Obviously, the bottom-line motivation for creating the commercial was to enhance the Chrysler brand and sell cars. That's the diffuse spectacle piece—the underlying reality that the consumer is not supposed to notice. But the ad captured people's imaginations as well and sparked conversations about Detroit, about American cities recovering from economic hardship, and a sense of hope. As stated by Oliver Francois of Chrysler, "We are humbled at the thought that the conversation continues and is generating a spark throughout the country."

By engaging people in a socially mediated conversation, selling T-shirts, and contributing to local charities, this ad campaign moves into the realm of *megaspectacle*. It also illustrates the challenges of controlling the effects of this type of spectacle once they are triggered. The "Imported from Detroit" merchandise proved so popular that other companies began to make and sell their own versions. Chrysler moved quickly to sue.

Chrysler's lawsuit against Pure Detroit, filed in March of 2011, stated:

Upon seeing Chrysler's stunning ad, capped off by the powerful tagline, defendants immediately and opportunistically sought to usurp Chrysler's goodwill and exploit Chrysler's investment for themselves. They both copied Chrysler's tagline exactly and used it on some of the very goods for which Chrysler had filed a trademark application, clothing. Falsely promoting themselves as an "exclusive" provider, and promoting their products by touting "the tagline that is making headlines across America!," defendants have sold huge numbers of T-shirts.[5]

Although this kind of merchandise is commonly sold in the music industry, it is a relative rarity for automobile manufacturers. The problem of knockoff merchandise, which generates no revenue for a performing artist, is not unusual. In this case however, as a result of the larger "conversation" inspired by the ad campaign, there was a significant backlash from the public to Chrysler's legal action.

As noted by Michigan journalist, Jeff T. Wattrick:

> Strange as it may sound, this marketing campaign is perceived as bigger than a commercial. It's become a kind of totemistic call to arms. That works in Chrysler's favor because buying a car isn't just about reliable transportation. It's about making a personal statement. Chrysler's marketing effort [that] connects its product to Detroit as an idea means, to a certain demographic, buying a Chrysler is an expression of an ethos.[6]

The challenge and the opportunity of operating in the realm of megaspectacle both come from the same place: the media that allow the message to diffuse widely and for people to participate in the conversation and to sharply disagree if they are offended by a company's actions. Or, as stated by a commenter in the *Detroit Free Press*, "Wow, taking a feel good slogan for our area into a profit-making, litigious slugfest in court."[7]

One of the key elements of the commercial is the presence of Eminem and his music. As a well-known musical artist, Eminem is readily identified not only with Detroit, but also with a specific, blue-collar culture found in that city. In addition, his film *8 Mile* emphasizes themes of ambition, courage, and redemption that underscore on a personal level the commercial's theme: a city that, through strength, courage, and hard work, is reclaiming its pride.

The "Imported from Detroit" story includes cars, Detroit, America, Eminem (local boy "makes good" and comes back home), decay and renewal, and more. But is it in any sense true? In the context of spectacle theory, factual accuracy matters less than the extent to which the audience accepts the story and how they feel about the commercial as part of the overall Super Bowl viewing experience.

The Chrysler/Eminem Super Bowl ad is an example of how music is used in the service of selling a nonmusical product. But what happens when we use layers of images that create a complex visual story when musical experience itself is the product?

SELLING MUSICAL SPECTACLE

In music, spectacle involves not only the theatrical elements of a concert performance, but also how the event and the artist are promoted to the public. How an artist's public persona can be leveraged to sell tickets to upcoming events was mapped out with great effectiveness by P. T. Barnum in relationship to the Jenny Lind tour he promoted (1850–1852).[8] Even in the context of this very early example, it is clear not only that musical performance is capable of being "spectacular," but so is a celebrity performer.

It is no accident that the twentieth-century music production model is based on the creation, promotion, and distribution of "hits" and "stars" using every available communications medium. As new media for distributing musical experience developed, there were recurring predictions of doom for the live performance business. In fact, however, mediated and in-person musical experience aligned effectively. The synergy of radio, recordings, television, film, and live shows made the global music industry of the twentieth century possible. By the time we got to Internet-based platforms for music, the concept of megaspectacle was fully realized and the production, distribution, and consumption of musical experience were rapidly transformed.

The modern tour as delivered by major recording artists depends on leveraging technical spectacle and celebrity across every available medium. A very good example is provided by the *On the Run Tours I* and *II* presented by Beyoncé and Jay-Z in 2014 and 2018 (see also chapter 5). Both artists have active solo recording and touring careers. In fact, OTR I was announced in April 2014, very shortly after they had both completed solo tours.

From one perspective, touring again so soon risked audiences not being motivated to see another performance. Bringing the performers together made the upcoming tour different, in that the music of the two artists is quite distinct. That said, their fan bases are also distinct, which could be another risk factor. But one of the most important spectacular elements of the joint tour was the relationship of the two stars. As husband and wife with a relatively high-profile "private" life and the opportunity to see "hip hop's royal couple" together onstage were factors that transcended musical performance.[9]

Consequently, the personal and professional relationship between Beyoncé and Jay-Z was integral to the promotion and production of the tour. The duo released a "mini-movie," *Run,* a month before the first date of the tour. In it, the artists portray action movie roles, possibly criminals. This connects to the name of the tour, which is in itself connected to the Jay-Z single "Part II (On the Run)," on which Beyoncé performed as a guest artist. Although presented as a movie trailer, as if promoting an upcoming film, it was clearly intended to promote the tour and the couple's brand in anticipation of it. Videos were also incorporated into the concerts themselves.

The spectacular elements of the shows were "epic," according to Omar Al-Joulani (VP of North American Touring for Live Nation) and included

> three staging systems hop-scotching across the route. Elements included a moving high-def screen, pyro, hyrdraulic lifts, and a B stage extended well into the audience. "Knock on wood—we started production load-in in San Francisco at noon today—every show has gone up on time, with no production issues," he says, adding that there were no weather issues or delays, either. The total production moved on 42 trucks, with about 150 crew.[10]

The On the Run II Tour, announced in March 2018, was another stadium tour that included twenty-one dates in the United States and fifteen in Europe. This tour was also announced by a (much shorter) film "trailer" showing the couple onstage, on a motorcycle, and featuring juxtaposed images of a wedding ring and handcuffs. The promotional materials for the tour emphasized the couple's personal relationship and marriage and included a "tour book" featuring intimate photos of the couple. During the shows videos of their children and other home movie–type content were displayed.

During the European leg of the tour, Jay-Z and Beyoncé released a video filmed in the Louvre of their song "APES—T." Within three weeks of its posting, the video had been viewed over sixty million times.[11] On one level, the release of video online while a live show is on tour is an example of the multimedia nature of spectacle. In addition, the Louvre created an online tour of the seventeen works of art featured in the video. According to Mark Zablow (CEO of Cogent Entertainment Marketing): "The Louvre is already a massive tourist attraction; now it is an Instagram attraction for all pop culture junkies."[12]

Pop culture scholar Robert Thompson of Syracuse University makes the case that the video takes OTR II and its fans to another level and across the threshold of megaspectacle:

> Beyoncé and Jay-Z have essentially become backdoor curators of one of the world's greatest art collections, because they have taken those 17 works and suddenly escalated them to the top of the Louvre. The Louvre's 17 must-see pieces are now the ones that they chose; their own greatest hits.[13]

The OTR II shows incorporate visual and structural elements that underscore the artistic and personal relationship of the performers. Designer Ric Lipson talks about the creative and engineering work of putting OTR II onstage:

> While the two catwalks separate Beyoncé and Jay-Z at the beginning of the show, "The Bridge" reconciles them at the end. This feat of engineering and design rises and coasts over the heads of the audience below, pumps out plumes of smoke to create "Club Carter" beneath. "Architecturally and engineering-wise the bridge is pretty special," says Lipson. "It weighs 26 tonnes and accommodates up to 15 dancers at once. I believe this is the first track bridge that elevates over the audience in an outdoor environment."[14]

While this kind of staging and the accompanying technologies are obviously designed for maximum visual impact, they must also serve as a practical platform for the performing artists, dancers, and backing band. There is, embedded in the architecture and technology, a musical performance going on. But it's not just the visual experience that is designed and manipulated in the modern concert environment. The music you hear is just as engineered, edited, and framed to produce a particular experiential result.

REDEFINING "LIVE"

The art of musical performance was at one time entirely dependent on the craft and artistry of the performer to make music in real time using only the resources of his or her body and musical instruments, if any. Good singers sounded better than bad ones. Likewise for good guitarists (and guitars). With the introduction of electronic amplification, some of the constraints of live performing were reduced. Soft singers could be made louder, guitars amplified, and so on. But the limitations of talent were not affected. If you were out of tune or out of time without an amp, you were also those things with one. Just louder.

Comparably, early recording technologies were intended to capture live performance and render a copy as close to the original as technologically possible. Electronic amplification also affected work in the studio. Reverb was used to change the sound of a voice, for example. Effect boxes were used to change the sound of guitars. But up to around 1960, recording and live performance were basically in the business of getting the best version of a live performance on record or to a live audience.

The advent of multitrack recording ushered in a significant—even profound—shift in the production of recordings and in the relative importance of performing skill versus sound engineering. The history of recording technology is outside the scope of this chapter, but suffice it to say that by the 1960s, it was possible to create musical effects on record and to sell them, and for such recordings to become iconic musical works. Because of this, the challenge flipped. Now live performers had to try to sound like the recording, instead of the other way round.

Sometimes this challenge was met by having more performers onstage, sometimes many more, if, for example, a recording had featured a full symphony orchestra. Sometimes extra instrumental performers and/or exotic instruments on a record could be addressed with electronic instruments. As synthesizer technologies became more sophisticated this became a more effective means to re-create a studio sound in a live environment.

In addition, live performance could be blended with prerecorded sounds. Doing so requires synchronization between the live and recorded performance elements. This includes being able to start/stop the record at precisely the right time in relationship to the live performance. Once triggered, the performers must be able to stay with the recording, because early recordings could not be adjusted to live performers. All of this tended, at least in early versions of the technology, to reduce the energy of the performance, making it less responsive to the moment, and eliminating any spontaneity.

In a sense, performing with a recording connects to the practice of lip-syncing. This was an artifact of the increasing importance of the record as the definitive version of a song as well as the relative complexity of managing audio for live performances in broadcast studios. Syncing was particularly common on television programs in the 1960s, like American Bandstand and others, where artists with hit records would be physically present in the television studio, but the music would be prerecorded.

This represents one extreme of the integration of prerecorded elements into performance with the only "live" element being the presence of the performers and their movements simulating making music. As the tools for synchronization improved, it became easier and more common for a singer to perform "live" with backing tracks, or a mix of live and recorded sounds to be blended together.

To some extent the motivation for this kind of reality-blending performance comes from the desire to present more consistent live shows. This can be particularly useful in terms of lead vocals. If a singer is having a bad allergy day, the show that night can be compromised. As explained by musician and writer Doc Coyle:

There are also cases of bands that use a mirror track for the lead vocal so you have the live vocal run parallel to a pre-recorded track. This can sound good, but almost too good. I am not sure where I stand on this approach, and will not post any examples because I am not sure if its fair to call bands out on this. In many cases, I am not sure where it's being used, but I can say that it is becoming very common. Bands tour with others bands that do it, and they copy them to keep up with the Jonses. It's like steroids in sports. People use them because they feel like they can't compete otherwise, and I sympathize with that. I have also seen this method used with bands adding extra guitars to beef up the tone.[15]

In the case of artists performing music that they've previously recorded, backing tracks can be a matter of making the live version sound more like the recording, something that audiences have come to expect, based on decades of discovering bands and solo artists via their studio recordings.

The issue of backing tracks in live shows has been a concern for many years. In 1989, Jon Pareles, music critic of the *New York Times,* stated in a concert review:

I wish it were a nightmare. As elaborate lights illuminated a stageful of smoke-machine smoke, on came a full band—singers, dancers, guitarists, keyboardists, a drummer. The first song had a big beat, layered vocal harmonies and a dance move for every line of lyrics. It didn't seem to bother anyone but a lone, cranky critic that the drum kit was untouched until five songs into the set, or that the backup vocals (and, it seemed, some of the lead vocals as well) were on tape along with the beat.[16]

Subsequent developments in DIY recording technologies have only intensified this issue. Coyle explains it this way:

In my view, all of this stems from overproduction on modern records. It is so easy to throw midi sounds and electronic elements directly into Pro Tools, Logic, and even Garageband sessions. You can add unlimited layers of guitars and pianos and whatever else you can conceive. You are often recording at home, at your leisure: no studio time or 2 inch tape to pay for. Vocals are doubled or quadrupled with several harmonies added, and then auto-tuned. We have painted ourselves into a corner. It's the equivalent of having Photoshopped and airbrushed photos on a dating site hiding all of your physical flaws. You don't look like that, but what happens when you actually show up on the date? That date is the live show. You don't really sound like that album either.[17]

Coyle goes on to suggest that the alternative to dependence on backing tracks for live shows is to "create more stripped down records: less layers, avoid doing vocal harmonies or guitar parts you don't have members to perform, and use auto-tune sparingly."[18] He also points out that this can be difficult to do when working with a producer with a reputation to maintain:

> They are afraid of putting out albums that aren't flawless because it may come off as unprofessional. I can sympathize with that as well. Listeners have come to expect perfect performances. This is the "modern" sound.

It has been "modern" for a long time now. In fact, we might call the progressing blurring of the distinction between "live" and "prerecorded" as postmodern. The study of postmodernity is where spectacle theory originates. One of the core characteristics of both is the progressive dedifferentiation between the spectacular and the ordinary, or in this case between performance and "pretending" to perform.

As observed by Jon Pareles, "Lip-syncing, and other canned 'live' performances, may well be the fastest-growing entertainment form of the 1980's."[19] The 1980s brought another entertainment innovation as well: the music video and a cable television channel dedicated to it.

THE DAY THE MUSIC DIED: FROM MTV TO REALITY TV

When, on August 1, 1981, MTV went on the air with "Video Killed the Radio Star" by the Buggles, music videos were certainly not new, nor was the idea of a television show devoted to playing music videos. It was new for a cable channel to have programming—24/7—exclusively devoted to music videos. What made the idea controversial was, in part, the limited number of videos available, but more significantly, the way music videos were understood at the time.

Short musical films had been around from the 1920s. A number of examples can be found on the web and they show how little the formula for a "musical short" changed over that time.[20] Even though musical styles had changed—as had fashion and the aesthetics and technologies of film and video—by 1981, the function of short musical clips had not: they were promotional in nature. In fact, they were called "promotional clips" in the industry and served as advertisements for live shows and albums while promoting the performer's celebrity style and brand.

It is now history of course that MTV was a commercial success, winning millions of subscribers by the end of the first year and then going far beyond. Further, the impact of heavy-rotation music videos on record sales helped transform business models for labels in the 1980s. In the earliest days, labels provided videos for free to MTV and they were often relatively low budget and crude. After the impact of MTV play became obvious, videos grew more elaborate and more expensive and labels began charging for their use. This shift is critical to understanding what MTV represented: evidence of a transformation of what had been advertising into programming content. Thus, musical "ads" became consumable art—another reflection of the blurring effects of postmodern, spectacle-infused culture.

Music videos also prompted changes in the way artists thought about live shows. A few years into the MTV era, Jon Pareles noted:

> Then along came music video. For many more people than could ever pack an auditorium, the image of the lip-syncing singer, smiling and sweatless in a club full of cute extras, became the image of a pop concert. Some performers tried to make live shows look like videos; some decided that audiences wouldn't like hearing the hits in raw, real-time, possibly out-of-tune form after they'd seen the lip-synced "performances" on television.[21]

Music videos and MTV not only prompted reframed business models and patterns of consumption. By focusing on a product that was a blended version of advertising and art (see the Sting and Jaguar comparison in "Further Discussion"), MTV underscored a fundamental truth. Just as we might consider music as always being a form of advertising (for itself if nothing else), Music Television was never just—or even primarily—about music. It was about a culture of celebrity and consumption.

The purchase of MTV by Viacom in 1986 is often considered the tipping point and the end of music videos as the programming focus for the channel. But it was not so much a change of direction as of focus. Viacom's MTV was more broadly concerned with all forms of popular (though the term "commercial" is in this case more accurate) culture. But it is more than that: Viacom was interested in the consumers of culture and in using MTV programming as a way to show consumers themselves.

While "I Want My MTV" had been the network's slogan since 1982 and had been interpolated into a song by Dire Straits in 1985, by 1986 "my MTV" meant something rather more specific. The original MTV had music videos performed by music "stars" whose careers had already been established or at least begun in other media. The Dire Straits song was sung by the internationally known Mark Knopfler and guest artist Sting. By contrast, the stars of Viacom's new MTV were the viewer.

Music remained a component of MTV and sister station VH1 programming, but music videos were increasingly marginalized. In their place came "Best of..." nostalgia programming, game shows, awards shows, movies, and, above all, reality television. The spectacle of music videos was increasingly replaced by programming that allowed the viewer to see themselves or at least others from their peer group "on television" in platforms ranging from *The Real World* debuting in 1992 to *The Hills.*

Sometimes music celebrities, like Ozzy Osbourne, Flavor Flav, and Bret Michaels, appeared on MTV/VH1 but they did so in platforms where emphases on music or musical talent were replaced by socially inappropriate behavior. In fact, the celebrities of the second MTV era—Heidi and Spencer of *The Hills* for example—had no discernible talent other than behaving badly on camera. Still, after her appearance on the VH1 Show *I'm a Celebrity Get Me Out of Here*, Heidi released an album, "Superficial" (which sold extremely poorly).

Even poor sales and scathing critical reviews were not the signs of a career on life support in the "reality TV" era, because music is not the product—celebrity is. "Famous for being famous" is a concept that dates back at least to the early 1960s.[22] Viacom/MTV turned this into a core principle for creating content and guiding their business model.

MTV clearly redefined celebrity through its "reality" and "celebreality" programming. From the perspective of spectacle theory, they deconstructed celebrity, just as their popularization of the broken-down distinctions between art/entertainment and advertising deconstructed programming content. Their reinterpretation of celebrity also set the stage for an even more far-reaching cultural shift: the transformation of consumers into producers and audience members into artists.

AUDIENCE TO ARTIST

For many years, the talent show concept successfully exploited a common dream: that, given the opportunity, anyone can become a star. The history of talent shows is beyond the scope of this discussion, but suffice it to say that by the first decade of the twenty-first century, the combined effect of talent shows like the long-running *American Idol, America's Got Talent, The X Factor,* and *The Voice,* plus the massive growth of user-created video hosting sites like YouTube (original motto, "Broadcast Yourself"), had changed the music/entertainment business environment and culture.

YouTube originally created no content in the traditional sense. Instead, it aggregated millions of DIY producers and connected them with hundreds of millions of viewers, also aggregated by the site. Although it initially may have appeared that YouTube's product was the large number of viewers, it was also—and even more critically—the amateur producers, who were also viewers themselves.

One consequence of this structure and the diffusion of "user-produced" content across the Web was a rise in what Alvin Toffler predicted (1970) to be "prosumers"[23] and what William Deresiewicz in 2015 labeled "producerism."[24] Toffler anticipated how emerging media—long before the Internet or even personal computing appeared—would empower people to increasingly produce the products they wished to consume.

In the realm of popular music enterprise, the shift toward producerism followed an arc of, first, aggregation beginning with labels aggregating songwriters and performers, to major labels aggregating independent ones, to digital music providers (of downloads and streams) aggregating labels. At this point, with a rise of DIY-supporting technologies, independent artists began attempting to aggregate themselves and, via online video hosting sites, fans began having expectations of becoming famous for broadcasting themselves.

By the final stage, facilitated by an interactive network of service providers marketing the concept of celebrity as being within the reach of everyone, "producerism" begins to become a personal brand and lifestyle. Because the majority of the consumers are members of a generation that is networked across both professional and personal life, that experience is "networked, curated, publicized, fetishized, tweeted, catered, and anything but solitary, anything but private."[25]

The consumers of the "production experience" aggregate themselves, reshaping the economy and the culture. As a result, the musical experience has never been more transactional, or more diversely produced, mediated, and consumed, or the roles of creator and consumer so blurred.

So when everyone is a famous musical artist, how is anyone going to make money from making music?

SELLING UGLY DUCKLINGS INSTEAD OF SWANS

We know this story. How a youngster that everyone sees as ungainly, ridiculous, and—frankly—ugly turns out to be a beautiful "swan" that everyone comes to admire and love. It would seem that the payoff—or, to use a term from contemporary reality television, "the reveal"—is when we see the inner swan come out.

But what about the "ugly" part? Can we have an effective reveal without having some preliminary "ugly" to set the stage? Further, must entertainment entrepreneurs wait for the happy accident—the odd and ungainly performer with great artistry—to emerge?

This is the key to the long history of talent shows, which depend upon two things. First, they provide amusement for the audience in that many amateur performers are not very good at what they do. So one can find a sad amusement in the awkward, brave attempt to perform. Or you can see an ugly duckling become a swan before your eyes. That's the story that turns out to be a key to driving success in the modern talent show and a principle underlying user-generated content platforms and producerism in general.

Consider a performance of a contestant on *Britain's Got Talent* on April 11, 2009.[26] The video reveals a familiar situation: a contestant is on stage in front of a live audience and a panel of judges. The contestant sings a version of a popular song. The video repeatedly cuts away from the performer to show reactions from the judges and audience members. The three judges (two male, one female, including Simon Cowell, most familiar to American audiences as the "stern" judge on *American Idol*) display contrasting affects: affable, emotional, and serious. It is obvious that *Britain's Got Talent* is closely related to the *American Idol* genre.

Susan Boyle is the contestant. Her performance of "I Dreamed a Dream" from *Les Miserables* was popularized on the Internet and drew swift and widespread attention, making her, suddenly, an internationally recognized figure. The video of Boyle's audition, posted on April 11, 2009, on YouTube by the production company, does more than capture a particular moment on a talent show. It is a staged scene—a carefully edited video short—intended to produce a particular kind of theater.

First, there is Susan Boyle's appearance. She looks middle-aged and has a hairstyle and clothing more suitable for a PTA meeting than a stage performance. Her demeanor is somewhat awkward onstage, a fact that is emphasized by the cutaways to backstage personnel, the judges, and the audience reacting in amused disbelief. It is clear that there is an expectation that the performance will not be good, perhaps even embarrassing.

Then comes the drama: Boyle has a brief interchange with the judges and then begins her performance. Based on the reaction shots as Boyle begins to sing, we are to believe that her voice is astonishingly good, made all the more amazing by the disparity with her appearance. The video clip is edited to ask the question, how can someone who looks like that sound so amazingly good? It is, in a way, the ugly duckling story and it is also a version of the "Gomer Pyle" effect, where a funny-looking, funny-talking, socially awkward individual sings beautifully and thrills listeners.[27]

It is evident that in this posted clip Susan Boyle's dramatic situation was carefully edited to capture the essence of the underlying drama of *Britain's Got Talent*. This theater piece—indisputably a type of spectacle—depends on the judges to play roles: supportive mentors and/or villains who stand between the common person and their dreams. It also depends on contestants who are characters we recognize (heroes, villains, clowns) and whose story connects with our own (rags to riches, ugly duckling, overcoming the odds, and others) positively or negatively.

In the eight years since it was posted, the official video of Susan Boyle's performance received nearly 230 million hits on YouTube, but that is only a fraction of the amount of attention paid to Susan Boyle across all media. As a result she became a household name. More critically and perhaps usefully for understanding this kind of media product, Boyle is the template for "wannabes" whose looks do not "fit" their performance impact. It is a pattern that has been used many times since.

The effect of talent shows—as well as the compelling narrative of finding "hidden" talent and the consequent rise from obscurity to fame—is a familiar artifact of the contemporary megaspectacle era. It embodies how spectacle has come to increasingly replace lived experience. Such talent shows are not only a means of discovery for new artists, or even platforms for establishing their brands. They are a framework for the experience of talent across a society, for understanding what "talent" means in America, Britain, and beyond.

This discussion of simulated realities in music has drawn two concepts from spectacle theory: pervasive spectacle progressively replacing reality and the dedifferentiation—of product and content, and between artists and audiences. The things that defined live performance for earlier generations—being able to play and sing your music in the moment—were changed by the capacity to edit and create sounds technologically, first in the studio, after a performance ended, and then as performance happened in real time.

On the one hand, this can be seen as enhancing performance. But from another perspective, you could argue that tools like synced prerecorded tracks and autotune, not to mention the various multimedia effects integrated into a "live" show, have deconstructed live performance and what it means to be a performer.

Perhaps the most significant deconstruction of music in the course of the twentieth and twenty-first century is to the creative/performative process itself. Traditionally the development of performance skills, say as a singer/guitarist, required effort over quite a bit of time. You sang around the house as a child. Someone gave you a guitar and showed you some chords. You experimented. You sounded bad. Your fingers hurt. A lot. You persisted and got better, or you did something else.

Becoming a performer that other people would enjoy hearing took more time and more effort still. A lot more. And the creative process—learning how to write a song, figuring out what you wanted to sing about and how to frame that musically—also required effort, over time.

The integration of technological tools that made the development of live performance skills unnecessary changed the equation. Loops made composition different, more of an assembly process. It's not that loop-based, computer/sequencer-assisted music production is not creative. It certainly can be. But the relationship between effort, sometimes painful, over time to create and making music has changed fundamentally. It has been deconstructed.

BEYOND LIVE

For nearly a century, communications media have made it possible to experience music while separated in space or time from the performance and performers. In that sense, live streaming a concert, for example, is not fundamentally different from a live radio broadcast. In both cases, access is provided for people who cannot physically be present at the performance. Also, both radio and streaming access have raised concerns about their potential to reduce revenue from live events or perhaps render them unnecessary.

Those questions are primarily economic in nature. Further, whether the medium is broadcast, satellite, or Internet, there is a musical performance somewhere. Only the means of access to it are changed. In this final section we look a step beyond mediation. What if, instead of facilitating distribution and production or assisting live performers interactively, technology makes the creative and production decisions? What happens when the machines make the music instead of people?

There are two additional technologies to consider in this context: virtual reality and holograms (for artificial intelligence and songwriting, see "Further Consideration"). Both of them have already impacted performance and touring, and both have the potential to profoundly disrupt music creation, production, and consumption going forward.

VIRTUAL REALITY

According to journalist Jen Sako:

> Virtual reality is a three-dimensional environment created by a combination of computer software and hardware. Anyone entering the environment

wearing sensory headgear and gloves can move objects around or otherwise cause an action. To the person immersed in this environment, objects
are perceived by the senses as being real, even though without the special
gear, they are not. VR technology extends beyond the basic senses to stim-
ulate our sense of balance and other physiological factors so that our brains
mediate the artificial environment as one where we are actually there.[28]

The potential applications of virtual reality (VR) technology to
music are both obvious and subtle. For example, it seems apparent that
a virtual version of a concert could make previous broadcast or streaming versions obsolete. In addition, since VR depends upon proprietary
software and hardware, access to virtual concerts would be easier to
control and to monetize.

Win, win.

On another level, VR technology is more than a more layered distri-
bution/access medium. Sako summarizes predictions about the impact
of VR on music this way:

> Virtual reality is going beyond the current applications of gaming and
> design to change the way music is encountered. The future music experi-
> ence looks to be fully interactive outside the limits of hearing and sight.
> Like a personal concert, except soaked with texture, action, and decision-
> making. Songs, conceived as events, can make listeners participants and
> leave them with an unforgettable impression.[29]

With VR the creative possibilities expand, as do opportunities to
develop artist–audience relationships. In addition, some performers/
producers are already considering the advantages of creating a VR performance experience instead of touring. This would reduce logistical
complexities and costs, as well as eliminate concerns about security in
large, public spaces.

At this stage in the development of commercial VR technologies, the
discussions tend to be utopian: all about the unprecedented possibilities. The difference between a novelty invention that has a limited
short-term impact on production and reception and one that is truly

disruptive and transformative has to do with whether or not people find it truly useful. Put another way, is VR is simply another way to stream a concert or something more?

According to media and entertainment journalist Cherie Hu:

> The boundary between observation and action continues to blur, and the music industry needs to pay more attention to how it can facilitate and draw more attention to this boundary. For example, as of now, live-streaming a concert from a VR device is only looking, not doing. Viewing an empty stadium through VR, on the other hand, is both looking *and* doing because you actively make a purchasing decision based on the images presented to you.[30]

That virtual reality technology blurs the distinction between "observation and action," between reception and participation, and between consumption and production is another manifestation of living in a spectacular society. It also, at least hypothetically, facilitates new creative methods and possibilities for human artists using sound, sight, and sensation. In that sense it is a new tool for creation, production, and presentation—in short, a new way to produce (and experience) a concert. That human musicians will make VR content is, at this point, a given. There is an older technology, however, that promises to be even more fundamentally disruptive of this point.

HOLOGRAMS

The technology for projecting images seemingly "in space" is well over one hundred years old. The means by which theatrical designers projected "ghostly" images on glass sheets are essentially the same as those used in such twenty-first-century applications as the 2006 Grammy performance of the hit "Feel Good, Inc." by cartoon band Gorillaz, integrated with live performers, De La Soul, and Madonna.[31] The more famous "appearance" at Coachella in 2012 by the late Tupac performing with a live Dr. Dre brought the technology more attention and sparked controversy over the ownership of celebrity images after their death.[32]

Though that event in 2012 spurred growth in the application of holographic technology to music performances, it was less disruptive than controversial in terms of intellectual property. Subsequent holographic integrations of deceased and living performers have produced similar results: a kind of novelty interest along with "pushback" from fans and/or artist estates about appropriate usage of an artist's image.

A more disruptive application of holograms to music is provided by Hatsune Miku, a character created in 2007 by Hiroyuki Itoh, CEO of Crypton Future Media, a music technology company based in Japan. According to technology writer Rebecca Greenfield: "Itoh envisioned her [Hatsune Miku] as an avatar for Crypton's voice synthesis software, which he built using Yamaha's Vocaloid 2 program. He commissioned an illustrator to make something 'cute but also slightly edgy.'"[33]

Hatsune Miku concerts, with the avatar projected via holographic technology and accompanied by a live backing band onstage, have been entirely successful since "her" debut in Tokyo in 2010. She has subsequently toured Asia, Europe, and North America. But concert revenue is just the tip of the iceberg, culturally and economically.

According to one reviewer of the Toronto performance on her tour in 2016:

> If an ordinary show's affinity is to theater, Hatsune Miku's is to film: both are coldly automatic, nonspontaneous, even projected, with bleeding-edge invention, onto a vast and gleaming silver screen. One sees Hatsune Miku perform live in much the same way one sees Iron Man fight Captain America in a Marvel movie. The Miku Expo isn't a concert—it's a robo-show, a concert simulacrum. Two thousand fans hop and scream as before them light and sound take on the shape of real experience.[34]

Nor are fan behaviors the only thing similar to a "real" concert in the Hatsune Miko experience. Merchandise is also incredibly important. According a Crypton employee at the Toronto event, "The VIP ticket holders are admitted to the venue early so they can be the first in line for merchandise. They've spent more money on their ticket just so they can spend more money."[35]

The real bottom line for Crypton is the Vocaloid synthesizer software, for which Miku was created to be the avatar. Sales of that software have been robust and worldwide. People who use it to write songs and program Miku's voice include millions who have no musical training or experience. This is a particularly significant factor in that fan-generated songs can become part of Miku's repertoire.

> "Hatsune Miku is installed on hundreds of thousands of computers all over the world," says Hiroyuki Itoh, CEO of Crypton, in the theater's bustling green room. "Every day you have new songs uploaded to the internet. And after a while the more popular ones and the less popular ones get naturally separated. For these concerts we like to choose the songs that already have the support of users. We give the fans what they want."[36]

Further, Crypton does not act as publisher of this music. In fact

> Hundreds of thousands of songs have been recorded using their software—and the Hatsune Miku image, free to use and modify as musicians see fit — Crypton doesn't own any of them, or indeed have any right to their reproduction or performance live. Miku is merely an instrument.[37]

CONCLUSIONS

Hatsune Miko and other technological developments that blur distinctions between the real and simulated in music inevitably raise questions about the future of concerts, of touring, of live performance, of what it means to be a performer and creative artist. On one hand, even the most cutting-edge technologies do not represent a new force in music production and consumption. Ever since the invention of recording technologies, there has been a tension between music that is produced and that which is performed. Jon Pareles, for example, saw it this way in 1989:

As far as I'm concerned, anything goes in the studio, since we expect the results to be artificial. Yet in a world filled with canned music, concerts offer a special (and expensive) privilege—a respite from studio perfection, a chance to see what can still be done with the naked hands and throat and hips and feet. Performances from gymnastics meets to Bartok string-quartet cycles to live news reports, are occasions to witness dexterity and daring, events in which humans overcome their own frailty and imperfection. A performer takes the risk, in public, of doing something difficult and rare, demonstrating skills beyond those of most of the audience.[38]

This almost thirty-year-old quotation—still relevant today—contains some assumptions that we need to examine. Certainly attending a live performance of high-level musical performers is a privilege and often quite expensive. Live shows remain the economic backbone of the industry. But Pareles implies that audiences continue to be engaged with the drama of performative skill:

Sometimes we expect the performers to make it look easy; sometimes, we prefer suspense. Rock, in particular, often enacts the struggle between the urge to express something and a performer's rudimentary musical technique. The strain only makes the music more exciting.[39]

This is no longer necessarily the case. As the distinction between live and computer-assisted performance has become more blurred and audiences lose the capacity to distinguish one from another, their reasons for attending an event will inevitably change. And this points out the challenge for any producer, consumer, critic, or student of popular music.

In 2012, sound engineer John Cooper was quoted as saying about the then upcoming Bruce Springsteen tour: "This is about the only live music left, with a few exceptions."[40] He was speaking particularly about the number of artists who used recorded backing tracks and other technologies to enhance their concert performances. Without debating either the accuracy of that assessment relative to other performers in 2012 or the extent to which any arena show depends on technological support, there is a critical issue to consider. NPR's music critic Ann Powers addresses it by stating that pop has fundamentally changed since the days when Springsteen was playing the Stone Pony. The electronic beats and samples at the core of hip-hop and dance music are now fundamental songwriting tools. In mainstream music, the old divide between "real" and "fake" ("rock" and "disco," "authentic" and "plastic") has collapsed. Music is truly cyborgian, and live performance continues to evolve to accommodate this reality.

There you have it. What may seem to be, from the perspective of one generation, a collapse of a system is actually the inevitable disruption of the old, followed by the creation of the new. What spectacle theory calls the deconstruction of familiar institutions, Schumpeter (chapter 8) labels creative destruction. Further, virtuoso from-scratch music-making skills have never been the only way that artists and audiences connect. Musical celebrity and successful musical brands have always been as much about emotional, kinetic, and human connection and shared experience as about "chops."

Obviously human music making and technology can coexist. They have done so from the early luthier handcrafting guitars to the kids learning how to build tracks using Fruity Loops and Ableton Live. The question remains what it has always been, regardless of the tools or the context: How do humans make and share music, musical experience, meaning, and value?

CRITICAL CONCEPTS

· Music has been consistently threaded through virtually every form of spectacle.

· Regardless of the technology employed or the production budget available, the purpose of adding spectacle to musical performances is to intensify the experience, engage and gratify the audience, and justify the cost of attendance.

· As spectacle becomes a more common feature of musical experience: (a) people begin to lose the capacity to tell the difference between real and artificial experience, and (b) people increasingly demand spectacular experiences.

- It is not just the visual experience that is designed and manipulated in the modern concert environment. The music you hear is just as engineered, edited, and framed to produce a particular experiential result.

- Key concepts from spectacle theory to apply to music enterprise: blurring or dedifferentiation of previously distinct ideas or activities and deconstruction of established ideas or activities and their reassembly in new forms.

FURTHER CONSIDERATION

From Audience to Artist

- Musical.ly Sells for $800 Million But Peaked by Being Too Silicon Valley

  https://musicindustryblog.wordpress.com/2017/11/10/musical-ly-sells-for-800-million-but-peaked-by-being-too-silicon-valley/

Autotune

- The Invention That Changed Music Forever

  www.cnn.com/2015/05/26/tech/autotune-inventor-mci/index.html

AI and Composition

- Music as a Commodity: Songwriting with Artificial Intelligence

  www.forbes.com/sites/jordanpassman/2017/03/03/music-as-a-commodity-songwriting-with-artificial-intelligence/

CONCEPTUAL PROTOTYPE QUESTIONS

The commercial production of music has historically depended upon performers having sufficient talent and charisma to connect with audiences. While these elements remain important, the means to achieving them have changed significantly. Today the creation, production, and consumption of music are not just parts of a complex system. That system operates inside a framework wherein corporate-designed, multimedia, and interactive spectacles have become normal and expected.

Thus, being able to create an effective enterprise in music, in a culture where everyone believes that they would be "world famous for fifteen minutes" if only they got the chance, depends upon the capacity to operate within a massively complex system of megaspectacle that is so pervasive that we scarcely notice it, except in its absence, in which case we are disappointed.

As a result, one must consider not only which model of capitalization and revenue to pursue, but also which kind of spectacular framework best suits what an artist is trying to create. Will it be full, concentrated spectacle—Pink, spinning above the crowd, performing "Glitter in the Air"—or antispectacle—Adele, standing on a bare stage in front of a piano, simply singing about love? Or will you pursue some alternative, disruptive course and change the world?

NOTES

I. INCEPTION: CREATION, PRODUCTION, RECEPTION

1. The historical pattern of music production crises is discussed, for example, in David Bruenger, *Making Money, Making Music,* University of California Press, (2016)

2. Donna Miller and David Bruenger, "Decivilization: Compressive Effects of Technology on Culture and Communication," *China Media Research* 3, no. 2 (April 2007).

3. For the importance of Instagram to the music business, see John Paul Titlow, "How Instagram Became the Music Industry's Secret Weapon," *Fast Company* (9–29–2017), www.fastcompany.com/40472034/how-instagram-became-the-music-industrys-most-powerful-weapon. Mark Mulligan, "Gen Z: Meet the Young Millennials," *A MIDiA Research report jointly commissioned by BPI and ERA* (June 2017), https://eraltd.org/media/27138/midia-research-gen-z-report.pdf.

4. Samuel Potts, "Record Labels Need a Change of Culture in the 'Dashboard Era' of the Music Industry," *Medium* (7–12–2016), https://medium.com/cuepoint/record-labels-need-a-change-of-culture-in-the-dashboard-era-of-the-music-industry-585e91f6de99.

5. As rated, for example, by Billboard's "Hot 100 Chart." Premiering in 1958, the Hot 100 measures weekly physical sales (and since 2005 digital downloads), radio play, and online streaming (since 2007).

6. See, for example, Ben Kaye, "Proof the 'Sophomore Album Slump' Is a Real Problem," *Consequence of Sound* (2–13–2015), https://consequenceofsound .net/2015/02/proof-the-sophomore-album-slump-is-a-real-problem/.

7. Nico Lang, "How U2 Became the Most Hated Band in America," *Salon* (9–8–2014), www.salon.com/2014/09/18/how_u2_became_the_most_hated_ band_in_america_partner/; or Erik Sherman, "Apple's $100 Million U2 Deba-cle" (9–19–2014), www.cbsnews.com/news/apples-100-million-u2-debacle/.

8. To make the issue even more challenging, any "formula" for economic success would not be the same as one for making good musical art—if such was possible. Creative genius is notoriously hard to "manage."

9. The seminal article defining both styles of expertise is G. Hatano and K. Inagaki, "Two Courses of Expertise," in *Child Development and Education in Japan,* ed. Harold W. Stevenson, Hiroshi Azuma, and Kenji Hakuta, WH Freeman/Times Books/Henry Holt (1986), 262–272.

10. Routine expertise is the basis for traditional approaches to learning how the music business works. Certainly learning best practices is both com-plicated and essential. No one should have to "reinvent the wheel" every time they want to copyright, publish, or license a song. This is the sphere in which justly influential music industry texts like those of Donald Passman, David Baskerville, and William Krasilovsky shine.

11. Valerie M. Crawford, Mark Schlager, Yukie Toyama, Margaret Riel, and Phil Vahey, "Report on a Laboratory Study of Teacher Reasoning: Char-acterizing Adaptive Expertise in Science Teaching" (presentation, the Ameri-can Educational Research Association Annual Conference, April 11–15, 2005, Montreal, Canada), 4.

12. See David Bruenger, *Making Money, Making Music,* for a closer look at issues surrounding Napster, the major labels, and Steve Jobs.

13. Sergey Smirnov, Hajo A. Reijers, Thijs Nugteren, and Mathias Weske, "Business Process Model Abstraction: Theory and Practice," in *Technische Berichte Nr. 35 des Hasso-Plattner-Instituts für Softwaresystemtechnik an der Univer-sität Potsdam,* Universitätsverlag Potsdam (2010).

14. Def Jam case and process model references: www.theguardian.com /music/2011/jun/13/def-jam-launched-simmons-rubin; https://nypost.com/2014 /10/11/the-wild-and-crazy-stories-behind-the-early-days-of-def-jam/; and www .openculture.com/2014/10/rick-rubin-revisits-the-origins-of-def-jam-records .html.

15. The d.school at Stanford site is here: https://dschool.stanford.edu; and an overview of Design Thinking as "a methodology for creative problem

solving" is here: https://dschool.stanford.edu/resources/getting-started-with-design-thinking.

16. The IDEO website is here: https://www.ideo.com; an overview of their Human-Centered Design Process is here: www.usertesting.com/blog/2015/07/09/how-ideo-uses-customer-insights-to-design-innovative-products-users-love/; and their Design Kit (including the Business Model Canvas) is here: www.designkit.org.

17. See *An Introduction to Design Thinking PROCESS GUIDE* at https://dschool-old.stanford.edu/sandbox/groups/designresources/wiki/36873/attachments/74b3d/ModeGuideBOOTCAMP2010L.pdf.

18. Noah Yoo, "The Full Transcript Of Jay Z's Tidal Q & A at the Clive Davis Institute of Recorded Music," *Fader* (Fall 2017), www.thefader.com/2015/04/01/the-full-transcript-of-jay-zs-qa-at-the-clive-davis-institute-of-recorded-music. More recent fee structures for the major streaming services are: Tidal—$9.99 or $19.99 for premium; Apple Music—$9.99 or $14.99 for six family members; Spotify—free, family $4.99, premium $10); from Jay McGregor, "Apple Music vs. Spotify vs. Tidal: Everything You Need to Know," *Forbes* (6–8-2015), www.forbes.com/sites/jaymcgregor/2015/06/08/apple-music-vs-spotify-vs-tidal-everything-you-need-to-know/#57333fdd415f.

19. See, for example, Jem Aswad, "Tidal Accused of Falsifying Beyonce and Kanye West Streaming Numbers," *Variety* (5–9-2018).

20. *An Introduction to Design Thinking PROCESS GUIDE.*

21. "Methodology," in *The Lean Startup*, http://theleanstartup.com/principles. For a more detailed discussion of Lean Startup and its impact on startup entrepreneurship, see Steve Blank, "Why the Lean Startup Changes Everything," *Harvard Business Review* (May 2013), https://hbr.org/2013/05/why-the-lean-start-up-changes-everything.

2. PRODUCTION: ART, SCIENCE, ENTERPRISE

1. Quoted by John Seabrook, "How Mike Will Made It," *New Yorker* (July 11 & 18, 2016), www.newyorker.com/magazine/2016/07/11/how-mike-will-made-it.

2. Quoted by J.J. Gould, "'The Musical Equivalent of Star Trek': Moby on Teaming, Touring, Sci-Fi," *Atlantic* (7–24–2012), www.theatlantic.com/entertainment/archive/2012/07/moby-star-trek/260261/.

3. Adam Smith, *An Inquiry into the Nature and Causes of the Wealth of Nations*, bk. 4, chap. 8, para. 49, www.econlib.org/library/Smith/smWN18.html.

4. For a variety of perspectives about the role and responsibilities of record producers, see "What Is A Record Producer?," *Music Producers Guild*, www .mpg.org.uk/about-mpg/what-is-a-record-producer/.

5. See, for example, Matt Wake, "Why Huge Tours Come to Alabama Arenas to Rehearse," *Al.com* (11–9-2017), www.al.com/entertainment/index.ssf/2017/11/ michael_jackson_kanye_carrie_u.html. For a take on pretour rehearsals being used as a commercial product, see Gill Kaufman, "Michael Jackson's Last Tour Rehearsals Filmed for Possible Release," *MTV News* (6–29–2009), www.mtv .com/news/1614882/michael-jacksons-last-tour-rehearsals-filmed-for-possible-release/.

6. For a consideration of the importance of art, social good, and economic viability across the nonprofit and for-profit musical sectors, see Bill Ivey, "America Needs a New System for Supporting the Arts," *Chronicle of Higher Education* (2–4-2005). For a discussion of subsidy and patronage in classical music, see David Bruenger, *Making Money, Making Music,* University of California Press (2016).

7. See "The 80/20 Rule? More Like 80/1 for Music Sales," *Punch-In at True-Fire.com* (4–4-2016), http://truefire.com/blog/inspiration/8020-rule-801-music-sales/; and Anita Elberse, *Blockbusters: Hit-Making, Risk-Taking, and the Big Business Of Entertainment,* Henry Holt and Company (2013).

8. Ivey, "America Needs a New System for Supporting the Arts," *Chronicle of Higher Education* (2–4-2005), www.chronicle.com/article/America-Needs-a-New-System-for/4621.

9. Quoted by Dylan Jones, "Icon Of The Year: Robbie Williams," *GQ* (10–1-2012).

10. From "Motown: The Sound That Changed America," *Motown Museum,* www.motownmuseum.org/story/motown/.

11. Helienne Lindvall, "Behind the Music: Motown—a Pop Factory with Quality Control," *Guardian* (11–26–2010), www.theguardian.com/music /musicblog/2010/nov/26/behind-music-motown-pop-factory. She writes about *The Record Producer's Motown Experience—the Secrets of the Classics,* a live event presented by the *Guardian* on November 20, 2010, featuring record producer Steve Levine, British radio broadcaster Richard Allinson, and Harry Weinger, A & R VP and manager of the Motown catalog at Universal Music Enterprises.

12. Lindvall, "Behind the Music."

13. Ibid.

14. Ibid.

15. Arthur Kempton, *Boogalo: The Quintessence of American Popular Music,* University of Michigan Press (2005), 213.

16. Ibid., 214.

17. "Motown's No. 1 Hits in One Box Set for the First Time: Celebrate Motown's 50th Anniversary with the 10-CD MOTOWN: THE COMPLETE NO. 1'S," *T4C, Top40 Charts/Universal Music Enterprises* (10–15–2008), http://top40-charts.com/news.php?nid=43528.

18. Tom Whitwell, "Why Do All Records Sound the Same," *Cuepoint* (1–9–2015),https://medium.com/cuepoint/why-do-all-records-sound-the-same-830ba863203.

19. Corey Moss, "Maroon 5 Film 'Wonder' Clip; Say Next One Is Bob Dylan Meets R. Kelly," *MTV News* (3–19–2007), www.mtv.com/news/1555064/maroon-5-film-wonder-clip-say-next-one-is-bob-dylan-meets-r-kelly/.

20. Whitwell, "Why Do All Records Sound the Same."

21. Ibid.

22. Jefferson Mao, "Godfather Lives Through: Hip-Hop's Top 25 James Brown Sampled Records," *egotripland.com* (5–3-2012), www.egotripland.com/hip-hop-james-brown-sampled-records/; Felix Contreras, "The Hip-Hop Influence Of Jab'o Starks, James Brown's Timekeeper," *All Songs Considered, NPR Music* (5–3-2018), www.npr.org/sections/allsongs/2018/05/03/607748562/the-hip-hop-influence-of-jabo-starks-james-brown-s-timekeeper.

23. For an in-depth discussion, see Lawrence Lessig, *Remix: Making Art and Commerce Thrive in the Hybrid Economy,* Penguin (2008).

24. See, for example, Ethan Hein, "Bittersweet Symphony," *Ethan Hein Blog* (11–23–2009), www.ethanhein.com/wp/2009/bitter-sweet-symphony/.

25. Reggie Uggwu, "Inside the Playlist Factory," *BuzzFeed* (7–12–2016), www.buzzfeed.com/reggieugwu/the-unsung-heroes-of-the-music-streaming-boom?utm_term=.dcMBm208w#.tnoV3NBzn.

26. For comparison purposes, *Apple Radio* streaming is omitted here. Were it included, it would belong with Spotify in the curation model category, as would Pandora and a number of other streaming and Internet "radio" entities.

27. Bono, "My Wish: Three Actions for Africa," *TED2005,* www.ted.com/talks/bono_s_call_to_action_for_africa/transcript; Samuel Potts, "Record Labels Need a Change of Culture in the 'Dashboard Era' of the Music Industry," *Cuepoint* (7–12–2016), https://medium.com/cuepoint/record-labels-need-a-change-of-culture-in-the-dashboard-era-of-the-music-industry-585e91f6de99. Quoted more fully in chapter 1.

28. According to a press release, Music Dealers was "built to bridge the gap between top brands and independent and emerging artists," combining "the world's largest, hand-selected catalog of pre-cleared, independent music with an amazing team of music and technology professionals to offer an unprecedented list of music-related services." It is an interesting curation model business that is now, however, closed. See Daniel Sanchez, "Music Dealers Suddenly Closes Doors, Leaving Many Artists without Pay," *Digital Music News* (7–28–2016), www.digitalmusicnews.com/2016/07/28/music-dealers-closes-doors/.

29. There is a massive amount of academic (and practical writing) on customer experience and the customer journey. This particular description—awareness, discovery, interest, interaction, purchase, use, cultivation, and advocacy—is widely used and is almost certainly derived from Bernd Schmidt, *Customer Experience Management: A Revolutionary Approach to Connecting with Your Customers,* Wiley (2003).

30. Potts, "Record Labels Need a Change of Culture."

31. Eric Sheinkop, "Music Strategy and the Consumer Experience Journey," *Music Ally* (3–18–2016), http://musically.com/2016/03/18/music-strategy-and-the-consumer-journey-guest-column/.

32. Potts, "Record Labels Need a Change of Culture."

33. Mark Mulligan, "After the Album: How Playlists Are Re-Defining Listening," *Music Industry Blog* (4–26–2016), https://musicindustryblog.wordpress .com/2016/04/26/after-the-album-how-playlists-are-re-defining-listening/.

34. Potts, "Record Labels Need a Change of Culture."

35. Sarah Kessler, "BuzzFeed's Jonah Peretti Is the Stephen Hawking Of Radical Skateboarding Birds," *Fast Company* (9–14–2012), www.fastcompany .com/3001308/buzzfeeds-jonah-peretti-stephen-hawking-radical-skateboarding-birds.

36. Potts, "Record Labels Need a Change of Culture."

3. RECEPTION: LISTENERS, FANS, CONSUMERS

1. Originally, Alvin Toffler, *The Third Wave,* Bantam (1980) and more recently, for example, this discussion of prosumerism and blockchain technology: Joel "DJ Deadly Budda" Bevaqua, "Are Cryptocurrencies Like Bitcoin the Solution to the Music Industry's Woes?," *LA Weekly* (7–11–2017). For more on cryptocurrency and its impact on the music business, see chapters 5 and 11.

2. See, for example, John Philip Sousa, "The Menace of Mechanical Music," *Appleton's Magazine* 8 (1906): 278–284, https://ocw.mit.edu/courses

/music-and-theater-arts/21m-380-music-and-technology-contemporary-history-and-aesthetics-fall-2009/readings-and-listening/MIT21M_380F09_read02_sousa .pdf.

3. For example, according to the National Association of Music Merchants, there were over sixty million amateur musicians in the United States in the 1990s. And, although electric guitar sales have declined in recent years, there are still approximately one million sold annually. For a discussion of this phenomenon, see Geoff Edgers, "Why My Guitar Gently Weeps," *Washington Post* (6–22–2017), www.washingtonpost.com/graphics/2017/lifestyle/the-slow-secret-death-of-the-electric-guitar/?noredirect=on&utm_term=.43c86c9d03b4.

4. "Music and Health," *Harvard Health Publishing* (July 2011), www.health .harvard.edu/staying-healthy/music-and-health.

5. Töres Theorell, *Psychological Health Effects of Musical Experiences: Theories, Studies and Reflections in Music Health Science,* Springer (2014), 33.

6. Ibid., abstract, https://link.springer.com/chapter/10.1007/978–94–017–8920–2_5.

7. Ibid.

8. Wake Forest Baptist Medical Center, "Music Has Powerful (and Visible) Effects on the Brain," *ScienceDaily* (4–12–2017), www.sciencedaily.com/releases /2017/04/170412181341.htm.

9. Ibid.

10. Quoted in ibid. For original research, see R. W. Wilkins, D. A. Hodges, P. J. Laurienti, M. Steen, J. H. Burdette, "Network Science and the Effects of Music Preference on Functional Brain Connectivity: From Beethoven to Eminem," *Nature: Scientific Reports* 4 (2014): 6130, www.nature.com/articles/srep06130.

11. Ibid.

12. Norman M. Weinburger, "Music and the Brain," *Scientific American* (9–1–2006), www.scientificamerican.com/article/music-and-the-brain 2006 09/.

13. For example, John Philip Sousa, "The Menace of Mechanical Music."

14. Overview of David Huron, *Sweet Anticipation: Music and the Psychology of Expectation,* MIT Press (2006), https://mitpress.mit.edu/books/sweet-anticipation.

15. David Huron, *Sweet Anticipation: Music and the Psychology of Expectation,* MIT Press (2006), vii.

16. Ibid., 2.

17. Dave Simpson, "Lamont Dozier: 'The Hits Just Kept Coming,'" *Guardian* (8–26–2015), www.theguardian.com/culture/2015/aug/26/lamont-dozier-the-songs-just-kept-coming.

18. Carlos Silva Pereira, João Teixeira, Patrícia Figueiredo, et al., "Music and Emotions in the Brain: Familiarity Matters," *PLOS One* (11–16–2011), http://journals.plos.org/plosone/article?id=10.1371/journal.pone.0027241.

19. From the research summary, "Why Some Songs Get Stuck in Your Head," www.dur.ac.uk/music/research/earworms/. For the original study, see Kelly Jakubowski, Lauren Stewart, Sebastian Finkel, and Daniel Müllensiefen, "Dissecting an Earworm: Melodic Features and Song Popularity Predict Involuntary Musical Imagery," *Psychology of Aesthetics, Creativity, and the Arts* 11, no. 2 (2017): 122–135.

20. Ibid.

21. Ibid.

22. "Reach for the stars" are the lyrics to the opening riff of "Moves Like Jagger," cited by Jakubowski et al., "Dissecting an Earworm."

23. Matthew Crawford, *The World Beyond Your Head: On Becoming an Individual in an Age of Distraction,* Farrar, Straus and Giroux (2015), 11.

24. Eric Sheinkop, "Music Strategy and the Consumer Experience Journey," *Music Ally* (3–18–2016), http://musically.com/2016/03/18/music-strategy-and-the-consumer-journey-guest-column/.

25. Quoted in "Sonic Boom Author Joel Beckerman on Power of Sound and Music in Media," *CBS News* (1–12–2015), www.cbsnews.com/news/sonic-boom-author-joel-beckerman-on-power-of-sound-and-music-in-media/.

26. Ibid.

27. Joel Beckerman and Tyler Gray, *The Sonic Boom: How Sound Transforms the Way We Think, Feel, and Buy,* Houghton Mifflin Harcourt (2014), xviii.

28. Ibid., 58.

29. Ibid., 23.

30. Ibid.

31. "Why Some Stongs Get Stuck in Your Head"; Jakubowski et al., "Dissecting an Earworm."

32. Beckerman and Gray, *The Sonic Boom,* xix.

33. Sue Devine, "How Music Impacts Our Lives in Ways We Don't Even Notice," *Playback, ASCAP* (12–1–2014), www.ascap.com/playback/2014/11/radar-report/joel-beckerman-sonic-boom.

34. "Sonic Boom Author Joel Beckerman."

35. The sound of Chili's fajitas being served as a sonic brand is often associated with Beckerman's work. It is discussed briefly in the article "Sonic Boom Author Joel Beckerman" and in more detail in Beckerman and Gray, *Sonic Boom.*

36. The JumboTron, developed by Sony, and newer LED-based large screens have become standard features of all sports arenas for both athletic and concert events. Although, they have been late adopters, classical organizations have begun to use this technology to bring the audience visually closer to the performers, moving "inside" the orchestra for a view that transcends even the best seat in the house. See, for example, Will Wlizlo, "JumboTrons for Concert Halls," *Utne Reader* (12–8–2010), www.utne.com/arts/music-scoreboards-for-concert-halls.

37. Radio call-in and request shows were attempts at making a one-way broadcast medium a more social experience. The practice began (in the United States) during the 1930s and was already being discussed by media theorists at around the same time.

38. For an early and influential discussion of "markets as conversation" in the Internet era, see David Weinberger, Rick Levine, Doc Searls, and Chistopher Locke, *The Cluetrain Manifesto: The End of Business as Usual*, Perseus Books (1999).

39. Brittany Spanos, "Fans to the Front: How Internet Fandoms Are Gaming the Music Industry," *Rolling Stone* (5–5–2017), www.rollingstone.com/music/news/how-internet-fandoms-are-gaming-the-music-industry-w480851.

40. Olivia Goldhill, "The Most Committed Fans in the World: One Directioners versus Beatlemania," *Telegraph* (11–18–2014), www.telegraph.co.uk/women/womens-life/11236700/The-most-committed-fans-in-the-world-One-Directioners-versus-The-Beatlemania.html.

41. Ibid. Will Cosme's Twitter account, *Pop Crave*, is here: https://twitter.com/PopCrave.

42. One Direction were contestants on the modern "hit factory" *The X Factor* (see chapter 2). Simon Cowell signed the band to Syco Records and had them make their first album at another "hit factory" icon, Cheiron Studios in Sweden.

43. Katie Buenneke, "One Direction Is Now a DIY Band," *LA Weekly* (5–18–2015), www.laweekly.com/music/one-direction-is-now-a-diy-band-5581248; Trevor Anderson, "One Direction Takes 'Control' at No. 1 on Billboard + Twitter Top Tracks Chart," *Billboard* (5–21–2015), www.billboard.com/articles/columns/chart-beat/6575675/one-direction-no-control-twitter-top-tracks.

44. Ibid.

45. Ibid.

4. COMMODIFICATION: PRODUCT, PROCESS, CULTURE

1. Tin Pan Alley was the nickname for the music publishing district in New York in the late 1800s and early 1900s. For a brief retrospective and some

twenty-first-century photos of what used to be Tin Pan Alley, see Luke J. Spence, "The Remnants of Tin Pan Alley," *Atlas Obscura,* www.atlasobscura.com/places/the-remnants-of-tin-pan-alley.

2. William Arms Fisher, *One Hundred and Fifty Years of Music Publishing in the United States,* Oliver Ditson (1933), 114.

3. "How Popular Song Factories Manufacture a Hit," *New York Times* (9–18–1910), http://sundaymagazine.org/2010/09/how-popular-song-factories-manufacture-a-hit/.

4. RIAA, US Sales Database, www.riaa.com/u-s-sales-database/, and for a more detailed analysis, see Mark J. Perry, "Recorded Music Sales by Format from 1973–2015, and What That Might Tell Us about the Limitations of GDP Accounting," AEI (9–15–2016), www.aei.org/publication/annual-recorded-music-sales-by-format-from-1973–2015-and-what-that-tells-us-about-the-limitations-of-gdp-accounting/.

5. The term "units" in the music industry refers to unit of measurement in tracking sales. The term is also combined with the verb "shift" to describe units sold or shipped to retailers. The expression "radio friendly unit shifter" was used ironically as the title to a song on Nirvana's album *In Utero,* released in 1993. See chapter 5, "Monetization," for a more in-depth discussion of music industry metrics of various kinds.

6. David Bruenger, *Making Money, Making Music: History and Core Concepts,* University of California Press (2016), 3.

7. B. Joseph Pine, II, and James H. Gilmore, *The Experience Economy: Work Is Theater & Every Business a Stage,* Harvard Business School Press (1999).

8. Ibid.

9. "Public Good," *Investopedia,* www.investopedia.com/terms/p/public-good.asp.

10. Ibid.

11. Ibid.

12. Ibid.

13. Ibid.

14. B. Joseph Pine, II, and James H. Gilmore, "Welcome to the Experience Economy," *Harvard Business Review* (July-August 1998), https://hbr.org/1998/07/welcome-to-the-experience-economy.

15. Peter DiCola, "The Economics of Recorded Music: From Free Market to Just Plain Free," *Future of Music Coalition* (7–16–2000), https://futureofmusic.org/article/economics-recorded-music.

16. Ibid.

17. Ibid.

18. Chong Hyun and Christie Byun, *The Economics of the Popular Music Industry,* Palgrave MacMillian (2016), 28.

19. Pine and Gilmore, "Welcome to the Experience Economy."

20. Spencer Kornhaber, "Starbucks's Failed Music Revolution," *Atlantic* (2–5-2015), www.theatlantic.com/entertainment/archive/2015/02/starbuckss-failed-music-revolution/385937/.

21. Melody, "A Starbucks History Lesson: HEAR Music Concept Stores," *Starbucks Melody: Unofficial Starbucks News and Culture* (5–6-2011), www.starbucksmelody.com/2011/05/06/hear-music-a-memorable-piece-of-starbucks-history/.

22. Valerie O'Neil, "Starbucks Refines Its Entertainment Strategy," *Starbucks Newsroom* (4–24–2008), archived at Internet Archive Wayback Machine, https://web.archive.org/web/20130116172638/http://news.starbucks.com/article_display.cfm?article_id=48.

23. RIAA, US Sales Database.

24. Peter Kafka, "The Music Business Is Growing Again—Really Growing—and It's Because of Streaming," *Recode* (9–20–2017), www.recode.net/2017/9/20/16339484/music-streaming-riaa-spotify-apple-music-youtube-2017-revenue-subscription/.

25. Mark Wycislik-Wilson, "Spotify Sells Your Personal and Playlist Data to Advertisers Making You the Product," *BetaNews* (7–22–2016), https://betanews.com/2016/07/22/spotify-sells-user-data-to-advertisers/.

26. "Soundtrack Business," www.soundtrackyourbrand.com/soundtrack-business?utm_expid=.EJF120cySym9RY5bGRKmsQ.1&utm_referrer=.

27. Samuel Potts, "Record Labels Need a Change of Culture in the 'Dashboard Era' of the Music Industry," *Cuepoint* (7–12–2016), https://medium.com/cuepoint/record-labels-need-a-change-of-culture-in-the-dashboard-era-of-the-music-industry-585e91f6de99.

28. Ibid.

29. Ibid.

30. Ibid.

31. Jody Rosen, "Oh! You Kid! How a Sexed-Up Viral Hit from the Summer of '09—*1909*—Changed American Pop Music Forever," *Slate* (6–2-2014), www.slate.com/articles/arts/culturebox/2014/06/sex_and_pop_the_forgotten_1909_hit_that_introduced_adultery_to_american.html.

32. Danny Ross, "8 Protest Songs since 2000 That Inspired Change (All The Way to the Bank)," *Forbes* (1–30–2017), www.forbes.com/sites/dannyross1

/2017/01/30/8-protest-songs-since-2000-that-inspired-change-all-the-way-to-the-bank/#515439881715.

33. Ibid.

34. See chapter 12, "Simulation," for further exploration of this concept in various iterations.

35. Potts, "Record Labels Need a Change."

36. Ibid.

5. MONETIZATION: PUBLISHING, PERFORMING, RECORDING

1. The distinction between copyrights and trademarks is legally compli-cated, but in simple terms a trademark is a brand name, image, or logo. For example, the music and lyrics to the song "Satisfaction" are copyrighted (as is the recording), while the Rolling Stone's "lips and tongue" logo is trade-marked and copyrighted. See, for example, "The Rolling Stones Sue German Clothing Company for Using Mouth Logo," *NME* (8–15–2013), www.nme.com /news/music/the-rolling-stones-128–1265367.

2. See, for example, Brandt Ranj, "5 Terms Buzzfeed Uses Internally That Reveal How It Works," *Business Insider* (2–16–2016), www.businessinsider .com/5-terms-buzzfeed-uses-internally-that-reveal-how-it-works-2016–2.

3. Heather McDonald, "Track Equivalent Albums Were Established to Measure Sales," *Balance Careers* (5–16–2018), www.thebalancecareers.com /track-equivalent-albums-2460947; Randall Roberts, "What Makes for a No. 1 Album in the on-Demand Age of Streaming?," *LA Times* (8–30–2016), www .latimes.com/entertainment/music/la-et-ms-music-charts-20160822-snap-story .html.

4. "Do Not Assume We Have Arrived at Our Destination," *Music Industry Blog* (6–15–2017), www.midiaresearch.com/blog/do-not-assume-we-have-arrived-at-our-destination/.

5. Paul Resnikoff, "Live Concerts + Streaming = 73% of the US Music Industry," *Digital Music News* (6–7–2017), www.digitalmusicnews.com/2017/06 /07/music-industry-concerts-streaming/.

6. The best sources of global information come from proprietary research organizations like Price-Waterhouse (PwC) and MIDiA Research. The reports they produce are based upon multiple large data sets and, because they are intended for business/industry use, are expensive. Other sources—also propri-etary—come from industry-specific organizations like LiveNation, Billboard

Box, and PollStar (all for live music) and the Recording Industry Association of American (RIAA) and the International Federation of the Phonographic Industry (IFPI) for recordings in their various forms.

7. Resnikoff, "Live Concerts + Streaming."

8. Ibid.

9. "Do Not Assume We Have Arrived At Our Destination."

10. "The Top 10 Benefits of Using RFID for Events," *Eventbrite,* www .eventbrite.com/blog/academy/the-top-10-benefits-of-using-rfid-for-events/.

11. Steve Gordon and Anja Puri, "The Current State of Pre-1972 Sound Recordings: Recent Federal Court Decisions in California and New York against Sirius XM Have Broader Implications Than Just Whether Satellite and Internet Radio Stations Must Pay for Pre-1972 Sound Recordings," *JIPEL* (5 4-2015), https://jipel.law.nyu.edu/vol-4-no-2-5-gordonpuri/.

12. "Herbert v. Shanley Co., 242 U.S. 591 (1917)," *Justia,* https://supreme .justia.com/cases/federal/us/242/591/case.html.

13. Ibid.

14. Frederick C. Boucher, "Blanket Music Licensing and Local Television: An Historical Accident in Need of Reform," *Washington and Lee Law Review* 44, no. 4 (Fall 1987), https://scholarlycommons.law.wlu.edu/cgi/viewcontent .cgi?article=2822&context=wlulr.

15. Ibid.

16. John Eggerton, "DOJ Antitrust Chief: We Are Reviewing ASCAP, BMI Consent Decrees," *Broadcasting & Cable* (3–28–2018), www.broadcastingcable .com/news/doj-antitrust-chief-reviewing-ascap-bmi-consent-decrees.

17. Ed Christman, "ASCAP and BMI Call on DOJ to Replace Consent Decrees: Open Letter," *Billboard* (2–28–2019), www.billboard.com/articles /business/8500472/ascap-bmi-open-letter-doj-consent-decrees-regulation.

18. "DOJ Takes Wait-and-See on ASCAP & BMI Consent Decrees," *Inside Radio* (6–14–2018), www.insideradio.com/free/doj-takes-wait-and-see-on-ascap-bmi-consent-decrees/article_8320cc50–6f9f-11e8-b5bf-5b88ac2c6845.html.

19. Similar arrangements were made in Britain in response to the mechanical copy and licensing issues. For more, see Ruth Towse, "Economics of Music Publishing: Copyright and the Market," *Journal of Cultural Economics* 41 (2017): 403–420.

20. Russell Sanjek, *American Popular Music and Its Business: From 1900 to 1984,* vol. 3, Oxford University Press (1988).

21. "CARP (Copyright Arbitration Royalty Panel) Structure and Process," Statement of Marybeth Peters the Register of Copyrights before the

Subcommittee on Courts, the Internet, and Intellectual Property, Committee on the Judiciary, United States House of Representatives, 107th Congress, 2nd Session (6–13–2002), www.copyright.gov/docs/regstat061302.html.

22. Ibid.

23. "Procedural Regulations for the Copyright Royalty Board," *Federal Register,* 70, 103 (5–31–2005), www.crb.gov/fedreg/2005/70fr30901.pdf.

24. Paula Parisi, "Production Music Conference: NMPA's David Israelite Takes Aim at 'Copyright Infringers,'" *Variety* (10–7–2017), https://variety.com/2017/music/news/production-music-conference-nmpa-david-israelite-keynote-1202583450/.

25. Ibid.

26. Ibid.

27. See, for example, the case of "Foreign & Domestic Music Corp. v. Licht et al, 196 F.2d 627 (2d Cir. 1952)," https://law.justia.com/cases/federal/appellate-courts/F2/196/627/15299/. This case concerns film soundtracks and refers to the songs recorded on a film soundtrack as "synchronized" and is cited as part of a larger study of a consideration of the synchronization "right" as an extension of the "derivative work" statues. See Carole A. Ellingson, "The Copyright Exception for Derivative Works and the Scope of Utilization," *Indiana Law Journal* 56, no. 1 (1980–1981), www.repository.law.indiana.edu/ilj/vol56/iss1/1.

28. Jason Peterson, "Music Licensing for Audio-Visual Content," *Digital EMA* (April 2015), www.entmerch.org/digitalema/white-papers/ema-music-rights-white-2.pdf.

29. Ibid.

30. Variety Staff, "Music Modernization Act Heads to President Trump for Signature," *Variety* (9–25–2018), https://variety.com/2018/music/news/music-modernization-act-president-trump-signature-1202957780/; Nate Rau, "Trump, Flanked by Nashville Artists, Signs Landmark Music Modernization Act into Law," *Nashville Tenneseean* (10–11–2018), www.tennessean.com/story/money/2018/10/11/trump-alongside-kid-rock-signs-music-modernization-streaming-act-into-law/1599350002/.

31. Marc Schneider, "'Truly a Historic Moment': Music Business Reacts to Music Modernization Act Becoming Law," *Billboard* (10–11–2018), www.billboard.com/articles/business/8479469/music-business-reactions-music-modernisation-act-law-signing.

32. Variety Staff, "Music Modernization Act."

33. RIAA, US Sales Database, www.riaa.com/u-s-sales-database/.

34. Gordon and Purjna, "The Current State of Pre-1972 Sound Recordings."

35. Ibid.

36. "The Digital Millennium Copyright Act Summary," *Pub. L. No. 105–304, 112 Stat. 2860 (10–28–1998), U.S. Copyright Office,* www.copyright.gov/legislation /dmca.pdf.

37. Gordon and Purjna, "The Current State of Pre-1972 Sound Recordings."

38. These are the sections of copyright law in the United States that cover temporary, "ephemeral" recordings made only to facilitate transmission (112) and performance rights in sound recordings (114), including digital services. "Licensing 101," *SoundExchange,* www.soundexchange.com/service-provider /licensing-101/.

39. Ed Christman, "SoundExchange Extends CEO Michael Huppe Through 2021," Billboard (1–10–2018), www.billboard.com/articles/business /8093735/soundexchange-ceo-michael-huppe-contract-2021.

40. Ibid.

41. Emma Griffiths, "Sync Licensing in 2017: A Look at the Trends and Figures," *SynchBlog* (12–22–2017), www.synchtank.com/blog/sync-licensing-in-2017-a-look-at-the-trends-and-figures/.

42. Joshua Friedlander, "News and Notes on 2017 RIAA Revenue Statistics," *RIAA,* www.riaa.com/wp-content/uploads/2018/03/RIAA-Year-End-2017-News-and-Notes.pdf.

43. Helienne Lindvall, "Behind the Music: The Real Reason Why the Major Labels Love Spotify," *Guardian* (8–17–2009), www.theguardian.com /music/musicblog/2009/aug/17/major-labels-spotify; Michael Arrington, "This Is Quite Possibly the Spotify Cap Table," *Tech Crunch* (8–7–2009), https:// techcrunch.com/2009/08/07/this-is-quite-possibly-the-spotify-cap-table/.

44. Alex Hearn, "Is Spotify Really Worth $20bn?" *Guardian* (3–2–2018), www.theguardian.com/technology/2018/mar/02/is-spotify-really-worth-20bn.

45. Nick Statt, "Spotify's IPO Was Both a Success and an Uncertain Forecast for the Future of Music," *Verge* (4–3–2018), www.theverge.com/2018/4 /3/17194208/spotify-ipo-nyse-music-streaming-market-valuation.

46. Lucas Shaw, "Record Labels Reap More Than $1 Billion Selling Spotify Stakes," *Bloomberg* (5–7–2018), www.bloomberg.com/news/articles/2018–05–07/record-labels-reap-more-than-1-billion-selling-spotify-stakes.

47. http://winformusic.org.

48. Richard Smirke, "Indie Labels Repeat Calls for 'Fair Share' of Spotify Equity Payout," *Billboard* (3–6–2018), www.billboard.com/articles/business /8232536/spotify-indie-labels-equity-sale-fair-share-win.

49. Tim Ingham, "Here's Exactly How Many Shares the Major Labels and Merlin Bought in Spotify—and What Those Stakes Are Worth Now," *Music Business Worldwide* (5–14–2018), www.musicbusinessworldwide.com/heres-exactly-how-many-shares-the-major-labels-and-merlin-bought-in-spotify-and-what-we-think-those-stakes-are-worth-now/.

50. Ingrid Lunden, "Spotify Strikes New Deal with Indy Giant Merlin 'Competitive' with Big Labels," *Tech Crunch* (4–20–2017), https://techcrunch.com/2017/04/20/spotify-strikes-new-deal-with-indy-giant-merlin-competitive-with-big-3-labels/.

51. Jacob Ganz, "The Concert Ticket Food Chain: Where Your Money Goes," *Record, NPR Music* (4–6-2011), www.npr.org/sections/therecord/2011/04/07/134851302/the-concert-ticket-food-chain-where-your-money-goes.

52. Ibid.

53. Ibid.

54. Ibid.

55. Ray Waddell, "Jay-Z and Beyonce's on the Run Tour Isn't Struggling," *Billboard* (6–19–2014), www.billboard.com/biz/articles/news/touring/6128489/jay-z-beyonce-on-the-run-tour-doing-bad-not-true.

56. Ibid.

57. Ibid.

58. Ibid.

59. Dave Brooks, "Beyoncé and JAY-Z's on the Run II Tour Could Do Double the Business Their 2014 Tour Did," *Billboard* (3–12–2018), www.billboard.com/articles/business/8240747/beyonce-jay-z-on-the-run-ii-tour-double-business-2014-tour.

60. Ibid.

61. Eric Frankenberg, "Beyonce & JAY-Z's on the Run II Tour Finishes with More Than $250 Million," *Billboard* (10–23–2018), www.billboard.com/articles/columns/chart-beat/8481384/beyonce-jay-z-on-the-run-ii-tour-sales-by-the-numbers.

62. Richard Morgan, "Taylor Swift's Concert Revenue up 39 Percent over Last Tour," *New York Post* (11–23–2018), https://nypost.com/2018/11/23/taylor-swifts-concert-revenue-up-39-percent-over-last-tour/.

63. Dave Brooks, "Taylor Swift Has Concert Industry Embracing 'Slow Ticketing' Model," *Billboard* (12–14–2017), www.billboard.com/articles/business/8070644/taylor-swift-concert-industry-slow-ticketing-model-sales.

64. Ibid.

65. Ibid.

66. Ibid.

67. "The Top 10 Benefits of Using RFID for Events."

68. Bret Weiss, "It's Only Rock and Roll But I Like It," *Antique Week* (12–21–2011), www.antiqueweek.com/ArchiveArticle.asp?newsid=2265.

69. Nathan Jolly, "The History Of Music Merch," originally published in *The Music Network* (5–24–2010), https://nathanjollywrites.wordpress.com/2016/02/10/the-history-of-music-merch/.

70. Robert Cordero, "Concert 'Merch' Comes of Age," *Business of Fashion* (4–18–2016), www.businessoffashion.com/articles/intelligence/concert-tour-merchandise-justin-bieber-rihanna-kanye-west.

71. Ibid.

72. Ibid.

73. Ibid.

6. LOCATION: SCENES, VENUES, LABELS

1. Richard Florida and Scott Jackson, "Sonic City: The Evolving Geography of the Music Industry" (working paper, January 2008), Martin Prosperity Institute, University of Toronto, www-2.rotman.utoronto.ca/userfiles/prosperity/File/Sonic%20City%20RF3.w.cover.pdf.

2. Ibid.

3. Ibid.

4. Calvin C. Rydbom, *The Akron Sound: The Heyday of the Midwest's Punk Capital*, Arcadia Publishing (2014).

5. "About Sun Records," *Sun Record Company: Where Rock and Roll Was Born*, www.sunrecords.com/about.

6. Randy Lewis, quoting Peter Guralnick in "New Biography Illuminates Life of Sun Records Founder Sam Phillips," *Los Angeles Times* (11–17–2015), www.latimes.com/entertainment/music/posts/la-et-ms-sam-phillips-biography-peter-guralnick-elvis-presley-20151117-story.html.

7. Elizabeth Kaye, "Sam Phillips: The Rolling Stone Interview," *Rolling Stone* (2–13–1986), www.rollingstone.com/music/music-news/sam-phillips-the-rolling-stone-interview-122988/.

8. Ibid.

9. Ron Thibodeaux, "My Smokey Valentine—the Irrepressible Robinson Will Romance Marksville Tonight," *Times-Picayune* (2–14–2009).

10. James Bates, "Berry Gordy Sells Motown Records for $61 Million," *LA Times* (6–29–1988), http://articles.latimes.com/1988–06–29/business/fi-4916_1_motown-records.

11. Dave Segal, "Bruce Pavitt's 'Visionary' '80s Music Criticism Gets Anthologized in *Sub Pop USA*," *Stranger* (10–24–14), www.thestranger.com/slog/archives/2014/10/24/bruce-pavitts-visionary-80s-music-criticism-gets-anthologized-in-sub-pop-usa.

12. Mark Yarm, "Going out of Business since 1988!," *Blender* (July 2008), www.revolutioncomeandgone.com/articles/7/sub-pop-history.php.

13. Tyler Gray, "Punk Rock Branding: How Bruce Pavitt Built Sub Pop in an Anti-Corporate Nirvana," *Fast Company* (11–29–2012), www.fastcompany.com/1681976/punk-rock-branding-how-bruce-pavitt-built-sub-pop-in-an-anti-corporate-nirvana.

14. Chris Kissel, "Sub Pop Founder Bruce Pavitt Recalls the Birth of 'Indie' and Reflects on Today's Music Industry," *Diffuser* (2–24–2015), http://diffuser.fm/sub-pop-bruce-pavitt-interview-2015/.

15. Steve Jelbert, "Labelled with Love; Sounds," *The Times* (8–2–2008), http://link.galegroup.com/apps/doc/A182437350/AONE?u=colu44332&sid=AO.

16. Richard Florida, "Why Making the Scene Makes Good Cents for the Rest of Us," *Creative Class* (12–29–2007), www.creativeclass.com/_v3/creative_class/2007/12/29/urban-sound-system-2/.

17. Ibid.

18. Ibid.

19. Ibid.

20. Daniel Silver, Terry Nichols Clark, and Lawrence Rothfield, "A Theory of Scenes: The Structure of Social Consumption," University of Chicago (11–5-2006), http://scenes.uchicago.edu/theoryofscenes.pdf.

21. Florida, "Why Making the Scene Makes Good Cents for the Rest of Us."

22. Ibid.

23. Ibid.

24. "University of Georgia Fact Book 1977," UGA Institutional Research, www.oir.uga.edu/fact_book.

25. Sub Pop's history has been marked by an extended series of financial crises and drives for emergency capital. See, for example, Yarm, "Going out of Business Since 1988!"

26. "Small Music Venues: A Straightforward Guide to Managing Bar Costs and Forecasts," *Eventbrite*, www.eventbrite.co.uk/blog/academy/small-music-venues-bar-costings-and-forecasts/.

27. See Dell, *Future Ready Economies*, www.futurereadyeconomies.dell.com /?section=future-ready-economies; and *Enabling Economies for the Future: Insight from the 2015 Strategic Innovation Summit at Harvard*, http://theinnovatorsforum .org/sites/default/files/EEF_Whitepaper_2015.pdf.

28. Florida and Jackson, "Sonic City."

29. Ibid.

30. "Preparing Local Economies for the Future," sponsored content (Dell and Intel), *Harvard Business Review* (1–12–2016), https://hbr.org/sponsored /2016/01/preparing-local-economies-for-the-future.

31. "5 Unexpected Cities Experiencing a Live Music Renaissance," *Eventbrite* (8–17–2017), www.eventbrite.com/blog/music-cities-best-music-scenes-ds00/.

7. DIFFUSION: HERE, THERE, EVERYWHERE

1. David Bruenger, *Making Money, Making Music*, University of California Press (2016).

2. For a detailed examination of bundling in the digital music era, see Byungwan Koh, Il-Horn Hann, and Srinivasan Raghunathan, "Digitization, Unbundling, and Piracy: Consumer Adoption amidst Disruptive Innovations in the Music Industry" (October 2015), Robert H. Smith School Research Paper, http://ssrn.com/abstract=2371943 or http://dx.doi.org/10.2139/ssrn.2371943.

3. The term "blockbuster" is primarily used in the film industry, and both film and television offer instructive comparisons for the music industry. The changes from video rental models, i.e., Blockbuster Video, to streaming services such as Netflix are both illustrative and predictive for the functionality and potential of streaming services in music as opposed to product downloads.

4. Joe Lynch, "1994 vs. 2014: Comparing the Top-Selling Albums," *Billboard* (10–20–2014), www.billboard.com/articles/6259342/1994-vs-2014-top-selling-albums-comparison.

5. Hugh McIntyre, "Not One Artist's Album Has Gone Platinum in 2014," *Forbes* (10–16–2014), www.forbes.com/sites/hughmcintyre/2014/10/16/not-one-artists-album-has-gone-platinum-in-2014/.

6. Keith Coulfield, "Taylor Swift's '1989' Beats 'Frozen' as Top Selling Album of 2014," *Billboard* (12–31–2014), www.billboard.com/articles/columns /chart-beat/6422411/taylor-swift-1989-beats-frozen-top-selling-album-2014.

7. Mose Buchele, "How Did Austin Become the 'Live Music Capital of the World'?," *KUT 91.5, Austin's NPR Station* (9–21–2016), http://kut.org/post/how-did-austin-become-live-music-capital-world.

8. Roland Swenson, "History Intro," *SXSW,* www.sxsw.com/about/history/.

9. Ibid.

10. Michael Theis, "SXSW Economic Impact up Slightly in 2016; Hotel Rates Hit New High," *Austin Business Journal* (9–7-2016), www.bizjournals.com /austin/news/2016/09/07/sxsw-economic-impact-up-slightly-in-2016-hotel .html.

11. "2016 Demographics," *SXSW,* www.sxsw.com/wp-content/uploads /2016/05/SXSW-2016-Demographics.pdf.

12. Andrew Flanagan, "The Struggles of Austin's Music Scene Mirror a Widened World," *Record, NPR* (2–24–2017), www.npr.org/sections/therecord /2017/02/24/516904340/the-struggles-of-austins-music-scene-mirror-a-widened-world.

13. Titan Music Group, *The Austin Music Census,* The City of Austin Economic Development Department, Music and Entertainment Division (2015).

14. Flanagan, "The Struggles of Austin's Music Scene."

15. Ibid.

16. Ashley Lopez, "How Arts and Culture Could Shape Louisville's Tech Future," *WFPI* (01–08–2016), http://wfpl.org/how-arts-and-culture-in-louisville-could-help-its-tech-future/.

17. Scott Preston, "Behind the Scenes with JK McKnight, Founder of the Forecastle Festival," *Cincy Groove* (4–12–2009), www.cincygroove.com/?p=5660.

18. Ibid.

19. Jeff Haden, "How Forecastle Festival Turned Music, Art, and Activism into a National Happening," *Inc.* (7–12–2018), www.inc.com/jeff-haden/how-forecastle-festival-turned-music-art-activism-into-a-national-happening.html.

20. Ibid.

21. Ibid.

22. Ibid.

23. Jeffrey Lee Puckett, "Poorcastle Is the 'Festival for the Rest of Us,'" *Louisville Courier Journal* (7–10–2015), www.courier-journal.com/story /entertainment/music/2015/07/07/poorcastle-festival-louisville/29805517/.

24. Ibid.

25. Syd Bishop, "Festival for the Rest of Us: An Oral History of Poorcastle," *LEO* (7–8-2015), www.leoweekly.com/2015/07/festival-for-the-rest-of-us-an-oral-history-of-poorcastle/.

26. Ibid.

27. Sara Havens, "Poorcastle Celebrates Six Years with 36 Bands This Weekend," *Insider Louisville* (7–5-2018), https://insiderlouisville.com/lifestyle_culture/poorcastle-celebrates-six-years-with-36-bands-this-weekend/.

8. DISRUPTION: PATTERN, DEVIATION, ADAPTATION

1. David Bruenger, "Complexity, Adaptive Expertise, and Conceptual Models in the Music Business Curriculum," *MEIEA Journal* 15, no. 1 (December 2015), 99–119.

2. Andrew Lippmann and David Reed, "Viral Communications," *Media Laboratory Research, MIT* (5–19–2003), http://dl.media.mit.edu/viral/viral.pdf.

3. Joseph Schumpeter, *Capitalism, Socialism, and Democracy*, first edition Harper and Brothers (1942), reference here from the Harper edition of 1976, 83.

4. Frank Rose, "The Father Of Creative Destruction," *Wired* (3–1-2002), www.wired.com/2002/03/schumpeter/.

5. Esben Sloth Andersen, "Schumpeter's Core Works Revisited: Resolved Problems and Remaining Challenges," *Journal of Evolutionary Economics* 22, no. 4 (2012): 621–625; reprinted version, 10.

6. Ibid.

7. Ibid.

8. Bruenger, "Complexity, Adaptive Expertise, and Conceptual Models," and see the seminal work on which most expertise education is based: G. Hatano and K. Inagaki, "Two Courses of Expertise," in *Child Development and Education in Japan*, ed. Harold W. Stevenson, Hiroshi Azuma, and Kenji Hakuta, WH Freeman/Times Books/Henry Holt (1986), 262–272.

9. Bruenger, "Complexity, Adaptive Expertise, and Conceptual Models."

10. Murray Gell-Mann and Seth Lloyd, "Effective Complexity," SFI Working Paper 2003–12–068, https://sfi-edu.s3.amazonaws.com/sfi-edu/production/uploads/sfi-com/dev/uploads/filer/a2/of/a2of7840–5eb8–40a2–9d49-eb5c3456a8b9/03–12–068.pdf.

11. Murray Gell-Mann, "Complex Adaptive Systems," in *Complexity: Metaphors, Models, and Reality*, Perseus Books (1999), https://authors.library.caltech.edu/60491/1/MGM%20113.pdf.

12. Ibid.

13. See, for example, this retrospective by Andrew Harrison, "The Lazarus Effect: How the Music Industry Saved Itself," *New Statesman America* (1–9-2019), www.newstatesman.com/2019/01/is-the-music-industry-dead.

14. Murray Gell-Mann, "Complex Adaptive Systems."

15. See, for example, David Lowery, "Meet the New Boss, Worse Than the Old Boss," *Trichordist* (4–15–2012), https://thetrichordist.com/2012/04/15/meet-the-new-boss-worse-than-the-old-boss-full-post/.

16. Daniel Sanchez, "What Streaming Music Services Pay (Updated for 2018)," *Digital Music News* (1–16–2018), www.digitalmusicnews.com/2018/01/16/streaming-music-services-pay-2018/.

17. Kabir Seghal, "Spotify and Apple Music Should Become Record Labels So Musicians Can Make a Fair Living," *CNBC* (1–26–2018), www.cnbc.com/2018/01/26/how-spotify-apple-music-can-pay-musicians-more-commentary.htm.

18. Sanchez, "What Streaming Music Services Pay."

19. Mark Mulligan, "Global Recorded Music Revenues Grew by $1.4 Billion in 2017," MIDiA Research (4–19–2018), www.midiaresearch.com/blog/global-recorded-music-revenues-grew-by-1-4-billion-in-2017/.

20. "Kickstarter Crowdfunding Site Officially Launches in Canada," *Canadian Press* (9–10–2013), www.cbc.ca/news/business/kickstarter-crowdfunding-site-officially-launches-in-canada-1.1703774.

21. Sarah McKinney, "Patreon: A Fast-Growing Marketplace for Creators and Patrons of the Arts," *Forbes* (4–10–2014), www.forbes.com/sites/sarahmckinney/2014/04/10/patreon-a-fast-growing-marketplace-for-creators-and-patrons-of-the-arts/.

22. Gerrit De Vynck, "Patreon Found a Way to Pay the Creative Class. Will It Work?," *Bloomberg* (1–17–2018), www.bloomberg.com/news/articles/2018–01–17/patreon-found-a-way-to-pay-the-creative-class-will-it-work.

23. "Terms of Use," Patreon, www.patreon.com/legal.

24. Francisco Bernardo and Luis Gustavo Martins, "Disintermediation Effects on Independent Approaches to Music Business," *International Journal of Music Business Research* 3, no. 2 (October 2014), https://musicbusinessresearch.files.wordpress.com/2013/06/bernardo_desintermediation-effects-in-the-music-business.pdf.

25. Satoshi Nakamoto, "Bitcoin: A Peer-to-Peer Electronic Cash System," Bitcoin.org (2008), https://bitcoin.org/bitcoin.pdf.

26. Ibid.

27. David Gerard, *Attack of the 50 Foot Blockhain: Bitcoin, Blockchain, Ethereum, & Smart Contracts,* David Gerard (2017), 13.

28. Matthew Ingraham, "Using the Blockchain to Reinvent the Music Business," *Fortune* (11–27–2015), http://fortune.com/2015/11/27/blockchain-music/.

29. Ibid.

30. George Howard, "Imogen Heap's Mycelia: An Artists' Approach for a Fair Trade Music Business, Inspired by Blockchain," *Forbes* (7–17–2015), www.forbes.com/sites/georgehoward/2015/07/17/imogen-heaps-mycelia-an-artists-approach-for-a-fair-trade-music-business-inspired-by-blockchain/#6b3472ce4969.

9. CONNECTION: ARTISTS, AUDIENCES, NETWORKS

1. See, for example, Jordan Runtagh, "Beatles' Famous Rooftop Concert: 15 Things You Didn't Know," *Rolling Stone* (1–29–2016), www.rollingstone.com/music/music-news/beatles-famous-rooftop-concert-15-things-you-didnt-know-58342/.

2. For examples of some twenty-first-century marketing plans that embody these principles, see Jill Haverkamp, "6 Case Studies on Successful Online Music Marketing," *Music Think Tank* (2–21–2011), www.musicthinktank.com/blog/6-case-studies-on-successful-online-music-marketing.html.

3. Mark Mulligan, "After The Album: How Playlists Are Re-Defining Listening," *Music Industry Blog, MIDiA* (4–26–2016), https://musicindustryblog.wordpress.com/2016/04/26/after-the-album-how-playlists-are-re-defining-listening/.

4. Quoted by Marc Hogan, "Up Next: How Playlists Are Curating the Future of Music," *Pitchfork* (7–16–2015), https://pitchfork.com/features/article/9686-up-next-how-playlists-are-curating-the-future-of-music/.

5. Ibid.

6. Eric Sheinkop, "Music Strategy and the Consumer Journey," *Music Ally* (3–18–2016), http://musically.com/2016/03/18/music-strategy-and-the-consumer-journey-guest-column/.

7. Ibid.

8. Ibid.

9. Ibid.

10. Joel Beckerman and Tyler Gray, *The Sonic Boom: How Sound Transforms the Way We Think Feel and Buy,* Houghton, Mifflin, Harcourt (2014).

11. Ibid.

12. John Abercrombe and Nicholas Longhurst, *Audiences: A Sociological Theory of Performance and Imagination,* Sage (1998).

13. Ibid.

14. Ibid.

15. "Scanning the Audio Demand Landscape," *Nielsen* (6–25–2014), www
.nielsen.com/us/en/insights/news/2014/scanning-the-audio-demand-landscape
.html.

16. Ibid.

17. Ibid.

18. Kyle Coroneos, "New Study Sees Difference between Passive & Active
Music Listeners," *Saving Country Music* (6–27–2014), www.savingcountrymusic
.com/new-study-sees-difference-between-passive-active-music-listeners/.

19. Nathan Hanks, "The Music That Unites Us," *MAX* (5–16–2018), www
.musicaudienceexchange.com/blog/the-music-that-unites-us/.

20. Gab Ginsburg, "Taylor Swift Braved the Torrential Downpour, Emerged
Victorious at New Jersey Show," *Billboard* (7–22–2018), www.billboard.com
/articles/columns/pop/8466473/taylor-swift-metlife-concert-new-jersey-rain-
recap.

21. Abercombie and Longhurst, *Audiences*, 113.

22. Jamie Primeau, "Taylor Swift's Rainy 'Reputation' Concert Was a 'Rare'
Treat for the Singer & Fans Alike," *Bustle* (7–22–2018), www.bustle.com/p
/taylor-swifts-rainy-reputation-concert-was-a-rare-treat-for-the-singer-fans-alike-
videos-9841469.

23. Abercrombie and Longhurst, *Audiences*, 121.

24. Jacob Ganz, "Dave Grohl: How to Make an Arena Feel Like a Punk
Club," *Record, NPR* (4–7–2011), www.npr.org/sections/therecord/2011/04/07
/133965436/dave-grohl-how-to-make-an-arena-feel-like-a-punk-club.

25. Ibid.

26. COS Staff, "A Guide to Music Festival VIP Experiences: Which Ones
Are Worth the Price of Admission?," *Consequence of Sound* (12–27–2016), https://
consequenceofsound.net/2016/12/a-critical-guide-to-the-music-festival-vip-
experience/.

27. "The Top 10 Benefits of Using RFID for Events," *Eventbrite*, www.eventbrite
.com/blog/academy/the-top-10-benefits-of-using-rfid-for-events/.

28. Andrew Lippmann and David Reed, "Viral Communications," *Media
Laboratory Research, MIT* (5–19–2003), http://dl.media.mit.edu/viral/viral.pdf.

29. Lauren Wirtzer Seawood, "What Instagram Discovered in Our First
Nielsen Music Study," *Cuepoint* (3–14–2016), https://medium.com/cuepoint
/what-instagram-discovered-in-our-first-nielsen-music-study-de1a2740c005.

30. Ibid.

31. Ibid.

32. Daniel Cavicchi, "Fandom before the Internet: The Fan Club Directory," *Ardent Audience* (7–31–2011), http://theardentaudience.blogspot.com/2011 /07/fandom-before-internet-fan-club.html.

33. Ibid.

34. Jake Hall, "Lady Gaga Pioneered Online Fandom Culture as We Know It," *Noisey* (9–30–2017), https://noisey.vice.com/en_au/article/pakq59/lady-gaga-online-fandom-culture-little-monsters.

35. Ibid.

36. Nancy Baym, "Book Excerpt: How Music Fans Built the Internet," *Wired* (7–10–2018), www.wired.com/story/book-excerpt-playing-to-the-crowd/.

37. Ibid.

38. Britanny Spanos, "Fans to the Front: How Internet Fandoms Are Gaming the Music Industry," *Rolling Stone* (5–5-2017), www.rollingstone.com /music/music-news/fans-to-the-front-how-internet-fandoms-are-gaming-the-music-industry-194067/.

39. Ibid.

40. Ibid.

41. Ibid.

42. Ibid.

43. William Deresiewicz, "The Death of the Artist—and the Birth of the Creative Entrepreneur," *Atlantic* (January/February 2015), www.theatlantic .com/magazine/archive/2015/01/the-death-of-the-artist-and-the-birth-of-the-creative-entrepreneur/383497/.

44. "The Sharing Economy: A New Way of Doing Business," *Rubicon, Knowledge@Wharton* (12–11–2015), http://knowledge.wharton.upenn.edu/article /the-sharing-economy-a-new-way-of-doing-business/.

45. Ibid.

46. Yochai Benkler, "Sharing Nicely: On Shareable Goods and the Emergence of Sharing as a Modality of Economic Production," *Yale Law Journal* (2004).

47. "The Sharing Economy."

48. Giana M. Eckhardt and Fleura Bardhi, "The Sharing Economy Isn't about Sharing at All," *Harvard Business Review* (1–28–2015), https://hbr .org/2015/01/the-sharing-economy-isnt-about-sharing-at-all.

49. "The Sharing Economy."

50. Eckhardt and Bardhi, "The Sharing Economy Isn't about Sharing at All."

51. See, for example, David Bruenger, *Making Money, Making Music,* University of California Press (2016).

10. INCORPORATION: PRODUCTION, MONETIZATION, AFFILIATION

1. Joyce, Joe Price, Alex Gardiner, and Graham Corrigan, "49 Independent Record Labels You Should Know," *Pigeons and Airplanes* (6–12–2018), https://pigeonsandplanes.com/in-depth/independent-record-labels-you-should-know/.

2. "The 80/20 Rule? More Like 80/1 for Music Sales," *Punch-In at TrueFire. com* (4-4-2016), http://truefire.com/blog/inspiration/8020-rule-801-music-sales/.

3. Evan Niu, "Steve Jobs Was Wrong about Music Streaming," *Motley Fool* (4-3-2018), www.fool.com/investing/2018/04/03/steve-jobs-was-wrong-about-music-streaming.aspx.

4. Yinka Andegoke, "Spotify CEO Daniel Ek on Hitting 10 Million Subs, Apple-Beats Deal, IPO (Q&A)," *Billboard* (5–21–2014), www.billboard.com/biz/articles/6092287/spotify-ceo-daniel-ek-10-million-subs-apple-beats-ipo?utm_source=twitter.

5. Brinkley Warren, "Lean Startup? Try Punk Rock Entrepreneurship," www.brinkleywarren.com/lean-startup-try-punk-rock-entrepreneurship/.

6. Gary Trust, "House Music: Your Living Room Might Be Your Next Concert Venue," *Billboard* (6–14–2013), www.billboard.com/articles/columns/chart-beat/1567029/house-music-your-living-room-might-be-your-next-concert-venue.

7. Ibid.

8. Ibid.

9. Cherie Hu, "Why Airbnb Is a Dark Horse in Live Music's Intimate Future," *Forbes* (6–19–2018), www.forbes.com/sites/cheriehu/2018/06/19/why-airbnb-is-a-dark-horse-in-live-musics-intimate-future/. While the AirBnB Concerts statistics for 2018 are not yet available and we can't confirm that prediction, the venture continues to be a vital part of the company's offerings and they are promoting it heavily via their blog. See, for example, https://blog.atairbnb.com/frequently-asked-questions-for-airbnb-concert-hosts/.

10. Hu, "Why Airbnb Is a Dark Horse in Live Music's Intimate Future."

11. Ibid.

12. Ibid.

13. Tim Sullivan, "Embracing Complexity," *Harvard Business Review* (September 2011 Issue), https://hbr.org/2011/09/embracing-complexity.

14. Edgar Morin, *On Complexity,* Hampton Press (2008), 49–50.

15. Joyce, Price, Gardiner, and Corrigan, "49 Independent Record Labels You Should Know." See also the label's website, https://mindofagenius.co.uk.

16. Ibid.

17. Ibid.

18. Ibid.

II. AGGREGATION: CONSUMPTION, PRODUCTION, PREDICTION

1. Jonathan Sale, "Sixty Years of Hits From Sinatra to ... Sinatra," *Independent* (1–5-1996), www.independent.co.uk/life-style/sixty-years-of-hits-from-sinatra-to-sinatra-1322429.html/.

2. Ibid.

3. Brian Wawzenek, "25 Years Ago: The Soundscan Era Rocks the Music Industry," *Ultimate Classic Rock,* http://ultimateclassicrock.com/billboard-soundscan/.

4. Ibid.

5. Ibid.

6. Chick Phillips, "The Accidental Chart Revolution: Pop Music: Billboard's New Method of Tracking Sales Is a Byproduct of a Once-Rival Market Research System," *Los Angeles Times* (5–30–1991), http://articles.latimes.com/1991–05–30/entertainment/ca-3677_1_market-research-system.

7. Wawzenek, "25 Years Ago."

8. Brian Moon, "From Spotify to Shazam: How Big-Data Remade the Music Industry One Algorithm at a Time," *Newsweek* (5–22–2017), www.newsweek.com/spotify-shazam-how-big-data-remade-music-industry-613325.

9. Ibid.

10. Derek Thompson, "The Shazam Effect," *Atlantic* (December 2014), www.theatlantic.com/magazine/archive/2014/12/the-shazam-effect/382237/.

11. Ibid.

12. Don Reisinger, "Here's How Many Subscribers Shazam Could Bring to Apple Music," *Fortune* (1–26–2018), http://fortune.com/go/tech/shazam-apple-music-subscribers/.

13. Thompson, "The Shazam Effect."

14. Ibid.

15. Josh Constine, "How Spotify Is Finally Gaining Leverage over Record Labels," *Tech Crunch* (3–18–2017), https://techcrunch.com/2017/03/18/dictate-top-40/.

16. "Most Popular Music Streaming Services in the United States as of March 2018, by Monthly Users (in Millions)," *Statista,* www.statista

.com/statistics/798125/most-popular-us-music-streaming-services-ranked-by-audience/.

17. Constine, "How Spotify Is Finally Gaining Leverage."

18. Felix Richter, "Spotify's Losses Widen as Royalty Costs Pile Up," *Statista* (3–1-2018), www.statista.com/chart/4894/spotify-revenue-vs-costs/.

19. Constine, "How Spotify Is Finally Gaining Leverage."

20. Ibid.

21. Steve Knopper, "How Apple Music, Tidal Exclusives Are Reshaping Music Industry," *Rolling Stone* (10–5-2016), www.rollingstone.com/music/music-news/how-apple-music-tidal-exclusives-are-reshaping-music-industry-106132/.

22. Hanna Karp, "Spotify Offers Managers, Artists Advances to License Music Directly to Its Streaming Service: Exclusive," *Billboard* (6–6-2018), http://musically.com/2018/07/26/spotify-talks-direct-artist-deals-licensing-content-doesnt-make-us-a-label/.

23. Ibid.

24. Ibid.

25. One possible outcome of the massive reorganization of music licensing for streaming under the Music Modernization Act (2018) is that Spotify becomes more free to license music directly from music makers—songwriters/performers—in addition to labels. Pursued even to a modest degree, this is potentially extremely disruptive to labels.

26. Stuart Dredge, "The Five Types of Music Discovery," *Guardian* (3–19–2014), www.theguardian.com/technology/2014/mar/19/music-discovery-spotify-apps-facebook.

27. Ibid.

28. Dhavanesh Adhiya, "15 Brilliant Apps to Discover Music on iPhone in 2018," *iGeeks Blog,* www.igeeksblog.com/brilliant-apps-to-discover-music-on-iphone/.

29. Stuart Dredge, "What's Next for Spotify? Perhaps Going 'beyond the Play Button,'" *Guardian* (3–11–2014), www.theguardian.com/technology/2014/mar/11/echo-nest-spotify-paul-lamere-sxsw.

30. Ibid.

31. Sasha Frere-Jones, "If You Care about Music, Should You Ditch *Spotify*," *New Yorker* (7–19–2013), www.newyorker.com/culture/sasmakingha-frere-jones/if-you-care-about-music-should-you-ditch-spotify.

32. Joel Warner, "Fueled by Venture-Capital Funding and a Love for Unknown Bands, Can Boulder's Next Big Sound Predict the Next Rock Star?,"

Westword (10–7–2010), www.westword.com/music/fueled-by-venture-capital-funding-and-a-love-for-unknown-bands-can-boulders-next-big-sound-predict-the-next-rock-star-5110133.

33. See www.nextbigsound.com/charts and then "Learn more about the science."

34. Warner, "Fueled by Venture-Capital Funding and a Love for Unknown Bands."

35. Bruenger, *Making Money, Making Music,* University of California Press (2016).

36. TuneCore was created to empower independent musicians by "partnering with digital stores to allow any musician to sell their songs worldwide while keeping 100% of their sales revenue." See www.tunecore.com.

37. See www.musicaudienceexchange.com. For a deeper discussion of Music Audience Exchange, see chapter 10, "Incorporation."

38. George Howard, "Imogen Heap's Mycelia: An Artists' Approach for a Fair Trade Music Business, Inspired by Blockchain," *Forbes* (7–17–2015), www.forbes.com/sites/georgehoward/2015/07/17/imogen-heaps-mycelia-an-artists-approach-for-a-fair-trade-music-business-inspired-by-blockchain/#6b3472ce4969.

39. Ibid.

40. Ibid.

41. http://myceliaformusic.org.

42. Ibid.

43. Howard, "Imogen Heap's Mycelia."

44. Ibid.

45. Imogen Heap, "Blockchain Could Help Musicians Make Money Again," *Harvard Business Review* (6–5–2017), https://hbr.org/2017/06/blockchain-could-help-musicians-make-money-again.

46. David Gerard, "Ujo Attempts Music on the Blockchain a Second Time With: EGO By RAC," *Hypebot* (11–1–2017), www.hypebot.com/hypebot/2017/11/ujo-attempts-music-on-the-blockchain-a-second-time-with-ego-by-rac.html.

47. Howard, "Imogen Heap's Mycelia."

48. David Gerard, "Why Spotify Wants Some Blockchain; How Music Industry Blockchain Dreams Work," *Rocknerd* (4–27–2017), https://rocknerd.co.uk/2017/04/27/why-spotify-wants-some-blockchain-how-music-industry-blockchain-dreams-work/.

49. Ibid.

50. Ibid.

51. Gerard, "Ujo Attempts Music on the Blockchain."

52. George Howard, "Bitcoin Can't Save the Music Industry Because the Music Industry Will Resist Transparency," *Forbes* (5–22–2015), www.forbes.com/sites/georgehoward/2015/05/22/bitcoin-cant-save-the-music-industry-because-the-music-industry-will-resist-transparency/.

53. Meghan Neal, "A Machine Successfully Predicted the Hit Dance Songs of 2015," *Motherboard* (12–17–2015), http://motherboard.vice.com/read/a-machine-successfully-predicted-the-hit-dance-songs-of-2015.

54. Ibid.

12. SIMULATION: CREATION, PRODUCTION, CONSUMPTION

1. David Boje, *Theatres of Capitalism,* n.p. (2002).

2. Ibid.

3. As of April 2, 2019, the view count was 18,538,077 on the Chrysler channel, https://youtu.be/SKL254Y_jtc.

4. Christina Rogers, "Building on the Buzz," *Detroit News* (3–16–2011).

5. Jeff T. Wattrick, "Chrysler Sues Pure Detroit for Selling 'Imported from Detroit' Merchandise," *MLive* (3–16–2011), www.mlive.com/auto/index.ssf/2011/03/chrysler_sues_pure_detroit_for.html.

6. Ibid.

7. Ibid.

8. For example, see David Bruenger, *Making Money, Making Music,* University of California Press (2016).

9. Stephanie Smith, "Beyoncé & Jay Z Touring Together This Summer," *Page Six* (4–15–2014), https://pagesix.com/2014/04/15/beyonce-and-jay-z-to-go-on-tour-this-summer/.

10. Ray Waddell, "Jay Z and Beyonce's on the Run Tour Tops $100 Million, 'Everybody's Winning,'" *Billboard* (8–5–2014), www.billboard.com/articles/business/6207007/jay-z-beyonce-on-the-run-tour-100-million.

11. Nicole Lyn Pesce, "The Louvre Unveils Beyoncé and Jay-Z-Themed Tour," *New York Post* (7–9–2018), https://nypost.com/2018/07/09/the-louvre-unveils-beyonce-and-jay-z-themed-tour/.

12. Ibid.

13. Ibid.

14. Harriet Thorpe, "Beneath the Stage with Beyoncé & Jay-Z," *Wallpaper,* www.wallpaper.com/architecture/beyonce-jay-z-tour-stage-design-by-stufish.

15. Doc Coyle, "What Are Backing Tracks and Why Do They Matter?," *Creative Live* (4–6-2015), www.creativelive.com/blog/backing-tracks-history-use/.

16. Jon Pareles, "Pop View; That Syncing Feeling," *New York Times* (4–9-1989), www.nytimes.com/1989/04/09/arts/pop-view-that-syncing-feeling .html?pagewanted=all&src=pm.

17. Coyle, "What Are Backing Tracks and Why Do They Matter?"

18. Ibid.

19. Pareles, "Pop View; That Syncing Feeling."

20. Examples of musical shorts include Dick Rich and His Melodious Monarchs (1926) and Louis Jordan, "Caledonia" (1946), www.youtube.com /watch?v=cAIHhkTdHMw and www.youtube.com/watch?v=OCH_n9CT-TbA, respectively.

21. Pareles, "Pop View; That Syncing Feeling."

22. For example, Daniel Boorstin described a celebrity as "a person who is known for his well-knownness" in *The Image: A Guide to Pseudo-Events in America*, Vintage (1961).

23. Alvin Toffler, *Future Shock, Random House* (1970).

24. William Deresiewicz, "The Death of the Artist and the Rise of the Creative Entrepreneur," *Atlantic* (January/February 2015), www.theatlantic. com/magazine/archive/2015/01/the-death-of-the-artist-and-the-birth-of-the-creative-entrepreneur/383497/.

25. Ibid.

26. www.youtube.com/watch?v=RxPZh4AnWyk.

27. See, for example, Jim Nabors (in character as Gomer Pyle) performing "Impossible Dream" from "The Show Must Go On" episode (11-3-1967) of *Gomer Pyle: USMC* (CBS/Ashland Productions), www.youtube.com/watch?v= r5KeGccP9Jk.

28. Jen Sako, "To Virtual Reality and Beyond: The Future of Music Experiences," *Music Development Agency* (12–28–2017), https://themusicda.com /virtual-reality-beyond-future-music-experiences/.

29. Ibid.

30. Cherie Hu, "Virtual Reality in the Music Industry Needs to Be a Tool, Not Just an Experience," *Forbes* (4–23–2016), www.forbes.com/sites/cheriehu /2016/04/23/virtual-reality-in-the-music-industry-needs-to-be-a-tool-not-just-an-experience/.

31. Keith Harris and Maura Johnston, "20 Weird and Wild Grammy Collaborations," *Rolling Stone* (2–9-2016), www.rollingstone.com/music/music-lists

/20-weird-and-wild-grammy-collaborations-26174/gorillaz-madonna-and-de-la-soul-feel-good-inc-hung-up-2006–26018/.

32. Gil Kaufman, "Tupac, Michael Jackson, Gorillaz & More: A History of the Musical Hologram," *Billboard* (3–9-2017), www.billboard.com/articles/columns/pop/7717042/musical-holograms-history-dead.

33. Rebecca Greenfield, "Meet Hatsune Miku, the Japanese Pop Superstar Who Is Entirely Virtual," *Fast Company* (10–24–2014), www.fastcompany.com/3037383/meet-hatsune-miku-the-japanese-pop-superstar-who-is-entirely-virtual.

34. Calum Marsh, "We Attended the Hatsune Miku Expo to Find Out If a Hologram Pop Star Could Be Human," *Thump/Vice* (5–27–2016), https://thump.vice.com/en_ca/article/ae87yb/hatsune-miku-crypton-show-feature.

35. Ibid.

36. Ibid.

37. Ibid.

38. Pareles, "Pop View; That Syncing Feeling."

39. Ibid.

40. David Remnick, "We Are Alive," *New Yorker* (7–30–2012), www.newyorker.com/magazine/2012/07/30/we-are-alive.

BIBLIOGRAPHY

"2016 Demographics." *SXSW*, www.sxsw.com/wp-content/uploads/2016/05/SXSW-2016-Demographics.pdf.

"5 Unexpected Cities Experiencing a Live Music Renaissance." *Eventbrite* (8–17–2017), www.eventbrite.com/blog/music-cities-best-music-scenes-ds00/.

"The 80/20 Rule? More Like 80/1 for Music Sales." *Punch-In at TrueFire.com* (4–4–2016), http://truefire.com/blog/inspiration/8020-rule-801-music-sales/.

Abercrombie, John, and Nicholas Longhurst. *Audiences: A Sociological Theory of Performance and Imagination*, Sage (1998).

"About Sun Records." *Sun Record Company*. www.sunrecords.com/about.

Adhiya, Dhavanesh. "15 Brilliant Apps to Discover Music on iPhone in 2018." *iGeeks Blog*, www.igeeksblog.com/brilliant-apps-to-discover-music-on-iphone/.

Adorno, Theodor W. "On Popular Music." In *Essays on Music*, 437–469. University of California Press (2002).

Andegoke, Yinka. "Spotify CEO Daniel Ek on Hitting 10 Million Subs, Apple-Beats Deal, IPO (Q&A)." *Billboard* (5–21–2014), www.billboard.com/biz/articles/6092287/spotify-ceo-daniel-ek-10-million-subs-apple-beats-ipo?utm_source=twitter.

Andersen, Esben Sloth. "Schumpeter's Core Works Revisited: Resolved Problems and Remaining Challenges." *Journal of Evolutionary Economics* 22, no. 4 (2012): 621–625.

Anderson, Trevor. "One Direction Takes 'Control' at No. 1 on Billboard + Twitter Top Tracks Chart." *Billboard* (5–21–2015), www.billboard.com

/articles/columns/chart-beat/6575675/one-direction-no-control-twitter-top-tracks.

Arrington, Michael. "This Is Quite Possibly the Spotify Cap Table." *Tech Crunch* (8–7-2009), https://techcrunch.com/2009/08/07/this-is-quite-possibly-the-spotify-cap-table/.

Aswad, Jem. "Tidal Accused of Falsifying Beyonce and Kanye West Streaming Numbers." *Variety* (5–9-2018).

"Auto-Tune and Vocal Processing Tools." www.antarestech.com/products/.

Bates, James. "Berry Gordy Sells Motown Records for $61 Million." *LA Times* (6–29–1988), http://articles.latimes.com/1988–06–29/business/fi-4916_1_motown-records.

Baym, Nancy. "Book Excerpt: How Music Fans Built the Internet," *Wired* (7–10–2018), www.wired.com/story/book-excerpt-playing-to-the-crowd/.

Beckerman, Joel, and Tyler Gray. *The Sonic Boom: How Sound Transforms the Way We Think, Feel, and Buy.* Houghton Mifflin Harcourt (2014).

Benkler, Yochai. "Sharing Nicely: On Shareable Goods and the Emergence of Sharing as a Modality of Economic Production." *Yale Law Journal* (2004).

Bernardo, Francisco, and Luis Gustavo Martins. "Disintermediation Effects on Independent Approaches to Music Business." *International Journal of Music Business Research* 3, no. 2 (October 2014), https://musicbusinessresearch.files .wordpress.com/2013/06/bernardo_desintermediation-effects-in-the-music-business.pdf.

Bevaqua, Joel. "Are Cryptocurrencies Like Bitcoin the Solution to the Music Industry's Woes?" *LA Weekly* (7–11–2017).

Bishop, Syd. "Festival for the Rest of Us: An Oral History of Poorcastle." *LEO* (7–8-2015), www.leoweekly.com/2015/07/festival-for-the-rest-of-us-an-oral-history-of-poorcastle/.

Blank, Steve. "Why the Lean Startup Changes Everything." *Harvard Business Review* (May 2013), https://hbr.org/2013/05/why-the-lean-start-up-changes-everything.

"BMI Members Say 'No' to 100% Licensing." *BMI.* www.bmi.com/advocacy /doj_letter.

Boje, David. *Theatres of Capitalism.* n.p. (2002).

Bollek, Brooks. "NAB Opens Fire on RIAA Royalty Drive." *Hollywood Reporter* (6–15–2007), www.hollywoodreporter.com/news/nab-opens-fire-riaa-royalty-138999.

Bono, "My Wish: Three Actions for Africa." *TED2005,* www.ted.com/talks /bono_s_call_to_action_for_africa/transcript.

Boorstin, Daniel. *The Image: A Guide to Pseudo-Events in America.* Vintage (1961).

Boucher, Frederick C. "Blanket Music Licensing and Local Television: An Historical Accident in Need of Reform." *Washington and Lee Law Review* 44, no. 4 (Fall 1987), https://scholarlycommons.law.wlu.edu/cgi/viewcontent.cgi?article=2822&context=wlulr.

Brooks, Dave. "Beyoncé and JAY-Z's On the Run II Tour Could Do Double the Business Their 2014 Tour Did." *Billboard* (3–12–2018), www.billboard.com/articles/business/8240747/beyonce-jay-z-on-the-run-ii-tour-double-business-2014-tour.

———. "Taylor Swift Has Concert Industry Embracing 'Slow Ticketing' Model." *Billboard* (12–14–2017), www.billboard.com/articles/business/8070644/taylor-swift-concert-industry-slow-ticketing-model-sales.

Bruenger, David. "Complexity, Adaptive Expertise, and Conceptual Models in the Music Business Curriculum." *MEIEA Journal* 15, no. 1 (December 2015): 99–119.

———. *Making Money, Making Music.* University of California Press (2016).

Buchele, Mose. "How Did Austin Become the 'Live Music Capital Of The World'?" *KUT 91.5, Austin's NPR Station* (9–21–2016), http://kut.org/post/how-did-austin-become-live-music-capital-world.

Buenneke, Katie. "One Direction Is Now a DIY Band." *LA Weekly* (5–18–2015), www.laweekly.com/music/one-direction-is-now-a-diy-band-5581248.

"CARP (Copyright Arbitration Royalty Panel) Structure and Process." *Statement of Marybeth Peters, the Register of Copyrights before the Subcommittee on Courts, the Internet, and Intellectual Property, Committee on the Judiciary, United States House of Representatives, 107th Congress, 2nd Session* (6–13–2002), www.copyright.gov/docs/regstat061302.html.

Cavicchi, Daniel. "Fandom before the Internet: The Fan Club Directory." *Ardent Audience* (7–31–2011), http://theardentaudience.blogspot.com/2011/07/fandom-before-internet-fan-club.html.

Christman, Ed. "ASCAP and BMI Call On DOJ to Replace Consent Decrees: Open Letter." *Billboard* (2–28–2019), www.billboard.com/articles/business/8500472/ascap-bmi-open-letter-doj-consent-decrees-regulation.

———. "Music Modernization Act Sails through Senate Judiciary Committee; Industry Reacts." *Billboard* (6–28–2018), www.billboard.com/articles/business/8463234/music-modernization-act-senate-judiciary-committee.

———. "SoundExchange Extends CEO Michael Huppe through 2021." *Billboard* (1–10–2018), www.billboard.com/articles/business/8093735/soundexchange-ceo-michael-huppe-contract-2021.

Constine, Josh. "How Spotify Is Finally Gaining Leverage over Record Labels." *Tech Crunch* (3–18–2017), https://techcrunch.com/2017/03/18/dictate-top-40/.

Contreras, Felix. "The Hip-Hop Influence Of Jab'o Starks, James Brown's Timekeeper." *All Songs Considered, NPR Music* (5-3-2018), www.npr.org/sections/allsongs/2018/05/03/607748562/the-hip-hop-influence-of-jabo-starks-james-brown-s-timekeeper.

"Copyright Act of 1976." *Public Law 94–553*, www.copyright.gov/history/pl94–553.pdf.

Cordero, Robert. "Concert 'Merch' Comes of Age." *Business of Fashion* (4–18–2016), www.businessoffashion.com/articles/intelligence/concert-tour-merchandise-justin-bieber-rihanna-kanye-west.

Coroneos, Kyle. "New Study Sees Difference between Passive & Active Music Listeners." *Saving Country Music* (6–27–2014), www.savingcountrymusic.com/new-study-sees-difference-between-passive-active-music-listeners/.

COS Staff. "A Guide to Music Festival VIP Experiences: Which Ones Are Worth the Price of Admission?" *Consequence of Sound* (12–27–2016), https://consequenceofsound.net/2016/12/a-critical-guide-to-the-music-festival-vip-experience/.

Coyle, Doc. "What Are Backing Tracks and Why Do They Matter?" *Creative Live* (4–6-2015), www.creativelive.com/blog/backing-tracks-history-use/.

Crawford, Matthew. *The World Beyond Your Head: On Becoming an Individual in an Age of Distraction*. Farrar, Straus and Giroux (2015).

Crawford, Valerie M., Mark Schlager, Yukie Toyama, Margaret Riel, and Phil Vahey. "Report on a Laboratory Study of Teacher Reasoning: Characterizing Adaptive Expertise in Science Teaching." Presentation, the American Educational Research Association Annual Conference, April 11–15, 2005, Montreal, Canada.

Deresiewicz, William. "The Death of the Artist and the Rise of the Creative Entrepreneur." *Atlantic* (January/February 2015), www.theatlantic.com/magazine/archive/2015/01/the-death-of-the-artist-and-the-birth-of-the-creative-entrepreneur/383497/.

Devine, Sue. "How Music Impacts Our Lives in Ways We Don't Even Notice." *Playback, ASCAP* (12–1-2014), www.ascap.com/playback/2014/11/radar-report/joel-beckerman-sonic-boom.

De Vynck, Gerrit. "Patreon Found a Way to Pay the Creative Class. Will It Work?" *Bloomberg* (1–17–2018), www.bloomberg.com/news/articles/2018–01–17/patreon-found-a-way-to-pay-the-creative-class-will-it-work.

DiCola, Peter. "The Economics of Recorded Music: From Free Market to Just Plain Free." *Future of Music Coalition* (7–16–2000), https://futureofmusic.org /article/economics-recorded-music.

"The Digital Millennium Copyright Act Summary." *Pub. L. No. 105–304, 112 Stat. 2860 (10–28–1998), U.S. Copyright Office,* www.copyright.gov/legislation /dmca.pdf.

"Digital Performance Right in Sound Recordings Act of 1995." Public Law 104–39, 109 Stat. 336 (11–1–1995), www.wipo.int/wipolex/en/text.jsp?file_id= 343768.

"Do Not Assume We Have Arrived At Our Destination." *Music Industry Blog* (6–15–2017), https://musicindustryblog.wordpress.com/tag/artist-income/.

Dredge, Stuart. "The Five Types of Music Discovery." *Guardian* (3–19–2014), www.theguardian.com/technology/2014/mar/19/music-discovery-spotify-apps-facebook.

———. "What's Next for Spotify? Perhaps Going 'beyond the Play Button.'" *Guardian* (3–11–2014), www.theguardian.com/technology/2014/mar/11/echo-nest-spotify-paul-lamere-sxsw.

Eckhardt, Giana M., and Fleura Bardhi. "The Sharing Economy Isn't About Sharing at All." *Harvard Business Review* (1–28–2015), https://hbr.org/2015/01 /the-sharing-economy-isnt-about-sharing-at-all.

Edgers, Geoff. "Why My Guitar Gently Weeps." *Washington Post* (6–22–2017), www.washingtonpost.com/graphics/2017/lifestyle/the-slow-secret-death-of-the-electric-guitar/?noredirect=on&utm_term=.43c86c9do3b4.

Eggerton, John. "DOJ Antitrust Chief: We Are Reviewing ASCAP, BMI Consent Decrees." *Broadcasting & Cable* (3–28–2018), www.broadcastingcable.com /news/doj-antitrust-chief-reviewing-ascap-bmi-consent-decrees.

Elberse, Anita. *Blockbusters: Hit-Making, Risk-Taking, and the Big Business Of Entertainment.* Henry Holt and Company (2013).

Ellingson, Carole A. "The Copyright Exception for Derivative Works and the Scope of Utilization." *Indiana Law Journal* 56, no. 1 (1980–1981), www.repository .law.indiana.edu/ilj/vol56/iss1/1.

"Enabling Economies for the Future: Insight from the 2015 Strategic Innovation Summit at Harvard." http://theinnovatorsforum.org/sites/default /files/EEF_Whitepaper_2015.pdf.

Fisher, William Arms. *One Hundred and Fifty Years of Music Publishing in the United States.* Oliver Ditson (1933).

Flanagan, Andrew. "The Struggles Of Austin's Music Scene Mirror a Widened World." *The Record, NPR* (2–24–2017), www.npr.org/sections/therecord

/2017/02/24/516904340/the-struggles-of-austins-music-scene-mirror-a-widened-world.

Florida, Richard. "Why Making the Scene Makes Good Cents for the Rest of Us." *Creative Class* (12–29–2007), www.creativeclass.com/_v3/creative_class/2007/12/29/urban-sound-system-2/.

Florida, Richard, and Scott Jackson. "Sonic City: The Evolving Geography of the Music Industry." Working paper, January 2008, Martin Prosperity Institute, University of Toronto, www-2.rotman.utoronto.ca/userfiles/prosperity/File/Sonic%20City%20RF3.w.cover.pdf.

"Foreign & Domestic Music Corp. v. Licht et al, 196 F.2d 627 (2d Cir. 1952)," https://law.justia.com/cases/federal/appellate-courts/F2/196/627/15299/.

Frere-Jones, Sasha. "If You Care about Music, Should You Ditch Spotify?" *New Yorker* (7–19–2013), www.newyorker.com/culture/sasmakingha-frere-jones/if-you-care-about-music-should-you-ditch-spotify.

Friedlander, Joshua. "News and Notes on 2017 RIAA Revenue Statistics," *RIAA*, www.riaa.com/wp-content/uploads/2018/03/RIAA-Year-End-2017-News-and-Notes.pdf.

"Future Ready Economies." Dell, www.futurereadyeconomies.dell.com/?section=future-ready-economies.

Ganz, Jacob. "The Concert Ticket Food Chain: Where Your Money Goes." *The Record, NPR Music* (4–6–2011), www.npr.org/sections/therecord/2011/04/07/134851302/the-concert-ticket-food-chain-where-your-money-goes.

———. "Dave Grohl: How to Make an Arena Feel Like a Punk Club." *The Record, NPR* (4–7–2011), www.npr.org/sections/therecord/2011/04/07/133965436/dave-grohl-how-to-make-an-arena-feel-like-a-punk-club.

Gell-Mann, Murray. "Complex Adaptive Systems." In *Complexity: Metaphors, Models, and Reality*. Perseus Books (1999), https://authors.library.caltech.edu/60491/1/MGM%20113.pdf.

Gell-Mann, Murray, and Seth Lloyd. "Effective Complexity." SFI Working Paper 2003–12–068, https://sfi-edu.s3.amazonaws.com/sfi-edu/production/uploads/sfi-com/dev/uploads/filer/a2/0f/a20f7840–5eb8–40a2–9d49-eb5c3456a8b9/03–12–068.pdf.

Gerard, David. *Attack of the 50 Foot Blockhain: Bitcoin, Blockchain, Ethereum, & Smart Contracts*. David Gerard (2017).

———. "Ujo Attempts Music on the Blockchain a Second Time with: EGO by RAC." *Hypebot* (11–1–2017), www.hypebot.com/hypebot/2017/11/ujo-attempts-music-on-the-blockchain-a-second-time-with-ego-by-rac.html.

————. "Why Spotify Wants Some Blockchain; How MusicIndustry Blockchain Dreams Work." *Rocknerd* (4–27–2017), https://rocknerd.co.uk/2017/04/27/why-spotify-wants-some-blockchain-how-music-industry-blockchain-dreams-work/.

Ginsburg, Gab. "Taylor Swift Braved the Torrential Downpour, Emerged Victorious at New Jersey Show." *Billboard* (7–22–2018), www.billboard.com/articles/columns/pop/8466473/taylor-swift-metlife-concert-new-jersey-rain-recap.

Goldhill, Olivia. "The Most Committed Fans in the World: One Directioners versus Beatlemania." *Telegraph* (11–18–2014), www.telegraph.co.uk/women/womens-life/11236700/The-most-committed-fans-in-the-world-One-Directioners-versus-The-Beatlemania.html.

Gordon, Steve, and Anja Puri. "The Current State of Pre-1972 Sound Recordings: Recent Federal Court Decisions in California and New York against Sirius XM Have Broader Implications Than Just Whether Satellite and Internet Radio Stations Must Pay for Pre-1972 Sound Recordings." *JIPEL* (5–4–2015), https://jipel.law.nyu.edu/vol-4-no-2-5-gordonpuri/.

Gould, J.J. "'The Musical Equivalent of Star Trek': Moby on Teaming, Touring, Sci-Fi." *Atlantic* (7–24–2012), www.theatlantic.com/entertainment/archive/2012/07/moby-star-trek/260261/.

Gray, Tyler. "Punk Rock Branding: How Bruce Pavitt Built Sub Pop in an Anti-Corporate Nirvana." *Fast Company* (11–29–2012), www.fastcompany.com/1681976/punk-rock-branding-how-bruce-pavitt-built-sub-pop-in-an-anti-corporate-nirvana.

Greenfield, Rebecca. "Meet Hatsune Miku, the Japanese Pop Superstar Who Is Entirely Virtual." *Fast Company* (10–24–2014), www.fastcompany.com/3037383/meet-hatsune-miku-the-japanese-pop-superstar-who-is-entirely-virtual.

Haden, Jeff. "How Forecastle Festival Turned Music, Art, and Activism into a National Happening." *Inc.* (7–12–2018), www.inc.com/jeff-haden/how-forecastle-festival-turned-music-art-activism-into-a-national-happening.html.

Hall, Jake. "Lady Gaga Pioneered Online Fandom Culture as We Know It." *Noisey* (9–30–2017), https://noisey.vice.com/en_au/article/pakq59/lady-gaga-online-fandom-culture-little-monsters.

Hanks, Nathan. "The Music That Unites Us." *MAX* (5–16–2018), www.musicaudienceexchange.com/blog/the-music-that-unites-us/.

Harris, Keith, and Maura Johnston. "20 Weird and Wild Grammy Collaborations." *Rolling Stone* (2–9-2016), www.rollingstone.com/music/music-lists /20-weird-and-wild-grammy-collaborations-26174/gorillaz-madonna-and-de-la-soul-feel-good-inc-hung-up-2006–26018/.

Harrison, Andrew. "The Lazarus Effect: How the Music Industry Saved Itself." *New Statesman America* (1–9-2019), www.newstatesman.com/2019/01/is-the-music-industry-dead.

Hatano, G., and K. Inagaki, "Two Courses of Expertise." In *Child Development and Education in Japan,* edited by Harold W. Stevenson, Hiroshi Azuma, and Kenji Hakuta, 262–272. WH Freeman/Times Books/Henry Holt (1986).

Havens, Sara. "Poorcastle Celebrates Six Years with 36 Bands This Weekend." *Insider Louisville* (7–5-2018), https://insiderlouisville.com/lifestyle_culture /poorcastle-celebrates-six-years-with-36-bands-this-weekend/.

Haverkamp, Jill. "6 Case Studies on Successful Online Music Marketing." *Music Think Tank* (2–21–2011), www.musicthinktank.com/blog/6-case-studies-on-successful-online-music-marketing.html.

Heap, Imogen. "Blockchain Could Help Musicians Make Money Again." *Harvard Business Review* (6–5-2017), https://hbr.org/2017/06/blockchain-could-help-musicians-make-money-again.

Hearn, Alex. "Is Spotify Really Worth $20bn?" *Guardian* (3–2-2018), www .theguardian.com/technology/2018/mar/02/is-spotify-really-worth-20bn.

Hein, Ethan. "Bittersweet Symphony." *Ethan Hein Blog* (11–23–2009), www .ethanhein.com/wp/2009/bitter-sweet-symphony/.

"Herbert v. Shanley Co., 242 U.S. 591 (1917)." *Justia,* https://supreme.justia.com /cases/federal/us/242/591/case.html.

Hogan, Marc. "Up Next: How Playlists Are Curating the Future of Music." *Pitchfork* (7–16–2015), https://pitchfork.com/features/article/9686-up-next-how-playlists-are-curating-the-future-of-music/.

Hoos, Willem. "Dutch Newspaper Details Stones' Financial Web." *Billboard* (8–7-1982), https://books.google.com/books?id=FiQEAAAAMBAJ&pg= PT68&lpg=PT68&dq=rolling+stones+promotour&source=bl&ots=EeEti CNHes&sig=EGjLCBBGTn5zsUPlmofOcPa7yUE&hl=en&sa=X&ved= oahUKEwiP-fS-4tPbAhUk_4MKHS3PCz44ChDoAQhPMAg#v=onepa ge&q&f=false.

Howard, George. "Bitcoin Can't Save the Music Industry Because the Music Industry Will Resist Transparency." *Forbes* (5–22–2015), www.forbes.com /sites/georgehoward/2015/05/22/bitcoin-cant-save-the-music-industry-because-the-music-industry-will-resist-transparency/.

————. "Imogen Heap's Mycelia: An Artists' Approach for a Fair Trade Music Business, Inspired by Blockchain." *Forbes* (7–17–2015), www.forbes .com/sites/georgehoward/2015/07/17/imogen-heaps-mycelia-an-artists-approach-for-a-fair-trade-music-business-inspired-by-blockchain/#6b3472ce4969.

Hu, Cherie. "Virtual Reality in the Music Industry Needs to Be a Tool, Not Just an Experience." *Forbes* (4–23–2016), www.forbes.com/sites/cheriehu/2016 /04/23/virtual-reality-in-the-music-industry-needs-to-be-a-tool-not-just-an-experience/.

————. "Why Airbnb Is a Dark Horse In Live Music's Intimate Future." *Forbes* (6–19–2018), www.forbes.com/sites/cheriehu/2018/06/19/why-airbnb-is-a-dark-horse-in-live-musics-intimate-future/.

Huron, David. *Sweet Anticipation: Music and the Psychology of Expectation*. MIT Press (2006).

Hyun, Chong, and Christie Byun. *The Economics of the Popular Music Industry*, Palgrave MacMillan (2016).

Ingham, Tim. "Here's Exactly How Many Shares the Major Labels and Merlin Bought in Spotify—and What Those Stakes Are Worth Now." *Music Business Worldwide* (5–14–2018), www.musicbusinessworldwide.com/heres-exactly-how-many-shares-the-major-labels-and-merlin-bought-in-spotify-and-what-we-think-those-stakes-are-worth-now/.

Ingraham, Matthew. "Using the Blockchain to Reinvent the Music Business." *Fortune* (11–27–2015), http://fortune.com/2015/11/27/blockchain-music/.

"An Introduction to Design Thinking PROCESS GUIDE." https://dschool-old .stanford.edu/sandbox/groups/designresources/wiki/36873/attachments/74b3d /ModeGuideBOOTCAMP2010L.pdf.

Ivey, Bill. "America Needs a New System for Supporting the Arts." *Chronicle of Higher Education* (2–4–2005).

Jakubowski, Kelly, Lauren Stewart, Sebastian Finkel, and Daniel Müllensiefen. "Dissecting an Earworm: Melodic Features and Song Popularity Predict Involuntary Musical Imagery." *Psychology of Aesthetics, Creativity, and the Arts* 11, no. 2 (2017): 122–135.

Jelbert, Steve. "Labelled with Love; Sounds." *The Times* (8–2–2008), http://link .galegroup.com/apps/doc/A182437350/AONE?u=colu44332&sid=AO.

Jolly, Nathan. "The History Of Music Merch." *Music Network* (5–24–2010), https://nathanjollywrites.wordpress.com/2016/02/10/the-history-of-music-merch/.

Jones, Dylan. "Icon Of The Year: Robbie Williams." *GQ* (10–1–2012), www .gq-magazine.co.uk/article/icon-of-the-year-robbie-williams.

Joyce, Joe Price, Alex Gardiner, and Graham Corrigan. "49 Independent Record Labels You Should Know." *Pigeons and Airplanes* (6–12–2018), https://pigeonsandplanes.com/in-depth/independent-record-labels-you-should-know/.

Kafka, Peter. "The Music Business Is Growing Again—Really Growing—and It's Because of Streaming." *Recode* (9–20–2017), www.recode.net/2017/9/20/16339484/music-streaming-riaa-spotify-apple-music-youtube-2017-revenue-subscription/.

Karp, Hanna. "Spotify Offers Managers, Artists Advances to License Music Directly to Its Streaming Service: Exclusive." *Billboard* (6–6–2018), http://musically.com/2018/07/26/spotify-talks-direct-artist-deals-licensing-content-doesnt-make-us-a-label/.

Kaufman, Gil. "Michael Jackson's Last Tour Rehearsals Filmed for Possible Release." *MTV News* (6–29–2009), www.mtv.com/news/1614882/michael-jacksons-last-tour-rehearsals-filmed-for-possible-release/.

———. "Tupac, Michael Jackson, Gorillaz & More: A History of the Musical Hologram." *Billboard* (3–9-2017), www.billboard.com/articles/columns/pop/7717042/musical-holograms-history-dead.

Kawashima, Dale. "NMPA CEO David Israelite Discusses the Recent Copyright Royalty Board Ruling and the Music Modernization Act." *Songwriter Universe* (2–7-2018), www.songwriteruniverse.com/david-israelite-nmpa-2018.htm.

Kaye, Ben. "Proof the 'Sophomore Album Slump' Is a Real Problem." *Consequence of Sound* (2–13–2015), https://consequenceofsound.net/2015/02/proof-the-sophomore-album-slump-is-a-real-problem/.

Kaye, Elizabeth. "Sam Phillips: The Rolling Stone Interview." *Rolling Stone* (2–13–1986), www.rollingstone.com/music/music-news/sam-phillips-the-rolling-stone-interview-122988/.

Kempton, Arthur. *Boogalo: The Quintessence of American Popular Music*. University of Michigan Press (2005).

Kessler, Sarah. "BuzzFeed's Jonah Peretti Is the Stephen Hawking of Radical Skateboarding Birds." *Fast Company* (9–14–2012), www.fastcompany.com/3001308/buzzfeeds-jonah-peretti-stephen-hawking-radical-skateboarding-birds.

"Kickstarter Crowdfunding Site Officially Launches in Canada." *Canadian Press* (9–10–2013), www.cbc.ca/news/business/kickstarter-crowdfunding-site-officially-launches-in-canada-1.1703774.

Kissel, Chris. "Sub Pop Founder Bruce Pavitt Recalls the Birth of 'Indie' and Reflects on Today's Music Industry." *Diffuser* (2–24–2015), http://diffuser .fm/sub-pop-bruce-pavitt-interview-2015/.

Knopper, Steve. "How Apple Music, Tidal Exclusives Are Reshaping Music Industry." *Rolling Stone* (10–5–2016), www.rollingstone.com/music/music-news /how-apple-music-tidal-exclusives-are-reshaping-music-industry-106132/.

Koh, Byungwan, Il-Horn Hann, and Srinivasan Raghunathan. "Digitization, Unbundling, and Piracy: Consumer Adoption amidst Disruptive Innovations in the Music Industry." Robert H. Smith School Research Paper (October 2015), http://ssrn.com/abstract=2371943 or http://dx.doi.org/10.2139 /ssrn.2371943.

Kornhaber, Spencer. "Starbucks's Failed Music Revolution." *Atlantic* (2–5–2015), www.theatlantic.com/entertainment/archive/2015/02/starbuckss-failed-music-revolution/385937/.

Lagorio-Chafkin, Christine. "The Company Reinventing How Bands Sell Merch This Festival Season." *Inc.* (7–25–2016), www.inc.com/christine-lagorio/band-tour-merchandise.html.

Lang, Nico "How U2 Became the Most Hated Band in America." *Salon* (9–8-2014), www.salon.com/2014/09/18/how_u2_became_the_most_hated_band_ in_america_partner/.

Lessig, Lawrence. *Remix: Making Art and Commerce Thrive in the Hybrid Economy.* Penguin Press (2008).

Lewis, Randy. "New Biography illuminates Life of Sun Records Founder Sam Phillips." *Los Angeles Times* (11–17–2015), www.latimes.com/entertainment /music/posts/la-et-ms-sam-phillips-biography-peter-guralnick-elvis-presley-20151117-story.html.

"Licensing 101." *SoundExchange,* www.soundexchange.com/service-provider /licensing-101/.

Lindvall, Helienne. "Behind the Music: Motown—a Pop Factory with Quality Control." *Guardian* (11–26–2010), www.theguardian.com/music/musicblog /2010/nov/26/behind-music-motown-pop-factory.

Lippmann, Andrew, and David Reed, "Viral Communications." *Media Laboratory Research, MIT* (5–19–2003), http://dl.media.mit.edu/viral/viral .pdf.

Lopez, Ashley. "How Arts and Culture Could Shape Louisville's Tech Future." *WFPI* (1–08–2016), http://wfpl.org/how-arts-and-culture-in-louisville-could-help-its-tech-future/.

Lowery, David. "Meet the New Boss, Worse than the Old Boss." *Trichordist* (4–15–2012), https://thetrichordist.com/2012/04/15/meet-the-new-boss-worse-than-the-old-boss-full-post/.

Lunden, Ingrid. "Spotify Strikes New Deal with Indy Giant Merlin 'Competitive' with Big Labels." *Tech Crunch* (4–20–2017), https://techcrunch.com/2017/04/20/spotify-strikes-new-deal-with-indy-giant-merlin-competitive-with-big-3-labels/.

Lynch, Joe. "1994 vs. 2014: Comparing the Top-Selling Albums." *Billboard* (10–20–2014), www.billboard.com/articles/6259342/1994-vs-2014-top-selling-albums-comparison.

Mao, Jefferson. "Godfather Lives Through: Hip-Hop's Top 25 James Brown Sampled Records." *egotripland.com* (5–3-2012), www.egotripland.com/hip-hop-james-brown-sampled-records/.

Marsh, Calum. "We Attended the Hatsune Miku Expo to Find Out if a Hologram Pop Star Could Be Human." *Thump/Vice* (5–27–2016), https://thump.vice.com/en_ca/article/ae87yb/hatsune-miku-crypton-show-feature.

McDonald, Heather. "Track Equivalent Albums Were Established to Measure Sales." *Balance Careers* (5–16–2018), www.thebalancecareers.com/track-equivalent-albums-2460947.

McGregor, Jay. "Apple Music Vs. Spotify vs. Tidal: Everything You Need to Know." *Forbes* (6–8-2015), www.forbes.com/sites/jaymcgregor/2015/06/08/apple-music-vs-spotify-vs-tidal-everything-you-need-to-know/#57333fdd415f.

McIntyre, Hugh. "Not One Artist's Album Has Gone Platinum in 2014." *Forbes* (10–16–2014), www.forbes.com/sites/hughmcintyre/2014/10/16/not-one-artists-album-has-gone-platinum-in-2014/.

McKinney, Sarah. "Patreon: A Fast-Growing Marketplace for Creators and Patrons of the Arts." *Forbes* (4–10–2014), www.forbes.com/sites/sarahmckinney/2014/04/10/patreon-a-fast-growing-marketplace-for-creators-and-patrons-of-the-arts/.

Melody, "A Starbucks History Lesson: HEAR Music Concept Stores." *Starbucks Melody: Unofficial Starbucks News and Culture* (5–6-2011), www.starbucksmelody.com/2011/05/06/hear-music-a-memorable-piece-of-starbucks-history/.

"Methodology." Lean Startup, http://theleanstartup.com/principles.

Miller, Donna, and David Bruenger. "Decivilization: Compressive Effects of Technology on Culture and Communication." *China Media Research* 3, no. 2 (April 2007).

Mitchell, Gail. "NMPA's David Israelite Keynotes the 2017 Production Music Conference: 'The Licensing System Is Broken,'" *Billboard* (10–6-2017), www

.billboard.com/articles/business/7990179/nmpa-david-israelite-keynote-2017-production-music-conference.

Moon, Brian. "From Spotify to Shazam: How Big-Data Remade the Music Industry One Algorithm at a Time." *Newsweek* (5–22–2017), www.newsweek.com/spotify-shazam-how-big-data-remade-music-industry-613325.

Morin, Edgar. *On Complexity*, Hampton (2008).

Moss, Corey. "Maroon 5 Film 'Wonder' Clip; Say Next One Is Bob Dylan Meets R. Kelly," *MTV News* (3–19–2007), http://www.mtv.com/news/1555064/maroon-5-film-wonder-clip-say-next-one-is-bob-dylan-meets-r-kelly/.

"Most Popular Music Streaming Services in the United States as of March 2018, by Monthly Users (in millions)." *Statista*, www.statista.com/statistics/798125/most-popular-us-music-streaming-services-ranked-by-audience/.

"Motown: The Sound That Changed America." *Motown Museum*, www.motownmuseum.org/story/motown/.

"Motown's No. 1 Hits in One Box Set for the First Time: Celebrate Motown's 50th Anniversary with the 10-CD MOTOWN: THE COMPLETE NO. 1'S." T4C, Top40 Charts/ Universal Music Enterprises (10–15–2008), http://top40-charts.com/news.php?nid=43528.

Mulligan, Mark. "After The Album: How Playlists Are Re-Defining Listening." *Music Industry Blog* (4–26–2016), https://musicindustryblog.wordpress.com/2016/04/26/after-the-album-how-playlists-are-re-defining-listening/.

———. "Gen Z: Meet the Young Millennials." A MIDiA Research report jointly commissioned by BPI and ERA, June 2017, https://eraltd.org/media/27138/midia-research-gen-z-report.pdf.

———. "Global Recorded Music Revenues Grew by $1.4 Billion in 2017." *MIDiA Research* (4–19–2018), www.midiaresearch.com/blog/global-recorded-music-revenues-grew-by-1-4-billion-in-2017/.

"Music and Health." *Harvard Health Publishing* (July 2011), www.health.harvard.edu/staying-healthy/music-and-health.

"Music Licensing Part One: Legislation in the 112th Congress." *Hearing before the Subcommittee On Intellectual Property, Competition, and the Internet of the Committee on the Judiciary, House of Representatives, One Hundred Twelfth Congress, Second Session*, www.gpo.gov/fdsys/pkg/CHRG-112hhrg77042/html/CHRG-112hhrg77042.htm.

Nakamoto, Satoshi. "Bitcoin: A Peer-to-Peer Electronic Cash System." *Bitcoin.org* (2008), https://bitcoin.org/bitcoin.pdf.

Neal, Meghan. "A Machine Successfully Predicted the Hit Dance Songs of 2015." *Motherboard* (12–17–2015), http://motherboard.vice.com/read/a-machine-successfully-predicted-the-hit-dance-songs-of-2015.

Niu, Evan. "Steve Jobs Was Wrong about Music Streaming." *Motley Fool* (4–3–2018), www.fool.com/investing/2018/04/03/steve-jobs-was-wrong-about-music-streaming.aspx.

O'Neil, Valerie. "Starbucks Refines Its Entertainment Strategy." *Starbucks Newsroom* (4–24–2008), archived at Internet Archive Wayback Machine, https://web.archive.org/web/20130116172638/http://news.starbucks.com/article_display.cfm?article_id=48.

Pallante, Maria A. "The Next Great Copyright Act." *Columbia Journal of Law & the Arts* 36, no. 3 (2013), www.copyright.gov/docs/next_great_copyright_act.pdf.

Pareles, Jon. "David Bowie, 21st-Century Entrepreneur." *New York Times* (6–9–2002), www.nytimes.com/2002/06/09/arts/david-bowie-21st-century-entrepreneur.html.

———. "Pop View; That Syncing Feeling." *New York Times* (4–9–1989), www.nytimes.com/1989/04/09/arts/pop-view-that-syncing-feeling.html?pagewanted=all&src=pm.

Parisi, Paula. "Production Music Conference: NMPA's David Israelite Takes Aim at 'Copyright Infringers.'" *Variety* (10–7–2017), https://variety.com/2017/music/news/production-music-conference-nmpa-david-israelite-keynote-1202583450/.

Parker, Chris. "The Economics of Music Festivals: Who's Getting Rich, Who's Going Broke?" *LA Weekly* (4–17–2013), www.laweekly.com/music/the-economics-of-music-festivals-whos-getting-rich-whos-going-broke-4167927.

Pereira, Carlos Silva, João Teixeira, Patrícia Figueiredo, et al. "Music and Emotions in the Brain: Familiarity Matters." *PLOS One* (11–16–2011), http://journals.plos.org/plosone/article?id=10.1371/journal.pone.0027241.

Perry, Mark J. "Recorded Music Sales by Format from 1973–2015, and What That Might Tell Us about the Limitations of GDP Accounting." *AEI* (9–15–2016), www.aei.org/publication/annual-recorded-music-sales-by-format-from-1973–2015-and-what-that-tells-us-about-the-limitations-of-gdp-accounting/.

Pesce, Nicole Lyn. "The Louvre Unveils Beyoncé and Jay-Z-Themed Tour." *New York Post* (7–9–2018), https://nypost.com/2018/07/09/the-louvre-unveils-beyonce-and-jay-z-themed-tour/.

Phillips, Chuck. "The Accidental Chart Revolution: Pop Music: Billboard's New Method of Tracking Sales Is a Byproduct of a Once-Rival Market

Research System." *Los Angeles Times* (5–30–1991), http://articles.latimes
.com/1991–05–30/entertainment/ca-3677_1_market-research-system.

Pine, B. Joseph, II, and James H. Gilmore. *The Experience Economy: Work Is Theater & Every Business a Stage*. Harvard Business School Press (1999).

———. "Welcome to the Experience Economy." *Harvard Business Review* (July-August 1998), https://hbr.org/1998/07/welcome-to-the-experience-economy.

Potts, Samuel "Record Labels Need a Change of Culture in the 'Dashboard Era' of the Music Industry." *Medium* (7–12–2016), https://medium.com/cuepoint /record-labels-need-a-change-of-culture-in-the-dashboard-era-of-the-music-industry-585e91f6de99.

Preston, Scott. "Behind the Scenes with JK McKnight, Founder of the Fore-castle Festival." *Cincy Groove* (4–12–2009), www.cincygroove.com/?p=5660.

Primeau, Jamie. "Taylor Swift's Rainy 'Reputation' Concert Was a 'Rare' Treat for the Singer & Fans Alike." *Bustle* (7–22–2018), www.bustle.com/p /taylor-swifts-rainy-reputation-concert-was-a-rare-treat-for-the-singer-fans-alike-videos-9841469.

"Procedural Regulations for the Copyright Royalty Board." *Federal Register, 70, 103* (5–31–2005), www.crb.gov/fedreg/2005/70fr30901.pdf.

"Public Good." *Investopedia,* www.investopedia.com/terms/p/public-good .asp.

Ranj, Brandt. "5 Terms Buzzfeed Uses Internally That Reveal How It Works." *Business Insider* (2–16–2016), www.businessinsider.com/5-terms-buzzfeed-uses-internally-that-reveal-how-it-works-2016-2.

Reisinger, Don. "Here's How Many Subscribers Shazam Could Bring to Apple Music." *Fortune* (1–26–2018), http://fortune.com/go/tech/shazam-apple-music-subscribers/.

Remnick, David. "We Are Alive." *New Yorker* (7–30–2012), www.newyorker .com/magazine/2012/07/30/we-are-alive.

Resnikoff, Paul. "Live Concerts + Streaming = 73% of the US Music Indus-try." *Digital Music News* (6–7-2017), www.digitalmusicnews.com/2017/06/07 /music-industry-concerts-streaming/.

Richter, Felix. "Spotify's Losses Widen as Royalty Costs Pile Up." *Statista* (3–1-2018), www.statista.com/chart/4894/spotify-revenue-vs-costs/.

Roberts, Randall. "What Makes for a No. 1 Album in the on-Demand Age of Streaming?" *LA Times* (8–30–2016), www.latimes.com/entertainment /music/la-et-ms-music-charts-20160822-snap-story.html.

Rogers, Christina. "Building on the Buzz." *Detroit News* (3–16–2011).

"The Rolling Stones Sue German Clothing Company for Using Mouth Logo." *NME* (8–15–2013), www.nme.com/news/music/the-rolling-stones-128-1265367.

Rose, Frank. "The Father Of Creative Destruction," *Wired* (3–1-2002), www.wired.com/2002/03/schumpeter/.

Rosen, Jody. "Oh! You Kid! How a Sexed-Up Viral Hit from the Summer of '09—1909—Changed American Pop Music Forever." *Slate* (6–2-2014), www.slate.com/articles/arts/culturebox/2014/06/sex_and_pop_the_forgotten_1909_hit_that_introduced_adultery_to_american.html.

Ross, Danny. "8 Protest Songs since 2000 That Inspired Change (All the Way to the Bank)." *Forbes* (1–30–2017), www.forbes.com/sites/dannyrossi/2017/01/30/8-protest-songs-since-2000-that-inspired-change-all-the-way-to-the-bank/#515439881715.

Runtagh, Jordan. "Beatles' Famous Rooftop Concert: 15 Things You Didn't Know." *Rolling Stone* (1–29–2016), www.rollingstone.com/music/music-news/beatles-famous-rooftop-concert-15-things-you-didnt-know-58342/.

Rydborn, Calvin C. *The Akron Sound: The Heyday of the Midwest's Punk Capital.* Arcadia (2014).

Sako, Jen. "To Virtual Reality and Beyond: The Future of Music Experiences." *Music Development Agency* (12–28–2017), https://themusicda.com/virtual-reality-beyond-future-music-experiences/.

Sale, Jonathan. "Sixty Years of Hits From Sinatra to … Sinatra." *Independent* (1–5-1996), www.independent.co.uk/life-style/sixty-years-of-hits-from-sinatra-to-sinatra-1322429.html/.

Sanchez, Daniel. "Music Dealers Suddenly Closes Doors, Leaving Many Artists without Pay." *Digital Music News* (7–28–2016), www.digitalmusicnews.com/2016/07/28/music-dealers-closes-doors/.

———. "What Streaming Music Services Pay (Updated for 2018)." *Digital Music News* (1–16–2018), www.digitalmusicnews.com/2018/01/16/streaming-music-services-pay-2018/.

Sanjek, Russell. *American Popular Music and Its Business: From 1900 to 1984.* Vol. 3. Oxford University Press (1988).

"Scanning the Audio Demand Landscape." *Nielsen* (6–25–2014), www.nielsen.com/us/en/insights/news/2014/scanning-the-audio-demand-landscape.html.

Schmidt, Bernd. *Customer Experience Management: A Revolutionary Approach to Connecting with Your Customers.* Wiley (2003).

Schneider, Marc. "'Truly a Historic Moment': Music Business Reacts to Music Modernization Act Becoming Law." *Billboard* (10–11–2018), www.billboard

.com/articles/business/8479469/music-business-reactions-music-modernisation-act-law-signing.

Schumpeter, Joseph. *Capitalism, Socialism, and Democracy.* Harper (1976).

Seabrook, John. "How Mike Will Made It." *New Yorker* (July 11 & 18, 2016), www.newyorker.com/magazine/2016/07/11/how-mike-will-made-it.

Seawood, Lauren Wirtzer. "What Instagram Discovered in Our First Nielsen Music Study." *Cuepoint* (3–14–2016), https://medium.com/cuepoint/what-instagram-discovered-in-our-first-nielsen-music-study-de1a2740c005.

Segal, Dave. "Bruce Pavitt's 'Visionary' '80s Music Criticism Gets Anthologized in Sub Pop USA." *Stranger* (10–24–14), www.thestranger.com/slog/archives/2014/10/24/bruce-pavitts-visionary-80s-music-criticism-gets-anthologized-in-sub-pop-usa.

Seghal, Kabir. "Spotify and Apple Music Should Become Record Labels So Musicians Can Make a Fair Living." *CNBC* (1–26–2018), www.cnbc.com/2018/01/26/how-spotify-apple-music-can-pay-musicians-more-commentary.htm.

Serwer, Andy. "Inside Rolling Stones, Inc." *Fortune* (7–21–2002), http://fortune.com/2013/07/21/inside-rolling-stones-inc-fortune-2002/.

"The Sharing Economy: A New Way of Doing Business." *Rubicon Knowledge@Wharton* (12–11–2015), http://knowledge.wharton.upenn.edu/article/the-sharing-economy-a-new-way-of-doing-business/.

Shaw, Lucas. "Record Labels Reap More Than $1 Billion Selling Spotify Stakes." *Bloomberg* (5–7–2018), www.bloomberg.com/news/articles/2018–05–07/record-labels-reap-more-than-1-billion-selling-spotify-stakes.

Sheinkop, Eric. "Music Strategy and the Consumer Experience Journey." *Music Ally* (3–18–2016), http://musically.com/2016/03/18/music-strategy-and-the-consumer-journey-guest-column/.

Sherman, Erik. "Apple's $100 Million U2 Debacle." *CBS News* (9–19–2014), www.cbsnews.com/news/apples-100-million-u2-debacle/.

Silver, Daniel, Terry Nichols Clark, and Lawrence Rothfield. "A Theory of Scenes: The Structure of Social Consumption." *University of Chicago* (11–5–2006), http://scenes.uchicago.edu/theoryofscenes.pdf.

Simpson, Dave. "Lamont Dozier: 'The Hits Just Kept Coming.'" *Guardian* (8–26–2015), www.theguardian.com/culture/2015/aug/26/lamont-dozier-the-songs-just-kept-coming.

"Small Music Venues: A Straightforward Guide to Managing Bar Costs and Forecasts." *Eventbrite*, www.eventbrite.co.uk/blog/academy/small-music-venues-bar-costings-and-forecasts/.

Smirke, Richard. "Indie Labels Repeat Calls for 'Fair Share' Of Spotify Equity Payout." *Billboard* (3–6-2018), www.billboard.com/articles/business/8232536/spotify-indie-labels-equity-sale-fair-share-win.

Smirnov, Sergey, Hajo A. Reijers, Thijs Nugteren, and Mathias Weske. "Business Process Model Abstraction: Theory and Practice." *Technische Berichte Nr. 35 des Hasso-Plattner-Instituts für Softwaresystemtechnik an der Universität Potsdam,* Universitätsverlag Potsdam (2010).

Smith, Adam. *An Inquiry into the Nature and Causes of the Wealth of Nations.* London: W. Strahan and T. Caddell (1776), www.econlib.org/library/Smith/smWN18.html.

Smith, Stephanie. "Beyoncé & Jay Z Touring Together this Summer." *Page Six* (4–15–2014), https://pagesix.com/2014/04/15/beyonce-and-jay-z-to-go-on-tour-this-summer/.

"Soundtrack Business." www.soundtrackyourbrand.com/soundtrack-business?utm_expid=.EJF120cySym9RY5bGRKmsQ1&utm_referrer=.

Sousa, John Philip. "The Menace of Mechanical Music." *Appleton's Magazine* 8 (1906): 278–284, https://ocw.mit.edu/courses/music-and-theater-arts/21m-380-music-and-technology-contemporary-history-and-aesthetics-fall-2009/readings-and-listening/MIT21M_380F09_read02_sousa.pdf.

Spanos, Britanny. "Fans to the Front: How Internet Fandoms Are Gaming the Music Industry." *Rolling Stone* (5–5-2017), www.rollingstone.com/music/music-news/fans-to-the-front-how-internet-fandoms-are-gaming-the-music-industry-194067/.

Spence, Luke J. "The Remnants of Tin Pan Alley." *Atlas Obscura,* www.atlasobscura.com/places/the-remnants-of-tin-pan-alley.

Statt, Nick. "Spotify's IPO Was Both a Success and an Uncertain Forecast for the Future of Music." *Verge* (4–3-2018), www.theverge.com/2018/4/3/17194208/spotify-ipo-nyse-music-streaming-market-valuation.

"Streaming Forward." DiMA-Digital Media Association Annual Music Report (March 2018), https://dima.org/wp-content/uploads/2018/04/DiMA-Streaming-Forward-Report.pdf.

Sullivan, Tim. "Embracing Complexity." *Harvard Business Review* (September 2011), https://hbr.org/2011/09/embracing-complexity.

Swenson, Roland. "History Intro." *SXSW,* www.sxsw.com/about/history/.

"Sync Licensing in 2017: A Look at the Trends and Figures." *SynchBlog* (12–22–2017), www.synchblog.com/sync-licensing-in-2017-a-look-at-the-trends-and-figures/.

"Terms of Use." *Patreon,* www.patreon.com/legal.

Theis, Michael. "SXSW Economic Impact up Slightly in 2016; Hotel Rates Hit New High, *Austin Business Journal* (9-7-2016), www.bizjournals.com /austin/news/2016/09/07/sxsw-economic-impact-up-slightly-in-2016-hotel .html.

Theorell, Töres. *Psychological Health Effects of Musical Experiences: Theories, Studies and Reflections in Music Health Scien*ce. Springer (2014).

Thibodeaux, Ron. "My Smokey Valentine—the Irrepressible Robinson Will Romance Marksville Tonight." *Times-Picayune* (2-14-2009).

Thompson, Derek. "The Shazam Effect." *Atlantic* (December 2014), www .theatlantic.com/magazine/archive/2014/12/the-shazam-effect/382237/.

Thorpe, Harriet. "Beneath the Stage with Beyoncé & Jay-Z." *Wallpaper*, www .wallpaper.com/architecture/beyonce-jay-z-tour-stage-design-by-stufish.

Titan Music Group. *The Austin Music Census.* The City of Austin Economic Development Department, Music and Entertainment Division (2015).

Titlow, John Paul. "How Instagram Became the Music Industry's Secret Weapon." *Fast Company* (9-29-2017), www.fastcompany.com/40472034 /how-instagram-became-the-music-industrys-most-powerful-weapon.

Toffler, Alvin. *Future Shock.* Random House (1970).

———. *The Third Wave.* Bantam (1980).

"The Top 10 Benefits of Using RFID for Events." *Eventbrite,* www.eventbrite .com/blog/academy/the-top-10-benefits-of-using-rfid-for-events/.

Towse, Ruth. "Economics of Music Publishing: Copyright and the Market." *Journal of Cultural Economics* 41 (2017): 403–420.

Trust, Gary. "House Music: Your Living Room Might Be Your Next Concert Venue." *Billboard* (6-14-2013), www.billboard.com/articles/columns/chart-beat/1567029/house-music-your-living-room-might-be-your-next-concert-venue.

Tucker, Jeffrey A. "The End of the US Piano Industry." *Mises Institute* (12-10-2008), https://mises.org/library/end-us-piano-industry.

Uggwu, Reggie. "Inside the Playlist Factory." *BuzzFeed* (7-12-2016), www .buzzfeed.com/reggieugwu/the-unsung-heroes-of-the-music-streaming-boom?utm_term=.dcMBm208w#.tnoV3NBzn.

"University of Georgia Fact Book 1977." *UGA Institutional Research,* www.oir.uga .edu/fact_book.

"U.S. Sales Database." *RIAA,* www.riaa.com/u-s-sales-database/.

Waddell, Ray. "Jay-Z and Beyonce's on the Run Tour Isn't Struggling." *Billboard* (6-19-2014), www.billboard.com/biz/articles/news/touring/6128489 /jay-z-beyonce-on-the-run-tour-doing-bad-not-true.

————. "Jay Z and Beyonce's on the Run Tour Tops $100 Million, 'Everybody's Winning.'" *Billboard* (8–5-2014), www.billboard.com/articles/business /6207007/jay-z-beyonce-on-the-run-tour-100-million.

Wake, Matt. "Why Huge Tours Come to Alabama Arenas to Rehearse." Al. com (11–9-2017), www.al.com/entertainment/index.ssf/2017/11/michael_jackson_kanye_carrie_u.html.

Wake Forest Baptist Medical Center. "Music Has Powerful (and Visible) Effects on the Brain." *ScienceDaily* (4–12–2017), www.sciencedaily.com /releases/2017/04/170412181341.htm.

Warner, Joel. "Fueled by Venture-Capital Funding and a Love for Unknown Bands, Can Boulder's Next Big Sound Predict the Next Rock Star?" *Westword* (10–7-2010), www.westword.com/music/fueled-by-venture-capital-funding-and-a-love-for-unknown-bands-can-boulders-next-big-sound-predict-the-next-rock-star-5110133.

Warren, Brinkley. "Lean Startup? Try Punk Rock Entrepreneurship," www .brinkleywarren.com/lean-startup-try-punk-rock-entrepreneurship/.

Wattrick, Jeff T. "Chrysler Sues Pure Detroit for Selling 'Imported from Detroit' Merchandise." *MLive* (3–16–2011), www.mlive.com/auto/index.ssf /2011/03/chrysler_sues_pure_detroit_for.html.

Wawzenek, Brian. "25 Years Ago: The Soundscan Era Rocks the Music Industry." *Ultimate Classic Rock,* http://ultimateclassicrock.com/billboard-soundscan/.

Weinberger, David, Rick Levine, Doc Searls, and Chistopher Locke. *The Cluetrain Manifesto: The End of Business As Usual.* Perseus Books (1999).

Weinburger, Norman M. "Music and the Brain." *Scientific American* (9–1-2006), www.scientificamerican.com/article/music-and-the-brain-2006–09/.

Weiss, Bret. "It's Only Rock and Roll But I Like It." *Antique Week* (12–21–2011), www.antiqueweek.com/ArchiveArticle.asp?newsid=2265.

"What Is a Record Producer?" Music Producers Guild, www.mpg.org.uk /about-mpg/what-is-a-record-producer/.

Whitwell, Tom. "Why Do All Records Sound the Same." *Cuepoint* (1–9-2015), https://medium.com/cuepoint/why-do-all-records-sound-the-same-830ba863203.

Wilkins, R. W., D. A. Hodges, P. J. Laurienti, M. Steen, J. H. Burdette. "Network Science and the Effects of Music Preference on Functional Brain Connectivity: From Beethoven to Eminem." *Nature: Scientific Reports* 4 (2014): 6130, www.nature.com/articles/srep06130.

Wlizlo, Will. "JumboTrons for Concert Halls." *Utne Reader* (12–8-2010), www .utne.com/arts/music-scoreboards-for-concert-halls.

Wycislik-Wilson, Mark. "Spotify Sells Your Personal and Playlist Data to Advertisers Making You the Product." *BetaNews* (7–22–2016), https:// betanews.com/2016/07/22/spotify-sells-user-data-to-advertisers/.

Yarm, Mark. "Going out of Business since 1988!" *Blender* (July 2008), www .revolutioncomeandgone.com/articles/7/sub-pop-history.php.

Yoo, Noah. "The Full Transcript of Jay Z's Tidal Q & A at the Clive Davis Institute of Recorded Music." *Fader* (Fall 2017), www.thefader.com /2015/04/01/the-full-transcript-of-jay-zs-qa-at-the-clive-davis-institute-of- recorded-music.

———. "How Popular Song Factories Manufacture a Hit." *New York Times* (9–18–1910), http://sundaymagazine.org/2010/09/how-popular-song- factories-manufacture-a-hit/.

INDEX

Founded in 1893,
UNIVERSITY OF CALIFORNIA PRESS
publishes bold, progressive books and journals
on topics in the arts, humanities, social sciences,
and natural sciences—with a focus on social
justice issues—that inspire thought and action
among readers worldwide.

The UC PRESS FOUNDATION
raises funds to uphold the press's vital role
as an independent, nonprofit publisher, and
receives philanthropic support from a wide
range of individuals and institutions—and from
committed readers like you. To learn more, visit
ucpress.edu/supportus.